ENGAGING

WITH

IRIGARAY

:

GENDER AND CULTURE

Carolyn G. Heilbrun and
Nancy K. Miller, editors

ENGAGING

WITH

IRIGARAY

. .

Feminist

Philosophy

and Modern

European

Thought

Edited by Carolyn Burke,
Naomi Schor, and
Margaret Whitford

COLUMBIA UNIVERSITY PRESS • NEW YORK

Columbia University Press

New York   Chichester, West Sussex

Copyright ©1994 Columbia University Press

All rights reserved

Library of Congress Cataloging-in-Publication Data

Engaging with Irigaray: feminist philosophy and modern European
    thought / edited by Carolyn Burke, Naomi Schor, and Margaret
    Whitford.
        p.   cm. — (Gender and culture)
    Includes bibliographical references and index.
    ISBN 0–231–07896–X — ISBN 0–231–07897–8 (pbk.)
    1. Irigaray, Luce.   2. Feminist Theory.   3. Philosophy, European.
    4. Philosophy, French—20th century.   I. Burke, Carolyn L.
    II. Schor, Naomi.   III. Whitford, Margaret.   IV. Series.
    B2430.I744E54   1994
    194—dc20   94–6815
                                                                CIP

Printed in the United States of America

c 10 9 8 7 6 5 4 3 2 1

CONTENTS

PART 2:
IRIGARAY AND/IN
PHILOSOPHY

PART 3:
TOWARD A NEW
SYMBOLIC ORDER

ACKNOWLEDGMENTS

The editors wish to express their gratitude to Janell Watson and Anna Gilcher for their invaluable help in bringing this volume to completion. Throughout the years it took to prepare the manuscript, they kept track of myriad details with exemplary tact and efficiency, staying in touch with far-flung contributors and editors, tracking down obscure references, and meticulously melding articles prepared according to different style sheets and using different computer software. We are also grateful to Jennifer Crewe for shepherding this manuscript, with all its predictable and unpredictable delays.

In addition, Carolyn Burke thanks the staff of the Word Processing Center at the University of California, Santa Cruz; Naomi Schor thanks Nancy K. Miller, who encouraged her to proceed with this project and performed her task as a series editor as the French feminist that she is and remains; and Margaret Whitford is grateful for the extensive support she has received from secretarial staff at Queen Mary and Westfield College, University of London, particularly from Celia Williams in the French Department.

INTRODUCTION

°

° *Naomi Schor*

PREVIOUS

ENGAGEMENTS:

THE RECEPTIONS

OF IRIGARAY

In a series of interviews conducted between May 1986 and November 1987 by Alice Jardine and Anne Menke with some of the major figures of the post-68 French intelligentsia, including Luce Irigaray, a recurrent question arises concerning what seems to be the distinctly American preoccupation with the canon.[1] In several instances this question highlights the misunderstandings between American academic feminists and French feminist writers, psychoanalysts, and academics, as the study of the canon has simply not been constituted as a critical field in France as it has been constituted in the United States. Irigaray, however, understands the question perfectly, and a strikingly confident portion of her answer provides an excellent starting place for this reconsideration of the reception(s) of Luce Irigaray. In response to the interviewers' question, "Do you think your oeuvre will be included in the twentieth-century canon?" Irigaray answers: "Once a dozen or so of one's books have been in book shops and public and private libraries for fourteen years and have been translated into several languages, they are likely to appear in the canon of the twentieth century."[2]

But what canon, if not the literary? Even arguing as Irigaray goes on to that the interviewers' questions are too restrictive, in assuming there exists only one canon and that it is cast in bronze by one's contemporaries, the question remains: What canon is Irigaray a part of? Is it, as Jardine and Menke wonder, a canon composed of works situated at the shifting boundaries "among disciplines and genres of writing" (p. 104)? Yes and no, responds Irigaray: whereas the proliferation of new "branches of knowledge and new technologies" (p. 104) has led only to the reinforcement of disciplinary boundaries, philosophers since Hegel have elaborated a "style that comes close to that of tragedy, poetry, the Platonic dialogues, the way in which myth, parables, and liturgies are expressed" (p. 105). And this return to originary forms goes hand in hand with a return "to the moment at which male identity constituted itself as patriarchal and phallocratic" (p. 105). Clearly, for Irigaray to "take her place in the cultural memory of the twentieth century" (p. 103) is to locate herself in the canon of modern archaeophilosophy and not, as one might expect, in the canon of feminist theory, not to mention women's writing. Or rather, feminist theory and writing are bound up with, indeed, models of modern philosophical thought.

Whatever her doubts about the nature of the canon, however, one thing is certain: Irigaray is confident of her place therein. What I find most striking about Irigaray's response is the long view it takes and the light it sheds on Irigaray's critical reception to date, especially but not exclusively in the United Kingdom and the United States, in the never-never land of "Anglo-America."

As the century draws to a close we must ask ourselves what lessons are to be learned from the critical swings of the past twenty years. Whereas the two other major French feminists with whom Irigaray was always linked in the early stages of importing and packaging French feminism for an anglophone audience—Hélène Cixous and Julia Kristeva—have remained active as writers and teachers, feminist theory as such will be seen in retrospect as having constituted a relatively brief episode in their respective intellectual trajectories. Whereas in the early stages of the development of French feminisms Irigaray's writings were almost always invidiously compared to those of Kristeva and Cixous, today, although Kristeva remains a major intellectual presence (especially in the field of psychoanalysis) and Cixous continues to exert her influence through her seminar, her fiction and playwriting, it is becoming apparent that, as the major French theoretician, Irigaray is actually Simone de Beauvoir's chief successor.

Many judgments and hierarchies set in place in the heat of a particular debate now seem strangely outmoded, not to say lopsided; figures whose every theoretical utterance held masses of eager disciples in their thrall have long since stopped doing serious feminist or even theoretical work. Others, such as Michèle Le Doeuff and Irigaray, have continued to patiently construct a feminist oeuvre, to pursue a lifelong project without courting popularity or monopolizing the media. It is perhaps now the case, as both Carolyn Burke ("Translation Modified: Irigaray in English") and Margaret Whitford ("Irigaray, Utopia, and the Death Drive") argue in different ways in this volume, that in her more recent work Irigaray too has succumbed to an entropy that spares few, but she has behind her a substantial body of work that remains to be reread, or rather simply read in many cases. In short: the reason why this confident assertion struck me when I read it is that it highlights what is distinctive about Irigaray's reception: its longevity. Which is not to say its uniformity. One of the lessons of this collection of essays is that just as Irigaray's writings have evolved over time, her reception has moved through different stages, appealed to different disciplinary constituencies, been taken up by differently situated communities of readers. This multilayered reception gives rise to several combinatories: e.g., the early reception of the early works, the delayed reception of the early work, the contemporary reception of the later works. What follows pertains essentially to the early stages of that critical reception, the one dominated by feminist literary critics in search of theories.

The story of "Irigaray and her critics"[3] is by now well known, at least in its broad outlines, and need not be rehearsed in detail here. Basing themselves unapologetically on a partial knowledge of her work, notably *Speculum* and *This Sex Which Is Not One*, and even more specifically on a few essays in *This Sex*, an astonishing variety of critics, many with little or no knowledge of French and of French culture, almost immediately roundly condemned Irigaray. As Margaret Whitford remarks, "It is one of the ironies of reception that stances for or against Irigaray were adopted well before any of her major work was available in translation."[4] It is worth pointing out, however, that not all early criticism of Irigaray emanated from anglophone feminist critics; francophone and especially native French speakers have also played an important role in the negative reception of Irigaray (as they did of course in her celebration). Reading Irigaray in French is no guarantee of interest, let alone of admiration.

Writing in France, the United States, and the United Kingdom, these early critics of early Irigaray (notably Monique Plaza, Ann Rosalind Jones, and Toril Moi), for the most part (though not exclusively) socialist feminists writing in the personal or conceptual orbit of Simone de Beauvoir, are bound to an extent that has become increas-

ingly apparent over the years by a shared horror of essentialism, understood here as biological. This is how Monique Plaza summarizes Irigaray's essentialism:

> The Irigarayan schema thus integrates three postulates:
>
> —"Woman" exists in an irreducible way as an essence hitherto unrec-
> ognized.
> —This feminine essence gives women the potential of a psychic exis-
> tence which the Occident crushes and hides.
> —This feminine essence of woman can only be discovered outside of
> the oppressive social framework, that is to say, *in the body of the
> woman.*
>
> The potential existence of woman thus depends on the discovery of her
> essence, which lies in the specificity of her body.[5]

And there is no separating the essentialism debates in feminism, which
escalated throughout the eighties, from the proper name *Irigaray* with
which it soon became synonymous, though, of course, other French
"feminists of difference," in Elizabeth Grosz's terms, were subject to the
same critique. By the same token and perhaps even more to the point,
there is no understanding these debates without taking the measure of
the influence of the feminist Left on the early critical reception of
French feminism, for this reception is grounded in a precise moment
not only in history but also in the history of postwar Marxism. As Brennan points out:

> This critique of essentialism was elaborated in the context of early 1970s
> shift within received views on Marxism, a shift away from a "humanist"
> reading of Marx's theory of ideology towards the structuralist interpre-
> tation that criticized the early Marx on epistemological grounds for his
> tacit reliance on the notion of a "human essence.". . . *Where Marxism
> was allied with feminism, the critique of essentialism carried over.*[6]

Indeed, in retrospect it appears that another one of the major ironies of
the reception of Irigaray is that arguments made more or less openly,
and with extreme self-righteousness, in the name of an Althusserian-
inspired revolutionary politics and against the ahistoricity and sociopolitical conservatism entailed by essentialism were themselves put forth
with little if any acknowledgment or awareness of their own historical
situatedness. With few exceptions, notably the Lacanians,[7] the critique
of Irigaray as a paradigm of essentialism was propounded by socialist
constructionists writing in a void, radically severed from any context,
historical, national, or otherwise. Furthermore, antiessentialist critiques

of Irigaray that took her to task for promoting as undifferentiated, universalist, metaphysical notion of Woman proceeded mimetically, as it were, by failing to temper and modulate their analyses by taking into account the differences among women (see my "This Essentialism Which Is Not One: Coming to Grips with Irigaray" in part 1). By the end of the eighties the very antiessentialism that had attacked essentialism for its universalism had assumed the status of a universal value.

To reexamine some of the earliest essays comprising the "reception" of early Irigaray is to become aware of the fact that the identification of Irigaray with essentialism was not at the outset the hegemonic reading. It is interesting to note, for example, that early on other critiques of Irigaray were made, but, like evolutionary paths not taken, were not followed up and further elaborated once the essentialism critique became dominant. As a result, problematic aspects of Irigaray's work targeted by her first readers were left to languish in their embryonic state. Consider the case of Irigaray's alleged Hegelianism. Writing in 1977 the presenters of an interview with Irigaray published in *Ideology and Consciousness* note that "*Speculum* has been criticised on the grounds of Hegelianism, and to some, such may seem to be the tone of the present text as well."[8] Some fifteen years later the crucial question of Hegel's influence on Irigaray remains to be dealt with.

Not coincidently, I think, the authors of this article place great emphasis on the "theoretical and political conjuncture, that of contemporary France" (p. 60) in which Irigaray is writing. They see their duty as attempting "to situate the interview in the context of French and continental political struggles, including (but not simply as a special category) that of the Women's Movement" (p. 58). By 1981, as Christine Fauré's "The Twilight of the Goddesses, or The Intellectual Crisis in French Feminism" makes clear, the critique of Irigaray's essentialism had come to the fore, stamping out all other critiques. Nevertheless, it was still joined to a historical and political contextualization. Unlike Irigaray's other Beauvoirian critics, e.g., the slashing Monique Plaza who launched the first and still timely constructionist attack on Irigaray cited above, Fauré can hardly be accused of ahistoricism. On the contrary: if anything, she overhistoricizes, overcontextualizes. Her critique of Irigaray is embedded in a dense genealogy of the women's movement's antiessentialism, going back to the lessons Beauvoir learned during the Second World War regarding the dangers of embodied difference (racism), through the new utopianism of the post-68 seventies, and looking forward to the gloomy perspectives of the dawning but already crepuscular eighties.

◦ The threat of global war and the formation of pressure blocks by the great powers mark the return of the old fashioned, Cold War conception of politics. Alignments, third force; the whispers of already terrorized public opinion coming together around the national interest can barely be heard. The 1980s are opening with a pessimism that confronts the individual, throws him back to a position of isolated refusal, outside the context of his work and his habits of life and thought.[9]

Nothing turned out to be less prescient than this analysis published only months before the Left's return to power in France, at the beginning of a decade that was to culminate in the cold war's demise and a resurgence of millenarian utopianism. And yet it does have the signal virtue of locating Irigaray's writings in a specific time and place and of making the link between Irigaray's "dated" utopianism and her apotheosis of difference clear. For ultimately Fauré reproaches the author of *This Sex* and *Marine Lover*, not with being a utopianist, rather with being the wrong kind.

This rigid devaluation of the temporal and historical dimension of women to the benefit of a single dimension—space, the female sex, that other place—takes on some of the characteristics of utopian thought: the idea that social change is initiated on the basis of the new forms of behavior, thus protecting against the risks of unforseeable chance and reducing individual responsibility for failure. But the post-1968 feminist utopias did not attempt to define their chances of success in this way. The explosion of writing, the multiplication of references were used in quite the opposite way, to suggest the diversity of outside influences and of states of freedom conquered or rediscovered. Jubilation in all directions over new ways of life! Luce Irigaray, by contrast, brings the most reactionary possible feelings into her work. . . . How could this changeless body be the source of a new destiny?[10]

The conclusion seems inescapable and yet surprising: as of "around 1981"[11] the essentialism/antiessentialism debates dominated academic feminism, and, however paradoxical this may seem, under their regime feminist theory lost its connection with the women's movement. The obsession with rooting out an embodied difference in the name of politics, perhaps even especially Marxist politics, went hand in hand with a depoliticization, a dematerialization of feminist theory.

As the seventies and eighties recede and we move toward the turn of a new century, the historical context in which Irigaray's utopian essentialism emerged comes ever more clearly into focus, and is further sharpened by a more subtle and nuanced account of the varying contexts of her reception, for reception like communication in a structuralist linguistic model is bipolar; it is not enough to situate the emittor's message, one must also situate the receiver's.[12] The receiver must be specified in terms of national intellectual traditions (e.g., American empiricism vs. French theoreticism), disjunctive political configurations (the at least nominal return of the Left to power in France vs. the rise of Thatcherism in the U.K. and Reaganism in the United States), etc. To take the measure of these differences is to acknowledge a series of time warps that are an essential component of reception studies. This emerges most clearly in Nancy Fraser's recent account of the differing contexts of production and reception of Irigaray's early writings:

> It helps to recall the social context in which the new French feminist theories emerged. These theories were generated in the Paris of the 1970s. . . .
>
> The French feminisms we debate today were spawned in this *gauchiste* milieu. The spirit of that milieu marks their basic theoretical postulates to this day. . . .
>
> That spirit is not unknown to U.S. feminists of a certain age, but it is not particularly salient here today. On the contrary, *the context in which we have received and sought to use new French feminism theories stands in marked contrast to the context of their production.* The difference is due chiefly to the time lag in reception. During the decade or so it took to convey and absorb French feminist writings here, massive political changes occurred in both societies, most notably the collapse of the New Left and the rise of a conservative backlash. In France the resurgence of "neo-liberalism" was preceded by, and tempered by, the ascension to power in 1981 of a (nominally) Socialist government. In the United States, in contrast, the eighties were the Reagan years, a time in which a triumphant neoconservatism managed to discredit even the mildest liberalism, to stall reform efforts, and to reverse some of the civil rights gains of the sixties.[13]

If Fraser admirably captures the complexities generated by the superimposition of the context of reception on the context of production, her account can nonetheless be faulted for its reinscription of the oldest and most exhausted paradigm in the book, the opposition of a French sphere of theoretical production and an anglophone sphere of reception. Once again we can observe the workings of mimeticism in the reduplication by the antiessentialists of the feminists of difference's failure to attend to differences. If Fraser acutely captures the specificities of the American context of reception, she does not offset her analysis by any acknowledgment of other contexts of reception, especially (but not exclusively) other European and non-European sites of feminist theoretical activity that have recently come to the fore: e.g., Italy, the Netherlands, Australia, and Canada. This failure to go beyond the

Anglo-American sphere goes hand in hand with a failure to attend to an aspect of the reception of Irigaray that both intersects with and cuts across national differences. I am referring here to differences located on the fault line between nationalism and sexuality. As Whitford observes: "radical or lesbian feminism" comprises "the strands of feminism which have on the whole been the most sympathetic to Irigaray up to now."[14] It would thus stand to reason that in national feminist contexts such as the Italian where heterosexual institutions have been subjected to a particularly thoroughgoing interrogation, Irigaray should be vastly more popular and influential than in cultural contexts where homophobia remains covertly rampant even among feminists. For contrary to what is now being alleged by certain gay male critics bent on outing previously closeted homosexual figures,[15] feminists of difference, far from engaging in some sort of homophobic cover-up, have instead made common cause with a theoretician of difference who has found her chief sponsors in the most radical spheres of feminist theory. As Teresa de Lauretis astutely remarks, "I would . . . suggest that what motivates the suspicion or the outright construction, on the part of Anglo-American feminists, of a fantom feminist essentialism, may be less the risk of essentialism itself than the further risk which that entails: the risk of challenging directly the social-symbolic institution of heterosexuality."[16]

The result of the substitution of what Margaret Whitford calls "pseudo-Irigaray" for the real one produced the most salient and distinctive feature of the reception of Irigaray; it immediately put Irigaray's admirers into a defensive posture. Against the onslaught of critics armed with the high theoretical tools of Marxism and Lacanian psychoanalysis, her *admirers* were positioned as her *defenders* deploying strategies—indeed for some Derridean feminists essentialism could be "risked" so long as it was (merely) *strategic*. Though many such feminists enlisted Derrida in the war against essentialism, in retrospect it would appear that deconstruction provided Irigaray's receptive readers with some of the most effective means for breaking the lock of antiessentialism, just as it had earlier provided Irigaray herself with the means of contesting phallogocentrism (see Burke, "Irigaray Through the Looking Glass").

Thus, in a subtle, pioneering article published in 1983, Jane Gallop demonstrated by attending to the logic of structuralist poetics that Irigaray's use of what we might call "body language" was not as naively essentialist as it was made out to be; because of the innately nonreferential nature of language, a key word in Irigaray's vocabulary such as *lips* can never not be figurative, not a catachresis. However, in a characteristic having-it-all deconstructive gesture, Gallop concludes: "Although

we cannot embrace simple unquestioned referentiality neither can we
unproblematically deny referentiality. . . . For if Irigaray is not just writing a non-phallomorphic text (. . .) but actually constructing a non-
phallomorphic sexuality then the gesture of a troubled but nonetheless
insistent referentiality is essential."[17] Turning once again to deconstructive strategies to enable her reading, but writing in the very different context of late poststructuralism, Diana Fuss has recently argued
that the "essentialist/constructionist binarism" (p. 55) can be undone
and therefore provides no secure defense against the perceived threat or
taint of essentialism. In what may be seen as a final deconstructive turn
still other readers of Irigaray (myself included, see below) have exposed
the illusory unitary nature of essentialism; alongside pseudo-Irigaray
and propping her up stands pseudoessentialism. And once that pseudoessentialism is exposed to view as a construct meant to paper over the
incoherencies of antiessentialism, it becomes possible to begin to truly
engage with Irigaray, for as Margaret Whitford has said, "I would argue
for *engagement* with Irigaray rather than the alternatives of dismissal or
apotheosis."[18]

Although Irigaray remains a controversial figure and the seemingly
intractable terms of the debate that has stifled Irigaray studies for so
long have yet to be relegated to the junk heap of contemporary thought,
the increasingly sophisticated work of Irigaray's readers has at last cul-
minated in the publication in 1991 of a major book-length study on
Irigaray, Margaret Whitford's *Luce Irigaray: Philosophy in the Feminine.*
Whitford's subtitle signals a trend that this collection of essays confirms: after years of appropriation by literary critics, Irigaray has at last
entered the age of the philosophers. But the Irigaray inducted into the
canon of philosophical texts by Whitford, a scholar trained in philosophy but housed in a department of French, is a far cry from the Irigaray
rejected by so many literary critics. Complex where the other is simple,
revolutionary where the other is conservative, Whitford's Irigaray is a
utopian feminist philosopher committed to a radical transformation of
the social and symbolic order, "a theorist of change" (p. 15), "a kind of
cultural prophet" (p. 33). By positively valorizing Irigaray's utopianism,
Whitford gives new meaning to her essentialism, which is here viewed
as not so much strategic as provisional. Or put another way: for Whitford mimeticism is the strategy, essentialism is the stage, and that stage
is obligatory if women are to become subjects in the symbolic. "Unlike
the philosophers, who can afford to argue that they are not essentialists,
Irigaray has no choice. . . . One cannot get 'beyond essentialism' at this
point without passing through essentialism" (p. 103). Whereas the male

○   philosophers are free because of their founding exclusion of the maternal-feminine to deny their own essentialism, as a philosopher in the
feminine Irigaray is obliged not only to pass through essentialism but
also to speak its language: "Even to state the problem at all, Irigaray is
obliged to use the language of onto-theology, the language of essentialism" (p. 136). The major misreading of Irigaray according to Whitford
consists then in taking her essentialism for the final stage, the last word,
when it is only part of a process: "Given the symbolic distribution of
functions, in which the body is allotted to woman, it is only by defend-
ing—symbolizing—the value of what has been placed outside the transcendental that some redistribution can take place. If this is interpreted
as essentialism or phallogocentrism, it is because what has been lost
sight of is the horizon. It is to fix a moment of becoming as if it were
the goal" (p. 143).

NOTES •

1. This is due in large part to the original context in which excerpts of most
of these interviews first appeared, a special issue of *Yale French Studies*
devoted to French women writers and the canon, entitled *The Politics of
Tradition: Placing Women in French Literature* (1988), no. 75, Joan
DeJean and Nancy K. Miller, eds. That special issue was published in
book form, *Displacements: Women, Tradition, Literatures in French,* Joan
DeJean and Nancy K. Miller, eds. (Baltimore: Johns Hopkins University
Press, 1991).
2. Alice A. Jardine and Anne M. Menke, eds. *Shifting Scenes: Interviews on
Women, Writing, and Politics in Post-68 France* (New York: Columbia
University Press, 1990), p. 102.
3. Diana Fuss, *Essentially Speaking: Feminism, Nature, and Difference* (New
York: Routledge, 1989), pp. 56–57. See also Maggie Berg, "Escaping the
Cave: Luce Irigaray and Her Feminist Critics," in Gary Wihl and David
Williams, eds., *Literature and Ethics: Essays Presented to A. E. Malloch*
(Kingston, Montreal: McGill Queen's University Press, 1988), pp. 62–76.
4. Margaret Whitford, ed., *The Irigaray Reader* (Oxford: Basil Blackwell,
1991), p. 2. Consider the following: *Speculum* was originally published
in French in 1974, in English in 1985, *This Sex* originally appeared in
1977, in translation in 1985. After another long interval, recently several
more Irigaray texts have appeared in English: *Amante Marine* (Paris:
Minuit, 1980), *Marine Lover of Friedrich Nietzsche* (New York: Columbia, 1991); *Je, tu, nous* (Grasset, 1990; Routledge, 1992). Even allowing
for the difficulties with which Irigaray's texts confront the translator, if
compared to the rhythm of translating the no less daunting texts of, say,
Derrida, these are significant delays. For more on Irigaray and translation
see Burke, "Translation Modified: Irigaray in English," this volume.

5. Monique Plaza, " 'Phallomorphic Power' and the Psychology of 'Woman':
   A Patriarchal Vicious Circle," *Feminist Issues* (Summer 1980), 1(1):73.
   This remarkable text was first published in French in *Questions féministes*,
   the Beauvoir-sponsored journal, and in 1978 in *Ideology and Consciousness*.
6. Teresa Brennan, "Introduction," in Teresa Brennan, ed., *Between Femi-
   nism and Psychoanalysis* (London: Routledge, 1989), pp. 6–7; emphasis
   added.
7. See in particular Marie-Christine Hamon, "Le langage-femme existe-t-il?"
   Ornicar? (1977), 11:37–50, and the spirited response by Marcelle Marini,
   "Scandaleusement autre . . . ," *Critique* (1978), 34(373–374):603–621.
   See also, Jacqueline Rose in Jacqueline Rose and Juliet Mitchell, eds.,
   Feminine Sexuality: Jacques Lacan and the école freudienne (New York:
   Norton, 1982), pp. 53–56.
8. Diana Adlam and Couze Venn, "Introduction to Irigaray," *Ideology and
   Consciousness* (1977), 1:57–61.
9. Christine Fauré, "The Twilight of the Goddesses, or The Intellectual
   Crisis of French Feminism," trans. Lillian S. Robinson, *Signs: Journal of
   Women in Culture and Society* (1981), 7(11):81.
10. Ibid., pp. 85–86. Once again we find that one of the texts criticizing Iri-
    garay, and especially her body-centered utopianism, emanates from a
    member of Beauvoir's inner circle. Thus Christine Fauré's piece was
    originally published in *Les Temps modernes*, the journal founded and
    edited by Jean-Paul Sartre and Simone de Beauvoir.
11. I am alluding here to Jane Gallop's periodization in *Around 1981: Acade-
    mic Feminist Literary Theory* (New York: Routledge, 1992).
12. In order not to repeat this error, I want to add to the many historical
    time frames surrounding this staggered reception yet one more frame,
    the spatiotemporal coordinates of my own enunciation: fall 1992 in
    North Carolina. There are odd and ominous references of the French
    Left's victory of 1981 with Bill Clinton's electoral victory in 1992. Hav-
    ing been in Paris in May 1981 and being in the United States on
    November 4, 1992, makes me devoutly wish that history will not repeat
    itself and I will not watch again as the joyful explosion of countercultural
    utopian forces pent up for too long turns to something grimmer and
    grayer, that the age of diversity so many salute will not mutate into the
    age of divisiveness and internecine violence which seems to loom on the
    world horizon.
13. Nancy Fraser, "Introduction: Revaluing French Feminism," in Nancy
    Fraser and Sandra Lee Barky, eds., *Revaluing French Feminism: Critical
    Essays on Difference, Agency, and Culture* (Bloomington: Indiana Univer-
    sity Press, 1992), pp. 2–3; emphasis added.
14. Margaret Whitford, *Luce Irigaray: Philosophy in the Feminine* (London:
    Routledge, 1991), p. 15.
15. I am alluding here to a passage in D. A. Miller's *Bringing Out Roland
    Barthes* (Berkeley: University of California Press, 1992), which I take

(perhaps wrongly) to be a veiled allusion inter alia to my essay, "Dreaming Dissymmetry: Barthes, Foucault, and Sexual Difference," in Alice Jardine and Paul Smith, eds., *Men in Feminism* (New York: Methuen, 1987), pp. 88–110. The issue here seems to be a "conflict of specificities," for, according to Miller, by ignoring the "discreet but discernible gay specificities of Barthes's text" (p. 16), feminists in search precisely of their own female specificities are guilty of homophobia: "Recognizing this logic must greatly diminish the persuasiveness of recent accounts (embraced by critics of both sexes, though—predictably—under the rule of a single sexuality) that equate the Barthesian neuter with a ruse for submerging, under general sexual indeterminacy, the specificity of women" (p. 17).

16. Teresa de Lauretis, "The Essence of the Triangle or, Taking the Risk of Essentialism Seriously: Feminist Theory in Italy, the U.S., and Britain," *differences* (1989), 1(2):32. Cf. the interview in *Ideology and Consciousness* (1977): "For many the views expressed by Irigaray will appear similar to the canonical arguments developed by certain 'radical feminists' " (p. 58).

17. Jane Gallop, *"Quand Nos Lèvres S'Ecrivent:* Irigaray's Body Politic," *Romanic Review* (1983), 74:77–83; reprinted in Jane Gallop, *Thinking Through the Body* (New York: Columbia University Press, 1988), pp. 92–100, 117–118, under the title "Lip Service."

18. Whitford, *Luce Irigaray*, p. 28.

° *Margaret Whitford*

READING

IRIGARAY

IN THE

NINETIES

Beyond Essentialism

Irigaray's complexity is such that it is probably not possible—and certainly not desirable—to provide the definitive account of her work. I have argued elsewhere[1] that interpretations may either operate a restrictive closure or, more productively, engage with Irigaray and open up the possibility of using her work as a feminist resource. The multiplicity for which she is celebrated should be a prescription for the reader as well.[2] The approaches that I shall sketch out below indicate the state of Irigaray studies to date, and, in their discussion of the various contributions to the present collection, attempt to identify fruitful lines of interpretation and invite to further reflection. But I don't want to claim that they are exhaustive.

Despite a proliferation of articles on Irigaray over a period of at least a decade, we have begun only recently to grapple with the real difficulties and issues that her work puts into play. Interpretation was blocked for a long while in the deadlock produced by the terms of the essentialist/antiessentialist debate. All versions of constructionist theory, whether in its psychoanalytic form, its sociological and political form, or its poststructuralist literary and political form, converge in opposing what they take to be assertions of a kind of ontological causality. For a while the accusation of essentialism united critics of Irigaray across the spectrum, from Lacanian feminists to socialist/materialist feminists who may have agreed on little else but their dismissal of essentialism. What has enabled a shift in the rather monolithic essentialist readings of Irigaray is, first, a climate in which the binary pair essentialism/antiessentialism has been put into question.[3] This enables essentialism to be interpreted as a *position* rather than as an ontology, and Irigaray to be interpreted as a strategist (even a postmodernist) rather than as an obscurantist prophet of essential biological or psychic difference. Second, greater attention is now being paid to the status of Irigaray's writing as *text*, that is to say, writing that employs rhetorical devices and strategies.

One of the most important of these interventions was Naomi Schor's 1989 essay, "This Essentialism Which Is Not One: Coming to Grips with Irigaray" (this volume), which showed the ways in which essentialism had been "essentialized." Schor argued that the label *essentialism* conflated a variety of positions that were not always mutually compatible. Schor's elegant unpicking of the different strands allowed one to look for the strengths and weaknesses of a range of polarized positions and to shift the debate onto a more open-ended stage. She suggests that when Irigaray talks about feminine specificity her main point is to discredit "the oppressive fiction of a universal subject." Schor goes on to speculate that "universalism may well be one of the most divisive and least discussed issues in feminism today." In this way she recontextualises Irigaray within the framework of the feminist "differences between women" debates and points to a tension in Irigaray's work between the sexual difference model (which argues for *two* subjects, a male and a female one) and the critique of universalism (which opens the way to a greater plurality of subject-positions).

It is no doubt because of the essentialist reading that the Derridean influence on Irigaray took so long to be generally discovered and its implications digested, since feminist Derrideans saw themselves as antiessentialist. As Carolyn Burke saw clearly as long ago as 1981 in "Irigaray Through the Looking Glass" (this volume), Derrida's deconstructive strategies were a vital resource for Irigaray. Derrida's tactic, destabilizing the metaphysical opposition by privileging the hierarchically inferior term, can be compared with Irigaray's claim in *This Sex Which Is Not One* that "one must assume the feminine role deliberately."[4] And her statement that "there is no simple, manageable way to leap to the out-side of phallogocentrism, *nor any possible way to situate oneself there, that would result from the simple fact of being a woman*"[5] parallels Der-rida's view that one cannot step outside the metaphysical enclosure. *Speculum* fuses, in a remarkable theoretical achievement, the psycho-analytic attention to what is repressed by culture with the Derridean account of the repression required by metaphysics. But whereas Derri-da tends to present deconstruction and feminism as alternatives, in which feminism is a metaphysic to be deconstructed,[6] Irigaray can probably be more usefully seen *both* as a deconstructionist *and* as a feminist.

There has as yet been no really extensive discussion of Irigaray's rela-tion to Derrida's work.[7] Elizabeth Grosz, for example, argues that Iri-garay's use of deconstruction is an exemplary feminist strategy for approaching patriarchal theory. More critically, Braidotti takes up the position that Derrida's work, despite its value as a critique of phallogo-centric metaphysics, appropriates women's right to speak for themselves, and in a sense substitutes itself for women's voice once again. Whereas Derrida *deconstructs* identity, Irigaray argues for the *construction* of a new identity.[8] Although, as Derrida's interpreters point out, the deconstruc-tion of identity does not necessarily mean that we can do without it,[9] nonetheless it is true that Derrida aspires to a "beyond" of sexual differ-ence that could well leave women feeling that their interests have been subordinated to philosophy.[10] From Irigaray's point of view, as I inter-pret her, Derrida's work may still be implicated in a patriarchal imagi-nary economy, in which woman remains the ground or condition of predication, so that although Irigaray may utilize deconstruction as a critical device, her aim is the reorganization of the symbolic economy.[11]

In addition, most discussions of Derrida and Irigaray focus on Iri-garay's debt to Derrida;[12] a question that has not really been raised yet is that of Derrida's debt to feminist thought. Insofar as Derrida is explic-itly utopian at certain moments in his work,[13] one cannot rule out a two-way process of intertextuality. There is certainly much more to be said on this issue, and the Derrida-Irigaray relationship clearly needs exploring more closely.

Elizabeth Weed's essay, "The Question of Style" (this volume), picks up the Derridean resonances of Irigaray's work, using the early piece on Lacan, "Così Fan Tutti," as an extended example. Both Irigaray and Derrida employ deconstructive readings that are "homeopathic,"[14] that is to say, they operate within what they are seeking to contest, and accept that there is no position *outside* metaphysics or language from which to disrupt metaphysics or language. However, Weed describes

°   Irigaray's difference from Derrida and Lacan as something that comes
      down to a question of tropes. Her subtle and intricate reading sets out
      to give an interpretation of the Irigarayan feminine specificity (or posi-
      tivity as she calls it here) that would elude the polarization of essential-
      ist and antiessentialist interpretations by appealing to figures of speech.

      Both Schor and Weed acknowledge their debt to Jane Gallop. One
      of the earliest accounts of Irigaray's "body poetics" was Gallop's pre-
      scient 1983 article entitled "*Quand Nos Lèvres S'Ecrivent*: Irigaray's
      Body Politic."[15] Gallop's paper warns, "Let us beware of too literal a
      reading of Irigarayan anatomy." She suggests that Irigaray was involved
      in a process of remetaphorizing the body, which nonetheless retained an
      insistent illusion of referentiality. She argued for a sort of Irigarayan
      "poetics of the body" that would set the body free—even if only
      momentarily—from the straitjacket of phallomorphic meanings.

      The question of the literal reading, with its essentialist implications,
      underlies Rosi Braidotti's comparison of Deleuze and Irigaray in her
      essay, "Of Bugs and Women" (this volume). Braidotti gives a reading of
      Irigaray that attempts to hold on to the materiality of the body while
      going beyond the impasse of essentialism. Her essay is an exploration of
      the tension between Irigaray's project of sexual specificity and Deleuze's
      "becoming-woman" of philosophy. Braidotti is a self-confessed Deleuz-
      ian. However, for Deleuze, women can be revolutionary subjects only
      to the extent that they develop a consciousness that is not specifically
      feminine; this is not a route that Braidotti wants to take. She retains a
      Deleuzian account of the body that has no metaphysical commitment
      to a "real" body beyond its representations, but draws conclusions that
      are more Irigarayan than Deleuzian. She argues for a materiality no
      longer understood as essentialist but as historically specific.

      We shall see that the turn from "essentialism" toward the identifica-
      tion of a kind of radical materialism, which Naomi Schor indicates in
      her essay and which is elaborated here by Braidotti, is picked up by
      some of the writers in part 2, notably Judith Butler, Philippa Berry, and
      Ellen Mortensen. Irigaray's move to put into question the metaphysical
      opposition "idealism"/"materialism," which was left unexplored (and
      often unnoticed) in the initial response to her work, now seems to be
      providing the focus for new directions both in feminist thought in gen-
      eral and in Irigarayan scholarship in particular.

Irigaray and/in Philosophy

As Naomi Schor points out in her introductory essay, Irigaray's warmest
reception was initially among literary scholars; philosophers have been

slow to recognize her as one of their number. The present collection marks a new phase in Irigaray studies, in its inclusion of a substantial number of essays on Irigaray and/in philosophy. Irigaray's relation to her philosophical predecessors raises interesting methodological questions. What does it mean to "romance the philosophers" as Carolyn Burke puts it,[16] to play the role of the "philosopher's wife"?[17] Her texts are often an extraordinary weave of intertextuality—particularly the more "poetic" works such as *Marine Lover* and *L'Oubli de l'air* (Forgetting the air). Given Irigaray's critique of Western philosophy, it is noteworthy that the philosophers (among whom one should include Freud and Lacan) are the writers with whom she engages most intensely.

One approach is the standard scholarly account, which looks for debts and influences. This can be invaluable exegetically. By displaying the strands that make up the intertextual network, it can be an enabling source for other readings. In certain cases it is indispensable; few of us are likely to have Irigaray's wide-ranging acquaintance with the philosophical culture, and we need to call on the resources of the feminist philosophical community. A second approach is to look for Irigaray's "transference" in relation to her chosen texts.[18] If one sees her work less as a relation of detached objectivity and more as a relation of passionate involvement, one will be less concerned with whether Irigaray has read "correctly" or "incorrectly" than with what her involvement allows her to bring into focus. The lover may not be objective, in the sense of "impartial," but does perceive what the more detached observer will never see. Michèle Le Doeuff has pointed out[19] that traditionally women's relation with philosophy was not mediated by the institution; it was mediated only by an individual. Women's access was seldom to *philosophy*, but only to one *philosopher*. As a result, women were expected at most to be faithful transcribers of the text. They could be trusted to produce exegesis, but they could not produce those "strong" readings that reconceptualized and revisioned the history of philosophy. There has been some argument about whether Irigaray is a "strong" reader or whether she is still too dependent on her mentors, particularly Lacan. I would argue here for "strong" *interpretations*: i.e., Irigaray will be as "strong" as we can make her, as we use her readings to reread in our turn.

One such "strong" interpretation is provided by Judith Butler's magisterial essay, "Bodies That Matter" (this volume). One of the central issues for feminist theory in the wake of poststructuralism is the question of the *grounding* of feminist politics. If the sexed specificity of the female body is no longer unproblematically available as an unquestioned experiential ground, what happens to feminism? The question

Butler raises is about the way in which certain categories—such as gender—are recognized to be cultural constructions, whereas others—such
as the materiality of sex—appear to be self-evidently irreducible or simply the raw material of cultural construction. Matter is a sign that has a
history, she writes, a history that is linked to the history of sexual difference. This is of course an Irigarayan question, raised both in *Speculum* and in *This Sex Which Is Not One*. By approaching Irigaray via Aristotle and Foucault, Butler shows how the form/matter binary appears
to include the feminine (as matter) while simultaneously excluding and
erasing it. There is the *specular* feminine (the other of the same) and the
excessive feminine (which falls outside the categories). Butler goes on to
identify the heterosexual matrix at work in the metaphysical tradition
(more on this later).

Another "strong" interpretation is that of Jean-Joseph Goux, whose
remarkable essay surveys the question of sexual difference in a broad
historical sweep. His essay challenges quite a few recent orthodoxies.
For Goux essentialism is no longer a real threat; its power to enforce
sexual difference, underpinned by a theological worldview, has long
since disappeared. The threat we should be more concerned about is
what he calls the logic of ultramodernity. His argument is that Irigaray's
work marks a new historical moment in the question of the relation
between the sexes, and can, justifiably, be called postmodernist with
much greater reason than the work of the poststructuralists, whom he
regards as ultramodernist. Whereas the logic of modernity—and a for-
tiori ultramodernity—tends toward the blurring and obliteration of the
difference between the sexes and hence the move toward a neutral sex
that conceals its masculinity, Irigaray opposes this logic; thus Goux sees
her as heralding a different and radically unpredictable future.

Nevertheless, despite the case that can be made for feminism's epistemological rupture, Irigaray does share a philosophical heritage with
French poststructuralist philosophers, particularly in her acknowledgment of the Nietzsche and Heidegger lineage. Several of the essays in
this collection present Irigaray as a reader and explore her philosophical intertextuality.

Joanna Hodge's essay raises the methodological problem. Given philosophy's self-conception, and given Irigaray's critique, where should we
situate Irigaray, and what exactly is her relation to philosophy? To what
extent is she inside/outside? Hodge suggests that Irigaray's critique of
philosophy is indebted to Heidegger. Irigaray endorses Heidegger's
analysis of the incompatibility between the perspective of time, situation, and history on the one hand, and, on the other, philosophy's conception of itself as concerned with timeless truth, a self-conception that

for Heidegger can be traced from its founding moment in Greece to the present epoch, and places philosophy outside history. "If philosophy consists in rigorous conceptual construction and history consists in processes of development, there can be no history in the history of European philosophy," Hodge points out. Instead, there is only a repetitious pattern in which "sameness" predominates. Hodge shows the extent to which Irigaray has made use of Heidegger's far-reaching critique of the "history" that philosophy has constructed for itself. She argues that Irigaray's problematic of sexual difference is foreshadowed and shaped by Heidegger's challenge to Kant, in the Heideggerian distinction between the *ontic* (what there is) and the *ontological* (what is possible, the conditions of possibility for what there is). For Heidegger "what there is" has an irreducible historical dimension that rules out the possibility of the timeless unspecific view from nowhere. Irigaray's work builds on the Heideggerian distinction when she argues that there has been a sexual subtext at work in philosophy whereby the distribution of philosophy to men leaves women bearing the weight of time, history, change, and mortality. This has allowed philosophers to preserve a Platonic distinction between reality (eternal) and appearance (ephemeral), and to devalue accordingly the bearers of the ephemeral. Hodge's paper is important in that it goes partway to responding to the persistent critique of Irigaray as ahistorical. Via the Heidegger connection Hodge is able to show her, in contrast, as crucially concerned with history.

Hodge's wide-ranging discussion is complemented by Ellen Mortensen's subtle and complex essay, which shows how Irigaray uses Heidegger to read Nietzsche while at the same time suggesting that Heidegger fails to confront woman's mater-iality. In *Marine Lover*, argues Mortensen, Irigaray indicates obliquely the failure of Nietzsche's "transvaluation of values" to leave the circle of the same. Nietzsche's "woman" remains trapped within the (t)autological circle of Western metaphysics, which is forgetful of its ground or conditions. Irigaray's Heideggerian approach reveals that the feminine can only appear in metaphysical language as that which it is not. Irigaray rejects phenomenology insofar as it assumes that appearance is the totality of what is. The feminine, she argues, may not have to appear in order to *be*. However, this rejection of phenomenology presents the reader with a number of difficulties. If the feminine in Irigaray is the ground, the elsewhere, the condition of appearance or the ontological, rather than the ontic, appearance, how can Irigaray speak about it, how can she gain access to it, or define it, without falling back into the metaphysical logos? Mortensen shows that Irigaray's problematic of sexual difference is indebted to the Nietzschean and Heideggerian formulations that Irigaray is contesting; she raises for discussion the extent to which Irigaray herself—in her attempt to retrieve the feminine without essentializing it—oscillates between a kind of Nietzschean will to power and a Heideggerian critique of metaphysics. Thus, although Mortensen and Butler, for example, use different theoretical frameworks to approach the question of matter, Butler beginning to explore the genealogy of matter, while Mortensen focuses on the inadequacy of a non-Heideggerian phenomenology, they both locate and problematize "matter" or "materiality" as a crucial and so far mostly unexamined area for further examination.

A third essay to pick up the Heidegger connection argues that Irigaray reappropriates Heidegger in a feminist way. Philippa Berry foregrounds Irigaray's image of fire, which, she suggests, deconstructs the dualism of light and darkness. This gives Irigaray a lever to open up to feminist investigation not only traditional Western metaphysics but also Heidegger's critique of metaphysics. The figure of the *miroir ardent* or burning glass undoes the opposition of matter and spirit, for the "feminine materiality" of the mirror is blended in a single image with the masculine "fire of spirit." And in place of a simple opposition between light (male vision) and darkness (female matter) there is the "darkness visible" or a dark and burning light, which reproduces the paradoxes of mysticism in a vocabulary used by both male and female mystics. In addition, Berry identifies the probable textual sources for the imagery of "La Mystérique" in fourteenth-century mystical writing (the first person, as far as I know, to track down Irigaray's source-texts here).

Irigaray exposes the sexual subtext in Heidegger—to be found in his *clearing* (the privileged space of the truth of being) and in his *disclosure* (unconcealment) of truth and the oblivion or shadow that accompanies the disclosure. Berry argues that one has to take into account the influence of Heideggerian phenomenology in examining Irigaray's deconstructive devices, in order to understand the full force of these. At the same time she warns us of the ethical and political associations of the "fires of spirit" in recent history that cannot be ignored by any thinker drawing on the Heideggerian legacy. Irigaray's debt to Heidegger is a central but relatively unexamined area of exploration, and it is thus rather unfortunate that Irigaray's "Heidegger" book, *L'Oubli de l'air*, is the only one of her untranslated works that is not currently being translated into English.

Thus, despite the problems of "including" Irigaray in the Western philosophical tradition, I don't think one can simply "exclude" her either. I would endorse Rosi Braidotti's argument, in *Patterns of Dissonance*, that we have to redefine philosophy so that it includes feminist thinking. I would thus argue for a creative relationship with the texts, in which Irigaray becomes in turn part of our feminist philosophical intertextuality.

Toward a New Symbolic: Irigaray and the Feminist Reader

One of the conditions for new readings of Irigaray is undoubtedly the availability of her work in translation. It is therefore appropriate that part 3 should be introduced by Carolyn Burke's article on "Translation Modified: Irigaray in English," where the pitfalls of reading Irigaray in translation are outlined. However, more important for this section, Burke also stresses Irigaray's address to the reader, her explicit appeal for response and dialogue as motors of change. Burke's new essay reminds us of the "transferential" possibilities of reading Irigaray, first sketched out in 1981 in her "Irigaray Through the Looking Glass" (this volume). I came to the same conclusion in 1986, when I wrote as follows:

> It seems to me . . . that we should treat Irigaray's work as literature . . . to the extent that its effect on us is *directly relevant* to its more apparently theoretical content. The transference of the reader is not a more or less accidental, "emotional" or subjective response which can be set aside to get at the "theory," but in fact gives a clue to what is at stake. If, as a reader, you "resist," then this resistance itself is worth analysing and exploring further. It is not in itself a guarantee of the theoretical "correctness" of Irigaray's work. . . . But it does indicate that you are not left indifferent, that your resistance is produced by something. If, in the interaction which takes place between you and Irigaray's work, you do not withdraw, to that extent she has succeeded and the scene is set for a possible exchange.[20]

I still think that "engaging with Irigaray" is one of the most productive ways to move beyond Irigaray, both to avoid being enclosed in the limitations of a single vision, and also to avoid the Scylla of idealization or the Charybdis of denigration. I developed this interpretation further with the help of Jane Gallop's valuable introduction to *Reading Lacan*.[21] It gave me the idea that one could map the two processes that Gallop identifies (interpretation as mastery, interpretation as transference) onto Irigaray's different "voices" and her image of the "amorous exchange"[22] to produce a dynamic reading strategy in which "male" and "female" *readings* engage in fertile intercourse.[23] The main point here is that the reader's openness "will participate in determining Irigaray's impact, indeed, her identity," as Elizabeth Hirsh (this volume) puts it.

○   Both Dianne Chisholm and Elizabeth Hirsh are extending in a most productive way the idea that reading Irigaray should be a dynamic process linked to change in the reader rather than a strategy of pinning down a fixed and already given meaning. In her unpublished work[24] and in her essay (this volume) on Irigaray's hysterical mimesis, Chisholm makes a distinction between psychoanalytic readings as a kind of formalist aesthetics[25] and psychoanalytic readings as a kind of feminist *therapy*. The danger of the former is that it neutralizes the radicalism of the psychoanalytic reading, whereas the emphasis on therapy and healing foregrounds the process of *change*: a feminist reading of Irigaray could be a political engagement that could change the situation of the reader. This brings to the fore the crucial element of transference (both positive and negative): transference is a crucible that may enable shifts in the deepest and most intractable psychic alignments. Chisholm argues that Irigaray mobilizes the woman reader's *negative* transference onto the male philosopher/psychoanalyst who has defined her as lacking or castrated; the negative transference thereby facilitates the refusal to be the patriarchal "feminine." The other side of the coin is the possibility of a more radical recovery of self-respect and identity through a "reserve of power"[26] lying in the unsymbolized desire of women, "a cultural reserve yet to come."[27] Chisholm writes, "Channeled into cultural production of symbolic systems that articulate women's difference and represent her autonomous desire, this 'reserve of power' could, Irigaray prognosticates, effect change and healing in society as well as in the individual." However, the process of mobilizing the negative transference is not without its dangers, and Chisholm sees collective feminist action as the indispensable third party that protects against an otherwise real risk of disintegration or "madness" at the individual or collective level.

    Elizabeth Hirsh develops a similar theme in her essay, "Back to Analysis: How to Do Things with Irigaray" (this volume). For Hirsh, too, the practice, or *praticable*, of psychoanalysis (defined more fully in her essay) constitutes "a privileged frame of reference for understanding the nature and operation of Irigaray's work." Like Chisholm, Hirsh examines the way in which psychoanalysis for Irigaray can be seen both as an instrument of critique and subversion and also as a means of healing and transformation. Whereas Chisholm concentrates on *Speculum* and *This Sex Which Is Not One*, Hirsh focuses specifically on the essays on psychoanalysis, and on Irigaray's argument that psychoanalysis is the scene in which *énonciation* itself is examined and transformed, so that it can shed light on the engendering of the male or female subject of enunciation. She explores the implications of Irigaray's distinctive

mode of intervention both for psychoanalytic practice and for feminist
theory, showing how the psychoanalytic encounter gives a more concrete meaning to Irigaray's claim in *Ethics of Sexual Difference* that we
need a new conception of time and space in order to bring the female
subject into existence. In addition, Hirsh argues that the understanding
of the relation between theory and practice provided by Irigaray's
account of the *praticable* may help us to negotiate the theoretical
impasse of essentialism and constructionism. The dynamic nature of
the encounter enabled by the *praticable* suggests new criteria of theoretical legitimacy.

The question of women's madness or "hysteria," which appeared to
some in the heyday of *écriture féminine* as women's only possible reaction to patriarchal culture, and its corollary, the question of the apparently contradictory and impossible position of the female subject, are
now reappearing in a less literary and more political context: that of
Italian feminism. It is only quite recently that we have become aware of
the link between Irigaray and Italian feminism and the remarkable theoretical work being produced in Italy.[28] Irigaray theorizes that it is a
condition of the coming-to-be of sexual difference that we create a
female homosexual economy and a maternal genealogy that would provide a counterweight to, and have an effect on, the male monosexual
economy that we know as patriarchy. Women need to learn to love
themselves and each other, she argues in *Ethics of Sexual Difference*. But
this love must take a public form, and not be confined to passional relationships at the individual level. The *collective* accession to symbolization is essential. It is a question of embodying sexual difference through
the representation of a different sex and a different genealogy—in language, culture, symbol, religion, social practices, civil and legal status,
and so on. It is in Italy that this vision has been taken the most seriously and where there have been concerted attempts to translate Irigaray's
ideas into political practice. Italian feminists associated with the Milan
Women's Bookstore Collective developed the controversial notion of
affidamento. One can briefly—though inadequately—define *affidamento* by saying that it is a practice that involves the symbolic recognition of women by each other. It is an attempt to go beyond the pitfalls
of both 1. individual emancipation at the cost of rejection of solidarity
with other women; or 2. a kind of merged relationship with other
women in the women's movement, in which any differences—particularly talents, skills, or success in the predominantly male world—are
perceived as threatening. The merged relation—equality in oppression—is said to lead to a kind of static separatism that prevents women
from ever having any real effect on the wider society. The idea of *affi-*

° *damento* was that *another woman* should provide the symbolic mediation between individual and society. It is an attempt—albeit not without pitfalls of its own perhaps—to give the mother-daughter relationship a social and symbolic form that rescues it from the invisibility of
the personal relationship and can therefore provide structures for social
change, by giving sexual difference a real existence at the sociosymbolic level. It rejects the stress on oppression, emancipation, and equality,
in favor of a "symbolic revolution," a kind of "social contract" between
women and a new definition of female freedom based on bonds
between women and an *explicit* acknowledgment of the debt to other
women, primarily to the mother, a debt that in patriarchy has been
invisible and taken for granted as a "natural resource." It thus prioritizes
relations between women over the relation between women and men,
and to this extent distances itself from Irigaray's later development, as
Luisa Muraro explains in her essay (this volume).

Luisa Muraro, one of the founding members of the Milan Women's
Bookstore Collective, argues that Irigaray's major contribution to
women's politics is her formulation of female genealogy and the symbolic woman-to-woman relationship. Thus Muraro sees Irigaray's
development from a politics of women-among-themselves to a politics
of the couple as a political shift with which she finds herself in disagreement. Tracing the itinerary of Irigaray's thought on the question
of female genealogies, she identifies a "turning point" in the 1986 lecture "L'Universel comme médiation" ("The Universal as Mediation";
reprinted in *Sexes and Genealogies*) that she likens to a "medieval fresco
of the end of the world" in its vision of a possible transition to a new
world. The turning point is the moment in Irigaray's thought when she
turns away from the exclusive emphasis on women-to-women relations
toward a broader vision that encompasses the construction of an ethical world of men and women together. Muraro relates the oscillation in
Irigaray's thought here to the oscillations in women's politics. She suggests that Irigaray's treatment of Antigone—a political heroine—indicates the different moments of her thought. For Irigaray Antigone is
originally an emblem of the patriarchal woman, the feminine in patriarchy; she "symbolizes the imprisonment of woman in a symbolic order
that is not her own and the paralysis of the women's world that is the
consequence of this" (Muraro). However, after the turning point
Antigone becomes a heroine, an exemplary figure who defended the
value of maternal genealogy at the cost of death. There is a move from
identity to *action*, a transition in Irigaray's thought toward the desire for
political efficacy and for women's agency in the transformation of the
world. The problems in the mother-daughter relationship, and in rela-

tions between women (the vertical and horizontal woman-to-woman relationships), then become an obstacle to this wider transformation. As Muraro points out, the problems are not solved. The risk of "madness," which Chisholm discusses and which figures prominently in Irigaray's early work, has been silently brushed under the carpet. Muraro's interpretation shows that Irigaray's work is not monolithic; it is marked by the oscillations and tensions that characterize feminist politics. One conclusion we could draw from this paper is that Irigaray herself is an exemplary figure whose work bears some of the signs of women's recent history and is not exempt from its contradictions. As Muraro puts it, we could see Irigaray as a kind of witness, for whom politics has become "demonstrative action and witnessing."

Irigaray's "turning point" must inevitably raise the question of Irigaray's controversial relation to lesbian politics.[29] Although Irigaray was seen at one time as a lesbian separatist, she has in recent years explicitly rejected a politics based on sexual object-choice in favor of the politics of sexual difference, i.e., the necessity for women to have a distinct sociosymbolic existence. This is a move that has not been without its critics. Liana Borghi, for example, argues that the theory of sexual difference suffers from the same problems as Adrienne Rich's notion of the lesbian continuum: they are both myths which reflect a dream of imaginary wholeness that glosses over the real differences and divisions between women: "The original formulation of the lesbian continuum encompassed all women, not just lesbians. The theory of sexual difference makes no distinction between lesbian and straight, white and black, rich and poor, so as to avoid the pitfall of categorising oppression."[30] In other words, Borghi is arguing that, so far, attempts to develop a woman-centered sociosymbolic practice have not succeeded in breaking free from a fantasy of conflict-free unity and harmony. However, the reservations do not detract from the radicality of the *aim*. The vision of a transformation of imaginary and symbolic to allow for an *other* sex, a different subject, is what gives Irigaray's work its utopian and mythical quality but also its reconstructive challenge.

The parameters of this challenge and its implications for lesbian politics are discussed by Elizabeth Grosz in her 1988 essay, "The Hetero and the Homo" (this volume). Grosz argues that Irigaray is redefining the meaning of the terms *homosexuality* and *heterosexuality* in her analysis of patriarchal culture as "hom(m)osexual," that is, an economy of the same, where only one sex is recognized. Thus what Judith Butler identifies as a heterosexual matrix, Irigaray sees as a patriarchal hom(m)osexuality.[31] The difference in vision here is crucial to the directions in which their respective analyses point. Where for Butler the figure of the lesbian is a central deconstructive lever in her destabilization of gender, in Irigaray's work there is a progressive shift in orientation toward a "politics of the couple,"[32] and its precondition "becoming-woman" (*devenir-femme*). In her account of Irigaray Grosz points out that lesbians within patriarchy are not free of the ramifications of patriarchal power. *All* relations between women, and particularly the most intense and intimate ones, are affected by the patriarchal rupture of the primitive mother-daughter bond. One can only identify with a phallic or castrated mother, i.e., with a mother as defined by the patriarchal economy. To become a woman in patriarchy means in effect abandoning the mother. Irigaray points out the urgent necessity of recognizing and giving symbolic existence to the archaic homosexual bond between mother and daughter. Thus while the politics of homosexuality under patriarchy may be *tactical*, as a political maneuver it can only be provisional for Irigaray, since her broader project is the transformation of society to make a place for women's existence. (For other essays in this volume offering further angles on the mother-daughter relationship, or the maternal genealogy, see Philippa Berry, Luisa Muraro, and Joanna Hodge).

Readings of Irigaray have tended to divide between those who regard her as a "sojourner in the imaginary"[33] (whether this is a cause for celebration or suspicion) and those who see her as intervening in the symbolic. However, the difference is not so clear-cut, since in practice the two are hard to separate. The symbolic is a *form* that depends on the imaginary for its content; the imaginary cannot take shape or existence without the structure of the symbolic.[34] It seems to me that the symbolic/imaginary division, like the essentialist/antiessentialist one, will be unhelpful here, if symbolic and imaginary are seen as mutually exclusive; it is time to leave this simplification behind.

Gail Schwab's essay, for example, engages in a detailed exploration of Irigaray's textual images, to focus precisely on "our struggles with the symbolic order." From this point of view she argues that Kristeva and Irigaray are both tackling the same kind of problems, and can most usefully be read as in continuity. The constitution of subjectivity and identity is a central issue for both Kristeva and Irigaray. But for Schwab, despite the importance of Kristeva's theorization of the semiotic, and her conception of prephallic difference, Kristeva remains within orthodox Freudian interpretation, and does not go as far as Irigaray is able to do. Schwab explores Irigaray's nonoedipal, nonphallic account of the body's relationship to subjectivity, through the bodily images of placenta and mucus and the figure of the angel. She reads Irigaray as attempting to symbolize a different, nonbinary imaginary through figures of mediation that put a nonphallic body or mediating space into play. Like Butler, she points to the possibility of the nonbinary. In Butler's case it is the intimation of something that exceeds the binary; in Schwab's case it is the mobilization of a ternary structure, in which the "space between" or "third party" loosens the all-or-nothing rigidity of the binary pair. Her article should also be read in conjunction with Luisa Muraro's discussion of mediation in a more political and philosophical context. These essays show that the idea of mediation in Irigaray's work appears in more than one register—both thematically and at the level of image.

In the final essay in the volume I discuss the ambiguity of Irigaray's images, particularly the utopian images, and suggest that some of their ambiguity derives from a difficulty that Irigaray—and perhaps feminism in general—has produced for herself. Irigaray argues that there is a patriarchal death drive, that patriarchy has been constructed on a sacrifice, an originary matricide, and that we need to bring the mother into symbolic existence. But she also comes dangerously close to suggesting the possibility that there might be a culture without sacrifice,[35] and her recent work, with its emphasis on love, explicitly turns its back on the shadows. (Philippa Berry's essay warns about the dangers of this.) This new form of political optimism can be interpreted in different ways, but it is not an unfamiliar phenomenon. It is easier to attribute violence to an *other* (like patriarchy) than to consider the implications of the inevitable violence at the heart of identity, which brings it closer to home. This leads me to consider one of the central tensions of feminism to be that between feminism as critique and feminism as construction. It seems to me that one of the most important underlying issues here is precisely that of the locus of violence. But it is seldom directly addressed. If Irigaray's recent work now evades that issue, her earlier work, from *Speculum* to *Ethics of Sexual Difference*, provides ample resources for beginning to think about the kind of alibi that patriarchal violence offers for feminism as critique, and the kind of difficulties that might lie in the way of fundamental symbolic reorganization (of which the conflicts engendered by differences between women is only the most obvious example).

In various ways many of the contributors to *Engaging with Irigaray* point toward the necessity or inevitability of radical social or symbolic transformation. Rosi Braidotti sees the redefinition of the subject Woman/women as no less than a change of civilization, of genealogy, and of sense of history. Luisa Muraro describes feminism as the manifestation of a structural change in our civilization. Jean-Joseph Goux, too, indicates that Irigaray is perhaps sketching out the shape of our

° possible future. Irigaray sees herself as announcing a new epoch of which the founding episteme would be sexual difference, marking an end to the episteme described by Heidegger as technology or by Foucault as the end of man and the demise of the subject. There is no doubt that she is envisaging the most far-reaching sociosymbolic reconstruction. Now that her work is becoming available in English, and its implications are being more fully debated, what kind of project will international readers of the nineties collectively create in their engagement with Irigaray?

NOTES •

1. Margaret Whitford, *Luce Irigaray: Philosophy in the Feminine* (New York and London: Routledge, 1991).
2. Jan Montefiore, *Feminism and Poetry: Language, Experience, Identity in Women's Writing* (London: Pandora, 1987), p. 152.
3. See in particular Diana J. Fuss, *Essentially Speaking* (London: Routledge, 1990); Moira Gatens, "A Critique of the Sex/Gender Distinction" in Sneja Gunew, ed., *A Reader in Feminist Knowledge* (New York and London: Routledge, 1991); Elizabeth Grosz, "A Note on Essentialism and Difference," in Sneja Gunew, ed., *Feminist Knowledge: Critique and Construct* (New York and London: Routledge, 1990); Eve Kosofsky Sedgwick, *Epistemology of the Closet* (Berkeley: University of California Press, 1990); and *differences* (1989), vol. 1, no. 2.
4. Irigaray, *This Sex*, p. 76/ *Ce Sexe*, p. 73.
5. Ibid., p. 162/157.
6. Jacques Derrida, "Deconstruction in America: An Interview with Jacques Derrida," James Creech, Peggy Kamuf, and Jane Todd, *Critical Exchange* (Winter 1985), 17:30–31.
7. Brief discussions may be found in Rosi Braidotti, *Patterns of Dissonance: A Study of Women in Contemporary Philosophy*, trans. Elizabeth Guild (Cambridge: Polity, 1991); Drucilla Cornell, *Beyond Accommodation: Ethical Feminism, Deconstruction, and the Law* (New York and London: Routledge, 1991); Elizabeth Grosz, "Derrida, Irigaray, and Deconstruction," in "Leftwright," *Intervention* (1986), 20:70–81; Toril Moi, *Sexual/Textual Politics: Feminist Literary Theory* (London: Methuen, 1985); Andrea Nye, *Feminist Theory and the Philosophies of Man* (London: Croom Helm, 1988); Whitford, *Luce Irigaray.*
8. Paul de Man points out that "[Derrida's] text is the unmaking of a construct. However negative it may sound, deconstruction implies the possibility of rebuilding." From Paul de Man, *Blindness and Insight: Essays in the Rhetoric of Contemporary Criticism* (New York: Oxford University Press, 1971), p. 140; quoted in Carolyn Burke, "Irigaray Through the Looking Glass," this volume).

9. Gayatri Chakravorty Spivak, " 'In a Word': Interview with Ellen Rooney," *differences* (1989), 1(2):124–156, for example.

10. Rosi Braidotti, *Patterns of Dissonance.*

11. Braidotti points out that male philosophers cannot have precisely the same place of enunciation as feminists. Braidotti, "Ethics Revisited: Women and/in Philosophy," in Carole Pateman and Elizabeth Grosz, eds., *Feminist Challenges: Social and Political Theory* (London: Allen and Unwin, 1986), pp. 44–60. See also her essay in this volume.

12. For further discussion of the relation between Derrida and feminism, see Elizabeth Grosz, *Sexual Subversions: Three French Feminists* (Sydney: Allen and Unwin, 1989); Alice Jardine, *Gynesis: Configurations of Woman and Modernity* (Ithaca and London: Cornell University Press, 1985); Gayatri Chakravorty Spivak, "Displacement and the Discourse of Woman," in *Displacement: Derrida and After* (Bloomington: Indiana University Press, 1983), pp. 169–195; Spivak, "Love Me, Love My Ombre, Elle," *Diacritics* (Winter 1984), 14(4):19–36; Spivak, "Feminism and Deconstruction, Again: Negotiating With Unacknowledged Masculinism," in Teresa Brennan, ed., *Between Feminism and Psychoanalysis* (New York and London: Routledge, 1989), pp. 206–223; Teresa de Lauretis, *Technologies of Gender* (Bloomington: Indiana University Press, 1987); Mary Ann Doane, "Veiling Our Desire: Close-Ups of the Woman," in Richard Feldstein and Judith Roof, eds., *Feminism and Psychoanalysis* (Ithaca and London: Cornell University Press, 1989), pp. 105–141; Ellie Ragland-Sullivan, "Seeking the Third Term: Desire, the Phallus, and the Materiality of Language," in *Feminism and Psychoanalysis*; Jacqueline Rose, "Where Does the Misery Come From? Psychoanalysis, Feminism and the 'Event,' " in Richard Feldstein and Judith Roof, eds., *Feminism and Psychoanalysis*; and *Feminist Studies* (1988) vol. 14, no. 1, a special issue on feminism and postmodernism.

13. Cornell, *Beyond Accommodation.*

14. Weed, "The Question of Style," this volume.

15. Jane Gallop, "*Quand Nos Lèvres S'Ecrivent*: Irigaray's Body Politic" in *Romanic Review* (1983), 74:77–83. Reprinted in Jane Gallop, *Thinking Through the Body*, New York: Columbia University Press (1988), pp. 92–100, 117–118, under the title "Lip Service."

16. Carolyn Burke, "Romancing the Philosophers: Luce Irigaray," in *Seduction and Theory: Readings of Gender, Representation and Rhetoric*, ed. Dianne Hunter (Chicago: University of Illinois Press, 1989), pp. 226–240.

17. Irigaray, *This Sex*, p. 151/*Ce Sexe*, p. 148.

18. See Gallop, *Feminism and Psychoanalysis: The Daughter's Seduction* (London: Macmillan, 1982); Suzanne Gearhart, "The Scene of Psychoanalysis: The Unanswered Questions of Dora," in Charles Bernheimer and Claire Kahane, eds., *In Dora's Case: Freud—Hysteria—Feminism* (New York: Columbia University Press, 1985, 1990; London: Virago, 1985), pp. 105–127.

19. Michèle Le Doeuff, "Women and Philosophy," in Toril Moi, ed., *French Feminist Thought: A Reader* (Oxford: Basil Blackwell, 1987), pp. 181–209.

20. Whitford, "Speaking as a Woman: Luce Irigaray and the Female Imaginary" *Radical Philosophy* (1986), 43:8.

21. Jane Gallop, *Reading Lacan* (Ithaca and London: Cornell University Press, 1985).

22. As far as I know, the term *amorous exchange* (*échange amoureux*) appears for the first time in "The Bodily Encounter with the Mother" in Margaret Whitford, ed., *The Irigaray Reader* (Oxford: Basil Blackwell, 1991), pp. 43–44. In subsequent writing it becomes a utopian figure for culture in general.

23. Whitford, "Luce Irigaray and the Problem of Feminist Theory," *Paragraph* (1986), 8:102–105.

24. Paper given at the Glasgow Feminist Theory conference, July 12–15, 1991.

25. Her example is Peter Brooks, "The Idea of a Psychoanalytic Literary Criticism," in Françoise Meltzer, *The Trial(s) of Psychoanalysis* (Chicago: University of Chicago Press, 1987), pp. 145–160.

26. Irigaray, *This Sex*, p. 138/ *Ce Sexe*, p. 136.

27. Ibid.

28. Most of the relevant literature is in Italian; however, for accounts in English, see Mirna Cicioni, " 'Love and Respect, Together': The Theory and Practice of *affidamento* in Italian Feminism," *Australian Feminist Studies* (1989), 10:71–83; Teresa de Lauretis, "The Essence of the Triangle or, Taking the Risk of Essentialism Seriously: Feminist Theory in Italy, the U.S., and Britain," *differences* (1989), 1(2):3–37; Liana Borghi, "Between Essence and Presence: Politics, Self, and Symbols in Contemporary Lesbian Poetry," in Dennis Altmann, Carol Vance, Martha Vicinus, and Jeffrey Weeks et al., eds., *Homosexuality, Which Homosexuality? International Conference on Gay and Lesbian Studies* (London: GMP Publishers, 1989), pp. 61–81; Rosi Braidotti, "The Italian Women's Movement in the 1980s," *Australian Feminist Studies* (1986), 3:129–135; Milan Women's Bookstore Collective, *Sexual Difference: A Theory of Social-Symbolic Practice* (Bloomington: Indiana University Press, 1990); *Italian Feminist Thought: A Reader*, ed. Paola Bono and Sandra Kemp (Oxford: Basil Blackwell, 1991).

29. For recent interpretations see Christine Holmlund, "The Lesbian, the Mother, the Heterosexual Lover: Irigaray's Recodings of Difference," *Feminist Studies* (1991), 17(2):283–308; and Anna Marie Jagose, "Irigaray and the Lesbian Body: Remedy and Poison," *Genders* (Spring 1992), 13:30–41.

30. Liana Borghi, "Between Essence and Presence," p. 65.

31. Some of the problems of this inversion—turning heterosexuality into homosexuality—are discussed in Sedgwick, *Epistemology of the Closet.*

32. Rosi Braidotti, "The Ethics of Sexual Difference: The Case of Foucault and Irigaray," *Australian Feminist Studies* (1986), 3:1–13.

33. Paul Smith, "Julia Kristeva et al.; or, Take Three or More," in Richard Feldstein and Judith Roof, eds., *Feminism and Psychoanalysis*, p. 102.

34. See Whitford, *Luce Irigaray*, chapter 4.

35. See in particular Irigaray, "Women, the Sacred, Money" in *Sexes and Genealogies*, pp. 73–88/"Les Femmes, le sacré, l'argent," *Sexes et parentés*, pp. 87–102.

PART 1

.

Beyond
Essentialism

IRIGARAY

THROUGH

THE

LOOKING GLASS

It is no longer possible to go looking for woman, or for woman's femininity or for female sexuality. At least, they can not be found by means of any familiar mode of thought or knowledge—even if it is impossible to stop looking for them.
—Jacques Derrida, *Spurs/Eperons*

Luce Irigaray is a philosopher, psychoanalyst, and essayist whose work explores the possibility and impossibility of understanding "woman." She has been active in the MLF (Mouvement de libération des femmes) in Paris since its early stages.[1] With the publication of *Speculum of the Other Woman* in 1974, her critiques of psychoanalytic and philosophical discourses began to be known by a limited audience outside of France. Her work has been inaccessible to English-speaking feminists, partly because there have been so few translations but, more importantly because of the conceptual and stylistic difficulties that her writing presents, even for those who are fluent in French. This situation is further complicated by the fact that her writing has been discussed, to some extent, out of context in a series of critiques of what is taken to be her position. Because Irigaray is concerned with the possibility of an analogy—a seductive one at that—between female sexuality and a *parler-femme*, or a "speaking (as) woman," it is important to examine her writing in context, to see how it functions and whether it lives up to its own expectations.

For some time Irigaray has been working on the premise that "lan-

•   guage and the systems of representation cannot 'translate' " woman's desire.[2] Her first book, *Le Langage des déments* (The language of dementia, 1973), studies the statements of schizophrenics of both sexes. As a result of this research Irigaray concludes that "sexual differences become embedded in language," that "there is a dynamics of statements which is different according to sex."[3] Although, in her view, male patients retained the ability to perform syntactic modifications and the use of metalanguage, women tended to articulate their condition physically, to "suffer it directly in their body."[4] Generally speaking, she asserts, women lack access to language appropriate to the expression of their desire. Consequently, in *Speculum,* she set out to understand why female sexuality could not be articulated within Western theoretical discourse. Taking examples from Plato to Hegel, Irigaray sees in this idealist tradition, which emphasizes the principles of identity, sameness, and visibility as conditions for representation in language, the philosophical assumptions underlying psychoanalytic discourse. Within this psychophilosophical system the female is defined "as nothing other than the complement, the other side, or the negative side, of the masculine."[5] Thus, the female subject is either assimilated to the male, as in Freud's account of infantile psychic development, or simply left out of theory, which assumes that it cannot be conceptualized. Because the female sex offers nothing to see, female sexuality becomes the "hole" in psychoanalytic theory. This lack scandalizes the philosopher in Freud, who suspects that it is indeed impossible to say what woman really wants.

   Speculum calls for a patient but radical "disconcerting" of language and logic, which is then enacted in *This Sex Which is Not One.* The sex which is not one is, of course, the female sex. In Irigaray's view the male sex has taken unto itself the privileged status of "oneness": that is, a unitary representation of identity in analogy with the male sexual organ. She asserts that "all Western discourse presents a certain isomorphism with the masculine sex: the privilege of unity, form of the self, of the visible, of the specularisable, of the erection."[6] Such a logic does not allow for the expression of the female sexual organs, which cannot be described, let alone represented in unitary terms. Just as the female genitals are "plural" or multiple—"always at least two . . . joined in an embrace"[7]—so women's language will be plural, autoerotic, diffuse, and undefinable within the familiar rules of (masculine) logic. Because Irigaray believes that female sexuality cannot be articulated within Aristotelian logic, her prose abandons the coherence and forcefulness of analytic argument. The result, in *This Sex Which Is Not One,* is a more fluid and sinuous style or styles that seek to keep "in touch" with a different form of sexuality.

A "speaking (as) woman" might articulate experiences that are devalued or not permitted by the dominant discourse: the most important, in Irigaray's view, are the sensual/emotional relationships of women with their mothers and with other women, which have been censured in psychoanalytic theory. Her next work, written in 1979, was a brief poetic text entitled *Et l'une ne bouge pas sans l'autre* ("And the One Doesn't Stir Without the Other") that takes as its theme the difficult relationship between a mother and daughter. Painfully, Irigaray's prose embodies their knotted relations and the guilt-ridden structures of their mutual desire. Returning in a different vein to the body language of women, she explores corporeal paralysis as a metaphor for lack of connection to the maternal. Written in 1980, Irigaray's most recent work, *Marine Lover of Friedrich Nietzsche*, conducts a subtle critique of the philosopher's theory, taken as a type of masculine thought. However, its lyrical, incantatory voice refuses to argue a thesis according to the traditional requirements for such language. It is as if she were speaking from another territory—the ocean, or the other side of the looking glass—where the familiar rules of logic have been reversed, deconstructed, and subjected to a sea change. To follow her trajectory this essay adopts the strategy of, first, locating her starting points and defining their intellectual ambience, then, imitating her progress in search of an ideological space for the *parler-femme*.

Irigaray might be described as a dissident Lacanian psychoanalyst whose feminist revision of psychoanalytic theory and "female style" may be situated in relation to Derridean deconstruction. However, such a description raises more questions than it answers for an American audience. Jaques Lacan and Jacques Derrida do not figure in her writing as straightforward "influences": indeed, *Speculum* mentions neither, and in *This Sex Which Is Not One* Irigaray hesitates to invoke the authority, or even the name, of Lacan. These two prominent intellectual forces are, to borrow a concept from deconstruction, present "intertextually"; they are interwoven into the web of her own text's unfolding. However, to locate the echoes of their writing in Irigaray's work, to describe their effects upon it, is a risky business, for any selection or summary is necessarily a distortion when one is dealing with such maddeningly abstruse thinkers. Risky, but unavoidable, if one wishes eventually to read with Irigaray rather than read about her.

Irigaray was a member of the Freudian School of Paris, the psychoanalytic institute founded by Jacques Lacan in 1964 when he and his followers broke from the more conservative French Psychoanalytic Society.[8] Members of the Freudian School also taught at Vincennes, the

• experimental, "left-wing" campus of the University of Paris, established in the wake of the 1968 political disturbances. From its inception the Vincennes Department of Psychoanalysis—the only one of its kind— was staffed by some of Lacan's close associates, including Irigaray. How- ever, after the publication of *Speculum*, when she proposed to examine some of its themes in her seminar, Irigaray learned that her seminar had been canceled by the new board of directors of the department: it did not appear to fit into their program for the development of a psycho- analytic "science."[9] When no explanation for her sudden dismissal was offered, many people felt that the publication of her book was the real reason, and, furthermore, that Lacan had used the reorganization of the department to express his personal displeasure at this feminist critique. Thus, to call Irigaray a "dissident Lacanian" raises the complicated his- tory of her theoretical and personal relations to the controversial psy- choanalyst. It calls for a discussion of her efforts to deal with the pres- ence of "le Maître," the position of Lacan as "Master" of the house of psychoanalysis.

The question of the disciples' relationship to Freud has played an enormously complicated role in the creation of a psychoanalytic estab- lishment. Critical of American interpretations of Freud, Lacan claims to return psychoanalysis to the spirit of the Master and accuses its American advocates of reducing Freud's subtle science to normative ego-psychology. As faithful disciple, Lacan defends and reinterprets his Master's word, but, as new Master, Lacan occupies the central position in his own branch of the psychoanalytic establishment. Although in their writings both Freud and Lacan undermine the traditional foun- dations of authority per se, their own magisterial positions within psy- choanalytic practice pose serious problems as a contradiction of their theory. Sherry Turkle, a sociologist of "psychoanalytic politics," has asked whether the master-disciple relationship built into psychoanaly- sis by means of the training analysis does not work, in the long run, to subvert what is most subversive about its own practices. She observes that Lacan's followers have been taxed with an allegiance to Lacan that overshadows any psychoanalyst's allegiance to Freud, and that, not sur- prisingly, the problem of "le Maître" has occupied a central place in their discussions.[10] One might expect, then, that questions of "mastery" and the "Master" would engage French feminists' attention: these con- cepts are loaded, or overdetermined, in their particular cultural context, and, for that reason, call out for a feminist demystification.

In Irigaray's view the general problem is further exacerbated when male masters speak as authorities on the subject of female sexuality. The first section of *Speculum* analyzes Freud's (fictive) lecture, "On Femi-

ninity," as the discourse of a master who cloaks his desire to dominate
his female subject(s) with the seductive formulations of phallocentric
theory.[11] In 1972–73 Lacan took as the theme for his famous public
seminar Freud's question *Was will das Weib* (What does Woman want?).
Lacan concluded that "there is a pleasure [*jouissance*] beyond the phallus,"[12] but insisted that women, even women analysts, would not or
could not make clear to him what this pleasure might be. Furthermore,
to add insult to injury, he added: "They don't know what they are saying, that's the whole difference between them and me."[13] Lacan, by
contrast, is the one who can "explain what it's all about."[14] But, Irigaray
"replied," in two essays published in 1975 and 1977, there is no place
for the female subject within Lacan's theoretical models. Although he
had already expelled her from the ranks of the faithful, she had by no
means gotten him out of her system. If "a Maître can play a dominant
role as much by his absence as by his presence,"[15] Irigaray's texts may be
haunted by Lacan. His unspoken name paradoxically embodies the
paternal authority of psychoanalytic "law."

Lacan is like the paterfamilias of the psychoanalytic family who
refuses to acknowledge the independent wisdom of his daughters. The
daughter, in turn, seeks a way out of her overdetermined transference
to this rejecting father-lover by turning upon the terms of her allegiance. Lacan's absent presence in Irigaray's writing resembles the
"Name-of-the-Father," his own concept of social identity as inscribed
in the subject, male or female, through the assumption of the patronym
within a patriarchal order.[16] Her work, then, becomes, in part, an
attempt to rename herself. She must divest herself of the patronym
Lacanian to reclaim an ideological space from which to "speak (as)
woman." Furthermore, this self-renaming would refuse the Name-of-
the-Father's prohibition against prolonged contact with the maternal,
which the congruence of "name" and "negative" [*nom et non*] implies in
the original French. Ridding language of this embodiment of the paternal law may free one to explore the "geography of feminine pleasure"[17]
and its ties to the preoedipal phase, when the child enjoys a sensual relationship to the mother's body. Irigaray suspects that it is with other
women that a woman may find the "means for overcoming that loss of
the first relationship with the mother's body,"[18] and that this recovery
can happen only in an ideological and textual space apart from the prohibitions represented by the Name-of-the-Father. This position leads to
a kind of separatism that is nevertheless troubled by the seductive
appeal of the paternal metaphor from which it is breaking away.

Irigaray derives considerable support in this undertaking from a
male philosopher who asserts that only "the 'man' . . believes in the

truth of woman, in woman-as-truth." This provocative statement appears in Jacques Derrida's essay, "La Question du style."[19] This text hovers, unmentioned, in the background of both *Speculum* and *This Sex Which Is Not One*, which amplify the charge that Lacanian discourse is phallocentric. Derrida's essay weaves its way around its subject, the relations of "woman" and "truth" as a question of style in Friedrich Nietzsche. It suggests that the apparently misogynistic Nietzsche may have sought, in spite of himself, to "describe a femininity that is not defined by a male desire to supply a lack."[20] Whether or not this was Nietzsche's project, it becomes Irigaray's. But, to come to it, she operates through the detour of deconstructive philosophy, which provides her with the methods to elaborate upon Derrida's charge against Lacan.

Derrida's vocabulary in "La Question du style" undergoes a slight but significant modification for Irigaray's purposes when he asserts that Lacanian theory places woman "back in the old [conceptual] machinery, in phallogocentrism."[21] His word weds *phallocentrism* to *logocentrism*: it implies that psychoanalytic discourse is guilty of identifying the phallus[22] with the *Logos* as transcendent and, therefore, unexamined (and unexaminable) grounds of signification, of assigning meaning. One may attempt to unpack his neologism. In Derrida's writing "logocentrism" designates the tendency in Western philosophy to interpret the Word (*Logos*) in its full theological sense ("In the beginning was the Word, and the Word was God"). Logocentrism also implies an attitude of nostalgia for a lost presence or a longing for some first cause of being and meaning. More recently, with the general diminution of religious belief, logocentric thinking has assigned this lost value to the activities of full self-consciousness ("thought thinking itself"). Logocentrism results from the human desire to posit a central presence as a locus of coherence and authenticity—whether in the form of God's statement "I am that I am" or the Cartesian "Cogito ergo sum." Derrida's coined word taxes Freudo-Lacanism with a double centrism when it puts the phallus in the central position as a kind of *Logos*, as the "signifier of all signifiers."

Expanding Derrida's critique, one could argue that because the phallus guarantees the possibility of the representation of both sexual difference and desire, it is the master term of psychoanalysis, or "God" within its own conceptual system. Derrida's *phallogocentrism*, then, "declares the inextricable collusion of phallocentrism with logocentrism . . . and unites feminism and deconstructive, grammatological philosophy in their opposition to a common enemy."[23] In psychoanalytic theory's longing for an authorizing principle resides its capacity for blindness about its own presuppositions. In a general way Derrida's medita-

tion on the relations of "truth" and "woman" suggests ways out of the
old conceptual machinery.

But what is deconstruction, let alone a feminist version of that enigmatic procedure? The deconstructor begins by finding "the point where
the text covers up,"[24] or "the moment that is undecidable in terms of
the text's apparent system of meanings."[25] Then "the task is to dismantle [*déconstruire*] the metaphysical and rhetorical structures at work in
(the text), not in order to reject or discard them, but to reinscribe them
in another way."[26] The structures in question are usually binary opposites such as "same/other," "subject/other," "identity/difference,"
"male/female." The aim is not to neutralize the oppositional structure,
but rather to demonstrate the inequality of the terms locked into opposition. In such a structure, according to Derrida, "one of the two terms
controls the other . . . holds the superior position. To deconstruct the
opposition is first . . . to overthrow [*renverser*] the hierarchy."[27] However, the task is not yet complete: "In the next phase of deconstruction,
this reversal must be displaced," and the "winning" term used without
giving it the privileged status that its opposite once possessed. The critic must be prepared to accept "the irruptive emergence of a new 'concept,' a concept which no longer allows itself to be understood in terms
of the previous regime."[28] In *Speculum* this strategy of reversal and displacement operates upon the conceptual hierarchies "identity/differ-
ence," "subject/object," "male/female." It also produces the fable of
female sexuality and writing enacted in *This Sex Which Is Not One* in
which the "inferior" terms of these structural pairs are reinscribed, but
with a different status and, presumably, without placing the formerly
devalued term in the position of its "oppressor."

The problematic status of this displacement, the way in which the
new concept means what it says once the operation of deconstruction
is complete, is beyond the scope of this essay, which returns now to the
subject of Irigaray, Irigaray as subject. At this point, however, one may
offer a final description of Derrida's strategy: "His text . . . is the unmaking of a construct. However negative it may sound, deconstruction
implies the possibility of rebuilding."[29] Both Derrida and Irigaray create new sexual fables of the process of signification. Derrida proposes
an account that replaces phallogocentrism with a "hymeneal" fable: one
that involves both sexes and sexual difference in its metaphorical representation of the creation of meaning. Irigaray, by contrast, omits the
male sex and valorizes female sexual sufficiency, in a fable that can be
described as "vulval" or "vaginal."[30] Her account emphasizes the multiple or plural styles of female sexuality and expression, in the figure of
the sexual lips that are constantly "in touch" with the diffuse sensuality

• of the female body. Although it would be interesting to compare Derrida's "hymeneal" fable with Irigaray's "vaginal" one, it suffices to
observe that, in both cases, a fable is offered in opposition to Lacan's figure of the phallus. Again, in both cases, it is important to note that
terms like *hymeneal* and *vaginal* are being used with an awareness of
their limitations as analogies, or as emerging "concepts" resisting the
possibility that they will be taken as new master terms. To put it differently, the reader of such texts must be willing not to "believe" in their
fables, to let go of them once they have become too useful.[31]

Is it possible or even desirable to adopt a frame of mind that does not
require a text to confer a final, reliable authority? Deconstructive writers assert, and intend their readers to understand, that they are creating
limited analogies without an absolute claim for their ontological status.
Certainly, this peculiar use of language creates a strain. Words are being
used without their authors' subscribing to the premise that the models
to which they refer might actually exist. The referential status of language is put into question, and, furthermore, each deconstruction can,
in turn, be deconstructed. In such a view "language bears within itself
the necessity of its own critique."[32] One may observe, at this point, that
deconstruction's basic stance is antiauthoritarian: it is suspicious of
master concepts and explanations that assert their own finality. Indeed,
if one adopts the strategies of deconstruction, then no single text,
including this one, can pretend to have made a definitive statement.
With this predicament in mind the critic is tempted to imitate Irigaray's
move from the "hard" language of theoretical discourse to the more
"fluid" languages of poetry and fable in her recent writing. This transformation—but the word is too dramatic to describe the gradual shift
that occurs in Irigaray's prose—can be observed as it happens in her
work. At this point in my own text, therefore, I follow on her path,
while keeping my distance, to speak of *This Sex Which Is Not One* in its
own language(s).

This Sex Which Is Not One is a chorus of voices, in which Freud, Lacan,
Derrida, various unnamed speakers, and, unexpectedly, Lewis Carroll,
reverberate and are transposed into a different mode. As readers we are
invited not to begin objectively, outside the text, but rather to start
inside and work our way out into its complex web of textual relations.
We recognize our own textuality while adjusting to the quality of intertextuality that inhabits Irigaray's writing. To become the reader of *This
Sex Which Is Not One* is to recognize that we are all implicated in this
discourse. This realization may then generate a new critical attitude:
one that rejects the lonely fiction of superiority over a text.

If we can abandon the illusion that it is possible to speak from a position of mastery, we may be tempted by the subversive notion of an "other" view—an underview. We may follow Irigaray when, in the preface, she goes underground with Lewis Carroll's Alice, seeking a place from which she may (re)learn to speak. That place is found after the book's prolonged journey through the looking glass, to what she imagines as the "other side," a conceptual realm beyond the law of the *Logos*. Woman's place, she tells the men, is not where you think it is: we are beyond the mirror of your languages in a new psychic space. Her "other" view is, then, something like the dizzying perspective of an adult Alice, and her "other side," an ideological space beyond the psychic economy of patriarchy. Irigaray is trying to imagine a realm—at once emotional and intellectual—in which woman is no longer defined in relation to man as his negative, other, or as lack.

However, in the country of *This Sex Which Is Not One* the rules of logic are not simply inverted as in Carroll's *Through the Looking Glass*. Rather, Irigaray questions the structures of logic in which the female as concept has been suppressed, then displaces the whole system. Deconstructing structural polarities that assign priority to the first term and devalue the second, she attempts to leave behind the conceptual universe of the *Logos* and its symbolic policeman, the phallus. This new ideological place of Irigaray's writing could be described as preoedipal or postpatriarchal, or, as the place of a desire. It is a site where women's relations to each other might acquire appropriate expression.

Some of the difficulties confronting one who would discuss Irigaray on her own terms may be apparent by now. In a sense, there is a lack of "content." Unlike Hélène Cixous or Monique Wittig, Irigaray does not invent (or reinvent) for us female characters, heroines, or myths in opposition to patriarchal culture. Her deconstructive procedure is puzzling, because she is chiefly concerned with questioning familiar modes of thought and interrogating the concepts of logic and the rules of discourse. Once we realize that this procedure is, in part, her content, we are on the right track. At the same time, her attempt to rethink woman without resorting to limiting or essentialist definitions puts a strain on our reading habits, as when Irigaray suggests, but does not make absolute claims for, a relation between the geography of female sexuality and the shape of her own writing. As my discussion interweaves with her texts, I trust that this performance will convey something of their procedures and strategies, while sketching the shape of her "speaking (as) woman."

On the unexpected order of *Speculum*, which begins with Freud and ends with Plato, Irigaray commented, "The architectonics of the text,

• or texts, confounds the linearity of an outline, the teleology of discourse, within which there is no possible place for the 'feminine' except the traditional place of the repressed, the censured."[33] In that work her desire was to disturb the "phallogocentric" order of argumentation, in which the end is clearly predetermined by the beginning. It is not surprising, then, that the form of *This Sex Which Is Not One* is difficult to describe. Like *Speculum*, it begins in an unexpected manner: its preface is a film review entitled "The Looking Glass, from the Other Side." This preface is doubly reminiscent, for it reviews a recent Swiss film, *Les Arpenteurs* (The surveyors), whose heroine is named Alice in a subtle parallel with the Alice of Wonderland. The film's "Alice" seems to have elected a dwelling place somewhere on the "other side," in Irigaray's new geography of female desire. Her activities, and the opposition they soon encounter, provide the rich thematic material that Irigaray teases out in the rest of the book. After this curious preface she traces "Alice's" journey backwards, via "a long detour by way of the analysis of the various systems of oppression brought to bear upon her," so that she may once again "reach the place where she knows pleasure as a woman."[34] This detour includes the title essay on female sexuality,[35] an evaluation of psychoanalytic theory, and an essay on the power of language and the subordination of the female as a concept. After a series of dialogues with various interlocutors, Irigaray pursues her analyses with an essay on "the traffic in women" (which suggests that female homosexuality must be rethought outside the psychosexual economy of patriarchy)[36] and a discussion of pornography. Her book concludes, although it does not seem to end, with a poetic prose essay evoking a love relationship between women, "When Our Lips Speak Together."[37]

If *Speculum* challenged Freud by deconstructing his theory of female sexuality, *This Sex Which Is Not One* adopts Lacan's own tactics to question the discourse of the Master: it contains two remarkably subtle replies to Lacan. Interestingly, however, Irigaray rarely mentions him by name in these two essays. She prefers to bring his system into question by exposing the ways in which it gives him the magisterial role. The first essay, "Così Fan Tutti," does Lacan the curious honor of quoting him against himself, to demonstrate his incapacity to hear what women say. Irigaray again insists that in his psychoanalysis "the feminine occurs only within models and laws devised by masculine subjects."[38] Although she cites Lacan throughout the text, his name—the symbol of his authority—is relegated to the bottom of the page, where it appears in a footnote.

The second essay, "The 'Mechanics' of Fluids," indicts the Master and his system for their lack of interest in the geography of female pleasure. However, Irigaray does this in an insidiously indirect manner, again weaving her way around Lacan while citing him in the footnotes only. Ostensibly, she discusses the physics of fluids, which have not been explained by the language suited to the discussion of solids. Here, of course, "fluids" is partly an analogy with female expression, and "solids" with the dry self-consistency of male logic, including the logic of psychoanalysis. In an artfully flowing style she unravels the "long-standing complicity" between rationality and "solids," which has result-ed in a privileging of that which is firm, quantifiable, and measurable. In this system of physics (and metaphysics) "every psychic economy is organized around the phallus (or Phallus)."[39] It is not surprising, then, that the fluidity of the female is deemed unworthy of attention. Because female language flows beyond the boundaries of logical discourse, it is seen as unstable, in excess of solidifiable sense, and, therefore, outside the discourse of the Master. Because "woman" speaks "fluid,"[40] her meanings can not be frozen into static images or metaphors. With tremendous stylistic fluidity, Irigaray slips away from Lacan's fiefdom while paying an ironic *hommage* to the Master.[41]

Because her writing seeks to stir up this fluid current within language and open up the closure of its logical and syntactic systems, it is useful to focus upon her strategies of beginning and ending, or, "preface" and "conclusion." Both "The Looking Glass, from the Other Side" and *This Sex Which Is Not One* begin with an epigraph from *Alice's Adventures Through the Looking-Glass* (chapter 3):

> . . . she suddenly began again. "Then it really *has* happened, after all! And now, who am I? I *will* remember, if I can! I'm determined to do it." But being determined didn't help her much, and all she could say, after a great deal of puzzling, was "L, I *know* it begins with L."[42]

The original Alice finds herself alone in the wood where things have no name. The rules of logic do not yet prevail, for no name-bestowing Adam is present. This is Alice's question about her identity, and her observation that "it begins with L." There is no answer other than her self-renaming. "L" is, of course, multiple in Irigaray's reading: Alice, "Alice," Luce, and, for a French speaker, *elle/elles*—the third person fem-inine, both singular and plural. To begin with *elle(s)* means to learn that the female self is multiple, that we are all written into the text. Once through the looking glass, the unified self is seen as an illusion. In the shifting tones and styles of *This Sex Which Is Not One*, "je" is trying to speak as "elle(s)," to establish through language the communication that she desires among "nous: toute(s)"—the final words of the book.

Irigaray suggests that our naming system has always hindered this

•   communion. Names appropriate identity and cloister us within the
networks of family relations. Like Lewis Carroll's Alice, the film's
"Alice" does not use a family name, for she seeks to live beyond the
Name-of-the-Father. She hopes to live apart from the categories of the
"proper," "property," and "propriety." Irigaray examines the logical
requirements of this cluster of concepts and demystifies its effects upon
the status of women within the economy of language.[43] It follows that
elle must demystify her proper name, the one that she was "given" within the system that saw her as a form of property. Since her father's death
"Alice" has situated herself in relation to her mother, who is her closest
neighbor and "the only one who seems to know who Alice is."[44] This
special knowledge suggests an identity shared with, or derived from, the
mother. Soon another woman appears in "Alice's" house, and becomes
first her double, then her accomplice. The two women refuse the surveyors' "patriarchal" attempts to separate them or demarcate their
sphere as private property. Through their deliberate rejection of such
values, they establish a fragile community among themselves. However, the old laws concerning identity, property, and what is proper soon
reassert themselves, when the surveyors threaten to destroy their privileged territory.

This new geography of female relations reappears only in the final
essay, which has a therapeutic aim. Irigaray wants to make room for a
language of love among women, of sexual pleasure beyond the law of
the phallus. These relations partake of the preoedipal relations between
mother and daughter, without, however, recreating their roles. Resur-
rected in the present, this lost paradise of mutual affection does not
resemble the psychoanalysts' description of preoedipal crises over the
need for individuation. There is no need to seal off the self from the
other. For the space of an essay, mutuality exists among women, for
each woman is herself multiple and speaks a variety of tongues. "Elle"
speaks to her lover in a mode that reinvents the female subject as
"tu/je," "you/I." Here language is trying to unlearn its requirements for
a unified subject and to set aside the subject-object paradigm as a model
of human relations. "Tu" is the equal of "je"; their mutuality is signaled
in writing by their double inscription as subject(s). Untrammeled by
the delimiting function of proper names, the lovers reject the demands
of appropriation as literally inappropriate to their relations. "When
Our Lips Speak Together" may be described as a love poem in prose and
a fable of female relations in the optative mood: it is written "as if" we
could forget the logical and emotional requirements of the phallic economy. Irigaray wagers that once language has been taught to lower its
resistance, it may then learn to generate another mode of signification.

•

Allow me to open a parenthesis within this opening. In her dream of an "other side," Irigaray's writing again shows affinities with that of Derrida. Like Derrida, Irigaray returns to the current in Freud that could enable us to decode the neurosis-producing structures of the oedipal family, the guilty relations of this central Western fable. However, if one abandons the oedipal model, what remains as a figure of truth? Is there a "feminist" fable through which we can work out the relations of woman and truth, woman's truth? Irigaray and Derrida have both taken up Antigone, that difficult daughter of Oedipus who defied the laws of the city. In their different interpretations the Antigone myth describes a break with the teleology of Oedipus within his own family.[45] In *Speculum* Irigaray reads Antigone's defiance of the law—the edicts of Creon—as the assertion of her maternal lineage. In her view, Antigone buries Polynices not because he is her brother, but because he is her mother's son. She wishes to honor their shared connection to the mother, in opposition to the surrogate father, Creon. She analyzes the Sophoclean drama as testimony of the transition from matriarchal to patriarchal values. Then, in the startling analogies of *This Sex Which Is Not One*, Irigaray's "Alice" shows affinities with Antigone, the antagonist whose going underground subverts the laws of the fathers. Describing the project that preceded her dismissal from Vincennes, Irigaray explains that she intended to examine the myth of Antigone in the work of Sophocles, Hoelderlin, Hegel, and Brecht. Her seminar would have analyzed what this heroine's opposition to the law brings into focus, "that other 'face' of discourse which provokes a crisis when it appears in broad daylight."[46] In this reading Antigone's example prompts us to rethink the reasons behind her sentence: the law's requirement that she be silenced to save the constituent necessities of rationality.

Both Irigaray and Derrida, however, bring into question these logical necessities in their attempts to counter the closed circle of theoretical discourse. Rejecting teleological closure, both create unfamiliar sequences of argument and demonstration. Although at this point I close my parenthesis concerning Derrida in Irigaray's text, I reopen the question of its opening. *This Sex Which Is Not One* begins with a preface that is not a preface: a review that repeats or rehearses the rest of the book in another key. In the sequence that follows "Alice" is transformed into "elle(s)," the antagonist of closed structures of meaning. For Irigaray the metamorphoses of the female self can occur only in an open structure, one in which neither beginning nor end is quite what we expect. Once the rhetorical and metaphysical structures requiring closure have been deconstructed, the critic can reinscribe her meaning in

• a new way. Irigaray's book ends without closing, as befits the image of "ce sexe": the female one whose lips are both closed and open. Through them flows the current of what "woman" is saying. "Yet one must know how to listen otherwise than in good form(s) to hear what it says."[47]

Irigaray's texts know how to listen, for "Alice" is also "an/alyste" and her work, "an/alyse." Her writing is an extension of the performance of psychotherapy, for female self and other. As such, it accepts the hesitations and silences of unfamiliar meanings. "Questions," for example, transcribes a number of interviews or exchanges in a mode that is between speech and writing, as befits her subject(s). Questions echo throughout her writing, but when they go unanswered silence is not oppressive. It waits for an opening, as in the indecisions, pauses, and blank spaces of "When Our Lips Speak Together." Reserving a space for the reader, her concluding essay offers "the site of a listening attention,"[48] or what the analyst provides for the analysand. In a more general way *This Sex Which Is Not One* as a whole opens itself to the reader, that other self. The book calls for a complicity between reader and writer not unlike that which may occur in the analytic situation between a nonsubordinate analysand and a nonauthoritarian analyst. Reading Irigaray is like taking part in a process in which neither participant is certain of the outcome. Because "termination" suggests (fore)closure, this analysis may well be interminable, but my own is now coming to an end.

But how, the nagging voice persists, do we learn to play with language in this fashion? And how shall we rescue our own writing from the mark of Oedipus, from the guilt and neurosis of "absence" and "lack"? Can we rid ourselves of the yoke of "authority" and desubjugate the female self simply by altering the languages in which we have learned to express our understanding? Is there anything here that translates into our contexts? One may observe that Irigaray's writing is not immediately "useful" or prescriptive, and that in its very nondirectiveness lies its importance. We can not extract from her work an all-encompassing feminist theory, although we can learn that "trick of rereading,"[49] the habit of mind that is called deconstructive. Furthermore, we may conclude that deconstruction, "which teaches one to question all transcendent idealisms," is a critical approach eminently suitable to feminists: surely, we have less to lose and more to jettison in the traditions of critical distance, authority, and mastery.[50] And, finally, it may come as a relief to find that one may use the available languages without fully subscribing to their premises, that one may question the metaphysics of their questions.

•

However, an important problem for readers of Irigaray remains: does her writing manage to avoid the construction of another idealism to replace the "phallogocentric" systems that she dismantles? Do her representations of a *parler-femme* in analogy with female sexuality avoid the centralizing idealism with which she taxes Western conceptual systems? Although feminists' criticism of her work has come, generally speaking, from quarters not in sympathy with the deconstructive strategies she employs, their different readings are, in their own ways, instructive. In one such reading Irigaray is charged with an essentialist celebration of the female body, differing little from the patriarchal definitions she proposes to dismantle: "To found a field of study on this belief in the inevitability of natural sex differences can only compound patriarchal logic and not subvert it."[51] However, as another critic asserts, to dismiss Irigaray's arguments in this reductive fashion "is to fail to register their full impact and the range of devices at their disposal."[52] One might respond to the first criticism by commenting that it reduces the subtlety of Irigaray's thought to a simple argument "from the body," in order to then point out that such arguments are, indeed, essentialist. This strategy ignores Irigaray's suggestion that female writing may be produced in analogy *with* the body and her awareness that it does not simply flow from it. Furthermore, in thus reducing her arguments, it disregards their manner, even though questions of style and strategy go to the heart of their matter.

A more useful critique argues that "to invoke the rhythms of the body is only to extend the sphere of existent speech, not invent a new one."[53] In this view the *parler-femme* simply extends the terrain of what can be expressed, and the dream of an "other side" of language is unrealizable. Although this observation is probably correct, it too focuses upon the problematic figure of the body in Irigaray's writing at the expense of other features: its mode of address, its stylistic fluidity, its deconstructive tactics. In her use of conscious or deliberate analogies, Irigaray intends to avoid the reification of which such critiques would convict her: she stresses "not so much the anatomy but . . . the morphology of the female sex."[54] The lips of "When Our Lips Speak Together," for example, should not be reduced to a literally anatomical specification, for the figure suggests another mode rather than another model. It implies plurality, multiplicity, and a mode of being "in touch" that differs from the phallic mode of discourse. Similarly, her "vaginal" fable does not simply replace the "phallic" one, and one should recall that both are probably simulacra, or representations of ideas in the mind. Important questions that have not been raised by Irigaray's critics concern the nature and use of her figurative language: whether it is mimetic or referential, whether it hovers or shifts back and forth between these two types of significa-

• tion, and whether it is used consistently. Only once these questions have been fully discussed can we begin to understand the problematic inter-section of sexuality and representation. On the subject of philosophy's "proud, delusive knowledge" (the assumptions that allow us to ask such questions), Nietzsche wondered whether all philosophy "has not been merely an interpretation of the body and a misunderstanding of the body."[55] To reverse Nietzsche, one might ask whether the representation of the body does not depend upon the undecidability of these philo-sophical questions. At this point, once again, the language of theory cedes tactfully to the language of fable.

Such fables can only be read: they do not provide a basis for action. However, although we can not "apply" Irigaray's writing in any direct fashion, we may find that we emerge from this difficult reading process with our minds, literally, changed. We may become interested in a kind of writing that encourages us "to question privileged explanations even as explanations are generated."[56] Furthermore, such writing is itself generative in its power to set language in motion. It is liberating to find that one may transgress the demands of univocal signification by letting in the linguistic "accidents" that don't fit into logical discourse—the puns, conjunctions of opposites, and coinages that open up the realm of meaning. At the same time, we may learn to participate in the play of self-unfolding within writing, for once the requirement of objectivi-ty is demystified, we come to the salutary admission of the autobio-graphical necessities of our own work. The transformations of "L"/Alice/"Alice"/Luce/"analyste" perform an instructive mimesis of self-discovery: Irigaray's insertion of this multiple signature runs counter to the Name-of-the-Father and goes beyond the enclosures of patriarchal naming. Through such play with language the conceptual systems that have determined the representation of the female may be deconstructed as the machinery of masters reluctant to recognize their actual lack of mastery. Let us dream, with Irigaray, that the story of O may yet be erased by the story of *elle*(*s*).

NOTES   •

This article is reprinted in modified form from Feminist Studies (1981), 7(2):288–306, by permission.

1. On this context and her relation to other French feminist writers, see the following in *Signs* (Summer 1978), vol. 3, no. 4: Elaine Marks, "Women

and Literature in France," pp. 832–842; and Carolyn Burke, "Report from Paris: Women's Writing and the Women's Movement," pp. 843–855.

2. Irigaray, "Women's Exile," p. 71.

3. Ibid., p. 74.

4. Ibid.

5. Ibid., p. 63.

6. Ibid., p. 64. "Specularisable": that which can be represented, as in a mirror or reflection.

7. Ibid., p. 65.

8. Jacques Lacan's selected essays are available in translation: *Ecrits: A Selection*, trans. Alan Sheridan (New York: Norton, 1977). On his work, see *Yale French Studies* (1972), vol. 48; Juliet Mitchell, *Psychoanalysis and Feminism* (New York: Pantheon, 1974); Jane Gallop, "The Ghost of Lacan, the Trace of Language," *Diacritics* (Winter 1975), 5(4):18–24; Anika Lemaire, *Jacques Lacan*, trans. David Macey (London: Routledge and Kegan Paul, 1977); Martha Noel Evans, "Introduction to Jacques Lacan's Lecture: The Neurotic's Individual Myth," *Psychoanalytic Quarterly* (1979), 48:386–404, among others. My account is indebted to Sherry Turkle, *Psychoanalytic Politics: Freud's French Revolution* (New York: Basic Books, 1978).

9. See Turkle, *Psychoanalytic Politics*, pp. 164–188, passim, on Lacan's attempt to base psychoanalytic "science" on the use of mathematical formulas, or *mathemes*.

10. Ibid., especially p. 120ff.

11. Irigaray, *Speculum*, pp. 41–42. See also Jane Gallop, "The Ladies' Man," *Diacritics* (Winter 1976), 6(4):28–34; and her *The Daughter's Seduction: Feminism and Psychoanalysis* (London: Routledge, 1982).

12. Jacques Lacan, *Le Séminaire XX: Encore* (Paris: Seuil, 1975), p. 69. All translations are my own, unless otherwise noted.

13. Irigaray cites Lacan's provocative judgment as the epigraph for "Così Fan Tutti," in *This Sex*, pp. 86–105/*Ce Sexe*, pp. 85–101, in which she implies that Lacan does not know how to listen.

14. Lacan, *Séminaire XX*, p. 54.

15. Turkle, *Psychoanalytic Politics*, p. 130.

16. For a full account of the Name-of-the-Father in relation to the Oedipus complex, see Lemaire, *Jacques Lacan*, pp. 78–92; and Evans, "Introduction," pp. 386–404n.12.

17. Irigaray, *This Sex*, p. 90/*Ce Sexe*, p. 88.

18. Irigaray, "Women's Exile," p. 76.

19. Derrida's essay, "La question du style," first appeared in *Nietzsche aujourd'hui? I: Intensités* (Paris: 10/18, 1973). Slightly revised, it is available in a bilingual edition: *Spurs: Nietzsche's Styles/Eperons: Les Styles de Nietzsche*, trans. Barbara Harlow, introduction by Stefano Agosti (Chicago: University of Chicago Press, 1979). The citation from Derrida appears on p. 249, "La Question du style," and pp. 62–65, *Spurs/Eperons*.

- 20. Gayatri Chakravorty Spivak, "Translator's Preface," to her translation of Derrida's *Of Grammatology* (Baltimore: Johns Hopkins University Press, 1976), p. xxxvii. I am greatly indebted to her account of his thought.
- 21. Derrida, "Question du style," pp. 247–248; *Spurs/Eperons*, p. 61, where "phallogocentrism" is, unfortunately, translated as "phallocentrism."
- 22. Lacan's exegetes point out that the phallus is not simply the penis; it is, rather, a simulacrum or mental image that functions in the psycholinguistic representation of sexual desire. Moreover, it is not so much a symbol as it is a mode of meaning, for the phallus expresses the realization of lack as a structural factor in the understanding of sexual difference. Freud's infamous "penis envy" might, then, more properly be called "phallus envy," and it might apply equally but differently in the psychic development of males and females. The phallus is "the signifier of all signifiers," or "the signifier of desire," that is, of the instauration of the need to express desire for what is lacking through and by means of language. On this difficult concept see Lacan, "The Signification of the Phallus," in *Ecrits*, pp. 281–291; and Irigaray, *This Sex*, pp. 60–62, 67, 110–111/*Ce Sexe*, pp. 57–59, 63, 108–109.
- 23. Gallop, "The Ladies' Man," p. 30.
- 24. Spivak, "Translator's Preface," p. lxxiii.
- 25. Ibid., p. xlix.
- 26. Derrida, cited in Spivak, "Translator's Preface," p. lxxv.
- 27. Ibid., p. lxxvii.
- 28. Ibid. See also Derrida, "Signature Event Context," *Glyph* (1977), 1:195.
- 29. Paul de Man, *Blindness and Insight: Essays in the Rhetoric of Contemporary Criticism* (New York: Oxford University Press, 1971), p. 140; cited in Spivak, "Translator's Preface," p. xlix.
- 30. Here again, according to Spivak, in her "Translator's Preface," pp. xxi–xxvii, Derrida's practice is Nietzschean when he adapts the concept of the philosopher-artist. Nietzsche observed that philosophical discourse is rhetorical or figurative language that has forgotten its own metaphorical status. Thus, he argued, its "truths are illusions of which one has forgotten that they are illusions." Philosophical fables such as those imagined by the philosopher-artists Derrida and Irigaray might function, then, as illusions that have a certain truth value as long as one remembers that they are illusions. Of his coined word, "hymeneal," for example, Derrida writes, "This word . . . is not indispensable" (quoted in *Of Grammatology*, p. lxxi).
- 31. See Spivak, "Translator's Preface," pp. xiv–xx, on Derrida's practice of writing *sous rature* (under erasure). This strategy allows one to use terms while putting into question their premises.
- 32. Derrida, cited in Spivak, "Translator's Preface," p. xviii. Deconstructive

philosophy puts one in the awkward/exhilarating critical position of the
mise en abîme (placing/being placed in the abyss or infinite regress of
meaning), in which no final account is possible even though one must
offer her provisional account—such as this one—as if she "believes" in
it. (See Spivak, "Translator's Preface," pp. lxxvii–lxxviii, on this intellectual "double bind.")

33. Irigaray, *This Sex*, p. 68/*Ce Sexe*, p. 67.
34. Ibid., p. 31/30.
35. Irigaray, "This Sex," pp. 99–106; *This Sex*, pp. 23–33/*Ce Sexe*, pp.
    23–32.
36. Irigaray, "Commodities Among Themselves," pp. 107–110; *This Sex*,
    pp. 192–197/*Ce Sexe*, pp. 189–193.
37. Irigaray, "When Our Lips," pp. 66–79; *This Sex*, pp. 205–218/*Ce Sexe*,
    pp. 205–217.
38. Irigaray, *This Sex*, p. 86/*Ce Sexe*, p. 85.
39. Ibid., p. 110/108.
40. Ibid., p. 111/109.
41. Ibid., p. 116/114. On this question see Jane Gallop, "Impertinent Ques-
    tions: Irigaray, Sade, Lacan," *Sub-Stance* (1980), 26:57–67.
42. Irigaray, *This Sex*, p. 9/*Ce Sexe*, p. 9.
43. Cf. Spivak's discussion in "Translator's Preface," p. lxxiii, of Derrida's
    somewhat different problematization of "proper" and "proper name."
44. Irigaray, *This Sex*, p. 10/*Ce Sexe*, p. 10.
45. Derrida and Irigaray both reread Hegel on Antigone (*The Phenomenology
    of Mind*). See Derrida, *Glas* (Paris: Editions Galilee, 1974); Gayatri
    Chakravorty Spivak, "*Glas*-Piece: a Compte Rendu," *Diacritics* (Autumn
    1978), 7(3): 2–14.
46. Irigaray, *This Sex*, p. 167/*Ce Sexe*, p. 162.
47. Ibid., p. 111/109. The rhetorical status of the *parler-femme* and Irigaray's
    sexual metaphors is not easily defined, partly because of her deliberate
    decision to elude the rigidity of definitions. The problem is discussed at
    the conclusion of this essay.
48. The phrase is used to describe Lacanian psychoanalysis by Stephen
    Heath, whose analysis of sexual difference and representation is influ-
    enced by Irigaray. See his "Difference," *Screen* (Autumn 1978), 19(3):52.
49. Gayatri Chakravorty Spivak, "Explanation and Culture: Marginalia,"
    Humanities in Society (Summer 1979), 2(3):204.
50. Ibid., p. 202. The forthcoming publication of Spivak's *Deconstruction,
    Feminism, and Marxism: Theory and Practice in the Humanities* is
    announced in the contributors section of this issue of *Humanities in
    Society*.
51. Monique Plaza, " 'Phallomorphic Power' and the Psychology of
    'Woman,' " *Ideology and Consciousness* (1978), vol. 4, no. 8. This essay
    was first published in *Questions féministes* (1978), vol. 1.

• 52. Beverley Brown and Parveen Adams, "The Feminine Body and Feminist
       Politics," *m/f* (1979), 3:36.
  53. Ibid., p. 37.
  54. Irigaray, "Women's Exile," p. 64.
  55. Cited in Spivak, "Translator's Preface," p. xxv.
  56. Spivak, "Explanation and Culture," p. 218.

· *Naomi Schor*

THIS

ESSENTIALISM

WHICH IS NOT

ONE: COMING

TO GRIPS WITH

IRIGARAY

As Jacques Derrida pointed out several years ago, in the institutional model of the university elaborated in Germany at the beginning of the nineteenth century no provision was made, no space allocated for the discipline of women's studies: "There was no place foreseen in the structure of the classical model of Berlin for women's studies."[1] Women's studies, a field barely twenty years old today, is a belated add-on, an afterthought to the Berlin model taken over by American institutions of higher learning. For Derrida the question then becomes: What is the status of this new wing? Does it function merely as an addition, or rather as a supplement, simultaneously within and without the main building: "With women's studies, is it a question of simply filling a lack in a structure already in place, filling a gap?"[2] If the answer to this question were yes, then in the very success of women's studies would lie also its failure. "As much as women's studies has not put back into question the very principles of the structure of the former model of the university, it risks being just another cell in the University beehive."[3] The question, in other words, is: Is

• women's studies, as it has from the outset claimed to be, in some essential manner *different* from the other disciplines accommodated within the traditional Germanic institutional model of the university, or is it in fact more of the same, different perhaps in its object of study, but fundamentally alike in its relationship to the institution and the social values it exists to enshrine and transmit? What difference, asks Derrida, does women's studies make in the university: "What is the difference, if there is one, between a university institution of research and teaching called 'women's studies' and any other institution of learning and teaching around it in the university or in society as a whole?"[4] Derrida goes on to strongly suggest that in the accumulation of empirical research on women, in the tenuring of feminist scholars, in the seemingly spectacular success of women's studies the feminist critique of the institution has been scanted. In the eyes of deconstruction women's studies *is* perilously close to becoming "just another cell in the University beehive."

Derrida's account of the relationship of women's studies to the institution is perhaps not entirely fair, not sufficiently informed: women's studies—if one can generalize about such a vast and heterogeneous field—has been neither as successful nor as easily co-opted as Derrida makes it out to be, no more or less so than deconstruction, with which, as he points out, it is often linked by their common enemies. My concern, however, lies elsewhere: what I continue to find perplexing about Derrida's remarks, remarks that were made at a seminar given at Brown University's Pembroke Center for Teaching and Research on Women, is his failure to articulate the grounds on which women's studies would found its difference. My perplexity grows when I read in the published transcription of the seminar, which I both attended and participated in, the following:

> This is a question of the Law: are those involved in women's studies—teachers, students, researchers—the guardians of the Law, or not? You will remember that in the parable of the Law of Kafka, between the guardian of the Law and the man from the country there is no *essential difference*, they are in oppositional but symmetric positions. We are all, as members of a university, guardians of the Law. . . . Does that situation repeat itself for women's studies or not? Is there in the abstract or even topical idea of women's studies, something which potentially has the force, if it is possible, to deconstruct the fundamental institutional structure of the university, of the Law of the university?[5]

Is what Derrida is calling for then, that potentially deconstructive *something*, on the order of an essential difference? Is what he is calling for a women's studies that would be *essentially different* from its brother and sister disciplines? How, given the antiessentialism of deconstruction, about which more in a moment, to found an essential difference between feminine and masculine guardians of the law? How can women's studies be essentially different from other disciplines in a philosophical system that constantly works to subvert all essential differences, all essentializing of differences?

These questions are of special concern to me because the conflict *within* the faculty of women's studies has from its inception been to a large extent a conflict—and a very violent one—over essentialism, and it is to this conflict that I want to turn in what follows. I will first consider the critiques of essentialism that have been advanced in recent years, then compare briefly Simone de Beauvoir and Luce Irigaray, the two major French feminist theoreticians, who are generally held to exemplify respectively antiessentialist and essentialist positions. Finally, in the space I hope to have opened up for a new look at Irigaray, I will examine her troping of essentialism.

I. This Essentialism Which Is Not One

What revisionism, not to say essentialism, was to Marxism-Leninism, essentialism is to feminism: the prime idiom of intellectual terrorism and the privileged instrument of political orthodoxy. Borrowed from the time-honored vocabulary of philosophy, the word *essentialism* has been endowed within the context of feminism with the power to reduce to silence, to excommunicate, to consign to oblivion. Essentialism in modern-day feminism is anathema. There are, however, signs, encouraging signs in the form of projected books, ongoing dissertations, private conversations, not so much of a return of or to essentialism, as of a recognition of the excesses perpetrated in the name of antiessentialism, of the urgency of rethinking the very terms of a conflict that all parties would agree has ceased to be productive.[6]

What then is meant by essentialism in the context of feminism and what are the chief arguments marshaled against it by its critics? According to a standard definition drawn from the *Dictionary of Philosophy and Religion*, essentialism is the belief that things have essences. What then is an essence? Again from the same dictionary: "that by which a thing is what it is," and further, "the more permanent and fixed aspects of a thing."[7] Essentialism in the specific context of feminism consists in the belief that woman has an essence, that woman can be specified by one or a number of inborn attributes that define across cultures and throughout history her unchanging being and in the absence of which she ceases to be categorized as a woman. In less abstract, more practical terms an essentialist, in the context of feminism, is one who instead of carefully holding apart the poles of sex and gender maps the feminine onto femaleness, one for whom the body, the female body, that is, remains, in however complex and problematic a way, the rock of feminism. But by defining essentialism as I just have have I not in turn essentialized it, since definitions are by definition, as it were, essentialist? Antiessentialism operates precisely in this manner, that is, by essentializing essentialism, by proceeding as though there were one essentialism, an essence of essentialism. If we are to move beyond the increasingly sterile conflict over essentialism, we must begin by deessentializing essentialism, for, no more than deconstruction, *essentialism is not one.*[8] The multiplicity of essentialisms—one might, for example, want to distinguish French essentialism from the native variety, naive essentialism from strategic essentialism, heterosexual from homosexual—is revealed by the multiplicity of its critiques. Now most often these critiques are imbricated—so tightly interwoven in the space of an article or a book that they appear to form one internally consistent argument directed against one immutable monolithic position. And yet if one takes the trouble for purely heuristic purposes to disentangle the various strands of these critiques—I will distinguish four such critiques—it becomes apparent that they serve diverse, even conflicting interests and draw on distinct, often incompatible conceptual frameworks. However much in practice these critiques may overlap and intersect, when separated they turn out to correspond to some of the major trends in feminist theory from Beauvoir to the present.

1. The Liberationist Critique: this is the critique of essentialism first articulated by Beauvoir and closely identified with the radical feminist journal, *Questions féministes,* which she helped found. "One is not born, but rather becomes a woman," Beauvoir famously declared in *The Second Sex.*[9] This is the guiding maxim of the culturalist or constructionist critique of essentialism, which holds that femininity is a cultural construct in the service of the oppressive powers of patriarchy. By promoting an essential difference of woman grounded in the body, the argument runs, essentialism plays straight into the hands of the patriarchal order, which has traditionally invoked anatomical and physiological differences to legitimate the sociopolitical disempowerment of women. If women are to achieve equality, to become fully enfranchised persons, the manifold forms of exploitation and oppression to which they are subject, be they economic or political, must be carefully analyzed and tirelessly interrogated. Essentialist arguments that fail to take

into account the role of society in producing women are brakes on the
wheel of progress.

2. The Linguistic Critique: this is the critique derived from the writings and seminars of Lacan and promoted with particular force by
Anglo-American film critics and theoreticians writing in such journals
as *Screen, m/f,* and *Camera Obscura.* What society is to Beauvoir and her
followers, language is to Lacan and Lacanians. The essentialist, in this
perspective, is a naive realist who refuses to recognize that the loss of the
referent is the condition of man's entry into language. Within the symbolic order centered on the phallus there can be no immediate access to
the body: the fine mesh of language screens off the body from any
apprehension that is not already enculturated. Essentialism is, then, in
Lacanian terms an effect of the imaginary, and it is no accident that
some of the most powerfully seductive evocations of the feminine,
notably those of Irigaray and Cixous, resonate with the presence and
plenitude of the prediscursive preoedipal. In the symbolic order ruled
by the phallus "there is no such thing as The Woman," as Lacan gnom-
ically remarks.[10] What we have instead are subjects whose sexual
inscription is determined solely by the positions they occupy in regard
to the phallus, and these positions are at least in theory subject to
change. The proper task of feminist theory is, however, not to contribute to changing the status of women in society—for the Law of the
symbolic is posited as eternal—but rather to expose and denaturalize
the mechanisms whereby females are positioned as women.

3. The Philosophical Critique: the reference here is to the critique
elaborated by Derrida and disseminated by feminist Derrideans rang-
ing from Irigaray and Cixous to some of the major transatlantic feminist critics and theoreticians. Essentialism, in this view, is complicitous
with Western metaphysics. To subscribe to the binary opposition
man/woman is to remain a prisoner of the metaphysical, with its illusions of presence, Being, stable meanings, and identities. The essentialist in this scheme of things is not, as for Lacan, one who refuses to
accept the phallocentric ordering of the symbolic, rather one who fails
to acknowledge the play of difference in language and the difference it
makes. Beyond the prison house of the binary, multiple differences play
indifferently across degendered bodies. As a strategic position adopted
to achieve specific political goals, feminist essentialism has, however, its
place in deconstruction.

• *4. The Feminist Critique:* I have deliberately reserved this rubric for the only critique of essentialism to have emerged from *within* the women's movement. No proper name, masculine or feminine, can be attached to this critique as its legitimating source; it arises from the plurivocal discourses of black, Chicana, lesbian, first and third world feminist thinkers and activists. The recent work of Teresa de Lauretis, *Alice Doesn't,* and the edited volume of conference proceedings, *Feminist Studies/Critical Studies,* might, however, be cited as exemplifying this trend.[11] Essentialism, according to this critique, is a form of "false universalism" that threatens the vitality of the newly born women of feminism. By its majestic singularity Woman conspires in the denial of the very real lived differences—sexual, ethnic, racial, national, cultural, economic, generational—that divide women from each other and from themselves. Feminist antiessentialism shares with deconstruction the conviction that essentialism inheres in binary opposition, hence its displacement of woman-as-different-from-man by the notion of internally differentiated and historically instantiated women.[12]

Unlike deconstruction and all the other critiques of essentialism I have reviewed all too briefly here, the feminist is uniquely committed to constructing specifically female subjectivities, and it is for this reason that I find this critique the most compelling. It is precisely around the issues of the *differences* among as well as within women that the impasse between essentialism and antiessentialism is at last beginning to yield: for just as the pressing issues of race and ethnicity are forcing certain antiessentialists to suspend their critiques in the name of political realities, they are forcing certain essentialists to question their assertion of a female essence that is widely perceived and rightly denounced by minority women as exclusionary.[13]

II. Beauvoir and Irigaray: Two Exemplary Positions

Quelle femme n'a pas lu *Le Deuxième sexe?*   —Irigaray, *Je, tu, nous*

The access of women to subjectivity is the central concern of the two major French feminist theoreticians of the twentieth century: Simone de Beauvoir and Luce Irigaray.[14] Indeed, despite their dramatically opposed positions, both share a fundamental grounding conviction: under the social arrangement known as patriarchy the subject is exclusively male: masculinity and subjectivity are coextensive notions. Consider these two celebrated assertions, the first drawn from Beauvoir's *The Second Sex,* the second from Irigaray's *Speculum*: "He is the Subject, he is the Absolute;"[15] "Any theory of the 'subject' has always been appropriated by the 'masculine.' "[16] Almost immediately the suspicion arises that though both are centrally concerned with the appropriation of subjectivity by men, Beauvoir and Irigaray are not in fact speaking about the same subject. Subjectivity, like essentialism, like deconstruction, is not one. There is a world of difference between Beauvoir's subject, with its impressive capitalized *S*, reinforced by the capitalization of *Absolute*, its homologue, and Irigaray's subject, with its lower case *s* and the relativizing quotation marks that enclose both *subject* and *masculine*. Beauvoir's subject is the familiar Hegelian subject of existentialist ethics, a heroic figure locked in a life and death struggle with the not-self, chiefly the environment and the Other:

> Every subject plays his part as such specifically through exploits or projects that serve as a mode of transcendence; he achieves liberty only through a continual reaching out toward other liberties. There is no justification for present existence other than its expansion into an indefinitely open future. Every time transcendence falls back into immanence, stagnation, there is a degradation of existence onto the "en-soi"—the brutish life of subjection to given conditions—and of liberty into constraint and contingence. This downfall represents a moral fault if the subject consents to it; if it is inflicted upon him, it spells frustration and oppression. In both cases it is an absolute evil.[17]

Subjectivity is, for Beauvoir, activity, a restless projection into the future, a glorious surpassing of the iterativity of everyday life. The dreadful fall from transcendence into immanence is woman's estate. Consigned by the masterful male subject to passivity and repetition, woman in patriarchy is a prisoner of immanence. Beauvoir's theory of subjectivity, thus, as has been often observed, dismally reinscribes the most traditional alignments of Western metaphysics: positivity lines up with activity, while passivity and, with it, femininity are slotted as negative. At the same time, however, Beauvoir's exemplary antiessentialism works to break the alignment of the transcendent and the male; by leaving behind the unredeemed and unredeemable domestic sphere of contingency for the public sphere of economic activity, women too can achieve transcendence. Liberation for women in Beauvoir's liberationist macronarrative consists in emerging from the dark cave of immanence "into the light of transcendence."[18]

Deeply implicated in the radical reconceptualization of the (male) subject that characterizes post-Sartrean French thought, Irigaray's subject is a diminished subject that bears little resemblance to the sovereign and purposeful subject of existentialist philosophy. For Irigaray—and this displacement is crucial—the main attribute of the subject is not activity but language. The *homo faber* that serves as Beauvoir's model gives way to *homo parlans*. Thus Irigaray's subject is for all practical purposes a speaking subject, a pronoun, the first-person singular *I*. And that pronoun has under current social arrangements been preempted by men: "The I thus remains predominant among men."[19] The much touted death of the subject—which can only be the male subject[20]—leaves Irigaray singularly unmoved: "And the fact that you no longer assert yourself as absolute subject does not change a thing. The breath that animates you, the law or the duty that leads you, are they not the quintessence of your subjectivity? You no longer cling to [*ne tiens pas à*] your "I"? But your "I" clings to you [*te tient*]."[21]

For women to accede to subjectivity clearly means becoming speaking subjects in their own right. It is precisely at this juncture that the major difference between Beauvoir and Irigaray begins to assert itself, and once again I take them as representative of what Anthony Appiah has called the "classic dialectic": whereas for Beauvoir the goal is for women to share fully in the privileges of the transcendent subject, for Irigaray the goal is for women to achieve subjectivity without merging tracelessly into the putative indifference of the shifter. What is at stake in these two equally powerful and problematic feminist discourses is not the status of difference, rather that of the universal, and universalism may well be one of the most divisive and least discussed issues in feminism today. When Irigaray projects women as speaking a sexually marked language, a *parler-femme,* she is, I believe, ultimately less concerned with theorizing feminine specificity than with debunking the oppressive fiction of an universal subject. To speak woman is, above all, *not* to "speak 'universal' ";[22] "No more subject which is indifferent, substitutable, universal";[23] "I have no desire to take their speech as they have taken ours, nor to speak 'universal.' "[24] For Beauvoir, on the other hand, it is precisely because women have been prevented from speaking universal, indeed because they have "no sense of the universal," that they have made so few significant contributions to the great humanist tradition. Mediocrity is the lot of those creators who do not feel "responsible for the universe."[25]

My task here is not to adjudicate between these two exemplary positions I am outlining, but to try to understand how, starting from the same assumptions about women's exile from subjectivity, Beauvoir and Irigaray arrive at such radically different conclusions, and, further, to show that Irigaray's work cannot be understood without situating it in relationship to Beauvoir's. In order to do so Beauvoir's and Irigaray's theories of subjectivity must be reinserted in the framework of their broader enterprises. Beauvoir's project throughout *The Second Sex* is to lay bare the mechanisms of what we might call, borrowing the term from Mary Louise Pratt, "othering": the means by which patriarchy fixed women in the place of the absolute Other, projecting onto women a femininity constituted of the refuse of masculine transcendence.[26] Otherness in Beauvoir's scheme of things is utter negativity; it is the realm of what Kristeva has called the abject. Irigaray's project is diametrically opposed to Beauvoir's but must be viewed as its necessary corollary. Just as Beauvoir lays bare the mechanisms of othering, Irigaray exposes those of what we might call, by analogy, "saming." If othering involves attributing to the objectified other a difference that serves to legitimate her oppression, saming denies the objectified other the right to her difference, submitting the other to the laws of phallic specularity. If othering assumes that the other is knowable, saming precludes any knowledge of the other in her otherness. If exposing the logic of othering—whether it be of women, Jews, or any other victims of demeaning stereotyping—is a necessary step in achieving equality, exposing the logic of saming is a necessary step in toppling the universal from his/(her) pedestal.

Since othering and saming conspire in the oppression of women, the workings of *both* processes need to be exposed. And yet to date the articulation of these two projects has proved an elusive, indeed insuperable task for feminist theoreticians, for just as Beauvoir's analysis precludes theorizing difference, or rather—and the distinction is crucial—difference as positivity, Irigaray's proves incapable of not theorizing difference, that is difference as positivity. One of the more awkward moments in Beauvoir comes in the closing pages of *The Second Sex*, when she seeks to persuade the reader that women's liberation will not signify a total loss of difference between men and women, for the entire weight of what precedes militates against theorizing a positive difference, indeed against grounding difference, since the body and the social have both been disqualified as sites of any meaningful sexual difference. Beauvoir gives herself away in these final pages when speaking of women's failure to achieve greatness in the world of intellect: "She can become an excellent theoretician, can acquire real competence, but she will be forced to repudiate whatever she has in her that is 'different.'"[27] Similarly, by relentlessly exposing the mechanisms of saming, the economy of what she calls the "echonomy" of patriarchy, Irigaray exposes herself to adopting a logic of othering, precisely what has been called—her protestations notwithstanding—her essentialism.[28] What I am suggesting here is that each position has its own inescapable logic, and that that inescapability is the law of the same/other. If all difference is attributed to othering then one

•   risks saming, and conversely: if all denial of difference is viewed as resulting in saming then one risks othering. In other words, it is as disingen-
uous to reproach Beauvoir with promoting the loss of difference
between men and women as it is to criticize Irigaray for promoting,
indeed theorizing that difference. And yet the logic I am trying to draw
out of these two exemplary feminist discourses seems to have escaped Irigaray's most incisive critics, who have repeatedly sought to sever her brilliant exposure of the specular logic of phallocentrism from her theorization of a specifically feminine difference. Toril Moi's formulation is in
this regard typical: "Having shown that so far femininity has been produced exclusively in relation to the logic of the same, she falls for the
temptation to produce her own positive theory of femininity. But, as we
have seen, to define 'woman' is necessarily to essentialize her."[29]

My argument is *a contrario*: that Irigaray's production of a positi-
theory of femininity is not an aberration, a sin (to extend the theological metaphor), rather the logical extension of her deconstruction of the
specular logic of saming. What is problematic about Irigaray's theorization of the feminine—which, it should be pointed out, is in fact only
one aspect or moment of her work—is indicated by Moi's use of the
word "positive." For finally the question posed by Irigaray's attempts to
theorize feminine specificity—which is not to be confused with "defining" woman, a task she writes is better left to men—is the question of
the difference *within* difference. Irigaray's wager is that difference can be
reinvented, that the bogus difference of misogyny can be reclaimed to
become a radical new difference that would present the first serious historical threat to the hegemony of the male sex. Irigaray's wager is that
there is a (*la/une femme*) woman *in* femininity: "Beneath all those/her
appearances, beneath all those/her borrowed finery, that female other
still sub-sists. Beyond all those/her forms of life and death, still she is living."[30] Mimesis is the term Irigaray appropriates from the vocabulary of
philosophy to describe her strategy, transforming woman's masquerade,
her so-called femininity into a means of reappropriating the feminine:

> One must assume the feminine role deliberately. Which means already
> to convert a form of subordination into an affirmation, and thus to
> begin to thwart it. . . . To play with mimesis is thus, for a woman, to try
> to recover the place of her exploitation by discourse, without allowing
> herself to be simply reduced to it. It means to resubmit herself—inas-
> much as she is on the side of the "perceptible," of "matter"—to "ideas,"
> in particular to ideas about herself that are elaborated in/by a masculine
> logic, but so as to make "visible," by an effect of playful repetition, what
> was supposed to remain invisible: the cover-up of a possible operation of
> the feminine in language. It also means to "unveil" the fact that, if

women are such good mimics, it is because they are not simply resorbed in this function. *They also remain elsewhere.*[31]

Mimesis (*mimétisme*) in Irigaray has been widely and correctly interpreted as describing a parodic mode of discourse designed to deconstruct the discourse of misogyny through effects of amplification and rearticulation that work, in Mary Ann Doane's words, to "enact a defamiliarized version of femininity."[32] But there is yet another aspect of mimesis—a notoriously polysemic term[33]—that has been largely misread, and even repressed, because it involves a far more controversial and riskier operation, a transvaluation rather than a repudiation of the discourse of misogyny, an effort to hold onto the baby while draining out the bathwater. For example, in *Le Corps-à-corps avec la mère*, Irigaray writes: "We are historically the guardians of the corporeal, we must not abandon this charge but identify it as ours, by inviting men not to make of us their body, a guarantee of their body."[34] Irigaray's use of the word *mimesis* mimes her strategy, bodies forth her wager, which might be described as an instance of what Derrida has termed paleonymy: "the occasional maintenance of an *old name* in order to launch a new concept."[35] In the specific context of feminism, the old mimesis, sometimes referred to as masquerade, names women's alleged talents at parroting the master's discourse, including the discourse of misogyny. At a second level, parroting becomes parody, and mimesis signifies not a deluded masquerade but a canny mimicry. Finally, in the third meaning of mimesis I am attempting to tease out of Irigaray's writings, mimesis comes to signify difference as positivity, a joyful reappropriation of the attributes of the other that is not in any way to be confused with a mere reversal of the existing phallocentric distribution of power. For Irigaray, as for other new French antifeminists, reversal—the coming into power of women that they view as the ultimate goal of American-style feminists—leaves the specular economy she would shatter in place. The mimesis that lies beyond masquerade and mimicry—a more essential mimesis, as it were, a mimesis that recalls the original Platonic mimesis—does not signify a reversal of misogyny but an emergence of the feminine, and the feminine can only emerge from within or beneath—to extend Irigaray's archeological metaphor—femininity, within which it lies buried. The difference within mimesis *is* the difference within difference.

III. Coming to Grips With Irigaray

> Est-ce qu'il n'y a pas une fluidité, quelque déluge, qui pourrait ébranler cet ordre social?
> —Irigaray, *Corps-à-corps*
>
> Où sont, au présent, les fluides?
> —Irigaray, *L'Oubli de l'air*

• Few claims Irigaray has made for feminine specificity have aroused more virulent accusations of essentialism than her "outrageous" claim that woman enjoys a special relationship with the fluid. One of the earliest such assertions occurs in *This Sex Which Is Not One*, where in the heyday of *écriture féminine* Irigaray characterizes both women's writing and speech as fluid. "And yet that woman-thing speaks. But not 'like,' not 'the *same*,' not 'identical with itself' nor to any x, etc. . . . It speaks 'fluid.' "[36]

So uncomfortable has this assertion made certain feminist theoreticians that they have rushed to ascribe it to Irigarayan mimicry as ironic distancing rather than to the positive form of mimesis I have delineated above: "Her association of femininity with what she refers to as the 'real properties of fluids'—internal frictions, pressures, movement, a specific dynamics which makes a fluid nonidentical to itself—is, of course, merely an extension and a mimicking of a patriarchal construction of femininity."[37] And yet as Irigaray's linking up of feminine fluidity with flux, nonidentity, proximity, etc., indicates, the fluid is highly valorized in her elemental philosophy: "Why is setting oneself up as a solid more worthwhile than flowing as a liquid from between the two [lips]";[38] "*My* life is nothing but the mobile flexibility, tenderness, uncertainty of the fluid."[39]

Where then does this notion of the fluidity of the feminine, when not the femininity of the fluid, come from? Undeniably it is appropriated from the repertory of misogyny: "Historically the properties of fluids have been abandoned to the feminine."[40] What is worse, for the antiessentialists, it appears to emanate from an unproblematized reading out of the female body in its hormonal instanciation. It is, indeed, triply determined by female physiology:

> The anal stage is already given over to the pleasure of the "solid." Yet it seems to me that the pleasure of the fluid subsists, in women, far beyond the so-called oral stage: the pleasure of "what's flowing" within her, outside of her, and indeed among women.[41]
>
> The marine element is thus both the amniotic waters . . . and it is also, it seems to me, something which figures quite well feminine jouissance.[42]

The ontological primacy of woman and the fluid are for her one of the represseds of patriarchal metaphysics; the forgetting of fluids participates in the matricide that according to Irigaray's myth of origins founds Western culture: "He begins to be in and thanks to fluids."[43] Unquestionably then Irigaray's linking up of the fluid and the feminine rests on a reference to the female body.[44]

The antiessentialist would stop here, dismiss Irigaray's claims as misguided and turn away—and few of Irigaray's sharpest critics have bothered with the work published after 1977, which is to say the bulk of her writing.[45] In so doing they miss another and equally troublesome, but ultimately more interesting aspect of her work. And that is her reliance on the universe of science, notably physics (but also chemistry to the extent that the borders between them cannot always be clearly drawn), which enjoys a strange and largely unexamined privilege in Irigaray's conceptual universe.[46] Indeed, in her writings on the repressed feminine element of water, the referential reality that Irigaray most ardently invokes to ground her assertions is not so much physiological as physical; it is on the rock of materialism and not of essentialism that Irigaray seeks to establish the truth of her claim. Thus, in an essay entitled "The Language of Man," she writes: "But still today this woma(e)n's language [*langage de(s) femme(s)*] is censured, repressed, ignored . . . even as the science of the dynamic of fluids already provides a partial interpretation of it."[47] The real in Irigaray is neither impossible, nor unknowable: it is the fluid. Thus, further in the same essay, Irigaray insistently associates the fluid and the real, speaking of "the real of the dynamic of fluids" and "an economy of *real fluids*."[48] Two remarks are in order here: first, given all that I have said before, this new criticism of Irigaray may appear curious. But my desire in this essay is neither to "defend" Irigaray nor promote essentialism, but rather to dehystericize the debate, to show how the obsessive focus on what is so loosely termed the *biological* has worked to impoverish the reading of as challenging and ambitious a thinker as is Irigaray. Second, there is, on the other hand, nothing particularly surprising from the perspective of antiessentialism about the complicity of essentialism and scientism, in that both imply at least at some level a fundamental materialism. But because of the red flag (when it is not a red herring) of essentialism, the question of Irigaray's mater-ialism is never really addressed. It is as though certain feminists were more comfortable evacuating the body from the precincts of high theory—thereby, of course, reinforcing the very hierarchies they would dismantle—than carefully separating out what belongs to the body and what to the world of matter.

To say that science enjoys a special status in Irigaray's writings is not to say that science, the master discourse of our age, has escaped Irigaray's feminist critique. It has not. Laughter and anger are Irigaray's reactions to the supposed neutrality of scientific language, a form of writing that, like all writing, is inflected by gender but that, more so than any other, disclaims subjectivity. Science's failure to acknowledge the gendering of language results in its failures to adequately theorize

•   that which it aligns with the feminine, notably the elements, notably
the liquid. Thus, in "The 'Mechanics' of Fluids," Irigaray takes "science" to task for its failure to elaborate a "theory of fluids." And yet, in
some of her more recent writings, while remaining highly critical of the
ideology of science, she constantly invokes scientific theories as models,
analoga for female sexuality. For example: rejecting as more adequate to
male than to female sexuality the thermodynamic principles that
underlie Freud's theory of libido, Irigaray writes:

> Feminine sexuality could perhaps better be brought into harmony *if one
> must evoke a scientific model*—with what Prigogine calls "dissipating"
> structures that operate via the exchange with the external world, struc-
> tures that proceed through levels of energy. The organizational princi-
> ple of these structures has nothing to do with the search for equilibrium
> but rather with the crossing of thresholds. This would correspond to a
> surpassing of disorder or entropy without discharge.[49]

Similarly, later in the same essay Irigaray suggests that recent work in
physics as well as in linguistics might shed light on the specificities of
women's relationship to enunciation: "Some recent studies in discourse
theory, *but in physics as well,* seem to shed light upon the locus from
which one could or could not situate oneself as a subject of language
production."[50] Whatever her questions to the scientists, and some of
them—as in "Is the Subject of Science Sexed?"—are impertinent, Irigaray repeatedly attempts to anchor the truth of her theories in the latest scientific knowledge. She knows that scientific discourse is not neutral, but nevertheless she looks to it as the ultimate source of legitimation. Science is Irigaray's fetish.

   Why then is science, and especially physics, privileged in Irigaray's
writings? The answer emerges from a consideration of the pivotal role
of Descartes in Irigaray's writings. As Moi has noted, the Descartes
chapter in *Speculum* is located at the "exact center of the 'Speculum' section (and of the whole book) . . . Descartes sinks into the innermost
cavity of the book."[51] This chapter is, as Moi further remarks, traditional at least in its presentation of the subject of the Cogito: the "I" of
the Cogito is self-engendered, constituted through a radical denial both
of the other and of man's corporeal origins: "The 'I' thinks, therefore
this thing, this body that is also nature, that is still the *mother*, becomes
an extension at the 'I' 's disposal for analytical investigations, scientific
projections, the regulated exercise of the imaginary, the utilitarian practice of technique."[52] What is at stake here is the constitution of an
ontology that excludes all considerations having to do with the physical world: "The same thing applies to the discussions of woman and

women. Gynecology, dioptrics, are no longer by right a part of meta-physics—*that supposedly unsexed anthropos-logos whose actual sex is admitted only by its omission and exclusion from consciousness*, and by what is said in its margins."[53] How surprising then to discover in *Ethique de la différence sexuelle* another Descartes, a Descartes whose treatise on the passions of the soul contains the concept of admiration that fully realizes Irigaray's most cherished desire, the (re)connection of the body and the soul, the physical and the metaphysical:

> We need to reread Descartes a little and remember or learn about the role of movement in the passions. We should also think about the fact that all philosophers—except for the most recent ones? and why is this so?—have always been physicists and have always supported or accom-panied their metaphysical research with cosmological research. . . . This scission between the physical sciences and thought no doubt represents that which threatens thought itself.

It is, then, in Descartes's treatise that Irigaray finds the alliance of the physical and the metaphysical, the material and the transcendental that represents for her the philosophical ideal. Little matter that in elaborating his notion of admiration Descartes does not have sexual difference in mind: "Sexual difference could be situated here. But Descartes doesn't think of it. He simply asserts that what is different attracts."[55]

> He does not differentiate the passions according to sexual difference. . . . On the other hand he places admiration first among the passions. Passion forgotten by Freud? Passion which holds open a path between physics and metaphysics, corporeal impressions and movements toward an object be it empirical or transcendental.[56]

Thus in Irigaray Descartes functions both as the philosopher who irrev-ocably sunders body from soul and the one who most brilliantly reunites them. Physics is here placed in service of Irigaray's radical materialism, her desire to return to a pre-Socratic (but also post-Nietzschean and Bachelardian) apprehension of the four generic elements as foundation-al, which is—I repeat—not the same thing as essentialism. But there is more: Irigaray's ultimate goal is not, so to speak, to put the physics back in metaphysics, but rather the ruining of the metaphysics of being through the substitution of a physics of the liquid for a physics of the solid. Heidegger names that moment in the history of philosophy when a possible questioning of the primacy of the solid remains earth-bound, grounded in the very soil of metaphysics. The ruining of metaphysics is bound up with an anamnesis, a remembering of the forgotten elements:

•   Metaphysics always supposes, somehow, a solid earth-crust, from which
       a construction may be raised. Thus a physics which privileges or at least
       has constituted the solid plane. . . . So long as Heidegger does not leave
       the earth, he does not leave metaphysics. Metaphysics does not inscribe
       itself either on/in water, on/in air, on/in fire. . . . And its abysses, both
       above and below, doubtless find their interpretation in the forgetting of
       the elements which don't have the same density. The end of metaphysics
       would be prescribed by their reinvention in contemporary physics?[57]

Finally, calling into question Irigaray's relationship to science returns us
to the question of the institution, for what emerges from a reading of
Parler n'est jamais neutre is that her interventions cannot be read without taking into account their institutional context. It is altogether striking in this regard to consider the difference between two of the most
powerful essays in the volume, "The Poverty of Psychoanalysis" and "Is
the Subject of Science Sexed?" In the first of these essays, where Irigaray's addressees are the male guardians of the (Lacanian) psychoanalytic institution, her tone is from the outset self-assured, truculent, out-
raged. How different is the tone of her speech to the scientists. Addressing the members of the "seminar on the history and sociology of
scientific ideas and facts" of the University of Provence, Marseilles, Irigaray confesses to a rare attack of stage fright: "For a long time I have
not experienced such difficulties with the notion of speaking in public,"[58] she tells her audience. The problem is a problem of address:
whereas the text to the analysts begins with a peremptory "Messieurs les
analystes," the speech to the scientists begins by interrogating the very
act of address: "How does one talk to scientists?"[59]

       Standing before the scientists, Irigaray stands like a woman from the
country before the law:

       Anxiety in the face of an absolute power floating in the air, of an author-
       itative judgment: everywhere, yet imperceptible, of a tribunal, which in
       its extreme case has neither judge, nor prosecutor, nor accused. But the
       judicial system is in place. There is a truth there to which one must sub-
       mit without appeal, against which one can commit violations . . . unwill-
       ingly or unknowingly. The supreme instance is exercised against your
       will.[60]

According to Derrida's reading of Kafka's parable there is no essential
difference between the man from the country and the guardians of the
law. Their positions in regard to the law are opposite but symmetrical:
"The two protagonists are both attendant to the law but opposing one
another," writes Derrida.[61] But what if the man from the country is
replaced by a woman? Is there no essential difference between the

woman from the country, here the feminist philosopher Luce Irigaray, and the guardians of the law, in this instance the scientists whose faculty is to a very large extent hegemonic in our universities today?[62] If the man from the country is replaced by a woman, can one so easily speak of positions that are opposite and *symmetrical* without risking relapsing into a logic of saming, precisely what Irigaray has called an "old dream of symmetry"?

There can be no easy answers to these questions, which are immensely complicated by the very powerful interpretation Derrida has advanced of the law in Kafka's parable. If, however, Irigaray can be taken here as exemplifying the feminist intervention in the institution, then one can, however tentatively, discern the difference that women's studies can make: for instead of simply addressing the guardians of the law—if indeed any address is ever simple—Irigaray transforms the very conditions of the law's production and enforcement. In raising the question of the gender of the producers of knowledge, women's studies always involves a radical questioning of the conditions of the production and dissemination of knowledge, of the constitution of the disciplines, of the hierarchical ordering of the faculties within the institution. Further, by allying herself with the most radical elements in science, Irigaray points the way to what, paraphrasing Prigogine—who borrows the phrase from Jacques Monod—we might call a "new alliance" between women's studies and the law, one that would go beyond mere opposition. In other words, it is finally by insisting on the *dissymmetry* of the positions occupied by the guardians and the woman from the country in regard to the law that women's studies, at least in its "utopian horizon," can never be "just another cell in the University beehive."

NOTES •

What precedes is the revised text of a paper I delivered at a conference held at the University of Alabama, at Tuscaloosa, entitled "Our Academic Contract: The Conflict of the Faculties in America." This conference has since achieved footnote status in the history of poststructuralism because it was on the occasion of this gathering that the scandal of Paul de Man's wartime journalism broke in the United States. I wish to thank Richard Rand for having invited me to participate in this event and Jacques Derrida for his response to my remarks, as well as for all his other gifts. I also wish to thank the members of my feminist reading group: Christina Crosby, Mary Ann Doane, Coppélia Kahn, Karen Newman, Ellen Rooney—as well as Elizabeth Weed, Nancy K. Miller, and Kaja Silverman for their various forms of support and criticism.

•   1. Jacques Derrida, "Women in the Beehive: A Seminar with Jacques Derrida," in Alice Jardine and Paul Smith, eds., *Men in Feminism* (New York: Methuen, 1987), p. 190. When it was originally published in the Brown student journal *subjects/objects* (Spring 1984), pp. 5–19, in keeping with Derrida's wishes, the transcript of the seminar was prefaced by a cautionary disclaimer (reprinted in *Men in Feminism*), which I want to echo, emphasizing the text's undecidable status "somewhere between speech and writing," "authorized but authorless" (p. 189). All references will be to the reprinted version of the text.

2. Ibid., p. 190.

3. Ibid., p. 191.

4. Ibid., p. 190.

5. Ibid., pp. 191–192; emphasis added.

6. I refer here in turn to Teresa Brennan, ed., *Between Feminism and Psychoanalysis* (London: Routledge, 1989), and Diana Fuss, *Essentially Speaking* (New York: Routledge, 1989), which started out as a dissertation at Brown University. The keynote to this new deal for essentialism was perhaps sounded in the footnote to a paper given at a recent feminist conference by Mary Russo, who writes: "The dangers of essentialism in posing the female body, whether in relation to representation or to 'women's history' have been well stated, so well stated, in fact, that *antiessentialism may well be the greatest inhibition to work in cultural theory and politics at the moment, and must be displaced*" (*Feminist Studies/Critical Studies*, ed. Teresa de Lauretis [Bloomington: Indiana University Press, 1986], p. 228; emphasis added).

7. William J. Reese, *Dictionary of Philosophy and Religion: Eastern and Western Thought* (New Jersey: Humanities Press, 1980), p. 155.

8. Repeatedly in the course of an interview with James Creech, Peggy Kamuf, and Jane Todd, Derrida insists on the plural of deconstruction: "I don't think that there is something like one deconstruction"; ". . . it is difficult to define the one deconstruction [*la déconstruction*]. . . . Personally I would even say that its best interests are served by keeping that heterogeneity" ("Deconstruction in America: An Interview with Jacques Derrida," *Critical Exchange* [Winter 1985], 17:4, 6). Finally he concludes that it is more accurate to speak of deconstructions than a singular deconstruction.

9. Simone de Beauvoir, *The Second Sex*, trans. H. M. Parshley (New York: Vintage, 1974), p. 301.

10. Jacques Lacan, *Feminine Sexuality: Jacques Lacan and the école freudienne*, ed. Juliet Mitchell and Jacqueline Rose, trans. Jacqueline Rose (New York: Norton, 1982), p. 144.

11. Teresa de Lauretis, *Alice Doesn't: Feminism, Semiotics, Cinema* (Bloomington: Indiana University Press, 1984); de Lauretis, *Feminist Studies/Critical Studies*.

12. There is an extreme form of antiessentialism, a candidate for a fifth cri-

tique, that argues that the replacement of woman by women does not solve but merely displaces the problem of essentialism. This is the position represented by Denise Riley, who suggests, in a chapter entitled "Does Sex Have a History?": "Not only 'woman' but also 'women' is troublesome. . . . We can't bracket off either 'Woman,' whose capital letter alerts us to her dangers, or the more modest lower-case 'woman,' while leaving unexamined the ordinary, innocent-sounding 'women' " (*Am I That Name? Feminism and the Category of "Women" in History* [Minneapolis: University of Minnesota Press, 1988], p. 1). Cf. Donna Haraway, who, in her "A Manifesto for Cyborgs: Science, Technology, and Socialist Feminism in the 1980s," remarks: "It is no accident that woman *disintegrates* into women in our time" (*Socialist Review* [1985], 80:79; emphasis added). This is perhaps the place to comment on a critique whose conspicuous absence will surely surprise some: a *modern* Marxist critique of essentialism. I emphasize the word *modern* because of course Beauvoir's critique of essentialism in *The Second Sex* is heavily indebted to the Marxism she then espoused. Though the writings of Louis Althusser and Pierre Macherey, to cite the major Marxist theoreticians contemporaneous with Lacan and Derrida, inform some pioneering studies of female-authored fictions, they have not to my knowledge generated a critique of essentialism distinct from the critiques already outlined. This seeming absence or failure of a strong recent Marxist critique of essentialism is all the more surprising, as clearly the critique of essentialism was at the outset appropriated by Beauvoir (and others) from Marxism. If Riley's book and Haraway's article are at this point in time the only articulation we have of a postmodernist Marxist critique of essentialism, then it might be said that for them the essentialist is one who has not read history.

13. Ironically, in rejecting the ideal of a universal subject in favor of a subject marked by the feminine, Irigaray has, like other bourgeois white feminists, only managed to relocate universality, to institute a new hegemony. The question that arises is: How theorize a subjectivity that does not reinscribe the universal, that does not constitute itself by simultaneously excluding and incorporating others?

14. For Irigaray on Beauvoir, see "A Personal Note: Equal or Different?" in *Je, tu, nous*, pp. 9–14/pp. 9–15. Unfortunately, this text appeared too late to be taken into account in this article. It sets forth in unusually personal terms the differences between Beauvoir's feminism of equality and Irigaray's feminism of difference.

15. Beauvoir, *The Second Sex*, p. xix.

16. Irigaray, *Speculum*, p. 133/p. 165.

17. Beauvoir, *The Second Sex*, p. xxxiii.

18. Ibid., p. 798.

19. Irigaray, "L'Ordre sexuel du discours," *Langages* (March 1987), 85:83.

20. Nancy K. Miller, "Changing the Subject: Authorship, Writing, and the Reader," in de Lauretis, *Feminist Studies/Critical Studies*, pp. 102–120.

- 21. Irigaray, *Passions élémentaires*, p. 101.
22. Irigaray, *Corps-à-corps*, pp. 63–64.
23. Irigaray, *Parler n'est jamais neutre*, p. 9.
24. Irigaray, *Corps-à-corps*, pp. 63–64.
25. Beauvoir, *The Second Sex*, p. 793.
26. Pratt, "Scratches on the Face of the Country: or, What Mr. Barrow Saw in the Land of the Bushmen," in Henry Louis Gates, Jr., ed., *"Race," Writing, and Difference* (Chicago: University of Chicago Press, 1986), p. 139.
27. Beauvoir, *The Second Sex*, p. 788.
28. Irigaray's most explicit rejection of essentialism occurs in the "Veiled Lips" section of *Marine Lover*, where she writes: "She does not set herself up as *one*, as a (single) female unit. She is not closed up or around [*se referme sur ou dans*] one single truth or essence. The essence of a truth remains foreign to her. She neither has nor is a being" (p. 86/p. 92). Irigaray's best defense against essentialism is the defiant plurality of the feminine; there can be no essence in a conceptual system that is by definition antiunitary.
29. Toril Moi, *Sexual/Textual Politics* (London: Methuen, 1985), p. 139.
30. Irigaray, *Marine Lover*, p. 118/*Amante marine*, p. 126.
31. Irigaray, *This Sex*, p. 76/*Ce Sexe*, pp. 73–74.
32. Mary Ann Doane, *The Desire to Desire: The Woman's Film of the 1940s* (Bloomington: Indiana University Press, 1987), p. 182.
33. See Paul Ricoeur, "Mimesis and Representation," *Annals of Scholarship* (1981), 2:15–32. Irigaray gives this polysemy full play, reminding us for example in a passage of *This Sex* that in Plato mimesis is double: "There is *mimesis* as production, which would lie more in the realm of music, and there is the *mimesis* that would be already caught up in a process of *initiation, specularization, adequation* and *reproduction*. It is the second form that is privileged throughout the history of philosophy. . . . The first form seems always to have been repressed. . . . Yet it is doubtless in the direction of, and on the basis of, that first *mimesis* that the possibility of women's writing may come about" (p. 131/pp. 129–130). The question is, to paraphrase Yeats: How can you tell mimesis from mimesis?
34. Irigaray, *Corps-à-corps*, p. 29.
35. Derrida, *Positions*, trans. Alan Bass (Chicago: University of Chicago Press), p. 71.
36. Irigaray, *This Sex*, p. 111/*Ce Sexe*, p. 109.
37. Doane, *The Desire to Desire*, p. 104; emphasis added.
38. Irigaray, *Elemental Passions*, p. 15–16/*Passions élémentaires*, p. 18.
39. Ibid., p. 28.
40. Irigaray, *This Sex*, p. 116/*Ce Sexe*, p. 113.
41. Irigaray, *This Sex*, p. 140/*Ce Sexe*, p. 137.
42. Irigaray, *Corps-à-corps*, p. 49
43. Irigaray, *L'Oubli de l'air*, p. 36.

44. In a brilliantly turned defense of Irigaray against her antiessentialist critics, Jane Gallop cautions us against "too literal a reading of Irigarayan
anatomy" ("Lip Service," in *Thinking Through the Body* [New York:
Columbia University Press, 1988], p. 94). For example, when Irigaray
speaks of the plural lips of the female sex, the word she uses, *lèvres*, is a
catachresis, an obligatory metaphor that effectively short-circuits the referential reading of the text: "Irigaray embodies female sexuality in that
which, at this moment in the history of the language, is always figurative,
can never be simply taken as the thing itself" (p. 98). As brilliant as are
Gallop's arguments against a naively referential reading of the Irigarayan
textual body, in the end she recognizes that "the gesture of a troubled but
nonetheless insistent referentiality" is essential to Irigaray's project of
constructing a "non-phallomorphic sexuality" (p. 99).

45. It is no accident that one of the most thoughtful and balanced recent
articles on Irigaray is one based on a reading of her complete works and
not, as many (though not all) of the highly critical analyses, merely on
the works currently available in translation; see Margaret Whitford,
"Speaking as a Woman: Luce Irigaray and the Female Imaginary," *Radical Philosophy* (1986), 43:3–8.

46. On this point I would want to qualify Whitford's assessment of the place
of science in Irigaray's discourse: "Her account of Western culture runs
something like this. Our society is dominated by a destructive *imaginary*
(whose apotheosis is the ideology of science elevated to the status of a
privileged truth)"("Luce Irigaray and the Female Imaginary," p. 5). My
claim is that while condemning the imperialism of a neutered science, a
science cut off from the life-giving female body, and which threatens us
with "the many forms that destruction takes in our world" (*Ethics*, p. 5/
Ethique, p. 13; cf. the pronounced ecological strain in Luce Irigaray,
"Equal to Whom?" trans. Robert L. Mazzola, *différences* [Summer 1989],
1(2):59–76), Irigaray continues to look to science as a locus of "privileged truth."

47. Irigaray, *Parler n'est jamais neutre*, pp. 290–291; see also p. 289.

48. Ibid., p. 291.

49. Irigaray, "Is the Subject of Science Sexed?" p. 81; emphasis added. The
reference here is to the Nobel prize-winning research by Ilya Prigogine
on dissipative structures. For more on Prigogine's theories, whose influence on Irigaray has been significant, see Prigogine and Stengers. Shortly
after I first presented this article I received a letter from Katherine Hayles
telling me that, working out of the perspective of the relationship of
modern literature and science, she had been struck "by certain parallels
between the new scientific paradigms and contemporary feminist theory," notably that of Irigaray. I am most grateful to her for this precious
confirmation of my argument.

50. "Is the Subject of Science Sexed?" p. 86; emphasis added.

51. Moi, *Sexual/Textual Politics*, p. 131.

52. Irigaray, *Speculum*, p. 186/p. 232.

53. Ibid., p. 183.

54. Irigaray, *Ethics,* p. 72/ *Ethique de la différence sexuelle,* p. 75.

55. Ibid., p. 81.

56. Ibid., p. 84.

57. Irigaray, *L'Oubli de l'air*, p. 10.

58. Irigaray, *Parler n'est jamais neutre*, p. 74.

59. Ibid., p. 73.

60. Ibid., p. 308.

61. Derrida, "Devant la loi," trans. Avital Ronell, in Alan Udoff, ed., *Kafka and the Contemporary Critical Performance: Centenary Readings* (Bloomington: Indiana University Press, 1987), p. 139.

62. The question of gender is raised by Derrida in his reading, but not as regards the "two protagonists." For Derrida what is problematic is the gender of the law, in German *das Gesetz* (neutral), in French *la loi* (feminine) ("Devant la loi," p. 142).

THE

QUESTION

OF STYLE

The question of style
The title for this lecture was to have
been *the question of style.*
However—it is woman who will be
my subject.
Still, one might wonder whether
that doesn't really amount to the
same thing—or is it to the other?
The "question of style" is, as you
have no doubt recognized, a quotation.   —Jacques Derrida

There is a very stereotyped leftist
discourse that is . . . unacceptable to
me—as language. A newspaper like
Libération, which is very well done
and which I like a great deal, pur-
veys a type of discourse with the
same themes, the same stereotypes. I
always view problems in terms of
language. That's my particular
limit. An intellectual cannot directly attack the powers that be, but he
can inject new styles of discourse to
make things change.
                    —Roland Barthes

Until recently, Irigaray has been under-
translated. For some years now Anglophone readers have known her work primarily through *Speculum* and *This Sex
Which Is Not One.* As a number of her
other texts begin to appear in English, it
will be interesting to see how they are
received. They may well seem out of style
to many U.S. feminists today. When
today's feminist critics use the term
woman it almost always carries with it its
history as a critical concept, speaking its
role in an earlier stage of feminist criticism that could see the ends of
man but was blind to the future of women. In Irigaray's work, woman
does not heuristically lead to women. Irigaray may write about women
and their political, economic, psychic, and bodily betterment, but it is
through woman that she speaks. Moreover, the texts she reads are nothing if not Eurocentric and canonical, and categories of racial or ethnic
difference play little part in her work.

•   At the same time, Irigaray may well have something to say to today's feminist critics as her large corpus of writings becomes available in English translation. When *Speculum* and *This Sex Which Is Not One* first appeared in English in 1985, they figured often in Anglophone feminist debates about French feminism and essentialism, all the more so, perhaps, because they were read as *both* essentialist and antiessentialist. Irigaray's subsequent texts have opened up different ways to read her, including ways to reread her earliest writings. It is this somewhat different Irigaray, this differently read Irigaray, who may present challenges and possibilities to critical feminism.

In earlier debates it was the materiality of the female body that demarcated the critical positions around Irigaray. For some, Irigaray's lips and membranes and fluids spelled essentialism; others found within them the protocols of a different reading, that of mimesis, which, as Mary Ann Doane has said, was seen as a useful textual strategy serving "to enact a defamiliarizing version of femininity."[1] It is unlikely that such a neat critical split can recur. For one thing, the essentialist/antiessentialist opposition has lost its salience. For another, Irigaray's subsequent writings have made it more and more difficult to read her feminine corporeality as no more than a denaturalizing of the male symbolic order. Irigaray's "ethic of sexual difference" repeatedly affirms not only the feminine but the female body. Consider this passage from "The Culture of Difference": "The difficulties women have in gaining recognition for their social and political rights are rooted in this insufficiently thought out (*pensée*) relation between biology and culture. At present, to deny all explanations of a biological kind—because biology has paradoxically been used to exploit women—is to deny the key to interpreting this exploitation."[2] Or, from *Sexes et parentés*:

> *Division by sex* [*sexuation*], which represents one of the essential characteristics of living matter, has not been fostered in our society for centuries, and the technological era that we living through now aims to eliminate it. I am not simply referring to methods of artificial reproduction but to the whole mass of mechanical conditioning and environment that is ours today and that is gradually neutering us as living, sexual beings. The importance given to the problem of new reproductive techniques seems to me just one way of forcing women back into their role as mothers and defining the couple as merely a reproductive unit. . . . The identity of the human female is unknown or has become unknown.[3]

How are such passages to be read if the old essentialist/antiessentialist split no longer pertains? I will start by looking at the question from two

directions, first from within the critical context of Irigaray's writing and
then from the perspective of the current U.S. critical scene.

More than most, Irigaray's texts permit multiple and, as we have
seen, often contradictory readings. And this for very good reasons: her
rhetorical techniques are various and wily and she does not hesitate to
mystify, to mislead. According to her well-known critique of Western
cultural investments, the signifying structures within which we must
operate are produced at the expense of women. If woman remains Irigaray's category of analysis—woman not fractured into women—it is
because woman is for her the abstracted category of a cultural logic, not
a phenomenologized subject of epistemology. And that cultural logic,
the cultural logic of the West, which operates at the expense of real
women, incurs a debt that calls for extreme measures:

> But no clear univocal utterance, can in fact, pay off this mortgage since
> all are already trapped in the same credit structure. All can be recuper-
> ated when issued by the signifying order in place. It is still better to speak
> only in riddles, allusions, hints, parables. Even if asked to clarify a few
> points. Even if people plead that they just don't understand. After all,
> they never have understood. So why not double the misprision to the
> limits of exasperation?[4]

To disrupt the syntax of Western logic and to associate that disruption with woman is to appeal to a very old story. Indeed, the criticism
contemporaneous with Irigaray's—deconstruction, Lacanian psychoanalysis, other French feminisms—has been of interest to feminists precisely because it put some new spins on modernism's troping of the
feminine as reason's repressed other. But the spins are not all the same,
and Irigaray's woman is not Kristeva's (m)other, nor Derrida's figure of
undecidability, nor Lacan's woman-as-symptom. Irigaray's way of
undermining propositional logic through woman is different and perhaps unique. But hers is not a difference that easily reveals itself through
a straightforward examination of her theoretical propositions. With a
theorist who values misprision as Irigaray does the coherence yielded by
such means is always gained at a price. I will look, rather, at Irigaray's
style in order to locate what is unique about her and how her writings
might serve as a counterweight to some of today's prevailing critical
styles.

In seeing Irigaray's difference as a question of style, I am taking *style*
to mean something quite specific. I use style here the way Irigaray
develops it in the early interview "The Power of Discourse and the Subordination of the Feminine": "The issue is not one of elaborating a new
theory of which woman would be the *subject* or the *object*, but of jam-

• ming the theoretical machinery itself, of suspending its pretension to the production of a truth and of a meaning that are excessively univocal."[5] To jam the machinery of onto-theo-logy, this feminine must not renounce its "style":

> Which, of course, is not a style at all, according to the traditional way of looking at things. This "style," or "writing" of women tends to put the torch to fetish words, proper terms, well-constructed forms. . . . [It] resists and explodes every firmly established form, figure, idea or concept. Which does not mean that it lacks style, as we might be lead to believe by a discursivity that cannot conceive of it. But its "style" cannot be upheld as a thesis, cannot be the object of a position.[6]

It is in this same interview that Irigaray speaks of her famous mimetic style, and here also that she points to the explicitly Derridean character of woman's style:

> How, then, are we to redefine this language work that would leave space for the feminine? Let us say that every dichotomizing—and at the same time redoubling—break . . . has to be disrupted. Nothing is ever to be *posited* that is not also reversed and caught up again in the *supplementarity of this reversal.* To put it another way: there would no longer be either a right side or a wrong side of discourse, or even of texts, but each passing from one to the other would make audible and comprehensible even what resists the recto-verso structure that shores up common sense.[7]

How close Irigaray's formulation of woman's style is to Derrida's:

> From the moment the question of woman suspends the decidable opposition between the true and the nontrue, from the moment it installs the epochal regime of quotation marks for all the concepts that belong to the system of philosophical decidability, when it disqualifies the hermeneutical project of postulating a true sense for the text and liberates reading from the horizon of the meaning or the truth of being, of the values of production and produced, of the presence and the present—from that moment on, it becomes the question of style as the question of writing, the question of a spurring operation, more powerful than any content, any thesis, any meaning.[8]

Irigaray's theory of style is indeed so close—shall we say indebted?—to Derrida's that I will spend a moment on the similarities between the two in order presently to put in relief their difference.

Pointing to their commonality is not to say that Irigaray's and Derrida's manners of writing, their "styles" in the familiar sense of the word—their tropes and rhetorical turns, their rhythms and syntax—are the same; far from it.[9] Where they come together is on the *question* of style, where style, woman's style, is the deconstructive encounter of texts. This is an encounter that always entails a breakdown of the boundaries between reading and writing, between the text being written and the text being read. And that breakdown in turn renders the discursive frame undecidable, and with it the familiar conventions of rational discourse, the conventions of intelligibility.

This deconstructive encounter, long criticized as merely—or irresponsibly—ludic, has its theoretical foundations. As Derrida has often argued, we live the history of metaphysics: "We have no language—no syntax and no lexicon—which is alien to this history; we cannot utter a single destructive proposition which has not already slipped into the form, the logic, and the implicit postulations of precisely what it seeks to contest."[10] Nor is Derrida's position without its history. As Barbara Johnson has pointed out, deconstructive reading belongs to the long tradition of critique, that is, a reading that seeks to expose not a system's flaws but rather the grounds of that system's possibility, including the "insistent but invisible contradiction or differance (the repression of) which is necessary for and in the text's very elaboration."[11]

Of special interest here is the relation between the critique and its object. In the tradition of Marxist ideology-critique, as Peter Bürger argues, the critique takes place in the *nexus between* theory and its object, between the grasping of the historical possibilities of the unfolding of the object and the categories through which the object is theorized, "in the fact that the unfolding of the object and the elaboration of categories are connected."[12] Deconstructive critique involves a similar connection between the reading and what is read. "If," as Johnson says, "the traditional logic of meaning as an unequivocal structure of mastery *is* Western metaphysics, the deconstruction of metaphysics cannot simply combat logocentric meaning by opposing some other meaning to it. Differance is not a 'concept' or 'idea' that is 'truer' than presence. It can only be a process of textual *work*, a strategy of *writing*"[13]—or, quoting Irigaray, of language work.

Faced with her inevitable implication in the logic she aims to expose, Irigaray takes a homeopathic approach to the problem. If there is no metadiscourse, and if women especially can only repeat, then repetition it will be. Reading Irigaray's work of two decades, it becomes evident that her mimetic reading-writing practice is generalized throughout, that hers is a radical citationality. When she takes on the critical texts of the Western canon, it is those texts—Freud, Nietzsche, Marx, Hegel, Plato, and so on—that supply the language, that is to say the concep-

tual economies of her writing. She always cites, usually without attribution, and often ventriloquizes. For her, taking on a writer means
more than intertextuality; it means inhabiting his text. She does not
write on Heidegger, she writes Heidegger.[14]

Irigaray thus stages the commonplaces of the deconstructive critique: in her writing there is no *hors-texte* and there is (for women) no
metalanguage. At the same time, her texts can seem deceptively open;
they can invite the reader in *as if* the frame of intelligibility were intact.
And yet they mislead. Even familiar diacritical signs can be deceiving,
as with quotation marks that both do and do not signal the limits of
citation, and techniques of address that inadequately represent the relations between textual interlocutors. The cunning Irigarayan text invites
the reader in but then refuses to display the protocols of its reading. It
cannot be said to bar intelligibility, but rather always to problematize it.

It is here, around the question of intelligibility, that I will look at Irigaray for a moment from the other direction, from that of current U.S.
critical fashion. What makes Irigaray's texts particularly hard to read
today is precisely their relationship to the intelligible. In the U.S. the
politicization of criticism has been construed more and more as criticism's congruence with the politics of the social field. So great is that
congruence that much of current criticism seems inscribed in a kind of
instrumentalism, in a conviction that the route between naming a
problem and changing it is, though not always direct, at least chartable.
In such circumstances intelligibility is of the utmost importance; on it
seems to depend the very possibility of political change. For Irigaray,
however, the intelligible is more often than not the problem, the lure
that keeps one from reading the workings of the cultural system.[15]

One way of appreciating Irigaray's distance from prevailing critical
styles is to look at the present popularity of thematic criticism. Like an
out-of-date fashion that comes back into style—in a updated form, of
course—so have thematics returned to critical prominence. The most
innovative of today's thematic criticism is no longer concerned so much
with reading the thematic organization of a given work but with
putting thematics at the service of theory, or better, with making thematics into a theory. The recently popular "queer theory" is an example. In many of its manifestations it aims to put a new spin on a familiar cluster of semantic associations in order to produce fresh and, it is
hoped, unexpected readings of cultural texts that displace the categories
of hetero- and homosexuality.

Irigaray puts this hope into question. For her, it is precisely the
thematizable, the demonstrable, the formalizable, as she says in *This
Sex*, that one must write against.[16] In these terms the degree to which a

•

thematic theory takes its force from semantic association is the degree
to which it can only fail to open up the new. And as Jonathan Culler
pointed out a number of years ago, in his discussion of the deconstructive critique of thematics, it is not through semantic richness but only
through a semantic impoverishment that the deconstructive reading
permits us to see the inexorable workings of syntax, which is to say, the
philosophical apparatus.[17]

To look at current critical views on the intelligible is to look primarily at Foucault and his legacy. While much of the work done under his
influence does look at the historical conditions of intelligibility of a
given object of study (sexuality, the body, identities of various sorts),
rare is the critical text that problematizes its own comprehending and
comprehensible status. Moreover, work that too quickly reads Foucault's historicizing of epistemological breaks, and his theorizing of the
apparatus, can too simply frame the unthinkable as the merely suppressed, as something already present in culture but inexpressible within dominant structures of power/knowledge.[18]

Irigaray has something quite different to offer debates on intelligibility. Situated as she is with regard to deconstructive and psychoanalytic criticism, and not without her ties to the Marxist, she offers a very
particular critical frame in which to look at the feminist theoretical
enterprise. The frame is in some ways an old one, developed in the
1960s and seventies, but in light of both current critical trends and Irigaray's recent writings, it has new resonances. It provides us with a critical model very different from overly thematized theory. And it also
provides us with a way of thinking about something that no Fou-
cauldian criticism does—the question of ideology.[19]

As Irigaray attests in a 1988 interview, her theoretical analysis of
economic and social problems remains effectively constant from her
earliest through her latest works.[20] She remains consistently opposed to
mainstream women's movements that seek only to gain for women the
same rights as those held by men. For her now, as in 1977, "women's
'liberation' requires transforming the economic realm, and thus necessarily transforming culture and its operative agency, language."[21]

In Irigaray's view neither culture nor economics is determinant; the
two are necessary to each other for the full functioning of the system.
Moreover, because men have historically controlled the production of
both the cultural and the economic, the system is gendered. One would
have to be an "unbridled defender of idealism," writes Irigaray, to be
surprised at the sexed nature of language: "It is always men who have
spoken and above all written; in the sciences, philosophy, religion, and
politics."[22] But change cannot come about simply by giving power to

• women as agents, for the very logic of the culture forecloses positivity
for the feminine and, hence, for women. For Irigaray, without changing "the general grammar of culture, the feminine will never take place
in history."[23]

What is unique, one might say outrageous, about Irigaray is that she
chooses not to stop at a deconstructive reading of this cultural logic. In
the preceding essay of this volume, "This Essentialism Which Is Not
One: Coming to Grips with Irigaray," Naomi Schor shows that Irigaray's celebrated mimetic style does more than denaturalize and expose
phallocentrism. Breathing the scandal back into Irigaray's work, Schor
finds another mimesis, one that has been "largely misread, and even
repressed, because it involves a far more controversial and riskier operation, a transvaluation rather than a repudiation of the discourse of
misogyny." She calls this mimesis "positive." This

> mimesis comes to signify difference as positivity, a joyful reappropriation
> of the attributes of the other that is not in any way to be confused with a
> mere reversal of the existing phallocentric distribution of power. . . . The
> mimesis that lies beyond masquerade and mimicry . . . does not signify a
> reversal of misogyny but an emergence of the feminine, and the feminine
> can only emerge from within or beneath—to extend Irigaray's archaeo-
> logical metaphor—femininity, within which it lies buried. The differ-
> ence within mimesis *is* the difference within difference.

The positive mimesis Schor finds is doubly scandalous. First, according to the old feminist antiessentialist argument, it spells essentialism.
Schor cites Toril Moi as representative of that position: for Moi, Irigaray "falls for the temptation to produce her own positive theory of
femininity. But, as we have seen, to define 'woman' is necessarily to
essentialize her."[24] The other challenge Irigaray poses is to the larger
deconstructive project itself. In the deconstructive exposure of specular
logic, to take a positive turn is to leave the austerity of displacement for
the lure of the dialectic: struggling against Western logic means resisting the machinery that produces new positivities of the same. How can
Irigaray's scene of sexual difference, so crucial to her theorizing, escape
that dialectical machinery?

I want to suggest, following Schor, that in evoking a female positivity Irigaray always remains engaged in the deconstructive project while,
at the same time, extending it beyond its limits. The positivity she
evokes is one that cannot be summed up; it is not thematizable, trans-
latable into some kind of formula, however utopian. The positivity she
promotes, indeed her whole project, is to be grasped through her style.
Moreover, I am especially interested in the extent to which Irigarayan

positivity is produced through her readings of the blind spots in the
most radical critiques of epistemology—that is, through the texts of
Derrida, Lacan, Heidegger, Nietzsche, Marx, Freud, and so on. The
blind spots differ from text to text, but they are always sexed and always
related, at whatever a remove, to a disavowal of the (female) materiality blocked by even the most self-conscious critique of the symbolic
order. It is in displaying those blind spots that the Irigarayan "woman's
style" parts company with the styles of Derrida, Lacan, and those of her
other contemporaries.[25]

I choose one brief piece of Irigaray's as a starting point, her "Così Fan
Tutti (1975)," which deals with Lacan and psychoanalysis, specifically
with Lacan's seminar *Encore*. I pick an early text because Irigaray's later
writings all draw on the readings she did in that period; I choose a piece
on Lacan because the female positivity in Irigaray is produced largely
through a psychoanalytic frame.[26] As to psychoanalysis—that old
adversary of intelligibility—the psychoanalysis I want to discuss here is
less that of the analytic scene than that of the critique of epistemology.
The two cannot be separated, of course, in that the analytic scene is the
privileged site of psychoanalysis's critique of the Cartesian subject. But
Irigaray, like Lacan, regularly brings psychoanalysis to bear on epistemology in ways not at all dependent on the specificity of individual
analysis. And it is this critical use of psychoanalysis that makes visible
the very split or tension in psychoanalysis itself, that tension between a
discourse that aspires to science and one that relentlessly reads the
workings of a naturalized rationality. The Lacan that Irigaray addresses
in "Così Fan Tutti," then, is one who, like herself, aims not to consolidate but to interrogate systematicity, including the system of psychoanalysis.[27]

A Man of His Word

"Così Fan Tutti" is the essay in which Irigaray brings feminism's questions to the door of Lacanian psychoanalysis. Where do women stand
with regard to psychoanalytic discourse? Do castration and the Phallus
tell us the deep Truths of Western culture or just the truth of how things
are and might not always be? In other words, what is the relationship of
psychoanalysis to history?

The questions are clear, but not so the answers. "Così Fan Tutti" may
well be set up to test psychoanalysis's truth, but the reader soon realizes
that the most compelling question the text poses is how to tell the difference between Irigaray's discourse and Lacan's. Where does his leave
off and hers begin? This is a crucial question in reading Irigaray. We

• know she brings a psychoanalytic critique to bear on the blind spots of
philosophical and scientific discourse, and we know she distances her
own analytic readings from the blind spots she reads in Freud. But
where does she stand on Lacan? The question is a tricky one and Irigaray gives us little help with its answer.

Of course, Irigaray has reason to be at odds with Lacan; let us not
forget that "Così Fan Tutti" was published in August 1975 and that Irigaray was expelled from the Ecole freudienne shortly after her publication of *Speculum* in 1974. Still, we do not need the precise details of Irigaray's extratextual relations with the Law to know that the essay is cast
in a sardonic mode. The title "Così Fan Tutti" (All men are like that)
evokes Mozart's *Così Fan Tutte* (All women . . .), and its unsavory Don
Alfonso, a "cynical old philosopher," who, as Jane Gallop says "knows
all about women," who knows "communication between the sexes is
unreliable," and who profits from that knowledge.[28] We are set up,
then, for the exposure of Don Jacques, with the epigraphs from *Encore*
serving as props:

> "The one who I presume has knowledge is the one I love."
>   "Women don't know what they are saying, that's the whole differ-
> ence between them and me."[29]

The epigraphs are paired to display a Lacan who can only love the
one who knows—and women don't know. This whole set-up depends
on a "literal" reading of Lacan's words. However, the epigraphs also
yield another reading: a reading of a Lacanian subject who knows that
he knows only by not knowing. If Lacan himself uses the literal with
such relish, it is because he can do so much with it, including derail our
reasonable search for truth and meaning, for intelligibility. As he says in
another seminar, speaking with characteristic irony, "We shall be dealing with the most ordinary terms, idealization, identification. . . . These
are not easy terms to handle and it is not made any easier by the fact
that they already have meanings."[30] This is what Derrida calls paleonymy, giving old words new meaning, a practice in which Lacan
delights because it displays so well his theories of knowledge as repetition and return.

Miming Lacan, then, Irigaray puts the literal to work in the very
frame of her essay, which is to say she frames the essay itself as a problem of literality. This leaves the reader searching for the line of demar-
cation between her and Lacan. Read with a "knowledge" of Lacan, the
two opening lines say nothing Irigaray herself hasn't said in one form or
another: woman is excluded from the epistemological scene of mastery,
foreclosed by the specular return of phallic language. Of course, Lacan

says "women" and not "woman," but Irigaray need not take this seriously since she knows he doesn't mean what he says. It is the very task of psychoanalysis to show that mastery is a psychic investment, with the return on the investment denied to both male and female subjects.

Lacan would not deny that male subjects have a relationship to that lack of mastery that differs from the female's: he sees the knowledge (*savoir*) involved in symbolic processes as indissociable from the knowledge (*connaissance*) produced in the early, imaginary demarcations of "psyche" and "body," a *connaissance* that is, in turn, activated differently in the symbolic depending on whether the subject is sexed through language as male or female. If anything, Lacan sees women as knowing they don't know what they are saying—by virtue of their position in the symbolic order—while men are dupes of Truth. Which leaves Lacan, as Gallop so aptly put it, playing the prick and not the phallus. Moreover, and to turn the screw one more time, since Lacan knows enough to play the prick, he knows that it is little more than *woman* that he plays after all. And, as Irigaray says, "it is useless . . . to trap women in the exact definition of what they mean, to make them repeat (themselves) so that it will be clear; they are already elsewhere in that discursive machinery where you expected to surprise them."[31]

This is what Irigaray knows about Lacan and what she, for her part, plays with in "Così Fan Tutti." It is evident from the first lines that the essay is about delivering women from the hands of old men; Irigaray is explicit about the need for change. At the same time, it is not at all clear where her readings of sexual indifference differ from Lacan's, which do not at all seem to read for change. Where can one locate their difference and, hence, change itself? A rhetorical ambiguity dominates the essay. Consider one of the opening passages. Irigaray has just commented on Freud's phallocentric model and turns her attention to Lacan:

> But the truth of the truth about female sexuality is restated even more rigorously when psychoanalysis takes *discourse itself* as the object of its investigations. Here, anatomy is no longer available to serve, to however limited an extent, as proof-alibi for the real difference between the sexes. The sexes are now defined only as they are determined in and through language. Whose laws, it must not be forgotten, have been prescribed by male subjects for centuries.
>
> This is what results: "There is no woman who is not excluded by the nature of things, which is the nature of words, and it must be said that, if there is something they complain a lot about at the moment, that is what it is—except that they don't know what they are saying, that's the whole difference between them and me."

The statement is clear enough. Women are in a position of exclusion.[32]

• Irigaray's point does, indeed, seem clear: though Lacan takes as the object of his analysis not anatomy but discourse, little is gained for women; women's "exclusion is *internal* to an order from which nothing escapes: the order of (man's) discourse."[33] Yet just where does Irigaray's criticism of Lacan take her? When she cites Lacan's own words, the better to indict him, what does she gain? Lacan is past master of the style that undermines all critical frames. If he reduplicates women's exclusion, his is a staged reduplication that displays the work of the symbolic order as precisely man's discourse. Thus, the Lacanian analysis that takes discourse as its object of study finds that woman, or anything one might call "woman's own sexuality," is foreclosed by a logic that exposes itself as self-reflexively male. The sense is clear and Irigaray's own work says as much.

And if the logic Lacan mimes seems to foreclose the possibility of change, as Irigaray claims in the essay, where, then, is that change to come from? How is it to be theorized? Again, there is no easy answer in an essay that itself seems to have no end to its own miming game. In order presumably to take Lacan at his own game, Irigaray repeats his wily ways, speaking literally with no regard for the truth. One must ask where it leads her, if she is not in the end miming the very process by which women's discourse is always caught within the recursive structure of man's.

A careful page-by-page analysis of "Così Fan Tutti" only multiplies the questions. Irigaray cites abundantly from the *Séminaire XX*, surrounding most of the citations with quotation marks in the first half of the essay, using fewer marks in the second. Either way, her procedure remains the same. Virtually every element of the essay—the title would be an exception—comes from the twentieth *Séminaire*. Every problem or critique of a problem, every trope or figure comes from Lacan, from woman as not-all to negative theology to courtly love. We recognize as Lacanian that language excludes "bodies," that language exists but women don't, that there is no prediscursive reality to be found, that God occupies the place of being and not-being (having his being only to bar it, to divest himself of predicates), that woman's pleasure is never spoken except by man, that there is no law for women's pleasure, no relation between the sexes, no love possible that is not the love of the subject for himself, that there is no apparent end to the homo-sexual regime, and so on and on. All are Lacanian themes that say too little or too much when detached from the analytic discourse that produces them. All are Lacanian readings that allow themselves to be read *simultaneously* as symptomatic of a problematic cultural organization presumably subject to change *and* as determinant Truth.

Moreover, in Irigaray's text the Lacanian ambiguity is redoubled, for it is never clear for very long which truth (truth or Truth) is being underwritten or undermined.

It is one thing, then, for Irigaray to read Freud's blind spot, quite another for her to take on Lacan. To pin down Lacan and display him as culpable she must again and again take him at his word. This is not a simple strategy, given, first, that Lacan's discourse precisely cannot be reduced to what it says, and, second, that Irigaray and Lacan share fundamentally the same theoretical critique of the phallic order. And though some would dispute the latter claim—whether Lacanians who see Irigaray as misreading Lacan or feminists who read a greater difference between the two—I suggest that what separates Irigaray and Lacan cannot be found in theses or theories but rather in the Irigarayan positivity of woman, which is, once again, a question of style. To locate the specificity of that style is to find what makes Irigaray's argument in "Così Fan Tutti" work.

Since to locate that style one must be wary of positive terms that falsely illuminate, I will follow Irigaray's lead and take a circuitous route, approaching her style through Lacan. *Encore*, Lacan's twentieth *Séminaire*, and his eleventh, *The Four Fundamental Concepts of Psychoanalysis*, are the texts through which I will pass. And what I find there—what will help me suggest the difference in Irigaray's style—is a trope.

"Let us append here the question of the fetish.
Question of (the) style. Of pastiche . . . "[34]

Séminaire XX is a collection of seminars from 1972–73, with the collective title of *Encore*. There Lacan "returns" to the question of woman, but the seminars deal as much with epistemology as with femininity. Lacan might speak of femininity, women, love, and bodies, but, like Derrida, he is *also* speaking of knowledge, that is, that other love called philosophy. This concern of Lacan's runs throughout *Encore* and is, of course, nothing new. What could be older than that cultural knot of sexuality and epistemology narrativized by Oedipus? It is something Lacan has always talked of. However, Lacan has a rather particular way of returning to old topics. He has a way of working and reworking the same ground that amounts to a return, but always to a different place. By *Encore* Lévi-Strauss's theories of kinship and women as exchange have long since ceased to energize his readings, and earlier readings of the sexing of the subject in language have given way to different concerns. No longer is his focus on the continuous and never achieved process of producing a sexed subject, which is to say a subject *tout court*,

- but more on the failures of the sexual relation, of love, and of knowledge.

The topic is well suited, of course, to Lacan's notorious style, for nowhere in his work does he allow a theory to be simply adequate to its object.[35] On the contrary, he goes to great lengths to reveal the unreliability of his truths. In particular, he stresses the closed circularity of his discourse, the dependency of the analysis on the object analyzed, and the impossibility of mastery. Again and again, in his readings, Lacan inscribes his discourse as inadequate, where nothing ever meets its mark. Thus it is that throughout his corpus his analysis takes as its objects always failed processes: a subject that is always only a subject-effect, a desire that never possesses its object, knowledge that never knows what it knows *and* in not knowing mirrors the analysis that produces it.[36]

It is in speaking of love's failure that Lacan uses the trope that helps me to read Irigaray—the trope of meiosis. For Lacan no sexual relation exists, no relation between the sexes, and in "God and the *Jouissance* of The̶ Woman" he sets out to show what in the symbolic order stands in for that relationship: "Today I will be elaborating the consequences of the fact that in the case of the speaking being the relation between the sexes does not take place, since it is only on this basis that what makes up for the relation can be stated."[37] Of course, throughout history, according to Lacan, the culture speaks of *nothing but* that relationship, figuring it as the "relationship of the One"—the One that claims to be the union of two. This is the One of copulation, of Aristophanes' celebrated androgyne in the *Symposium*, that once-happy androgyne split into sexual halves now eternally seeking to have their two become one again.[38] Lacan finds this sexual combinatory everywhere, especially in notions of knowledge, where up to now "nothing has even been conceived of which did not share in the fantasy of the sexual tie." Witness, he says, "the terms active and passive which dominate everything which has been thought up on the relationship of form to matter . . . this crude polarity, which makes matter passive and form the agency which brings to life."[39]

Lacan asks rhetorically if this persistence of the sexual combinatory throughout history, the persistence of redemptive copulation, might not suggest that human signification itself rose out of "sexual reality," that it might be, in other words, biologically determined. After all, he says, the biological process of meiosis (which he here calls mitosis) could support that:[40]

> What would make it legitimate to maintain that it is through sexual reality that the signifier came into the world—that man learnt to think—is

the recent field of discoveries that begins by a more accurate study of mitosis [*sic*]. There are then revealed the modes according to which the maturation of cells operates, namely, the double process of reduction. What is involved, in this reduction, is the loss of a certain number of visible elements, chromosomes. This, of course, brings us to genetics. And what emerges from this genetics if not the dominant function, in the determination of certain elements of the living organism, of a combinatory that operates at certain of its stages by the expulsion of remainders?[41]

"Where is all this leading?" asks Lacan finally. "It is leading us to the question as to whether we must regard the unconscious as a remanence of that archaic junction between thought and sexual reality."[42]

The answer is no. Where the archaic connection really leads us, Lacan goes on to say in the eleventh seminar, is to Jungian archetypes. And for Lacan, one must look not to "some archaic relation, some primitive mode of access of thoughts," but precisely to Freud's theory of the libido. There we find not the shades of the biological past, some "ancient world surviving in ours," but something different at work.[43] For Lacan the work of biology, kept alive through ancient figures of the combinatory, is culture's imaginary and it is precisely that which Freud disrupts.[44]

Again in the twentieth seminar Lacan points to this Freud, the Freud who offers an alternative to biological determinism. There again he endorses Freud's One which is not the sum of two but which is also not identical to itself: "There is something of One" (*Y a d'l'Un*). To understand this concept of the One, we can look, Lacan says, to Freud's concept of Eros in *Beyond the Pleasure Principle*. There Eros is seen as a fusion making one out of two, even making one out of a vast multitude: "But just as it is clear that even all of you . . . not only do not make one but have no chance of doing so . . . so Freud had to raise up another factor as obstacle to this universal Eros, in the shape of Thanatos, which is reduction to dust."

What I want to underline is the passage that follows, in which Lacan again invokes a biological process—here called meiosis—but this time in a contrary direction, as a process that seems to have enabled *Freud's* thinking:

Clearly this [Eros and Thanatos] is a metaphor allowed to Freud by the fortunate discovery of the two units of the germen, the ova and the spermatozoa, whose fusion, crudely speaking, engenders—what? a new being. With this qualification, that the thing does not come about without a meiosis, a quite manifest subtraction for at least one of the two just before the conjunction is effected, a subtraction of certain elements which are not without their place in the final operation.[45]

• And yet, after this seeming endorsement of the role of meiosis in the Freudian metaphor, Lacan goes on directly to say that although facilitated by biology, the whole question of the One must nonetheless be interrogated at the level of *language*, thereby seeming to disavow the very connection just established and thoroughly confounding the reader in the process.

Of course, this is not the first time Lacan confounds the boundary between language and biology. In *The Four Fundamental Concepts* he declares that "sexuality is represented in the psyche by a relation of the subject that is deduced from something other than sexuality itself," after which he presents us with his famous theory of the split subject— a theory that resembles nothing as much as meiosis:

> Sexuality is established in the field of the subject through the way of lack.
>
> Two lacks overlap here. The first emerges from the central defect around which the dialectic of the advent of the subject to his own being in the relation to the Other turns—by the fact that the subject depends on the signifier and that the signifier is first of all in the field of the Other. This lack takes up the other lack, which is the real, earlier lack, to be situated at the advent of the living being, that is to say, at sexed reproduction. The real lack is what the living being loses, that part of himself *qua* living being, in reproducing himself through the way of sex. This lack is real because it relates to something real, namely, that the living being, by being subject to sex, has fallen under the blow of individual death.[46]

It appears that meiosis is a useful trope for Lacan himself, but just what is the status for him of a biological trope? What side is it on—language or biology? It is these questions—of language and biology, discourse and materiality, signifiers and sex—knotted as they are around meiosis, that will lead me presently back to Irigaray and her scandalous positivity. But first I must remain yet a moment with Lacan and the vexed problem of the split subject.

According to Lacan it is the doubly split subject that describes the human condition, not Aristophanes' misleading androgyne, for Lacan's subject seeks its complement not in the other, but in that "part of himself, lost forever, that is constituted by the fact that he is only a sexed living being, and that he is no longer immortal."[47] That is, Lacan's subject seems to reenact, on the psychic level, the drama of the sexed reproduction of living matter. In that drama there is no life without splitting and death, and no simple copulation of male and female can make up for that splitting. It is the subject's own loss that characterizes the organization of the living being in language.

•

In *The Four Fundamental Concepts* and *Encore* this lost part of the subject is figured by Lacan's *objet petit a*. And this *objet a*, this lost part, is, perhaps more than anything, what separates Lacan from Freud, or better, what enables Lacan to read Freud differently.[48] In this age of "discourse theory" it is easy to forget what an analytically and philosophically ambitious project Lacan took on in attempting to recast Freud's texts. Freud's theories of the psychic life of the human subject are in no way contained by the discourse of intersubjectivity, and yet they are so often read through the limits of that discourse and phenomenologized in the process. It is, then, just that ground of intersubjectivity that Lacan seeks to displace by driving a wedge of discourse between himself and Freud. Lacan's aim is to better theorize the unconscious, that is to say, the Other of the discourse of mastery, all that consciousness and reason cannot know. For Lacan the intersubjective as such is all too visible, too evident; it forces everything into its field. As long as the Other retains some degree of ontological status, so does the subject, or better, so does the naturalized subject-object couple along with the massively sedimented history of its relationships: "Mapping the subject in relation to reality, such as it is supposed to constitute us, and not in relation to the signifier, amounts to falling already into the degradation of the psychological constitution of the subject."[49] It amounts as well, Lacan says, to falling into sociology or phenomenology or any analysis that posits the relations between "beings in the real, including all of you animated beings out there," as "produced in terms of inversely reciprocal relations."[50] To read Freud out of intersubjectivity is to derail discourses of mastery, which, in recirculating the all too visible reciprocal relations of subject and object, domesticate Freud and deliver him back into the grip of the readily intelligible.[51]

The imaginary "imaginary" is what allows Lacan to set up an obstacle to two commonplaces of the symbolic economy: 1. the love of subject and other and 2. the subject's knowledge of the object. It is here that he uses the *objet petit a* to figure the trace of a process whereby the living being is as a child produced in and into signification, where the "subject" is "detached" from itself while still attached, whether the "detached part" is "its own body," another's body, or an external object. With the *objet a* Lacan rereads Freud's *fort-da*, with the crucial difference being that for Lacan the "reel is not the mother reduced to a little ball by some magical game" but "a small part of the subject that detaches itself from him while still remaining his, still retained."[52] Thus, Lacan's little object is *not simply an object*, a substantive, but the reeling in and out, the *splitting* that takes its effect—wholeness—with it. And,

• because it takes its wholeness with it, the splitting is not simply a splitting, but more of a cleaving—a cleaving that both sunders and clings.

By naming the phenomenon *objet petit a* Lacan figures it as a subset of *A(utre)*, but at the same time it is used to suggest a certain remainder produced in the division of the *subject*. It is thus, as remanence of the subject *and* produced through the Other, that the *objet petit a* is called on to figure that most difficult of concepts: a relationality that both brings together and exceeds the dialectical relations of subject-other and of subject-object.[53]

Let us return now to Lacan's use of meiosis and his equivocation as to language and biology. Of course, in reading Lacan one is never far from equivocation. The evasion inherent in the equivocal *is* Lacan's game, particularly the evasion of that which is always there to be seen. Indeed, there is something in meiosis waiting to be seen, the trick of meiosis as it were. Under the biological term of *meiosis* one can find another meaning, its rhetorical meaning of "litotes" or "understatement," of affirmation through negation. In that context, the rhetorical context, meiosis understates through diminishment. While the biological meiosis produces life through what is sometimes called "reduction division," the rhetorical meiosis affirms through negation, as in the trope that is not not biological.[54]

Now, like the *objet petit a*, like all of Lacan's figures and tropes, meiosis is called on to do the hardest of critical work. In *Four Fundamental Concepts* and in *Encore* it stages the conundrum of language and biology, of sexed reproduction as the riddle of life. In short-circuiting the copula through the trope of meiosis, Lacan seems to block both the language of the interpersonal, of communication, and the ontological *is* of epistemology.

When he associates the two-stage reduction division of meiosis with his two-stage rendering of the split subject, he also accomplishes a great deal: he exposes the androgyne model as a fantasy of a simple combinatory not borne out by biology, and then appropriates meiosis as a model of the subject's constitution in lack, all the while denying any biological determinism, a denial itself borne out by the figural nature of the concept of meiosis. On one level this is a language game, no more than language chasing its own tail. However, in that very game is a lesson about the subject's relation to biology, a relation we can recognize as fetishistic, one of knowing and not knowing. Moreover, Lacan gives a special turn to the fetishistic operation, a turn that speaks to the biology/language divide and that takes us, finally, back to the Irigaray we never left.

Meiosis (not not biological and not not rhetorical) is a perfect trope for figuring fetishism, that dominant operation of cultural logic. Meiosis actually offers us a better rendering, perhaps, of the classic psychoanalytic fetishist. He is the one who manages his anxiety by simultaneously knowing and not knowing. Meiosis shows us someone even more anxious, someone who sees the woman as both not having and not not having the phallus. Meiosis, then, shows us a special kind of positivity. Even a simple positive is subtended by the negative, but the cleaving positive of meiosis brings with it always the double trace of the negative. The only way it can *be* is by not not being.

Most important, this formulation gives us a way of seeing what is perhaps the hardest to see: that Lacan's own fetishistic formulations are above all a *reading* of the fetish as cultural symptom. Lacan equivocates about meiosis, because whether the subject-sexed-through-language is seen as *repeating* the death-in-life of the organism or whether the subject's constitution in language is seen as *cut off* from biology is, literally, all the same to him. They amount to the same thing because they both display the fetishistic nature of the production of the subject in discourse. Lacan's famous split subject is, then, a reading of the anxious formation of subjectivity within our cultural order, an anxious formation that, though not determined by biology, is permeated by it. Viewed this way his figurations of the split subject and the *objet a* aim not to naturalize the trope of the split but rather to expose the extent to which the split, as generalized trope and its effects, blocks the thinking of other possible relationalities.[55]

It is, after all, the mission of psychoanalysis, in dismantling the reign of rationality, to think "body" and "mind," but also "consciousness" and "matter" differently. Lacan displays over and over how obsessive is the investment in *not* doing that. The *objet a* is there to figure the "subject's" relation not only to its "body" but also to other bodies, to matter, to the world itself; and the *objet a* persists, it clings, *as if it were really something lost*, as if it were a wound. Lacan's subject-produced-through-language is a symptomatic reading of a cultural fixation with being and not-being, death and matter. And, since being or presence is itself the problem, or the fictive imaginary, the subject who does not and cannot know is driven continually to seek ways to not not know.[56]

"The Future of Sexual Difference"

Reading Lacan after "Così Fan Tutti," one has two strong impressions: that Lacan's and Irigaray's theories of sexual difference are both very similar and very different. Their similarity lies in their insistence on the need to open up and separate the culturally collapsed terms of sexual difference and biological reproduction. For Lacan it is culture's anxious relation to the death-in-life of biology and discourse that stands in the way of the sexual relation. He sees Western discourse, with its phallic organization, as both proclaiming and denying the fetishistic logic by which the subject's other—his other—is constituted by stand-ins for the *objet a*, namely woman or mother. Irigaray takes this reading of Lacan's and pushes it further. For her the stand-in that forever nourishes phallic speculation is "mother-matter-nature."[57] If Lacan reads the *fort-da* game as one that stages the splitting or cleaving of the subject and the *objet a*, Irigaray reads it as a staging of the child's effort to appropriate to *himself*, to master, the relationship between mother and child that is itself figured by a veil or a membrane. It is thus that "the body which gives life never enters into language."[58] This "matricide," this discursive disavowal of the (male) subject's relationship to the material takes many forms, including the idealization of the mother, which "erase[s] birth by an infinite love of the Other('s) ideality."[59]

The solution to the erasure of birth is not more birth. Like Lacan, Irigaray reads against the culture's obsession with the fantasy of copulation and finds sexed reproduction to be at the very heart of the cultural logic of the fetish. Her critique of Freud turns in part around this question:

> Now, is there any more obvious device or more explicit way of banishing the auto-erotic, homosexual, or indeed fetishistic character of the relationship of man to woman than to stress the production of a child? Is the appeal to biological materialism brought in to cover up the fantasy system governing the sexual economy of the couple?[60]

The answer to Irigaray's rhetorical question is not simply yes, but yes and no. Freud's appeal to biological materialism does "to some extent unwittingly"[61] repeat the Western tradition of covering over "the fantasy system governing the sexual economy of the couple." But at the same time—and this is what both Irigaray and Lacan read—it displays a cultural anxiety about the biological that is expressed *through* the collapse of sexual difference onto sexual reproduction. This is the anxiety Lacan reads in the Western tropes of form and matter, "a relationship which is so fundamental and which Plato, and then Aristotle, refer to at every step they take regarding the nature of things. It is visibly, palpably the case that these propositions are only upheld by a fantasy of trying to make up for what there is no way of stating, that is, the sexual relation."[62]

Of course, the sexual relation is just what Irigaray writes about.

Lacan says over and over that there is no sexual relation. And Irigaray
agrees. Yet Irigaray writes about the sexual relation nonetheless, and it
is her insistence on positive sexual difference, what she calls the ethic of
sexual difference, that marks the difference between Lacan and her.
Near the end of "Così Fan Tutti" she writes:

> That the sexual relation has no *as such*, that it cannot even be *posited* as
> such: one cannot but subscribe to such affirmations. They amount to
> saying that the discourse of truth, the discourse of "demonstration,"
> cannot incorporate the sexual relation within the economy of its logic.
> But still, does that not amount to saying that there is no possible sexual
> relation, claiming that there is no exit from this *logos*, which is wholly
> assimilated to the discourse of knowledge?
>
> Is it not, therefore, the same thing as judging the historical privilege
> of the *demonstrable*, the *thematizable*, the *formalizable*, to be a-histori-
> cal?[63]

Where Irigaray faults Lacan, then, is in his failure to posit any discourse beyond the logocentric, a failure that makes logocentrism appear
ahistorical. This is a serious indictment of a theorist who himself pits
psychoanalysis against the ahistorical, particularly against the ahistoricity particular to historicism (which Lacan simply calls "history"). For
Lacan psychoanalysis reads against both the eternal return of the archaic in the present (as with Jungianism or Aristophanes' androgyne) and
the inevitable unfolding of history (as in Hegelianism or "orthodox"
Marxism).[64]

Lacan's psychoanalysis is the analysis of signification and the culture's investment in signification, and neither signification nor the
investment in it is timeless. Moreover, for Lacan, psychoanalysis too
is historically produced. Not a "*Weltanschauung,* nor a philosophy
that claims to provide the key to the universe. It is governed by a particular aim, which is historically defined by the elaboration of the
notion of the subject."[65] Lacan is here inscribing psychoanalysis as a
form of dialectical critique. That is to say, the conditions of possibility that produce psychoanalysis as a critique—the emergence of the
modern subject and all of its historical concomitants such as rationalism or scientism—are the very questions that form the object of that
critique.

Irigaray's particular focus within this dialectical project is on the
phallic culture, which, though old, takes on an intensely visible importance with the elaboration of the modern subject.[66] For her psychoanalysis is particularly important in reading how that phallic culture
erases the history that produces it, and how the real historical relations

• between women and men—diverse, complex, and contradictory—are always subsumed under the categories of reproduction by a symbolic economy that fetishistically covers over historical relationality and contradiction.

It is this fetishizing culture that Lacan displays so dazzlingly, within a critical discourse that mirrors the discourse he reads, that never permits of an outside, that neutralizes all critique, as always, inevitably implicated in his own. And Irigaray's response to that powerful Lacanian discourse is that it may well tell the truth about the culture, but its effect is to make the logos seem itself inevitable, ahistorical. Of course, Irigaray is not alone in making this argument, but where she stands apart is in what she does with it. Rejecting the temptation to appeal either to an archaic prior to metaphysics or to a utopian positivity that could only defamiliarize, she remains within a present signifying history and writes her female positivity and her positive sexual relation through other texts and other traces.

Since terms like woman, matter, mother, nature, are indeed stand-ins for fetishizing operations, they cannot carry "truly" positive meanings outside their symbolic history. They are precisely not thematizable. It is this "historical privilege of the *demonstratable*, the *thematizable*, the *formalizable*" that belongs to phallic discourse and that all critiques of that discourse aim to displace. The difference between Irigaray's and Lacan's critiques—and, for that matter, Derrida's—can be said to come down to a question of troping. Lacan's dominant tropes remain, as it were, negatively symptomatic. His readings are dominated by the split, that is to say, the split-effect, much as Derrida's are dominated by the hymen and other figures of undecidability.

Irigaray refuses to stop with these tropes. Her psychoanalytic readings may be rooted in Lacan's. Her style may be indebted to Derrida's—and it is, after all, Derrida's shifting of critique from a dialectical reading for contradiction to a deconstructive reading for *différance* that enables Irigaray's work. But while the texts of Lacan and Derrida expose the phallic order in their different ways, they remain, through their splits and folds, within the bounds of their critiques, not venturing further into the unthinkable. Irigaray displays no such critical prudence. Where Lacan and Derrida expose the effects of the phallic economy and figure their critiques as "feminine," Irigaray attempts to write what is blocked by phallic categories of reading and writing and calls what she does "woman's style."

In Derridean terms Irigaray mobilizes the trace to "positive" ends, and she does this in a mode that is not unlike meiosis. It is here, finally, that the Lacanian meiosis—that borrowed and ambivalent term—is at its most useful in figuring Irigaray's style. Lacan invokes it to discuss the aporia of discourse and biology. So, too, can we bring it to bear on Irigaray's approach to the problem. Just as Irigaray does not stop at the impossibility of the sexual relation, so she strains at the catachresis that forever separates "brute" matter from discourse. If catachresis is not to be cured at least she can display and try to displace the cultural obsession that always reproduces it. It is thus that in Irigaray's writing the materiality of "bodies" and "nature" takes on substance with and against the cleaving split that produces the material as an effect. In Irigaray matter is always *not not matter*. That is, any "positive" term in Irigaray, whether lips or fluids or women or the sexual relation, bears the trace of its history—both its discursive history through other texts of the culture *and* its deconstructive history as a term that is posited, reversed, and "caught up again in the supplementarity of its reversal."[67] What Irigaray allows the reader to see, then, is several registers of historically and textually specific signification at work simultaneously. But that is not all. Because Irigaray *also* uses terms as if they could signify in some straightforward way, because she multiplies the misprision, covering her traces, so to speak, she displays what splits and hymens do not make as visible: a cultural logic that does its work, has its concrete effects on real women, and is at once both inescapable and subject to historical change.

Returning to "Così Fan Tutti" we see there an opportunistic text that plays Lacan's games and wins on its own terms. Lacan's game is with mastery. In his texts analysis and mastery are in endless pursuit of each other. But mastery ultimately wins in Lacan. The discourse that can always take its interlocutor by surprise ("they hear, but unfortunately they understand, and what they understand is a little too hasty"),[68] that resists excision by always being elsewhere, *is*, finally, its own master, and in mastery loses its power to unsettle.

In pinning Lacan down, in taking him to mean what he and his tropes say, Irigaray and her style do their work.[69] Irigaray is thus able to write the culture's symptoms *and* to evoke a different symbolic organization. Her own theoretical figuring of the relationality of the conscious and unconscious unequivocally permits of change. Consciousness has a history—perhaps, Irigaray observes, the logic of consciousness and the logic of history "add up to the same thing in the end, in a way"[70]—and that history can change and be changed. And, of course, to change the logic of consciousness is to change the relationship of conscious/unconscious: "Since the recognition of a 'specific' female sexuality would change the monopoly on value held by the masculine sex alone, in the final analysis by the father, what meaning

• could the Oedipus complex have in a symbolic system other than patriarchy?"[71]

In the years since "Così Fan Tutti" was published, in reading after reading, Irigaray has produced an elaborate thematics of sexual difference: a figurative thematics that works against the thematizable, a couple that works against the copula, a sexual difference rich in discursive positivity. This is the sexual difference that Irigaray posits for the future. And what does she offer today's feminists? Certainly not some old style to be taken up as a new critical model for all to use. Rather she reminds us that there is a tradition of radical critique that does not inscribe itself fully inside bourgeois epistemology, with its preference for the rational, the phenomenological, the systematizable. She reminds us of that different tradition and suggests that it might well be time to revive it.

NOTES •

My thanks to Christina Crosby for her insightful readings of this essay; to Mary Ann Doane, Naomi Schor, and Joan Wallach Scott for their helpful comments; and to Judith Butler for offering me the occasions to present versions of it.

1. Mary Ann Doane, *The Desire to Desire: The Woman's Film of the 1940s* (Bloomington: Indiana University Press, 1987), p. 182.
2. Irigaray, *Je, tu, nous*, p. 46/p. 56.
3. Irigaray, *Sexes and Genealogies*, p. 188/*Sexes et parentés*, pp. 202–203. Translations from *Sexes et parentés* are by the author.
4. Irigaray, *Speculum*, p. 143/p. 178.
5. Irigaray, *This Sex*, p. 78/*Ce Sexe*, p. 75.
6. Ibid., pp. 78–79/p. 76.
7. Ibid., pp. 79–80/pp. 76–77.
8. Derrida, "The Question of Style," in David B. Allison, ed., *The New Nietzsche* (Cambridge: MIT Press, 1985), p. 188. Derrida's "La Question du style," first published in *Nietzsche aujourd'hui* (1973), was revised and expanded into *Eperons*.
9. See Barbara Johnson, "Translator's Introduction," in Jacques Derrida, *Dissemination* (Chicago: University of Chicago Press, 1981), particularly "Derrida's Styles," pp. xvi–xvii.
10. Derrida, "Structure, Sign, and Play in the Discourse of the Human Sciences," in Richard Macksey and Eugenio Donato, eds., *The Structuralist Controversy: The Language of Criticism and the Sciences of Man* (Baltimore: Johns Hopkins University Press, 1972), p. 250.
11. Johnson, "Translator's Introduction," pp. xv–xvi.

12. Peter Bürger, *Theory of the Avant-Garde*, trans. Michael Shaw (Minneapolis: University of Minnesota Press, 1984), p. 16.

13. Johnson, "Translator's Introduction," p. xvi.

14. Even those writings that seem more expository, more like criticism than critique (like those in *Parler n'est jamais neutre* or some of the lectures in *Sexes et parentés*) are complexly citational. They mobilize themes and concepts such as the "natural" or the "divine" that seem accessible but are in fact produced by her earlier readings, which—in the very work of reading-writing—have "put a torch to fetish words [and] proper terms." See Margaret Whitford's discussion of Irigaray and the concept (in *Luce Irigaray: Philosophy in the Feminine* [London: Routledge, 1991], pp. 37, 155–56). While Whitford admirably follows the numerous trajectories taken by Irigaray's critique of the concept, I would modify her view that Irigaray's project is one of the invention of terms. Neither invention nor even paleonymy seems adequate to the multiple traces Irigaray puts into play in her readings, as I hope to show.

15. Though it seems evident that an uninterrogated intelligibility is precisely what a critique would aim to expose, the argument against the instrumentalization of critical work has its complexities, which I am not able to develop fully here, particularly with regard to the role of American pragmatism in current critical trends.

16. Irigaray, *This Sex*, pp. 99–100/ *Ce Sexe*, p. 97.

17. Jonathan Culler, *On Deconstruction* (Ithaca: Cornell University Press, 1982), pp. 206–212. Irigaray's critique of the thematizable is, of course, consistent with the larger psychoanalytic and deconstructive projects. Culler discusses, for example, Abraham's crucial reading of Freud's figures as "anasemia" (pp. 209–210).

18. In the more adept and far-reaching theoretical hands of Judith Butler, the intelligible is addressed by a notion of the performative that becomes a way of repeating the dominant structures of signification so as to displace and denaturalize them. See, for example, "Imitation and Gender Insubordination," in Diana Fuss, ed., *Inside/Out: Lesbian Theories, Gay Theories* (New York: Routledge, 1991). While the performative clearly provides a way of figuring Irigaray's writing, I want to stress that her particular notion of "language work" is crucial to any such reading. The trope of language work, fully grounded as it is in writing, may be seen to give ample room to the work of the trace, to the ineffability of the relationship between the conscious and the unconscious, and hence to the scope of Irigaray's call to change the symbolic order. In other words, Irigaray's theorizing guards against an overly optimistic view of what the performative might achieve. See Carolyn Burke on the seductiveness of Irigaray's performative writing, "Romancing the Philosophers," in Dianne Hunter, ed., *Seduction and Theory: Readings of Gender, Representation, and Rhetoric* (Urbana: University of Illinois Press, 1989), p. 236.

19. To raise the question of ideology is to look once again at how criticism

- tends to replicate the most evident, the most readable elements of the culture. See Schor's comments on today's criticism: "Indeed, this is a paradoxical moment, when despite the proliferation of differences, subjectivities, ethnicities, and sexualities, the theoretical discourse on these very notions has become monotholic, repetitious, almost entirely predictable." "The Righting of French Studies: Homosociality and the Killing of 'la pensée 68,' " in *Profession 92* (New York: MLA, 1992), p. 33.

20. Irigaray, *Je, tu, nous* p. 82/p. 102.

21. Irigaray, *This Sex*, p. 155/ *Ce Sexe*, p. 151.

22. Irigaray, *Parler n'est jamais neutre*, p. 311.

23. Irigaray, *This Sex*, p. 155/ *Ce Sexe*, p. 151.

24. Toril Moi, *Sexual/Textual Politics: Feminist Literary Theory* (London: Methuen, 1985), p. 139.

25. Whitford makes the important point that "the reception of Derrida, whatever its ambivalences, has been characterized by a relative openness and readiness to engage that has been lacking in the reception of Irigaray," and that many of her readers "fail to appreciate her complex relationship with philosophy" (*Luce Irigaray*, p. 126). My reading of Irigaray sees the "misreading" of her works as due in part to her style, which is *simultaneously* more and less "intelligible" than Derrida's.

26. I am not alone in thinking there is more to say about Irigaray and Lacan. See Maggie Berg, "Luce Irigaray's 'Contradictions': Postmodernism and Feminism," *Signs* (1991), 17(1):50–70.

27. See the differences between "Così Fan Tutti," with its treatment of Lacan's reading of culture, and Irigaray's "Misère de la psychanalyse" (1977, in *Parler n'est jamais neutre*), which is a vigorous attack on psychoanalytic practice, on the psychoanalytic establishment, and, in this context, on Lacan.

     With regard to Lacan, see Juliet Flower MacCannell, *Figuring Lacan: Criticism and the Cultural Unconscious* (New York: Routledge, 1986): "The fact that we generally are prepared to read psychoanalytic discussions as centered on an individual ego, from whose viewpoint all social and symbolic relationships are to be constructed and reconstructed, must be rethought in the case of Lacan. Lacan supplements the 'psychoanalytic ego' with the anthropological one" (pp. 5–6). For another slant on the question see Elisabeth Roudinesco, *Jacques Lacan & Co.: A History of Psychoanalysis in France, 1925–1985*, trans. Jeffrey Mehlman (Chicago: Chicago University Press, 1990), who sees Lacan reading Saussure first through Lévi-Strauss and then through Heidegger, with no clear breaks between successive rearticulations (especially pp. 297–298). See Warren Montag's "The Emptiness of a Distance Taken: Freud, Althusser, Lacan," *Rethinking Marxism* (1991), 4(1):31–36, which reads Lacan's project as one of defending psychoanalysis from the "philosophical apparatuses that sought to occupy the theoretical space that Freud had opened" (p. 36).

28. Jane Gallop, *The Daughter's Seduction* (Ithaca: Cornell University Press, 1982), p. 82.

29. Irigaray, *This Sex*, p. 86/*Ce Sexe*, p. 85.

30. Jacques Lacan, *The Four Fundamental Concepts of Psychoanalysis*, trans. Alan Sheridan, ed. Jacques-Alain Miller (New York: Norton, 1978), p. 244.

31. Irigaray, *This Sex*, p. 29/*Ce Sexe*, p. 28.

32. Ibid., pp. 87–88/p. 86.

33. Ibid., p. 88/p. 86.

34. Derrida, *Glas*, trans. Barbara Harlow (Chicago: University of Chicago Press, 1979), p. 222.

35. For a discussion of Lacan's style, as I am using the term here, and of his styles, see Jane Gallop, *Reading Lacan* (Ithaca: Cornell University Press, 1985), especially chapter 5.

36. It is this Lacan that is crucial to an understanding of Irigaray's project. As Montag argues, an effort (including Lacan's own at the end) to find a systematic, coherent "Lacanianism," adequate to its object, runs counter to Lacan's whole endeavor to resist the philosophical apparatus, to *analyze* the ruses of cogito. I see my reading of Lacan as quite similar to Montag's (which I discovered after completing this essay), though in a very different mode. See Montag: "We may examine the functioning of Lacan's key notions not as concepts immanent in the domain of psychoanalytic practice but as theoretical devices that may in some sense be the extrascientific or philosophical doubles of these concepts. Such theoretical devices or apparatuses, far from providing the axiomatic foundation for a progressively coherent body of knowledge, instead work actively in the domain of philosophy, perpetually removing philosophical obstacles to the development of psychoanalysis or barring the way to false, regressive (because philosophical) solutions to the problems that it encounters." (Montag, "The Emptiness of a Distance Taken," p. 36.) It is in her theoretical, analytical relationship to philosophy that Irigaray so resembles this Lacan.

37. Lacan, "God and the *Jouissance* of The Woman," in Jacqueline Rose, trans., *Feminine Sexuality: Jacques Lacan and the Ecole Freudienne* (New York: Norton, 1983), p. 138.

38. Lacan, *The Four Fundamental Concepts*, p. 205.

39. Lacan, "God and the *Jouissance*," p. 153.

40. Lacan's renderings of these biological processes are hardly orthodox. Mitosis is the "process of nuclear division of a living cell by which the hereditary carrier, or chromosome, is exactly replicated and the two parts distributed to the daughter nuclei. Mitosis is almost always accompanied by cell division . . . and the latter is sometimes considered a part of the mitotic process" (*New Columbia Encyclopedia*, ed. William H. Harris and Judith S. Levey [New York: Columbia University Press, 1975], p. 1796). Lacan's insistence in this passage on the double process of reduction

• seems more appropriate to meiosis, which designates the cell division entailed in the formation of gametes, or ova and sperms, and is necessary to prevent the doubling of cells in successive generations. "In the first stage of meiosis, called reduction division, the numbers of each pair of homologous chromosomes, which are double-stranded, lie side by side. Each member of the pair then moves away from the other toward opposite ends of the dividing nucleus, and two nuclei, each with the haploid [half] number of double-stranded chromosomes are formed. In the second meiotic sequence, called equational division, each haploid cell nucleus contains double-stranded chromosomes, the halves of the original homologous pairs. The chromosomes in the nucleus separate into their single strands and the strands move toward opposite ends of the dividing nucleus. The result of meiotic division is four cells, each haploid, with one chromosome of each pair" (*New Columbia Encyclopedia*, pp. 1740–1741).

41. Lacan, *The Four Fundamental Concepts*, p. 151.

42. Ibid., p. 152.

43. Ibid., p. 153.

44. Kaja Silverman sees Lacan as far less critical of the androgyne model. See her discussion in *The Subject of Semiotics* (New York: Oxford University Press, 1983), pp. 151–157. Note that Freud associates the androgyne and biological reproduction, in James Strachey, ed. and trans., *Beyond the Pleasure Principle* (New York: Norton, 1961), pp. 69–74, the text Lacan endorses in his underwriting of the libido. Lacan's reading can perhaps be illuminated by Jean Laplanche, who comments that the androgyne is necessary to Freud's theorizing of psychic reflexivity: "We shall simply add, in this context, that within *Beyond the Pleasure Principle*, the life-drive or Eros, the force that maintains narcissistic unity and uniqueness, can be deduced as a return to a prior state only through an appeal to mythology: the fable of the androgyne, proposed by Aristophanes in Plato's Symposium. So it will go as well for the death drive: here the priority of the reflexive phase, which was solidly affirmed concerning masochism in the sexual sense, will begin proliferating or fissioning in relation to origins" (Laplanche, *Life and Death in Psychoanalysis*, trans. Jeffrey Mehlman [Baltimore: Johns Hopkins University Press, 1976], p. 112). See Whitford's discussion of Irigaray and the death drive in *Luce Irigaray*, pp. 95–97 et passim, and see Irigaray's comments on the androgyne in "Belief Itself"/"La Croyance même."

45. Lacan, *Feminine Sexuality*, pp. 138–139. Lacan's reference here to "a quite manifest subtraction for at least one of the two just before the conjunction is effected," seems to be to the sex chromosomes. That would be incorrect.

46. Lacan, *The Four Fundamental Concepts*, p. 205.

47. Ibid., p. 205.

48. See Flower MacCannell's astute comments on Lacan's reading of Freud: "Lacan characterized his own enterprise as 'commenting' on the texts of

Freud, a layering of another text over his. The two form an allegorical relationship in Walter Benjamin's sense of the term. If we read Freud 'through' (in the sense of via, by means of) Lacan we can also reverse the process. Such a reading is aimed at bringing certain things to center-stage, things that remain occulted or hidden by the lucidity of the one, the obscurity of the other." *Figuring Lacan*, p. xiv.

49. Lacan, *The Four Fundamental Concepts*, p. 142.

50. Ibid., p. 206.

51. The readily intelligible for Lacan would be, especially, U.S. ego psychology, but also all other discourses that phenomenologize and psychologize psychoanalysis.

52. Lacan, *The Four Fundamental Concepts*, p. 62.

53. In "God and the *Jouissance*" Lacan claims that the very objective of his teaching is "to dissociate the a and the O [better translated, perhaps, "the a and the A," *l'a(utre) et l'A(utre)*], by reducing the former to what belongs to the imaginary and the latter to what belongs to the symbolic" (pp. 153–154). In that relegation of the small object *autre* and the large *Autre* to seemingly distinct spheres, Lacan willfully hypostatizes—as he so often does—that and the other divisions entailed. In fact, there is not one but at least two "divisions" at work here.

54. And, just as the author of the biological term *meiosis* knew his rhetoric, so does Lacan know his. Indeed, he goes on to display that knowledge with a flourish at the end of the first quoted passage on meiosis: "quite manifest subtraction for at least one of the two just before the conjunction is effected, a subtraction of certain elements *which are not without their place* [*qui ne sont pas pour rien*; my emphasis] in the final operation" ("God and the *Jouissance*," p. 139).

55. Many readers of Lacan would argue that he sees the split subject as constitutively human rather than symptomatic of a historically specific culture. I can only respond by saying that if Lacan sees the coherent subject-adequate-to-itself as a subject-effect, the very figure of the split subject is itself the effect of that coherence.

56. Lacan's subject, unlike Hegel's, is alienated by a choice "whose properties depend on this, that there is, in the joining [as of two sets or two overlapping circles] one element that, whatever the choice operating might be, has as its consequence a *neither one, nor the other*. The choice, then, is a matter of knowing whether one wishes to preserve one of the parts, the other disappearing in any case. . . . If we choose being, the subject disappears, it eludes us, it falls into non-meaning. If we choose meaning, the meaning survives, only deprived of that part of non-meaning that is, strictly speaking, that which constitutes in the realization of the subject, the unconscious" (*The Four Fundamental Concepts*, p. 211).

57. Irigaray, *This Sex*, p. 77/ *Ce Sexe*, p. 74.

58. Irigaray, "La Croyance même," p. 385. I cite from *Les Fins de l'homme* in order to place "La Croyance même" in its context as part of a colloquium

• on Derrida, and because in that setting it provoked heated reactions. For an example of how Irigaray can quite effectively "exasperate" through her discourse, see Jean-François Lyotard's reactions to the piece (p. 393). *Les Fins de l'homme: à partir du travail de Jacques Derrida: colloque de Cerisy, 23 juillet–1 août 1980.* Direction Philippe Lacoue-Labarthe, Jean-Luc Nancy (Paris: Galilée, 1981).

59. Irigaray, *Speculum,* p. 31/p. 33.

60. Ibid., p. 32/p. 34. Irigaray continues along these lines: "The most subtle detour taken by life in the course toward death, as Freud explains it in *Beyond the Pleasure Principle,* would be to respect the link to the original place of corruption by progressively sublating it from the materiality of its beginning. To erase birth by an infinite love of the Other(s) ideality" (p. 31). What is particularly interesting is that Irigaray undertakes to displace reproduction while valorizing a "maternal genealogy." See, for example, *Le Temps de la différence,* pp. 101–123. See also her criticism of reproductive technologies, as in *Je, tu, nous,* pp. 101–104/pp. 125–128.

61. Irigaray, *This Sex,* p. 86/ *Ce Sexe,* p. 85.

62. Lacan, "God and the *Jouissance,*" p. 153. See Irigaray: "So if the [sexual] relation were to come about, everything that has been stated up to now would count as an effect-symptom of its avoidance" (*This Sex,* p. 91/ *Ce Sexe,* p. 89).

63. Irigaray, *This Sex,* p. 99/ *Ce Sexe,* p. 97.

64. Which is not to say against Marx. Lacan sees in Marx (who, he says, invented the symptom as a critical term ["God and the *Jouissance,*" p. 166]), not a "conception of the world" but precisely the contrary: "that people advance such a term [conception of the world] to characterize Marxism makes me laugh." For Lacan, Marx had something very different to announce, that is that "history inaugurates another dimension of history and opens up the possibility of completely subverting the function of discourse as such, and properly speaking, of philosophical discourse, inasmuch as on it rests a conception of the world" (*Encore,* pp. 32–33).

65. Lacan, *The Four Fundamental Concepts,* p. 77.

66. Whitford, *Luce Irigaray,* p. 160. "To return to Nietzsche, when he says that God is dead, it seems that the collapse of this keystone of a transcendental system leads to the carriers of the phallus becoming gods themselves. Why is the phallic culture so important after the fall of the gods? Because the carriers of the phallus want to be gods themselves" (*Luce Irigaray,* p. 161). See *Ethique de la différence sexuelle:* "According to Heidegger, each age has one issue to think through, and one only. Sexual difference is probably the issue in our time which could be our 'salvation' if we thought it through." (*Ethics,* p. 5/ *Ethique,* p. 13).

67. Irigaray, *This Sex,* pp. 79–80/ *Ce Sexe,* pp. 76–77.

68. Lacan, "God and the *Jouissance,*" p. 140.

69. Irigaray intervenes in Lacan's discourse to her own advantage. In taking

Lacan at his word, she can be said to be taking on her proper role in the relationship of transference. I am indebted in my thinking on this subject to Whitford's "Luce Irigaray and the Female Imaginary: Speaking as a Woman," *Radical Philosophy* (1986), 43(2):3–8, in which she stresses, among other things, the importance of transference in Irigaray's approach.

70. Irigaray, *This Sex*, p. 129/*Ce Sexe*, pp. 127–128.
71. Irigaray, *This Sex*, p. 73/*Ce Sexe*, p. 71.

• *Rosi Braidotti*

OF BUGS AND WOMEN:

IRIGARAY AND DELEUZE

ON THE

BECOMING-WOMAN

In order to become, it is essential to have a gender or an essence (consequently a sexuate essence) as *horizon*. Otherwise, becoming remains partial and subject to the subject. When we become parts or multiples without a future of our own this means simply that we are leaving it up to the other, or the Other of the other, to put us together. To become means fulfilling the wholeness of what we are capable of being.
—Luce Irigaray

Luce Irigaray's work is a systematic and multifaceted attempt to redesign our understanding of the thinking subject, in a language and a form of representation that adequately renders women's experience. Firmly implanted in the post-Lacanian landscape, Irigaray is already

A kind of order or apparent progression can be established for the segments of becoming in which we find ourselves; becoming-woman, becoming-child, becoming-animal, -vegetable, or -mineral; becoming-molecular of all kinds, becoming-particles.   —Gilles Deleuze

looking onto a universe where the regime of phallogocentrism is over. This utopian gaze is in fact a politically informed map of women's becoming, posited on the framework of a radical transformation of the entire process of becoming-subject. Irigaray's quest for an alternative female symbolic calls into question every step of the process of becoming-subject, from the relation to the origins and consequently the maternal, to the transcendental, to one's relation to time and history; Irigaray's project consequently sexualizes in the feminine the very structures of subjectivity. An elemental sort of female cosmology pervades Irigaray's work: a firm, even shocking determination to return to the female imaginary the colors, the shapes, and the tempo of woman's passions, her thoughts, her perceptions, and the specific patterns of inter-

• action that mark her as sexed female. A sensible transcendental foundation for a female process of becoming-subject.

In this essay I will present a cross-reading of Irigaray's notion of the becoming-woman with another powerful contemporary attempt to redraw the foundations of subjectivity: Deleuze's notion of becoming.[1] Deleuze and Irigaray share a common root in their stated desire to move beyond Lacanianism. Their critique of Lacanian psychoanalysis, however, takes different forms: Irigaray concentrates her work on attacking the Lacanian assumption of the inevitability of the phallogocentric system, which she proposes to replace with a female symbolic, expressed in an imaginary that is no longer mediated by the phallus.

Deleuze on the other hand suggests that we rethink subjectivity without reference to any one symbolic system. Vitalism, redefined in the light of the new electronic universe we inhabit; empiricism in its link to affectivity; desire as positivity, not as lack; theoretical practice as a typology of passions and subjectivity as a network of machinic connections are Deleuze's staple diet. They constitute the backbone of Deleuze's critique of Lacanian psychoanalysis, which in his eyes overemphasizes dialectical oppositions, the metaphysical illusion of substance and the teleological structures of identity.

Both Deleuze and Irigaray raise the issue of "becoming," but in different ways. Although Deleuze has not attracted much feminist commentary so far,[2] in my opinion, the comparison between his philosophy of difference, multiplicity and becoming-minority and Irigaray's practice of sexual difference, can be very enlightening. In pointing out both convergences and tensions between these two positions, I will aim at highlighting the difficulties involved in freeing the subject "woman" from the subjugated position of "other," that is to say, the self-effacing servant at the banquet of the Socratic club. As Irigaray points out, the issue at stake in the redefinition of female subjectivity is how to make the feminine express a "different difference," a pure difference, released from the hegemonic framework of oppositional, binary thinking within which Western philosophy had confined it. In this feminist perspective the focus is as much on the deconstruction of the phallogocentric representations of the feminine ("woman as other," also known as Woman), as on the experience and the potential becoming of real-life women, in their diverse ways of inhabiting the subject position of "woman."[3] In other words, the feminist issue is how to activate real-life women as the political and epistemological agents capable of alternative definitions of female subjectivity. The women thus defined are subjects who have taken their distance from the male-defined images of woman-as-other.[4]

The philosophy of Luce Irigaray has convinced me that it is unthinkable that the question of the deconstruction of phallo-logocentrism could be disconnected from the concrete changes taking place in women's lives. The two questions:

i) how to free woman from the icon-function to which phallologocentrism has confined her?

and:

ii) how to express a different, positive vision of female subjectivity?

are inseparable.

I will first explore the tension between Irigaray's project and Deleuze's notion of "difference" in the sense of the "becoming-woman" of philosophy. I will then illustrate the merits of Irigaray's position with the help of a textual analysis of Clarice Lispector's *The Passion According to G. H.*

Discontinuous becomings[5]

The concept of "becoming" is central to both Irigaray's and Deleuze's philosophical concerns. It is linked to what I see as a point of convergence between their two theoretical projects, namely, the aim of imaging the activity of thinking differently, i.e., of redefining the scene of philosophy. This aim coincides with Deleuze's stern rejection of the canonized, institutionalized history of philosophy as a repressive force: philosophy's Medusa-like head has the power to captivate and intimidate its beholders. In his effort to move beyond this dogmatic image of thought, and the anxiety of influence that it arouses, Deleuze proposes an image of thought as the nonreactive activity of thinking the present, the actual moment, so as to account adequately for change and changing conditions.

Deleuze's notion of becoming is adapted from Nietzsche's *Zarathustra*: becoming is neither the dynamic alternation of opposites nor the unfolding of an essence in a teleologically ordained process leading to a synthesizing identity.[6] Deleuzian becoming is the affirmation of the positivity of difference, meant as a multiple and constant process of transformation, a flux of multiple becomings. Accordingly, thinking is not, for Deleuze, the expression of the in-depth interiority of a "knowing" subject or the enactment of transcendental models of reflexive consciousness. Pursuing to a radical degree the paradoxical insight of psychoanalysis about the noncoincidence of the subject with his/her consciousness, Deleuze posits the subject as an affective or intensive entity, which psychoanalysis is guilty of colonizing in a phallogocentric vision.

• In *Nietzsche et la philosophie* Deleuze unveils the linear, self-reflexive mode of thought that is favored by phallo-logocentrism. He opposes to it ideas as events, active states that open up unsuspected possibilities of life. This new style of thought is called "nomadic," "rhizomatic," or "molecular." These images are chosen for their capacity to suggest weblike interaction and interconnectedness, as opposed to vertical distinction, and to present a view of the subject as flux of successive becomings.

Deleuze's radical epistemology suggests that, beyond the propositional content of an idea, there lies another category: the affective force, the level of intensity that ultimately determines its truth-value. The truth of an idea, in other words, is less in its propositional content or referential value than in the kind of affects that it releases: ideas are noble or lowly, active or reactive, depending on whether they mobilize one's powers of affirmation and joy over the forces of denial and negation.

The new images of thought that Deleuze proposes can therefore be seen as postphallogocentric figurations of the subject, where the notion of "figuration" expresses a conceptual and aesthetic desire to think differently. Alternative figurations of the subject, including different feminine and masculine subject positions, are figural modes of expression that displace the vision of consciousness away from phallogocentric premises. Figurations such as "rhizomes, becomings, lines of escape, flows, relays and bodies without organs" release and express active states of being that break through the conventional schemes of theoretical representation.

This "intensive" redefinition of the activity of thinking entails a vision of subjectivity as a bodily entity. The embodied-ness of the subject is not of the natural, biological kind: Deleuze shares with the poststructuralist generation the desire to deessentialize the body, which thus appears as a complex interplay of constructed social and symbolic forces. In so doing he moves beyond the psychoanalytic idea of the body as a map of unconscious inscriptions and of culturally enforced codes to propose a vision of the body as a play of forces, a transformer and relay of energy, a surface of intensities. The embodied subject is a term in a process of intersecting forces (affects) and spatiotemporal variables (connections).

On this point Deleuze and Irigaray part roads: Deleuze's vision of the subject does not rest upon a dichotomous opposition of masculine and feminine subject positions, but rather on a multiplicity of sexed subject positions. The differences in degree between these subject positions mark different lines and intensities of becoming.

For us . . . there are as many sexes as there are terms in symbiosis, as
many differences as elements contributing to a process of contagion. We
know that many beings pass between a man and a woman; they come
from different worlds, are born on the wind, form rhizomes around
roots; they cannot be understood in terms of production, only in terms
of becoming.[7]

These different degrees of becoming are diagrams of thought,
typologies of ethical passions, variations on intensive states. Multiplicity does not reproduce one single model—as in the Platonic mode of
representation—but rather creates and multiplies differences.

Deleuze's central figuration is a general becoming-minority, or
becoming-nomad, or becoming-molecular. The minority is the dynamic or intensive principle of change in Deleuze's theory; the heart of the
phallogocentric subject is dead, but at the periphery there roam youth-
ful gangs of the new nomads:

All becomings are already molecular. That is because becoming is not to
imitate or identify with something or someone. Nor is it to proportion
formal relations. Neither of these two figures of analogy is applicable to
becoming: neither the imitation of a subject nor the proportionality of
a form. Starting from the forms one has, the subject one is, the organs
one has, or the functions one fulfills, becoming is to extract particles
between which one establishes the relations of movements and rest,
speed and slowness that are *closest* to what one is becoming, and through
which one becomes.[8]

The space of becoming is therefore a space of affinity and symbiosis
between adjacent particles. Proximity is both a topological and a quan-
titative notion, which marks the space of becoming of subjects as sensitive matter. The space of becoming is one of dynamic marginality.

As I have noted, Deleuze's theory of the "becoming-minority/
nomad/molecular/bodies-without-organs/woman" is very ambivalent
on the actual issue of the position of woman. The sexual dichotomy
between man and woman is not just one dualistic opposition among
many: it is constitutive of Western thought in that it has been symbolized in language, mental habits of thought, and culture at large.
Consistent with his critique of the phallogocentric appropriation of
symbolic subjectivity, Deleuze agrees with Irigaray that man as the
privileged referent of subjectivity, the standard-bearer of the
norm/law/logos, represents the majority, i.e., the dead heart of the system. The consequences are, on the one hand, that masculinity is antithetical to the process of becoming, and can only be the site of deconstruction or critique, and, on the other hand, that the becoming-

• woman is a fundamental step in the process of becoming, for both sexes.

Deleuze states that all the lines of deterritorialization go necessarily through the stage of becoming-woman, which is not just any other form of becoming-minority, but is rather the key, the precondition, and the necessary starting point for the whole process of becoming.

Let us keep in mind, however, that the reference to *woman* in the process of *becoming-woman* does not refer to empirical females, but rather to topological positions. The becoming-woman is the marker for a general process of transformation: it affirms positive forces and levels of nomadic, rhizomatic consciousness.

> There is a becoming-woman, a becoming-child, that do not resemble the woman or the child as clearly distinct entities. . . . What we term a molecular entity is, for example, the woman as defined by her form, endowed with organs and functions and assigned as a subject. Becoming-woman is not imitating this entity or even transforming oneself into it. . . . Not imitating or assuming the female form, but emitting particles that enter the relation of movement and rest, or the zone of proximity, of a microfemininity, in other words, that produce in us a molecular woman, create the molecular woman.[9]

Clearly, the woman occupies a troubled area in this radical critique of phallogocentrism: insofar as woman is positioned dualistically as the other of this system, she is also annexed to it. Deleuze—not uncharacteristically ignorant of the basic feminist epistemological distinction between Woman as representation and women as concrete agents of experience—ends up making distinctions internal to the category of woman herself. At this point his difference from Irigaray grows wider and more irreparable than ever.

Deleuze, just like Derrida and other poststructuralists, opposes to the "majority/sedentary/molar" vision of woman as a structural operator of the phallogocentric system the woman as "becoming/minority/molecular/nomadic." Concludes Deleuze: all becomings are equal, but the becoming-woman is more equal than others. In so far as the male/female dichotomy has become the prototype of Western dualism, the process of decolonizing the thinking subject from this dualistic grip requires as its starting point the dissolution of all sexed identities based on the gendered opposition. Sexuality being the dominant discourse of power in the West, as Foucault taught us,[10] it requires special critical analysis. Thus, the becoming-woman is the necessary starting point for the deconstruction of phallogocentric identities precisely because sexual dualism and its corollary—the positioning of woman as figure of oth-

erness—are constitutive of Western thought. In other words, it is
because of historical and not biological reasons that sexed identities are
foregrounded in the process of deconstruction.

More significant still for feminist theory is Deleuze's next step: the
entire process of becoming aims at moving beyond sexual dualism or
gender dichotomy. The nomadic or intensive horizon is a subjectivity
beyond gender in the sense of being dispersed, not binary; multiple, not
dualistic; interconnected, not dialectical; in constant flow, not fixed.
This idea is expressed in figurations like: "polysexuality," "bodies without organs," and, of course, "the molecular woman."

Ultimately, what Deleuze finds objectionable in feminist theory is
that it perpetuates reactive-, molar-, or majority-thinking; in Nietzsche's scale of values feminists have a slave-morality.[11] I find that such
a judgment may suit the case of Beauvoir, but I wonder whether it
applies at all to sexual difference theorists like Irigaray.[12] Be that as it
may, in Deleuze's framework all feminists are lumped together, and, in
his opinion, emphasis on any one of the gender polarities, whether masculine or feminine, achieves the equally undesirable aim of reasserting
all that he is critical of: binary thinking as the support of phallogocentrism as the dominant image of thought.

Following Luce Irigaray I feel doubtful about Deleuze's call for the
dissolution of sexed identities by the neutralization of gender
dichotomies, because I think that it is both theoretically and historically dangerous for women. I am quite aware of the potentially paranoid
undertones of this position, in that it expresses a reactive attachment to
the very identity—woman—which, as a feminist, I am committed to
deconstructing. In the light of my poststructuralist leanings, however,
and following on this point de Lauretis,[13] I would rather approach the
issue of subjectivity in terms of the paradox of female feminist identity
at the end of this century, to which I will return.

Sexual difference as our historical horizon

Irigaray, in her defense of sexual difference against a hasty dismissal or
deconstruction by the poststructuralist philosophers, refers negatively
to the Deleuzian figuration of the "molecular woman" or "bodies-with-
out-organs." For Irigaray these notions refer to a state of dis-possession
of the bodily self, that is to say, an internally divided position that is historically the sad lot of women. She points out that notions such as loss
of self, dispersion, and fluidity are all too familiar to women: is not the
"body without organs" women's own historical condition?[14] Irigaray's
critique of Deleuze is radical: she points out that the dispersal of sexu-

•   ality into a generalized "becoming" results in undermining the feminist
claims to a redefinition, and consequently an empowering, of the
female subject.

Developing this insight further, I subsequently argued that one cannot deconstruct a subjectivity one has never been fully granted control
over; one cannot diffuse a sexuality that has historically been defined as
dark and mysterious.[15] In my opinion Deleuze gets caught in the contradiction of postulating a general becoming-woman that fails to take
into account the historical and epistemological specificity of the female
condition. This neglect results in flattening out the differences between
the sexes, thereby delegitimating the feminist struggles on behalf of
women. To be fair to Deleuze I must say that he does acknowledge
some difficulty with the woman issue. In *A Thousand Plateaux* he
shows both awareness and hesitation on this point. He writes, "It is, of
course, indispensable for women to conduct a molar politics, with a
view to winning back their own organism, their own history, their own
subjectivity. . . . But it is dangerous to confine oneself to such a subject,
which does not function without drying up a spring or stopping a
flow."[16] This position strikes me a form of denial, that is to say, of willful disavowal, which expresses a structural and systematic indecision.

Apart from being politically unacceptable by a feminist, this position
is also problematic theoretically, because it suggests a symmetry
between the sexes, which results in attributing the same psychic, conceptual, and deconstructive itineraries to both.

This alleged symmetry between the sexes is challenged most radically by Irigaray. In her perspective sexual difference cannot be considered
as one difference among many, but rather as a founding, fundamental
structural difference, on which all others rest, that cannot be dissolved
easily without causing psychic and social damage. This perspective is
determined by Irigaray's acute sense of the historicity of women's struggles; to explain it, let me make a digression on the question of time.

Gendered time

For Irigaray, as for most poststructuralists, the subject is not a substance
but rather a process of negotiation between material and semiotic conditions that affect one's embodied, situated self. In this perspective
"subjectivity" names the process that consists in stringing together—
under the fictional unity of a grammatical "I"—different forms of
active and reactive interaction with and resistance to these conditions.
The subject is a process, made of constant shifts and negotiations
between different levels of power and desire, constantly shifting

between willful choice and unconscious drives. Whatever semblance of
unity there may be is no God-given essence but rather the fictional
choreography of many levels into one socially operational self. It
implies that what sustains the entire process of becoming-subject is the
will to know, the desire to say, the desire to speak, as a founding, primary, vital, necessary, and therefore original desire to become.

In this perspective the only viable kind of unity is posited in terms
of time. A subject is a genealogical entity, possessing his/her own coun-
termemory, which in turn is an expression of unconscious desires and
identifications. Viewed spatially the poststructuralist subject may
appear as fragmented and disunited; on a temporal scale, however, its
unity is that of a continuing power to connect and to recollect. The
genealogical ties create a continuity among disconnected fragments: it
is a discontinuous sense of time, which falls under Nietzsche's sense of
the Dionysiac as opposed to the Apollonian. Nevertheless, it provides
the grounds for unity in an otherwise dispersed self. Deleuze, for
instance, follows Nietzsche and borrows from the ancient Greeks the
useful distinction between the molar sense of linear, recorded time
(*chronos*) and the molecular sense of cyclical, discontinuous time (*aion*).
The former is related to being/the molar/the masculine, the latter to
becoming/the molecular/the feminine.

Feminists have argued that a complexified time structure helps to
clarify the tension and the paradox inherent in the feminist position.
Thus, Irigaray rests on this analysis of the double structure of time her
call for women's sense of their own genealogies, based on a bond of
grateful recognition of the maternal as site of origin. Kristeva, on the
other hand, stresses the two-tiered level of time and—resting on the
same philosophical background as Deleuze—argues for a distinction
between the longer, linear model of history and the more discontinuous timing of personal genealogy and unconscious desire. Kristeva
couples this distinction with the analysis of various historical forms
taken by feminist subjectivity: a form of which fits in with linear historical time whereas others are more attuned to cyclical patterns of repetition. By identifying the first kind with the Enlightenment belief in
equality and the second with contemporary affirmations of difference,
Kristeva sexualizes historical sequences, developing a sense of women's
becoming.

Although this way of associating certain forms of female subjectivity with certain moments of historical consciousness has been criticized
for its Eurocentrism,[17] it still marks a deep divergence from Deleuze's
no less ethnocentric and considerably less feminist standpoint.

In other words, to paraphrase Deleuze, at the level of *chronos* femi-

• nist women, at this point in history, are legitimate in pursuing "molar" positions, claiming a woman-centered redefinition of their political subjectivity and identity. In this respect they cannot easily become "molecular"; maybe they cannot afford to undertake a full-scale deconstruction of their sex-specific identity. The feminist engagement with linear historical time, however, neither replaces nor encompasses women's relationship to the discontinuous time of becoming (*aion*).

It is to Deleuze's credit that he can see such a distinction in time sequences, but he fails to pursue it to its logical conclusion and thus envisage the genderization of both time and history. He thus fails to see the scope of the theoretical horizon opened by sexual difference.

Toward a female subject

For Irigaray the issues are a great deal simpler: she enacts a redefinition of the subject as equally though discontinuously subjected to the structuring effects of many complex and overlapping variables: sexual morphology, sense of genealogy, cultural identity, age, religion, etc. While acknowledging the complexity of the process of subjectification, Irigaray also acknowledges the privileged position granted to sexuality in Western practices of subjectivity. Sexuality is a site of resistance and contradiction, and because the implications of the phallogocentric institutionalization of sexuality are so much more negative for women, feminists cannot afford to merely cast off their sexed identity: they rather need to critically and thoroughly repossess it.

In other words, the signifier "woman" is both the concept around which feminists have gathered in their recognition of a general condition and also the concept that needs to be analyzed critically and eventually deconstructed. This is for Irigaray a historically situated statement: it is a suitable description of the condition of women in postmodern late capitalism. This period has seen a growing hiatus between Woman as representation, the projection of a male subject, and real women as agents of transformation in the name of the positivity of their difference. The emphasis thus placed by contemporary feminists on the need to assert sexual difference is therefore the effect of a certain historicity.

More than any other feminist thinker Irigaray has made it clear that the subversion of identity acquires sex-specific connotations in the feminist project of sexual difference. In my reading of Irigaray's strategy I have argued that her notion of "mimesis"[18] amounts to a collective repossession by women of the images and representations of "Woman" as they have been coded in language, culture, science, knowledge, and dis-

course and consequently internalized in the heart, mind, body, and
lived experience of women. Mimetic repetition as a textual and political strategy is the active subversion of established modes of the representation and expression of women's experience. In this respect the
redefinition of the subject Woman/women as both representation and
experience amounts to no less than a change of civilization, of genealogy, of a sense of history. Feminist countergenealogies are the inroads to
a new symbolic system by women. As Irigaray put it: "Indeed, it is not
a matter of changing such and such a thing within a horizon already
defined as human culture, it is a matter of changing the horizon itself.
It is a matter of understanding that our interpretation of human identity is theoretically and practically incorrect."[19]

Irigaray's notion of sexual difference rests on the idea that there is no
symmetry between the sexes. This dissymmetry functions as a revindi-
cation of radical difference not only at the psychic and conceptual level
but also at the political level. Politically, it implies that the identification
of points of exit from the phallogocentric mode takes dissymmetrical
forms in the two sexes.[20] The assertion of the positivity of sexual difference challenges the century-old identification of the thinking subject
with the universal and of both subjects with the masculine. It posits a
female, sexed, thinking subject who stands in a dis-symmetrical relationship to the masculine. The feminine thus defined is not the structural "other" of a dualistic system that equates the masculine with the
universal, but is rather radically and positively other. In the feminist
analysis, in other words, woman's position as designated other is radical-
ized into a speaking stance that is incommensurable with that of man.

Clearly this radical dissymmetry has been covered up, coded as
devalorized difference and transmitted in linear phallogocentric discourse. It has been made to rest on a linear, teleological sense of time.
History as we have come to know it is the master discourse of the white,
masculine, hegemonic, property-owning subject, who posits his consciousness as synonymous with a universal knowing subject and mar-
kets a series of "others" as his ontological props.

As Irigaray explained:

We can assume that any theory of the subject has always been appropriated by the "masculine." . . . Subjectivity denied to woman: indisputably
this provides the financial backing for every irreducible constitution as
an object: of representation, of discourse, of desire. Once imagine that
woman imagines and the object loses its fixed, obsessional character. As
a bench mark that is ultimately more crucial than the subject, for he can
sustain himself only by bouncing off some objectiveness, some objective. If there is no more "earth" to press down/repress, to work, to rep-

• resent, but also and always to desire (for one's own), no opaque matter which in theory does not know herself, then what pedestal remains for the ex-istence of the "subject"?[21]

Because this history is the dominant discourse, which has posited itself by exclusions and disqualifications of its "others," it has reduced women to "unrepresentability." For Irigaray this implies that a feminist theorist who wishes to repossess and reinvest images and representations of the female subject as Woman is really dealing with fragments and figments of the phallogocentric imaginary. Irigaray argues, however, that this imaginary image of Woman needs to be repossessed by women precisely because it is loaded with phallogocentric assumptions. The image of Woman, or of woman-as-other is a culture-specific, historical system of material and symbolic representation, against which feminist women are struggling. Moreover, insofar as this imaginary has been internalized by women and has constructed female identity, it is by no means external to women and cannot be cast off like an old garment. Discursive practices, like ideological beliefs, are tattooed on bodies, and unless women can change skin, like snakes, they have to take care that the process of subverting identity does not take too heavy a toll on them.

The discursive strategy that aims at repossessing the feminine through strategic repetitions engenders difference. For if there is no symmetry between the sexes, it follows that the feminine as experienced and expressed by women is as yet unrepresented, having been colonized by the male imaginary. Women must therefore speak the feminine, they must think it, write it, and represent it in their own terms.

Emphasis on sexual difference meant as the dissymmetry between the sexes is the great dividing line between feminists and poststructuralists. It allows Irigaray to remain close conceptually to Deleuze's thought, especially his emphasis on the positive role played by the unconscious in the production of theoretical discourse, while being opposed to his "becoming-woman" as a way of overcoming the sexual bipolarization. Where the two differ, in other words, is in the priority that must be granted to the elaboration of adequate systems of representation for an alternative female subject; this difference is conceptual as well as political.

Sexual difference as a feminist project

In Irigaray's perspective, which I have described as a radical feminist bodily materialism, the woman, like the earth, is the fundamental dimension on which the multilayered institution of phallogocentric subjectivity is erected. She is the primary matter and the foundation

stone, whose silent presence installs the master in his monologic mode.
The feminism of sexual difference argues that women have borne, both
materially and symbolically, the costs of the masculine privilege for
autonomous self-definition: they have been physically and symbolically dispossessed of a place from which to speak.

The grounds for legitimation of Irigaray's redefinition of female subjectivity is a new form of materialism that inherits the corporeal materiality of the poststructuralists but also emphasizes the sexually differentiated structure of the speaking subject. This position, however, also goes
one step further than the poststructuralists, positing the grounds for
female political agency. The assertion of the positivity of sexual difference means that, in feminism, one *speaks as* a woman, although the subject "woman" is not a monolithic essence defined once and for all, but
rather the site of multiple, complex, and potentially contradictory sets of
experience, defined by the overlapping variables of sex, race, and class.

The new feminist subject thus defined is one of the terms in a
process that should not and cannot be streamlined into a linear, teleological form of subjectivity. I would add that it is rather the site of intersection of subjective desire with willful social transformation. Irigaray
has a different emphasis: stressing that the root of the term materialism
is *mater*, she consequently reattaches it to its maternal foundations. She
thus reminds us that the material/maternal is the instance that expresses the specificity of female sexuality,[22] the sense of a female humanity
and also of her divinity.[23] Central to her project is the quest for an alternative female genealogy, by immersion into the maternal imaginary.[24]
For Irigaray this takes the form of the exploration of images that represent the female experience of proximity to the mother's body.

Irigaray's project is how to identify and enact points of exit from the
universal mode defined by man, toward a radical version of heterosexuality, that is to say, the full recognition of the two genders. More
specifically she wonders how to elaborate a site, that is to say, a space
and a time, for the irreducibility of sexual difference to express itself, so
that the masculine and feminine libidinal economies may coexist in the
positive expression of their differences. This positivity is both horizon-
tal/terrestrial and vertical/celestial and it entails the (re)thinking
through of gender-specific relations to space, time, and the interval
between the sexes, so as to avoid polarizing oppositions.

To sum up Irigaray's theory of sexual difference as a political and
epistemological project, I would emphasize the following features: first,
the belief that the subject Woman is that which has been excluded in
the masculine system of representation, because she is in excess of it and
as such she is unrepresentable. This Woman, revindicated as the rally-

• ing point of feminist-minded women, also opens the possibility of elaborating an-other system of representation.

Second, this belief is turned into the textual strategy of *mimesis*. As I stated earlier, Irigaray's mimesis is a way of retracing backwards the multilayered levels of signification, or representations, of women. The process of mimesis results in a strategic form of essentialism, that is to say, the temporary strategy that defines as Woman the stock of cumulated knowledge about the female, sexed subject—whose traits, qualities, and representations affect every woman. For each woman is the empirical referent of all that has been symbolized as femininity, the female subject, and the feminine.

Third, feminism as critical thought is a self-reflexive mode of analysis, aimed at articulating the critique of power in discourse with the affirmation of the female feminist subject.[25] It aims at the articulation of questions of individual gendered identity with issues related to political subjectivity. The interaction of identity with subjectivity also spells out the categorical distinction between dimensions of experience that are marked by desire, and therefore the unconscious, and others that are rather subjected to willful self-regulation.

Fourth, sexual difference posits the formulation of new general schemes for female subjectivity and, therefore, leads to issues of transcendence. For instance, Irigaray's work seems to move ineluctably toward issues of incorporeal materiality. This tendency is explicit in her work on the sensible transcendental and "the divine woman." Here she argues that the female subject can recognize and enact her specificity by granting symbolic importance to her bond to other women as fundamental mediators between herself and the world.

Although a great deal of this statement aims at postulating a social contract by and for women, it also contains an equally powerful transcendental charge.[26] In other words, what Irigaray points out is that the portion of being that a woman is is sexed female; it is sensible matter, endowed with sex-specific forms of transcendence. By advocating a feminine form of transcendence, through "radical immanence," Irigaray postulates a definition of the body not only as material but also as the threshold to a generalist notion of female being, a new feminist humanity.[27] The embodied materialism of sexual difference theories, in other words, is the assertion of the importance of a multiplicity that can make sense, i.e., grant symbolic recognition to women's way of being. Irigaray's "divine" aims at materializing the a priori conditions needed to achieve changes in our symbolic as well as material conditions.

Fifth, changes and transformations, such as the new symbolic system of women, cannot be created by sheer volition. The way to transform

psychic reality is not by willful self-naming: at best that is an extreme
form of narcissism, at worst it is the melancholic face of solipsism.
Rather, transformation can only be achieved through deessentialized
embodiment or strategically reessentialized embodiment: by *working
through* the multilayered structures of one's embodied self. Change has
to be achieved by careful working through: difference is not the effect
of willpower but the result of many, of endless repetitions.

As a consequence, sexual difference as the project defended by Irigaray raises the very real, i.e., conceptually plausible notion that the
process of becoming may be gender-specific. Becoming-woman, therefore, far from marking the dissolution of all identities into a state of flux
where different connections will e/merge, may itself be sex-specific, sexually differentiated, and consequently take different forms and different senses of time according to different gendered positions.

One side effect is that Deleuze's theory of becoming can be seen as
determined by his gender, that is to say, his location as an embodied
male subject for whom the dissolution of identities based on the phallus results in bypassing gender altogether, dispersing phallic identity
into a multiple sexuality. This, however, may not be the option best
suited to female embodied subjects. Let me explore this hypothesis with
the help of a literary example.

A genderized becoming: the case of Clarice Lispector

> Every woman is the woman of all women, every man is the man of all
> men and each one of them could present her/himself wherever the
> human is at stake.   —Clarice Lispector[28]

Clarice Lispector's *The passion according to G. H.* is by now a classic of
feminist theories of sexual difference. It reads to me as an exemplifica-
tion of the sexual-specific sense of time, of spatial connections, of transcendence and recognition of the other that Irigaray theoretically
defends. I also find that it enacts a mimetic strategy of disengaging one
woman's sense of self from the culturally given idea of Woman on
which her sense of identity used to rest.

The main character, G. H., is the image of postemancipation female
consciousness: a successful sculptress, living on the top floor of a luxu-
rious apartment block in a modern South American metropolis. She
enjoys all the advantages of class: elegance, leisure, economic indepen-
dence, and creativity. Moreover, she has gained the right to a room of
her own, both financially and sexually. She is the sole owner of this
space, having neither husband nor children.

The plot of the story consists in her crossing a series of thresholds,

- like steps, in a process of unraveling the levels of her subjectivity. The protagonist's voyage across the multilayered structure of her subjectivity is a mimetic repetition that opens up unsuspected paths of becoming. This process of touching the woman beneath the image of Woman also involves the questioning of G. H.'s relationship to the many levels of otherness that surround her as a series of differentiating variables: class/race/lifestyle/the inhuman/the animal/the cosmic. The process results, in fact, in the dissolution of her identity into a cosmic becoming. What catalyzes the process is her intimate encounter with an insect.

The first threshold G. H. crosses is the class boundary, which also stands for her public persona and is closely connected to race or ethnic identity.[29] The action takes place on the maid's day off: the maid is a native Brazilian woman, dark-skinned and absolutely not as Eurocentric as G. H. Prompted by the desire to tidy up what she expects to be a messy room, G. H. enters her maid's quarters. The whiteness and cleanliness of it will blind her and confront her with her own culture-specific color blindness.

This room is situated at the far end of her apartment, at the most distant remove of her house, at the back of the kitchen. The inner space of the house is, in this text, a projection of the female body, and the back of the kitchen is an area lying on the margins of conscious space: the process G. H. undertakes is therefore a plunge into the depths of her own self. This room is the counterpoint to the calm comfort of the flat; it lifts out or strips the ironic sense of distance that G. H. has wrapped up around herself as the perfect image of postemancipation Woman. Her sense of the void is awakened: this is a space of multiple becomings, where sexual difference will come into play.

The second threshold marks the collapse of the barriers between the human and its animal and inorganic others. Through a series of structural analogies with insects these barriers are systematically dissolved. This begins with the description of her house as "the top of a bee-hive", solid but aerial, and culminates with her encounter with the cockroach, to which I will return.

In the third step the linearity of time is dissolved. The process of becoming is described internally as the dissolution of the self, but also externally, through a series of analogies between individual, intimate time (*aion*) and historical, external time (*chronos*). Thus, in a visionary moment that expresses perfectly the passion for sexual difference that Irigaray writes about, G. H. remarks that one day all this will come to pass: the foundations of the present civilization will sink in, as in an earthquake, exposing its hidden foundations. Living, brute matter will come to the fore, a new elemental force will enter into action, which will redesign the shape of what we are accustomed to call civilization. Cyclical temporality, together with a reshuffling of the basic elements, will join forces in producing new terms of reference for a human, or posthuman consciousness,[30] that is to say a radical change in the sense of space and time and of how we are to inhabit them.

In the immediate, this awareness marks the return to a primordial state beyond or prior to the civilized veneer; the room is a microcosm, where time implodes into a continuous present. Progressive, linear time is short-circuited by the circular times of G. H.'s own process of becoming.

The fourth threshold leads the character to encounter, beyond the dissolution of the boundaries, a point of ascesis, or of opening out. The microcosmic room is the tip of a minaret, the heart of the desert, a space of its own that defies euclidian geometry; it is a space where anamorphosis and optical illusions accompany the collapse of linear time. As ancient as the earth, it is a prehistorical space, outside the humane, civilized sense of the self. Like a mystic on top of some sacred mountain, G. H. gazes into the depth and soon begins to see: she experiences the interconnectedness of beings: buildings are bodies, both are made of living matter—"everything is alive and made of the same matter" (p. 84). What we call the self is a carefully painted mask; civilization is matter worked through by the crafty hands of builders: of pyramids, temples, high-rise flats, acropolises, and sewerage systems.

Of bugs and women

The fifth, crucial moment concerns G. H.'s "becoming-insect." The encounter with the insect triggers off the loss of the last vestiges of her civilized self. The cockroach, hideous thing, is one of the oldest forms of life: "a drop of matter" (p. 60). They existed already at the time of the dinosaurs, thus they witnessed the creation of the mineral foundations of the earth. They can endure anything, and we now know that they can survive nuclear radiation: "For 350 million years, they perpetuated themselves without one transformation: the death-like stillness of matter" (p. 59).

The insect as a life form is a hybrid insofar as it lies at the intersection of different species: it is a winged sort of fauna, microcosmic. The insect also lies in between the imaginary and the scientific, "old like a fossilized fish. It was a cockroach as old as the salamanders, the chimeras, dragons and leviathans. It was as old as a legend" (p. 67). A full bestiary is included in this list of abject beings that are comparable to this bug in their power to cross and blur human boundaries.

•   As Kristeva points out in her commentary on Mary Douglas's work on the abject, this is a figure of mixity and intermediary states.[31] Most abject beings, animals, or states are also sacred, because they mark essential boundaries. First and foremost among them the boundary of origin, that is to say, the interface between life and death. The mother as life-giver is an abject figure: a symbolic signpost marking the road to sunny daylight and, thereby, also the way to dusty death. It is no wonder that most primitive religions are mother-based and fertility-bound. Abject beings are eternal in the sense of being the same as they were when they were created: they are essential and therefore sacred, feared, totemic. They correspond to hybrid and in-between states, and as such they evoke both fascination and horror, both desire and loathing.

Clarice Lispector acknowledges that she wrote *La Passion selon G. H.* following the experience of an abortion: consequently, the maternal is one of the horizons within which the deconstruction of Woman takes place in this story. As a matter of fact, the whole plot can be read as a ritual whereby Lispector cleanses her memory of the traces of that portion of organic matter generated within her female body. It also clearly marks the confrontation with the maternal as an abject and therefore sacred and in any case unavoidable site of female identity.

The encounter with the abject portion of being that is the cockroach brings about a return of G. H.'s repressed. It first reminds her of her childhood, living in insalubrious surroundings in the company of rats and cockroaches. Second, she discovers herself as a portion of being, of organic matter, which exists in a continuum with other animals. G. H. reconnects to her own materiality: "this unknown, happy, unconscious matter that I was" (p. 60).

G. H. initially confronts this abject thing, surveying it carefully. The abject is an object of intense fascination, capable of titillating some obscure sense of recognition, of curiosity: a layered body, made up of many different levels of wings, scales, stone-hard surfaces. Does it have blood? milk? a sex? many? Aristotle himself, in his work on animals, did not quite know how to classify insects on the scale of gender: male? female? both? neither? A living enigma, eminently fascinating, unbearably horrible. This borderline creature is life itself in its materiality.

Then the realization of the coextensivity of her being with that of organic matter of all sorts marks her becoming-alive, in the manner of living matter. Beyond humanity G. H. experiences drives and desires that are alien to the civilized human being. She discovers the *jouissance* and the fear of, for instance, the basic instinct to kill. Significantly, what she becomes aware of is not only the insect as an entity but, much more important, her own becoming-inanimate—her becoming-insect, too: "I was completely acid like the taste of metal on your tongue, like a crushed green plant" (p. 66).

This description of the becoming-insect is comparable to Deleuze's definition:

> Becoming-animal means precisely making the move, tracing the line of escape in all its positivity, crossing a threshold, reaching a continuum of intensities that only have value for themselves, finding a world of pure intensities, where all the forms get undone, as well as all the significations: signifiers and signifieds, in favor of matter yet un-formed, of deterritorialized flows, of a-signifying signs.[32]

In their analysis of another memorable encounter between a human and an insect, Kafka's *Metamorphosis*, Deleuze and Guattari develop a full theory of the becoming-animal as a form of universal becoming-minority, or deterritorialization, that is "never just reproduction or imitation" (p. 25). The becoming-animal is a question of connections, alliances, symbiosis: it is a question of multiplicity. In this respect the chain of becomings goes on: becoming-woman/child/animal/insect/vegetable/matter/molecular/imperceptible, etc., etc.

As in other stages of the argument about the process of becoming, however, Deleuze and Guattari do not take into account the variable of sexual difference in their analysis. In their commentary on the Kafka story the process of metamorphosis is not at all related to the embodied male subjectivity that provides the corporeal field for this transformation to occur.

In Clarice Lispector's story, on the other hand, the entire process of becoming, down to the crux of the encounter with the insect, is specifically sexed as female. References to sexuality, to motherhood, to body fluids, to the flow of milk, blood, and mucus are unmistakably female. At the same time, however, the structure of the successive becomings experienced by G. H. is in keeping with Deleuze's analysis of becoming as a symbiotic metamorphosis. G. H.'s encounter with the insect marks a change of space and speed in her experiential field: we are not dealing here with metaphors of insectlike subcutaneous sensibility, but rather with growing into different bodies, or growing different organs. G. H. becomes the insect itself; this occurs in different phases that also correspond to different degrees evoking new fields of forces or sensations or flows. What is at stake is not the representation of a different consciousness but its shattering into a dynamic field of transformations. Just like Deleuze, G. H. defines the process of becoming as the

• encounter of *eccéités*,[33] single individualities that share certain attributes and can merge with each other because of them.

This return to the magmalike foundations of her inanimate being makes G. H. aware of the fact that life, which she calls "I-being" is prior to and more ancient than the human itself. "The world is not human" (p. 80). She experiences the loss of her social self as a major change in perspective: "I was turning away from the law, in spite of the intuition that I was about to enter the hell of living matter" (p. 71).

Through this encounter it is her own prehistoric materiality that gets asserted as the foundation of her being. The void encountered by G. H., contrary to Sartrean nothingness, is a site of interconnectedness and mutual interdependence: "Life, my love, is one big seduction where all that is alive is seducing each other. This room which used to be deserted becomes life in its primary state. I had reached the void and the void was alive and moist."[34]

The space of this void has female sexual connotations, it is a vision of the void as a mucous space, "alive and moist."

In this recognition of her materiality she steps beyond conventional morality. Being an insect herself, murder becomes a mode of relation— a deathly encounter—but an encounter nevertheless: G. H. kills the bug.

The encounter with the abject bug reveals a deadly sort of organic affinity between the two forms of matter: G. H. and the cockroach, linked in their mutual ferocity. G. H. will kill, and the killing will be as much a gesture of connecting as of destruction. After she kills the cockroach a white substance oozes out from its crushed body: like primitive magma, like impure discharges, this organic matter pours out ineluctably. This moment, which marks the transgression of all boundaries, pushes G. H. outside the perimeters of civilized behavior and is described in a passage that reads like an extended commentary on Munch's painting *The Scream*.

In a flash, G. H. sees beyond the present to the possibility of a new civilization, but in this moment of great illumination she also confronts, more clearly than ever, her being-a-woman. The experience G. H. recounts is one of transcendence, from the abject to the primordial, with its sacred and even biblical references. She discovers a life outside the self, which does not coincide with the human.

This sense of the nonhumanity of all that lives and the irrelevance of the human to living matter finds a counterpart in the structure of time. The only time that counts is the immediacy of the present instant: "The immediate cannot be imagined; between me and the present there is no interval: it is now, in me" (p. 91). Our attention is drawn to the impersonality of the moment, the actual as a timeless sort of continuous present.

This sense of the immateriality of time has the effect of highlighting the event of the present. Is the white substance that oozes out of a dead cockroach ugly? No—it just is. It is the actual, the moment, the rawness of the now, it is beyond value judgments. It is the relentless materiality of all that, having been brought to life, simply lives on.

G. H. describes this experience also as a metamorphosis: "I am losing all that I used to have and what I used to have was myself—now I only have what I am: to be able to stand up to the horror. I do not understand and I am afraid of understanding, the matter of the world scares me, with its planets and its cockroaches" (p. 79).

The discovery of her deeply rooted affinity with living matter is a euphoric revelation: "love is the living matter" (p. 79). The part of life that is in her is not hers: G. H. used to be a woman, that is to say, a sentimentalized, psychological entity culturally constructed as feminine. Now life claims her out of her civilized neutrality; life bursts out of her like a dike that collapses and, in collapsing, sweeps everything aside.

This returning life is simply a force that demands to be expressed, and it is very intense. The realization that the human is superfluous scares her; the raw force of life is frightening. It is no wonder that the "sentimentalization" of life is necessary to cover up this rawness and disperse the fear. She describes her descent into the inanimate of primordial matter, plasma, "living neutrality," "the inexpressive," "the demonic," "the diabolical," "the prehuman" (p. 112).

G. H., however, decides to let herself go to this raw force, to let life sweep into her until she dehumanizes herself, losing all attachment to herself. To mark her communion with the living matter G. H. accomplishes the last act of her dehumanization by swallowing the dead carapace of the insect. She is the abject in all its splendor. She was a person, a woman, now she turns into a portion of living matter. She loses all ideas, to become corporeal intelligence, or sensitive matter. This is no Freudian return of the repressed, but rather the explosion of unsuspected, excessive forces.

This rediscovery of the life in her takes the form of the transcendence of the human. G. H. is the anti-Kafka in the emphasis she places on her powers of regeneration, that is to say on the all-encompassing force of her being sexed female.

This new life is governed by the intelligent communication of sensitive beings; as Irigaray suggests in her *An Ethics of Sexual Difference*, this is a redefinition of seeing, not as rapacious possession of the other, but as caress, that is to say, affinity and empathy. G. H. uses also

- metaphors of fertility to describe the interconnectedness of things: "The two eyes were as alive as two ovaries. . . . They fertilized my dead fertility" (p. 89). This is a case for embodied vision, as opposed to disembodied seeing,[35] for a sensible transcendental sexed female, as opposed to the solipsistic transcendental narcissism of the phallogo-centric subject.

This process of peaceful taking in of the world is described as an *Oratorio*: pure expression of passions, without prayers or requests—just a form of proximity to that which is. This is what she calls "God": the divine is the pure expression of the joy of/in being, stronger than any guilt or the sense of sin.

In this state G. H. is capable of remembering her abortion in positive terms rather than as being pregnant, that is to say, as being plunged into life, into the rawness of matter: both joyful and horrible. The abortion as act is described as suspending the new life, through the intervention of matter acting upon matter: "You break the envelope and all that's left is the dough of matter" (pp. 103–104).

At this point she is capable of foreseeing "the prehistory of a future" (p. 122): she becomes a cosmic principle, an organizer of space and time. Faced with the immensity and the holiness of all that is, she bows down and she adores. Adoration is the best mode of approach and perception of the other.

Difference as repetition

The Passion According to G. H. is so rich a text that it deserves far more attention than I can devote to it here. I have simply used it as an illustration of how the perspective opened by sexual difference allows for notions such as genderized becoming or gender-specific forms of transcendence. These contrast sharply with the sexually undifferentiated patterns of becoming that are advocated by the philosophers of difference like Deleuze. For instance, in her philosophical commentary on this text the Italian philosopher of sexual difference Adriana Cavarero[36] sees in the passion of G. H. the affirmation of a feminist brand of radical materialism. The life that, in one, does not bear one's own name, is a force that connects one to all other living matter. Cavarero reads this insight as the woman's attempt to disconnect her sense of being from the patriarchal logos. By positing the connectedness of living matter as the foundation for an alternative system of thought, Lispector, according to Cavarero, dislodges one of the central premises of Western thinking: that being and language are one. With G. H. life as a raw force is in excess of the logocentric grid.

Moreover, following the insight of Irigaray, Cavarero criticizes the
assimilation of the universal to the masculine and defends the idea of a
female-specific notion of being. That the living matter may not require
the thinking "I" to exist results in more emphasis being placed on the
centrality of the sexed nature of the "she-I." One's sexed identity is primordial and inextricable from one's being. Sexual difference is defini-
tional of the woman and not contingent: it is always already there.

In a very different reading of the same text, the French writer Hélène
Cixous (1986) reads the event as a parable for women's writing: *écriture
féminine* meant as the constitution of an alternative female symbolic
system. G. H.'s passion is for life without mastery, power, or domination; her sense of adoration is compared to the capacity for giving and
receptivity, not for Christian martyrdom. Cixous connects this faculty
to the ability to both give and receive the gift, that is to say, to receive
the other in all of his/her astounding difference.

In her ethical defense of the politics of subjectivity Cixous defines
the ability to accept otherness as a new science, a new discourse that is
based on the idea of respectful affinity between self and other. G. H.'s
passion is about belonging to a common matter: life, in its total deper-
sonalized manner. The term "approach" defines for Cixous the basis of
her ethical system, which is comparable to Irigaray's ethics of sexual difference: it designates the way in which self and other can be connected
in a new worldview where all living matter is a sensitive web of mutually receptive entities. The key terms are affinity and receptivity. The
other-than-human at stake here is that which, by definition, escapes the
domination of the anthropologocentric subject and requires that she/he
accepts her/his marginality. More specifically, the divine in all humans
is the capacity to see interconnectedness and empathy. For Cixous this
heightened sense of being is the feminine, it is the woman as creative
force: poet and writer. The divine is the feminine as creativity.

When compared with this analysis of the metamorphosis that takes
place in Lispector's tale of becoming, Deleuze's analysis of the "becom-
ing-woman/insect," in its sexually undifferentiated approach, comes
across as naive. How can a philosopher with the subtlety of Deleuze
not bring this contradiction further than the systematic indecision and
hesitation that mark his discussion of the becoming-women? May I
again be so bold as to suggest that Deleuze is "located" elsewhere: close
enough to the feminist claim to the empowerment of alternative
female subjectivity, but distant enough to solve it by avoidance: "I
know, but . . . "

I would like to stress that the point about being "located" does not
have to do with biological differences but with sociosymbolic position-

•   ing. Politics being no more than a theoretically informed map, Deleuze draws his own topology, and he is fully entitled to it. Speaking as a feminist I see this as confirming the importance of the "politics of location" and of sexual difference as marking asymmetrical positions between the sexes. The positioning that comes from our embodied and historically located subjectivities also determines the sort of political maps and conceptual diagrams we are likely to draw. This supports my belief that the quest for points of exit from identities based on phallogocentric premises is affected by sexual difference meant as the dissymmetry between the sexes. Consequently, one must work on the assumption that the process of going "beyond gender" may not be as unified and homogeneous as the philosophers of difference would want it to be.

In other words, to return to my opening remarks about the historical necessity of a feminist poststructuralist redefinition of the female subject, I would say that the practice of sexual difference identifies the female subject as the site of political struggle at precisely the point in history when the notion of Woman has been deessentialized and made available as a cultural construct that needs deconstructing. Woman therefore ceases to be the culturally dominant and prescriptive model of female subjectivity and turns instead into an identifiable topos of analysis. For Irigaray this crisis of fixed phallogocentric identities marks the possibility for an alternative female becoming, in the positivity of sexual difference. Feminism is the strategy of working through the layers and sedimentations of meaning that sustained Woman, at a time when the term has lost its substantial unity and been shown up as an imaginary construction. The myth of Woman is now an empty stage where feminist women can experiment with their subjective becoming. This project is fraught with perils and paradoxes, but it is historically necessary.

A paradox, moreover, need not be solved hastily, or dismissed furtively: it can instead function as the productive site of creative thinking. It may well be worth our while to linger on this site and confront the contradictions it engenders instead of rushing headlong, prompted by the desire to escape from the "essentialized feminine"[37] toward a point supposedly "beyond gender." As G. H. shows, the process of becoming is primarily a process of repetition, of mimesis, of cyclical returns.

As in the Freudian totemic meal, one has to assimilate the dead to produce the new living order: the apocalypse is from now on. Once this process is triggered there is little knowing where it will end, but all that matters is the process, the act of going, not the destination. An encounter with a cockroach may open the doors of perception of inscrutable heavens, as of unmentionable hells, but the process that it engenders is irreplaceable. It can only be hoped, therefore, that the last

word about women's radical processes of transformation, over the •
becoming-woman, may come from the *practice* of sexual difference as a
conceptual and political project.

NOTES •

1. This topic is one of the themes that I discuss in my next book, *Organs Without Bodies*, forthcoming with Routledge, 1994.

2. See Rosi Braidotti, "Féminisme et philosophie: la critique du pouvoir et la pensée féministe contemporaine," doctoral dissertation, Panthéon-Sorbonne University, Paris, 1981; Braidotti, "Femmes et philosophie: questions à suivre," *La Revue d'en Face* (1984), 13:23–33; Braidotti, "Modelli di dissonanza: donne e/in filosofia," in Patrizia Magli, ed., *Le Donne e i segni* (Urbino: Il Lavoro, 1985), pp. 23–37; Braidotti, *Patterns of Dissonance* (Cambridge: Polity, 1991); Alice Jardine, *Gynesis* (Ithaca: Cornell University Press, 1985); Judith Butler, *Subjects of Desire* (New York: Columbia University Press, 1987); Judith Butler, *Gender Trouble* (New York: Routledge, 1990); Karin Emerton, "Les Femmes et la philosophie: la mise en discours de la différence sexuelle dans la philosophie contemporaine," doctoral dissertation, Panthéon-Sorbonne University, Paris, 1986; "From Conducting Bodies to Natural Science," catalogue of Marilyn Fairskye, *Natural Science* (Sydney: Bench Press, 1989), pp. 17–25.

3. For an excellent analysis of the split between "Woman" as representation and "women" as experience, see Teresa de Lauretis, *Alice Doesn't* (Bloomington: Indiana University Press, 1984), pp. 158–186.

4. Irigaray, *Speculum*; de Lauretis, *Alice Doesn't*, and "The Essence of the Triangle; or, Taking the Risk of Essentialism Seriously," *differences* (1989), vol. 1, no. 2.

5. This is the title of an earlier version of this paper, portions of which appeared in the *Journal of the British Society for Phenomenology* (January 1993), 24(1):44–45.

6. I am grateful for the comments made by Nicholas Davey on the notion of "becoming," during the work of the conference on Deleuze organized by the British Society for Phenomenology in Oxford, December 1990.

7. Gilles Deleuze and Félix Guattari, *A Thousand Plateaux: Capitalism and Schizophrenia*, trans. Brian Massumi (Minneapolis: University of Minnesota Press, 1987), p. 242.

8. Deleuze and Guattari, *A Thousand Plateaux*, p. 272.

9. Ibid., p. 275.

10. Michel Foucault, *Surveiller et punir* (Paris: Gallimard, 1975); *Histoire de la sexualité, I: La Volonté de savoir* (Paris: Gallimard, 1976); *II: L'Usage des plaisirs* (Paris: Gallimard, 1984); *III: Le Souci de soi* (Paris: Gallimard, 1984). For a feminist analysis see Irene Diamond and Lee Quinby, eds., *Foucault and Feminism* (Boston: North Eastern University Press, 1988).

11. On this point see Wendy Brown, "Feminist Hesitations, Postmodern Exposures," *differences* (1991), 3(1):63–84.

12. See on this point Judith Butler, *Subjects of Desire.*

13. De Lauretis, "The Essence of the Triangle."

14. Irigaray, *This Sex*, p. 143/ *Ce sexe*, p. 140.

15. In Braidotti, "Envy; or, With My Brains and Your Looks," in Alice Jardine and Paul Smith, eds., *Men in Feminism* (London and New York: Methuen, 1987) and *Patterns of Dissonance.*

16. Deleuze and Guattari, *A Thousand Plateaux*, p. 276.

17. Gayatri C. Spivak, "In a Word," *differences* (1989), 1(2):124–156.

18. On this point I have been greatly inspired by the work of Adriana Cavarero in *Nonostante Platone* (Roma: Editori Riuniti, 1990).

19. Irigaray, "Love Between Us," pp. 167–177. Citation from p. 167.

20. For an excellent analysis of the point see Naomi Schor, "Dreaming Dissymmetry," in Jardine and Smith, *Men in Feminism.*

21. Irigaray, *Speculum*, p. 133/165.

22. See on this point the magisterial study by Margaret Whitford, *Luce Irigaray: Philosophy in the Feminine* (London: Routledge, 1991).

23. For a study of the aesthetics of sexual difference, see L. Guadagnin and V. Pasquan, eds., *Parola, Mater-Materia* (Venezia: Arsenale Editrice, 1989).

24. See Irigaray, *Le Temps de la différence.*

25. De Lauretis, ed., *Feminist Studies/Critical Studies* (Bloomington: Indiana University Press, 1986); de Lauretis, *Technologies of Gender* (Bloomington: Indiana University Press, 1987).

26. This notion was expressed most powerfully by the Italian feminists of the women's commission of the Communist Party who, following Irigaray, stated that "women's strength comes from other women." This is in "The Communist Women's Charter," translated into English in Paola Bono and Sandra Kemp, eds., *Italian Feminist Thought* (Oxford: Blackwell, 1991).

27. I am grateful to Anne Claire Mulder for this formulation, which is central to her theological research on the notion of incarnation in the work of Irigaray.

28. Clarice Lispector, *La Passion selon G. H.* (Paris: Des Femmes, 1978), p. 193. The English translation, by Ronald W. Sousa, is *The Passion According to G. H.* (Minneapolis: University of Minnesota Press, 1988). All references are to the French edition; translations are by the author.

29. The interconnection of social identity with ethnic or race identity was brought to the fore by black feminist theorists from the beginning of the seventies. For a recent formulation, see Patricia Hill Collins, *Black Feminist Theory* (London and New York: Routledge, 1991).

30. The most inspiring thinker of the posthuman condition in English is Donna Haraway, to whom I owe this expression.

31. Julia Kristeva, *Pouvoirs de l'horreur* (Paris: Seuil, 1977).

32. Gilles Deleuze and Félix Guattari, *Kafka: pour une littérature mineure* (Paris: Minuit, 1975), p. 24. Translation by the author.

33. Gilles Deleuze and Félix Guattari, *A Thousand Plateaux/Mille Plateaux* (Paris: Minuit, 1980).

34. Clarice Lispector, *La Passion selon G. H.*, p. 73.

35. For an in-depth defense of the privileges of partial vision, see Donna Haraway, "Situated Knowledges," in *Simians, Cyborgs, and Women* (London: Free Association Press, 1990).

36. Cavarero, *Nonostante Platone.*

37. On essentialism see Naomi Schor, "This Essentialism Which Is Not One," this volume; Diana Fuss, *Essentially Speaking* (New York: Routledge, 1990); Rosi Braidotti "The Politics of Ontological Difference," in Teresa Brennan, ed., *Between Feminism and Psychoanalysis* (London and New York: Routledge, 1989); Braidotti, "Essentialism," in Elizabeth Wright, ed., *Feminism and Psychoanalysis: A Critical Dictionary* (Oxford: Blackwell, 1992).

PART 2

:

Irigaray
and/in
Philosophy

BODIES

THAT

MATTER

If I understand deconstruction, deconstruction is not an exposure of error, certainly not other people's error. The critique in deconstruction, the most serious critique in deconstruction, is the critique of something that is extremely useful, something without which we cannot do anything.   —Gayatri Chakravorty Spivak,
"In a Word," interview with Ellen Rooney

. . . the necessity of "reopening" the figures of philosophical discourse . . . One way is to interrogate the conditions under which systematicity itself is possible: what the coherence of the discursive utterance conceals of the conditions under which it is produced, whatever it may say about these conditions in discourse. For example the "matter" from which the speaking subject draws nourishment in order to produce itself, to reproduce itself; the *scenography* that makes representation feasible, representation as defined in philosophy, that is, the architectonics of its theatre, its framing in space-time, its geometric organization, its props, its actors, their respective positions, their dialogues, indeed their tragic relations, without overlooking the *mirror*, most often hidden, that allows the logos, the subject, to reduplicate itself, to reflect itself by itself. All these are interventions on the scene; they ensure its coherence so long as they remain uninterpreted. Thus they have to be reenacted, in each figure of discourse away from its mooring in the value of "presence." For each philosopher, beginning with those whose names define some age in the history of philosophy, we have to point out how the break with material contiguity is made (il faut repérer comment s'opère la coupure d'avec la contiguïté materielle), how the system is put together, how the specular economy works.
—Luce Irigaray, "The Power of Discourse"

Within some quarters of feminist theory in recent years there have been calls to retrieve the body from what is often characterized as the linguistic idealism of poststructuralism. In another quarter philosopher Gianni Vattimo has argued that poststructuralism, understood as textual play, marks the dissolution of *matter* as a contemporary category. And it is this lost matter, he argues, that must now be reformulated in order for poststructuralism to give way to a project of greater ethical and political value.[1] The terms of these debates are difficult and unstable ones, for it is difficult to know in either case who or what is designated by the term *post-*

structuralism, and perhaps even more difficult to know what to retrieve under the sign of *the body.* And yet these two signifiers have for some feminists and critical theorists seemed fundamentally antagonistic. One hears warnings like the following: If everything is discourse, what happens to the body? If everything is a text, what about violence and bodily injury? Does anything *matter* in or for poststructuralism?

It has seemed to many, I think, that in order for feminism to proceed as a critical practice, it must ground itself in the sexed specificity of the female body. Even as the category of sex is always reinscribed as gender, that sex must still be presumed as the irreducible point of departure for the various cultural constructions it has come to bear. And this presumption of the material irreducibility of sex has seemed to ground and to authorize feminist epistemologies and ethics as well as gendered analyses of various kinds. In an effort to displace the terms of this debate I want to ask how and why *materiality* has become a sign of irreducibility, that is, how is it that the materiality of sex is understood as that which only bears cultural constructions and, therefore, cannot be a construction? What is the status of this exclusion? Is materiality a site or surface that is excluded from the process of construction, as that through which and on which construction works? Is this perhaps an enabling or constitutive exclusion, one without which construction cannot operate? What occupies this site of unconstructed materiality? And what kinds of constructions are foreclosed through the figuring of this site as outside or beneath construction itself?

In what follows what is at stake is less a theory of cultural construction than a consideration of the scenography and topography of construction. This scenography is orchestrated by and as a matrix of power that remains disarticulated if we presume constructedness and materiality as necessarily oppositional notions.

In the place of materiality one might inquire into other foundationalist premises that operate as political "irreducibles." Instead of rehearsing the theoretical difficulties that emerge by presuming the notion of the subject as a foundational premise, or by trying to maintain a stable distinction between sex and gender, I would like to raise the question whether recourse to matter and to the materiality of sex is necessary in order to establish that irreducible specificity said to ground feminist practice. And here the question is not whether or not there ought to be reference to matter, just as the question never has been whether or not there ought to be speaking about women. This speaking will occur, and for feminist reasons it must; the category of women does not become useless through deconstruction, but becomes one whose uses are no longer reified as "referents" and that stand a chance of being opened up, indeed, of coming to signify in ways that none of us can predict in advance. Surely, it must be possible both to use the term—to use it tactically even as one is, as it were, used and positioned by it—and also to subject the term to a critique that interrogates the exclusionary operations and differential power relations that construct and delimit feminist invocations of "women." This is, to paraphrase the citation from Spivak above, the critique of something useful, the critique of something we cannot do without. Indeed, I would argue that it is a critique without which feminism loses its democratizing potential through refusing to engage—take stock of, and become transformed by—the exclusions that put it into play.

Something similar is at work with the concept of materiality, which may well be "something without which we cannot do anything." What does it mean to have recourse to materiality, since it is clear from the start that matter has a history (indeed, more than one) and that the history of matter is in part determined by the negotiation of sexual difference? We may seek to return to matter as prior to discourse in order to ground our claims about sexual difference, only to discover that matter is fully sedimented with discourses on sex and sexuality that prefigure and constrain the uses to which that term can be put. Moreover, we may seek recourse to matter in order to ground or to verify a set of injuries or violations, only to find that *matter itself is founded through a set of violations*, ones that are unwittingly repeated in the contemporary invocation.

Indeed, if it can be shown that in its constitutive history this "irreducible" materiality is constructed through a problematic gendered matrix, then the discursive practice by which matter is rendered irreducible simultaneously ontologizes and fixes that gendered matrix in its place. And if the constituted effect of that matrix is taken to be the indisputable ground of bodily life, then it seems that a genealogy of that matrix is foreclosed from critical inquiry. Against the claim that poststructuralism reduces all materiality to linguistic stuff, an argument is needed to show that to deconstruct matter is not to negate or do away with the usefulness of the term. And against those who would claim that the body's irreducible materiality is a necessary precondition for feminist practice, I suggest that that prized materiality may well be constituted through an exclusion and degradation of the feminine that is profoundly problematic for feminism.

Here it is of course necessary to state quite plainly that the options for theory are not exhausted by *presuming* materiality, on the one hand, and *negating* materiality, on the other. It is my purpose to do

•
•   precisely neither of these. To call a presupposition into question is not
     the same as doing away with it, rather it is to free it from its meta-
     physical lodgings in order to understand what political interests were
     secured in and by that metaphysical placing, and thereby to permit
     the term to occupy and to serve very different political aims. To prob-
     lematize the matter of bodies may entail an initial loss of epistemo-
     logical certainty, but a loss of certainty is not the same as political
     nihilism. On the contrary, such a loss may well indicate a significant
     and promising shift in political thinking. This unsettling of "matter"
     can be understood as initiating new possibilities, new ways for bodies
     to matter.

     The body is always *posited* or *signified* as *prior*. This signification
     produces as an *effect* of its own procedure the very body that it never-
     theless and simultaneously claims to discover as that which *precedes* its
     own action. If the body signified as prior to signification is an effect of
     signification, then the mimetic or representational status of language,
     which claims that signs follow bodies as their necessary mirrors, is not
     mimetic at all. On the contrary, it is productive, constitutive, one
     might even argue *performative*, inasmuch as this signifying act delim-
     its and contours the body that it then claims to find prior to any and
     all signification.[2]

     This is not to say that the materiality of bodies is simply and only a
     linguistic effect that is reducible to a set of signifiers. Such a distinction
     overlooks the materiality of the signifier itself. Such an account also fails
     to understand materiality as that which is bound up with signification
     from the start; to think through the indissolubility of materiality and
     signification is no easy matter. To posit by way of language a materiali-
     ty outside of language is still to posit that materiality, and the material-
     ity so posited will retain that positing as its constitutive condition. Der-
     rida negotiates the question of matter's radical alterity with the follow-
     ing remark: "I am not even sure that there can be a 'concept' of an
     absolute exterior."[3] To have the concept of matter is to lose the exteri-
     ority that the concept is suppose to secure. Can language simply refer
     to materiality, or is language also the very condition under which mate-
     riality may be said to appear?

     If matter ceases to be matter once it becomes a concept, and if a con-
     cept of matter's exteriority to language is always something less than
     absolute, what is the status of this "outside"? Is it produced by philo-
     sophical discourse in order to effect the appearance of its own exhaus-
     tive and coherent systematicity? What is cast out from philosophical
     propriety in order to sustain and secure the borders of philosophy? And
     how might this repudiation return?

Matters of Femininity

The classical association of femininity with materiality can be traced to a set of etymologies that link matter with *mater* and *matrix* (or the womb) and, hence, with a problematic of reproduction. The classical configuration of matter as a site of *generation* or *origination* becomes especially significant when the account of what an object is and means requires recourse to its originating principle. When not explicitly associated with reproduction, matter is generalized as a principle of origination and causality. In Greek, *hyle* is the wood or timber out of which various cultural constructions are made, but also a principle of origin, development, and teleology that is at once causal and explanatory. This link between matter, origin, and significance suggests the indissolubility of classical Greek notions of materiality and signification. That which matters about an object is its matter.[4]

In both the Latin and the Greek, matter (*materia* and *hyle*) is neither a simple, brute positivity or referent nor a blank surface or slate awaiting an external signification, but is always in some sense temporalized. This is true for Marx as well, when "matter" is understood as a principle of *transformation*, presuming and inducing a future.[5] The matrix is an originating and formative principle that inaugurates and informs a development of some organism or object. Hence, for Aristotle, "matter is potentiality [*dynamis*], form actuality."[6] In reproduction women are said to contribute the matter; men, the form.[7] The Greek *hyle* is wood that already has been cut from trees, instrumentalized and instrumentalizable, artifactual, on the way to being put to use. *Materia* in Latin denotes the stuff out of which things are made, not only the timber for houses and ships but whatever serves as nourishment for infants: nutrients that act as extensions of the mother's body. Insofar as matter appears in these cases to be invested with a certain capacity to originate and to compose that for which it also supplies the principle of intelligibility, then "matter" is clearly invested with a certain power of creation and rationality that is for the most part divested from the more modern empirical deployments of the term. To speak within these classical contexts of *bodies that matter* is not an idle pun, for to be material means to materialize, where the principle of that materialization is precisely what "matters" about that body, its very intelligibility. In this sense to know the significance of something is to know how and why it matters, where "to matter" means at once "to materialize" and "to mean."

Obviously, no feminist would encourage a simple return to Aristotle's natural teleologies in order to rethink the "materiality" of bodies. I want to consider, however, Aristotle's distinction between body and

- soul, effecting a brief comparison between Aristotle and Foucault to
- suggest a possible contemporary redeployment of Aristotelian terminology. At the end of this brief comparison I will offer a limited criticism of Foucault, which will then lead to a longer discussion of Irigaray's deconstruction of materiality in Plato's *Timaeus*. It is in the context of this second analysis that I hope to make clear how a gendered
matrix is at work in the constitution of materiality (although it is obviously present in Aristotle as well), and why feminists ought to be interested, not in taking materiality as an irreducible, but in conducting a
critical genealogy of its formulation.

Aristotle/Foucault

For Aristotle the soul designates the actualization of matter, where matter is understood as fully potential and unactualized. As a result, he
maintains in *De Anima* that the soul is "the first grade of actuality of a
naturally organized body." He continues, "That is why we can wholly
dismiss as unnecessary the question whether the soul and the body are
one: it is as meaningless to ask whether the wax and the shape given to
it by the stamp are one, or generally the matter [*hyle*] of a thing and that
of which it is the matter [*hyle*]."[8] In the Greek, there is no reference to
"stamps," but the phrase, "the shape given by the stamp" is contained
in the single term, "*schema.*" *Schema* means form, shape, figure, appearance, dress, gesture, figure of a syllogism, and grammatical form. If
matter never appears without its *schema,* that means that it only appears
under a certain grammatical form and that the principle of its recog-
nizability, its characteristic gesture or usual dress, is indissoluble from
what constitutes its matter.

In Aristotle we find no clear phenomenal distinction between materiality and intelligibility, and yet for other reasons Aristotle does not
supply us with the kind of "body" that feminism seeks to retrieve. To
install the principle of intelligibility in the very development of a body
is precisely the strategy of a natural teleology which accounts for female
development through the rationale of biology. On this basis, it has been
argued that women ought to perform certain social functions and not
others, indeed, that women ought to be fully restricted to the reproductive domain.

We might historicize the Aristotelian notion of the *schema* in terms
of culturally variable principles of formativity and intelligibility. To
understand the *schema* of bodies as a historically contingent nexus of
power/discourse is to arrive at something similar to what Foucault
describes in *Discipline and Punish* as the "materialization" of the pris-

oner's body. This process of materialization is at stake as well in the final chapter of the first volume of *The History of Sexuality* when Foucault calls for a "history of bodies" that would inquire into "the manner in which what is most material and vital in them has been invested."[9]

At times it appears that for Foucault the body has a materiality that is ontologically distinct from the power relations that take that body as a site of investments. And yet in *Discipline and Punish* we have a different configuration of the relation between materiality and investment. There the soul is taken as an instrument of power through which the body is cultivated and formed. In a sense it acts as a power-laden schema that produces and actualizes the body itself.

We can understand Foucault's references to the "soul" as an implicit reworking of the Aristotelian formulation. Foucault argues in *Discipline and Punish* that the "soul" becomes a normative and normalizing ideal according to which the body is trained, shaped, cultivated, and invested; it is a historically specific imaginary ideal (*idéal spéculatif*) under which the body is effectively materialized. Considering the science of prison reform, Foucault writes,

> The man described for us, whom we are invited to free, is already in himself the effect of a subjection [*assujettissement*] much more profound than himself. A "soul" inhabits him and brings him to existence, which is itself a factor in the mastery that power exercises over the body. The soul is the effect and instrument of a political anatomy; the soul is the prison of the body.[10]

This "subjection," or *assujettissement*, is not only a subordination but a securing and maintaining, a putting into place of a subject, a subjectivation. The "soul brings [the prisoner] to existence"; and not fully unlike Aristotle, the soul described by Foucault as an instrument of power, forms and frames the body, stamps it, and in stamping it brings it into being. Here "being" belongs in quotation marks, for ontological weight is not presumed, but always conferred. For Foucault this conferral can take place only within and by an operation of power. This operation produces the subjects that it subjects; that is, it subjects them in and through the compulsory power relations effective as their formative principle. But power is that which forms, maintains, sustains, and regulates bodies at once, so that, strictly speaking, power is not a subject who acts on bodies as its distinct objects. The grammar that compels us to speak that way enforces a metaphysics of external relations, whereby power acts on bodies but is not understood to form them. This is a view of power as an external relation that Foucault himself calls into question.

•
•
    Power operates for Foucault in the *constitution* of the very materiality of the subject, in the principle that simultaneously forms and regulates the "subject" of subjectivation. Foucault refers not only to the materiality of the body of the prisoner but to the materiality of the body of the prison. The materiality of the prison, he writes, is established to the extent that [*dans la mesure où*] it is a vector and instrument of power.[11] Hence, the prison is *materialized* to the extent that it is *invested with power*, or, to be grammatically accurate, there is no prison prior to its materialization. Its materialization is coextensive with its investiture with power relations, and materiality is the effect and gauge of this investment. The prison comes to be only within the field of power relations, but, more specifically, only to the extent that it is invested or saturated with such relations, that such a saturation is itself formative of its very being. Here the body is not an independent materiality invested by power relations external to it, but it is that for which materialization and investiture are coextensive.

    "Materiality" designates a certain effect of power, or rather *is* power in its formative or constituting effects. Insofar as power operates successfully by constituting an object domain, a field of intelligibility, as a taken-for-granted ontology, its material effects are taken as material data or primary givens. These material positivities appear *outside* discourse and power, as its incontestable referents, its transcendental signifieds. But this appearance is precisely the moment in which the power/discourse regime is most fully dissimulated and most insidiously effective. When this material effect is taken as an epistemological point of departure, a sine qua non of some political argumentation, this is a move of empiricist foundationalism that, in accepting this constituted effect as a primary given, successfully buries and masks the genealogy of power relations by which it is constituted.[12]

    Insofar as Foucault traces the process of materialization as an investiture of discourse and power, he focuses on that dimension of power that is productive and formative. But we need to ask what constrains the domain of what is materializable, and whether there are *modalities* of materialization—as Aristotle suggests, and Althusser is quick to cite.[13] To what extent is materialization governed by principles of intelligibility that require and institute a domain of radical *unintelligibility* that resists materialization altogether or that remains radically dematerialized? Does Foucault's effort to work the notions of discourse and materiality through one another not only fail to account for what *is excluded* from the economies of discursive intelligibility that he describes but for what *has to be excluded* in order for those economies to function as self-sustaining systems?

This is the question implicitly raised by Luce Irigaray's analysis of the form/matter distinction in Plato. That argument is perhaps best known from the essay "Plato's Hystera," in *Speculum of the Other Woman*, but is trenchantly articulated as well in the lesser known essay, "Une Mère de Glace," also in *Speculum*.

Irigaray's task is to reconcile neither the form/matter distinction nor the distinctions between bodies and souls or matter and meaning. Rather, her effort is to show that those binary oppositions are formulated through the exclusion of a field of disruptive possibilities. Her speculative thesis is that those binaries, even in their reconciled mode, are part of a phallogocentric economy that produces the "feminine" as its constitutive outside. Irigaray's intervention in the history of the form/matter distinction underscores "matter" as the site at which the feminine is excluded from philosophical binaries. Inasmuch as certain phantasmatic notions of the feminine are traditionally associated with materiality, these are specular effects that confirm a phallogocentric project of autogenesis. And when those specular (and spectral) feminine figures are taken to be the feminine, the feminine is, she argues, fully erased by its very representation. The economy that claims to include the feminine as the subordinate term in a binary opposition of masculine/feminine excludes the feminine, produces the feminine as that which must be excluded for that economy to operate. In what follows I will consider first Irigaray's speculative mode of engaging with philosophical texts and then turn to her rude and provocative reading of Plato's discussion of the receptacle in the *Timaeus*. In the final section of this essay I will offer my own rude and provocative reading of the same passage.

Irigaray/Plato

The largeness and speculative character of Irigaray's claims have always put me a bit on edge, and I confess in advance that although I can think of no feminist who has read and reread the history of philosophy with the kind of detailed and critical attention that she has,[14] her terms tend to mime the grandiosity of the philosophical errors that she underscores. This miming is, of course, tactical, and the reenactment of philosophical error that she performs requires that we learn how to read her for the difference that her reading performs. Does the voice of the philosophical father echo in her, or has she occupied that voice, insinuated herself into the voice of the father? If she is "in" that voice for either reason, is she also at the same time "outside" it? How do we understand the being "between," the two possibilities as something

·   other than a spatialized *entre* that leaves the phallogocentric binary
·   opposition intact?[15] How does the difference from the philosophical
father resound in the mime that appears to replicate his strategy so
faithfully? This is, clearly, no place between "his" language and "hers,"
but only a disruptive *movement* that unsettles the topographical
claim.[16] This is a taking of his place, not to assume it, but to show that
it is *occupiable*, to raise the question of the cost and movement of that
assumption. Where and how is the critical departure from that patri-
lineage performed in the course of the recitation of his terms? If the task
is not a loyal or proper "reading" of Plato, then perhaps it is a kind of
overreading that mimes and exposes the speculative excess in Plato. To
the extent that I replicate that speculative excess here, I apologize, but
only halfheartedly, for sometimes a hyperbolic rejoinder is necessary
when a given injury has remained unspoken for too long.

When Irigaray sets out to reread the history of philosophy she asks
how its borders are secured: what must be excluded from the domain of
philosophy for philosophy itself to proceed, and how is it that the
excluded comes to constitute negatively a philosophical enterprise that
takes itself to be self-grounding and self-constituting? Irigaray then isolates the feminine as precisely this constitutive exclusion, whereupon
she is compelled to find a way of reading a philosophical text for what
it refuses to include. This is no easy matter. For how can one read a text
for what does *not* appear within its own terms but that nevertheless constitutes the illegible conditions of its own legibility? Indeed, how can
one read a text for the movement of that disappearing by which the textual "inside" and "outside" are constituted?

Although feminist philosophers have traditionally sought to show
how the body is figured as feminine, or how women have been associated with materiality (whether inert—always already dead—or
fecund—ever-living and procreative) where men have been associated
with the principle of rational mastery,[17] Irigaray wants to argue that in
fact the feminine is precisely what is excluded in and by such a binary
opposition. In this sense when and where women are represented within this economy is precisely the site of their erasure. Moreover, when
matter is described within philosophical descriptions, she argues, it is at
once a substitution for and displacement of the feminine. One cannot
interpret the philosophical relation to the feminine through the figures
that philosophy provides, but rather, she argues, through citing the
feminine as the unspeakable condition of figuration, as that which, in
fact, can *never be* figured within the terms of philosophy proper, but
whose exclusion from that propriety is its enabling condition.

No wonder then that the feminine appears for Irigaray only in catachresis, that is, in those figures that function improperly, as an improper transfer of sense, the use of a proper name to describe that which does not properly belong to it, and that return to haunt and co-opt the very language from which the feminine is excluded. This explains in part the radical citational practice of Irigaray, the catachrestic usurpation of the "proper" for fully improper purposes.[18] For she mimes philosophy—as well as psychoanalysis—and, in the mime, takes on a language that effectively cannot belong to her, only to call into question the exclusionary rules of proprietariness that govern the use of that discourse. This contestation of propriety and property is precisely the option open to the feminine when it has been constituted as an excluded impropriety, as the improper, the propertyless. Indeed, as Irigaray argues in *Marine Lover (Amante marine)*, her work on Nietzsche, "woman neither is nor has an essence," and this is the case for her precisely because "woman" is what is excluded from the discourse of metaphysics.[19] If she takes on a proper name, even the proper name of "woman" in the singular, that can only be a kind of radical mime that seeks to jar the term from its ontological presuppositions. Jane Gallop makes this brilliantly clear in her reading of the two lips as both synecdoche and catachresis, a reading that offers an interpretation of Irigaray's language of biological essentialism as rhetorical strategy. Gallop shows that Irigaray's figural language constitutes the feminine in language as a persistent linguistic impropriety.[20]

This exclusion of the feminine from the proprietary discourse of metaphysics takes place, Irigaray argues, in and through the formulation of "matter." Inasmuch as a distinction between form and matter is offered within phallogocentrism, it is articulated through a further materiality. In other words, every explicit distinction takes place in an inscriptional space that the distinction itself cannot accommodate. The thematization of matter as a *site* of inscription cannot be explicitly thematized. And this inscriptional site or space is, for Irigaray, a *materiality* that is not the same as the category of "matter" whose articulation it conditions and enables. It is this unthematizable materiality that Irigaray claims becomes the site, the repository, indeed, the receptacle of and for the feminine *within* a phallogocentric economy. In an important sense this second inarticulate "matter" designates the constitutive outside of the Platonic economy; it is what must be excluded for that economy to posture as internally coherent.[21]

This excessive matter that cannot be contained within the form/matter distinction operates like the supplement in Derrida's analysis of philosophical oppositions. In Derrida's consideration of the form/matter distinction in *Positions*, he suggests as well that matter must be redoubled, at once as a pole within a binary opposition and as that which exceeds that binary coupling, as a figure for its non-systematizability.

Consider Derrida's remark in response to the critic who wants to claim that matter denotes the radical outside to language: "It follows that if, and in the extent to which, *matter* in this general economy designates, as you said, radical alterity (I will specify: in relation to philosophical oppositions), then what I write can be considered 'materialist.' "[22] For both Derrida and Irigaray, it seems, what is excluded from this binary is also *produced* by it in the mode of exclusion and has no separable or fully independent existence as an absolute outside. A constitutive or relative outside is, of course, composed of a set of exclusions that are nevertheless *internal* to that system as its own nonthematizable necessity. It emerges within the system as incoherence, disruption, a threat to its own systematicity.

Irigaray insists that this exclusion that mobilizes the form/matter binary is the differentiating relation between masculine and feminine, where the masculine occupies both terms of binary opposition, and the feminine cannot be said to be an intelligible term at all. We might understand the feminine figured within the binary as the *specular* feminine and the feminine that is erased and excluded from that binary as the *excessive* feminine. And yet, such nominations cannot work, for in the latter mode the feminine, strictly speaking, cannot be named at all and, indeed, is not a mode.

For Irigaray the "feminine" that cannot be said to *be* anything, to participate in ontology at all, is—and here grammar fails us—set under erasure as the impossible necessity that enables any ontology. The feminine, to use a catachresis, is domesticated and rendered unintelligible within a phallogocentrism that claims to be self-constituting. Disavowed, the remnant of the feminine survives as the *inscriptional space* of that phallogocentrism, the specular surface that receives the marks of a masculine signifying act only to give back a (false) reflection and guarantee of phallogocentric self-sufficiency, without making any contribution of its own. As a topos of the metaphysical tradition this inscriptional space makes its appearance in Plato's *Timaeus* as the receptacle (*hypodoche*), which is also described as the *chora*. Although extensive readings of the *chora* have been offered by Derrida and Irigaray, I want to refer here to only one passage, which is about the very problem of passage: namely, that passage by which a form can be said to generate its own sensible representation. We know that for Plato any material object comes into being only through participating in a Form that is its necessary precondition. As a result material objects are copies of Forms, and exist only to the extent that they instantiate Forms. And yet, where does this instantiation take place? Is there a place, a site, where this reproduction occurs, a medium through which the transformation from form to sensible object occurs?

In the cosmogony offered in the *Timaeus* Plato refers to three natures that must be taken into account: the first, which is the process of generation; the second, that in which the generation takes place; and the third, that of which the thing generated is a resemblance naturally produced. Then, in what appears to be an aside, we may "liken the receiving principle to a mother, and the source or spring to a father, and the intermediate nature to a child" (50d).[23] Prior to this passage Plato refers to this receiving principle as a "nurse" (40b), and then as "the universal nature which receives all bodies," according to the Hamilton/Cairns translation. But this latter phrase might be better translated as "the dynamic nature (*physis*) that receives (*dechesthai*) all the bodies that there are (*ta panta somata*)" (50b).[24] Of this all-receiving function, Plato argues, she "must always be called the same, for inasmuch as she always receives all things, she never departs at all from her own nature (*dynamis*) and never, in any way or at any time, assumes a form (*eilephen*) like that of any of the things which enter into her . . . the forms that enter into and go out of her are the likenesses of eternal realities modeled after their own patterns (*diaschematizomenon*)" (50c).[25] Here her proper function is to receive, *dechesthai*, to take, accept, welcome, include, and even comprehend. What enters into this *hypodoche* is a set of forms or, better, shapes (*morphe*), and yet this receiving principle, this *physis,* has no proper shape and is not a body. Like Aristotle's *hyle, physis* cannot be defined.[26] In effect, the receiving principle potentially includes all bodies, and so applies universally, but its universal applicability must not resemble at all, ever, those eternal realities (*eidos*) that in the *Timaeus* prefigure universal forms, and that pass into the receptacle. There is here a prohibition on resemblance (*mimeta*), which is to say that this nature cannot be said to be like either the eternal Forms or their material, sensible, or imaginary copies. But, in particular, this *physis* is only to be entered, but never to enter. Here the term *eisienai* denotes a going toward or into, an approach and penetration, it also denotes going into a *place*, so that the *chora*, as an enclosure, cannot be that which enters into another enclosure; metaphorically, and perhaps coincidentally, this prohibited form of entry also means "being brought into court," i.e., subject to public norms, and "coming into mind" or "beginning to think."

Here there is also the stipulation not "to assume a form like those that enter her." Can this receptacle, then, be likened to any body, to

that of the mother, or to the nurse? According to Plato's own stipulation, we cannot define this "nature," and to know it by analogy is to
know it only by "bastard thinking." In this sense the human who would
know this nature is dispossessed of/by the paternal principle, a son out
of wedlock, a deviation from patrilineality and the analogical relation
by which patronym lineage proceeds. Hence, to offer a metaphor or
analogy presupposes a likeness between that nature and a human form.
It is this last point that Derrida, accepting Plato's dictum, takes as
salient to the understanding of the *chora*, arguing that it can never be
collapsed into any of the figures that it itself occasions. As a result, Derrida argues, it would be wrong to take the association of the *chora* with
femininity as a decisive collapse.[27]

In a sense Irigaray agrees with this contention: the figure of the
nurse, the mother, the womb cannot be fully identified with the receptacle, for those are specular figures that displace the feminine at the
moment they purport to represent the feminine. The receptacle cannot
be exhaustively thematized or figured in Plato's text, precisely because it
is that which conditions and escapes every figuration and thematization. *This receptacle/nurse is not a metaphor based on likeness to a human
form, but a disfiguration that emerges at the boundaries of the human both
as its very condition and as the insistent threat of its deformation; it cannot
take a form, a morphe, and in that sense, cannot be a body.*

Insofar as Derrida argues that the receptacle cannot be identified
with the figure of the feminine, Irigaray would seem to be in agreement.
But she takes the analysis a step further, arguing that the feminine
exceeds its figuration, just as the receptacle does, and that this unthema-
tizability constitutes the feminine as the impossible yet necessary foundation of what can be thematized and figured. Significantly, Julia Kristeva *accepts* this collapse of the *chora* and the maternal/nurse figure,
arguing in *Revolution in Poetic Language* that "Plato leads us" to this
"process . . . [of] rhythmic space."[28] In contrast with Irigaray's refusal
of this conflation of the *chora* and the feminine/maternal, Kristeva
affirms this association and further asserts her notion of the semiotic as
that which "precedes" (26) the symbolic law: "The mother's body is
therefore what mediates the symbolic law organizing social relations
and becomes the ordering principle of the semiotic *chora*" (27).

Whereas Kristeva insists upon this identification of the *chora* with
the maternal body, Irigaray asks how the discourse that performs this
conflation invariably produces an "outside" where the feminine *not* cap-
tured by the figure of the *chora* persists. Here we need to ask, how is this
assignation of a feminine "outside" possible within language? And is it
not the case that there is within any discourse, and thus within Irigaray's

as well, a set of constitutive exclusions that are inevitably produced by the circumscription of the feminine as that which monopolizes the sphere of exclusion?

In this sense the receptacle is not simply a figure *for* the excluded, but, taken as a figure, stands for the excluded and thus performs or enacts yet another set of exclusions of all that remains unfigurable under the sign of the feminine—that in the feminine which resists the figure of the nurse-receptacle. In other words, taken as a figure, the nurse-receptacle freezes the feminine as that which is necessary for the reproduction of the human but is itself not human, and is in no way to be construed as the formative principle of the human form that is, as it were, produced through it.[29]

The problem is not that the feminine is made to stand for matter or for universality; rather, the feminine is cast outside the form/matter and universal/particular binarisms. She will be neither the one nor the other, but the permanent and unchangeable condition of both—what can be construed as a nonthematizable materiality.[30] She will be entered, and will give forth a further instance of what enters her, but she will never resemble either the formative principle or that which it creates. Irigaray insists that here it is the female power of reproduction that is taken over by the phallogocentric economy and remade into its own exclusive and essential action. When *physis* is articulated as *chora*, as it is in Plato, some of the dynamism and potency included in the meaning of *physis* is suppressed. In the place of a femininity that makes a contribution to reproduction, we have a phallic Form that reproduces only and always further versions of itself, and does this through the feminine, but with no assistance from her. Significantly, this transfer of the reproductive function from the feminine to the masculine entails the topographical suppression of *physis*, the dissimulation of *physis* as *chora*, as place.

The word matter does not occur in Plato to describe this *chora* or *hypodoche*, and yet Aristotle remarks in *The Metaphysics* that this section of the *Timaeus* articulates most closely his own notion of *hyle*. Taking up this suggestion, Plotinus wrote the Sixth Tractate of the *Enneads*, "The Impassivity of the Unembodied," an effort to account for Plato's notion of the *hypodoche* as *hyle* or matter.[31] In a twist that the history of philosophy has perhaps rarely undergone, Irigaray accepts and rereads Plotinus's effort to read Plato through Aristotelian "matter" in "Une Mère de glace."

In that essay, she writes that for Plato matter is "sterile," "female in receptivity only, not in pregnancy . . . castrated of that impregnating power which belongs only to the unchangeably masculine."[32] Her read-

ing establishes the cosmogony of the Forms in the *Timaeus* as a phallic fantasy of a fully self-constituted patrilineality, and this fantasy of
autogenesis or self-constitution is effected through a denial and coop-
tation of the female capacity for reproduction. Of course, the "she"
who is the "receptacle" is neither a universal nor a particular, and
because for Plato anything that can be named is either a universal or a
particular, the receptacle cannot be named. Taking speculative license,
and wandering into what he himself calls "a strange and unwonted
inquiry" (48d), Plato nevertheless proceeds to name what cannot be
properly named, invoking a catachresis in order to describe the receptacle as a universal receiver of bodies even as it cannot be a universal,
for, if it were, it would be participate in those eternal realities from
which it is excluded.

In the cosmogony prior to the one that introduces the receptacle,
Plato suggests that if the appetites, those tokens of the soul's materiality, are not successfully mastered, a soul, understood as a man's soul,
risks coming back as a woman, and then as a beast. In a sense woman
and beast are the very figures for unmasterable passion. And if a soul
participates in such passions, it will be effectively and ontologically
transformed by them and into the very signs, woman and beast, by
which they are figured. In this prior cosmogony woman represents a
descent into materiality.

But this prior cosmogony calls to be rewritten, for if man is at the
top of an ontological hierarchy, and woman is a poor or debased copy
of man, and beast is a poor or debased copy of both woman and of man,
then there is still a *resemblance* between these three beings, even as that
resemblance is hierarchically distributed. In the following cosmogony,
the one that introduces the receptacle, Plato clearly wants to disallow
the possibility of a resemblance between the masculine and the feminine, and he does this through introducing a feminized receptacle that
is prohibited from resembling any form. Of course, strictly speaking,
the receptacle can have no ontological status, for ontology is constituted by forms, and the receptacle cannot be one. And we cannot speak
about that for which there is no ontological determination, or if we do,
we use language improperly, imputing being to that which can have no
being. So, the receptacle seems from the start to be an impossible word,
a designation that cannot be designated. Paradoxically, Plato proceeds
to tell us that this very receptacle must always be called the same.[33] Precisely because this receptacle can only occasion a radically improper
speech, that is, a speech in which all ontological claims are suspended,
the terms by which it is named must be consistently applied, not in
order to make the name fit the thing named but precisely because that

which is to be named can have no proper name, bounds and threatens the sphere of linguistic propriety, and, therefore, must be controlled by a forcibly imposed set of nominative rules.

How is it that Plato can concede the undesignatable status of this receptacle and prescribe for it a consistent name? Is it that the receptacle, designated as the undesignatable, *cannot* be designated, or is it rather that this "cannot" functions as an "ought not to be"? Should this limit to what is representable be read as a prohibition against a certain kind of representation? And since Plato does offer us a representation of the receptacle, one that he claims ought to remain a singularly authoritative representation (and makes this offer in the very same passage in which he claims its radical unrepresentability), ought we not to conclude that Plato, in authorizing a single representation of the feminine, means to prohibit the very proliferation of nominative possibilities that the undesignatable might produce? Perhaps this is a representation within discourse that functions to prohibit from discourse any further representation, one that represents the feminine as unrepresentable and unintelligible but that in the rhetoric of the constative claim defeats itself. After all, Plato *posits* that which he claims cannot be *posited*. And he further contradicts himself when he claims that that which cannot be posited ought to be posited in only one way. In a sense this authoritative naming of the receptacle as the unnameable constitutes a primary or founding inscription that secures this place as an inscriptional space. This naming of what cannot be named is itself a penetration into this receptacle that is at once a violent erasure, one that establishes it as an impossible yet necessary site for all further inscriptions.[34] In this sense the very *telling* of the story about the phallomorphic genesis of objects *enacts* that phallomorphosis and becomes an allegory of its own procedure.

Irigaray's response to this exclusion of the feminine from the economy of representation is effectively to say, Fine, I don't want to be in your economy anyway, and I'll show you what this unintelligible receptacle can do to your system; I will not be a poor copy in your system, but I will resemble you nevertheless by *miming* the textual passages through which you construct your system and showing that what cannot enter it is already inside it (as its necessary outside), and I will mime and repeat the gestures of your operation until this emergence of the outside within the system calls into question its systematic closure and its pretension to be self-grounding.

This is part of what Naomi Schor means when she claims that Irigaray mimes mimesis itself.[35] Through miming Irigaray transgresses the prohibition against resemblance at the same time that she refuses the notion of resemblance as copy. She cites Plato again and again, but the citations expose precisely what is excluded from them, and seek to show and to reintroduce the excluded into the system itself. In this sense she performs a repetition and displacement of the phallic economy. *This is citation, not as enslavement or simple reiteration of the original, but as an insubordination that appears to take place within the very terms of the original, and that calls into question the power of origination that Plato appears to claim for himself.* Her miming has the effect of repeating the origin only to displace that origin *as* an origin.

And insofar as the Platonic account of the origin is itself a *displacement* of a maternal origin, Irigaray merely mimes that very act of displacement, displacing the displacement, showing that origin to be an "effect" of a certain ruse of phallogocentric power. In line with this reading of Irigaray, then, the feminine as maternal does not offer itself as an alternative origin. For if the feminine is said to be anywhere or anything, it is that which is produced through displacement and returns as the possibility of a reverse displacement. Indeed, one might reconsider the conventional characterization of Irigaray as an uncritical maternalist, for here it appears that the reinscription of the maternal takes place by writing with and through the language of phallic philosophemes. This textual practice is not grounded in a rival ontology, but inhabits—indeed, penetrates, occupies, and redeploys—the paternal language itself.

One might well ask whether this kind of penetrative textual strategy does not suggest a different textualization of eroticism than the rigorously antipenetrative eros of surfaces that appears in Irigaray's "When Our Lips Speak Together": "You are not *in me.* I do not contain you or retain you in my stomach, my arms, my head. Nor in my memory, my mind, my language. You are there, like my skin."[36] The refusal of an eroticism of entry and containment seems linked for Irigaray with an opposition to appropriation and possession as forms of erotic exchange. And yet the kind of reading that Irigaray performs requires not only that she enter the text she reads, but that she work the inadvertent uses of that containment, especially when the feminine is sustained as an internal gap or fissure in the philosophical system itself. In such appropriative readings Irigaray appears to enact the very specter of a penetration in reverse—or a penetration elsewhere—that Plato's economy seeks to foreclose ("the 'elsewhere' of feminine pleasure can be found only at the price of *crossing back* (*retraversée*) through the mirror that subtends all speculation").[37] At the level of rhetoric this "crossing back" constitutes an eroticism that critically mimes the phallus—an eroticism

structured by repetition and displacement, penetration and exposure—
that counters the eros of surfaces Irigaray explicitly affirms.

The opening quotation of Irigaray's essay claims that philosophical
systems are built on "a break with material contiguity," and that the
concept of matter constitutes and conceals that rupture or cut (*la
coupure*). This argument appears to presume some order of contiguity
that is prior to the concept, prior to matter, and that matter works to
conceal. In Irigaray's most systematic reading of the history of ethical
philosophy, *Ethique de la différence sexuelle*, she argues that ethical relations ought to be based on relations of closeness, proximity, and intimacy that reconfigure conventional notions of reciprocity and respect.
Traditional conceptions of reciprocity exchange such relations of intimacy for those characterized by violent erasure, substitutability, and
appropriation.[38] Psychoanalytically, that material closeness is understood as the uncertain separation of boundaries between maternal body
and infant, relations that reemerge in language as the metonymic proximity of signs. Insofar as concepts, like matter and form, repudiate and
conceal the metonymic signifying chains from which they are composed, they serve the phallogocentric purpose of breaking with that
maternal/material contiguity. On the other hand, that contiguity confounds the phallogocentric effort to set up a series of substitutions
through metaphorical equivalences or conceptual unities.[39]

This contiguity that exceeds the concept of matter is, according to
Margaret Whitford, not itself a natural relation, but a *symbolic* articulation proper to women. Whitford takes "the two lips" as a figure for
metonymy,[40] "a figure for the vertical and horizontal relationships
between women . . . women's sociality."[41] But Whitford also points out
that feminine and masculine economies are never fully separable; as a
result, it seems, relations of contiguity subsist *between* those economies
and, hence, do not belong exclusively to the sphere of the feminine.

How, then, do we understand Irigaray's textual practice of lining up
alongside Plato? To what extent does she repeat his text, not to augment
its specular production, but to cross back over and through that specular mirror to a feminine "elsewhere" that must remain problematically
within citation marks?

There is for Irigaray, always, a matter that exceeds matter, where the
latter is disavowed for the autogenetic form/matter coupling to thrive.
Matter occurs in two modalities: first, as a metaphysical concept that
serves a phallogocentrism; second, as an ungrounded figure, worri-
somely speculative and catachrestic, that marks for her the possible linguistic site of a critical mime.

> To play with mimesis is thus, for a woman, to try to recover the place of her exploitation by discourse, without allowing herself to be simply reduced to it. It means to resubmit herself—inasmuch as she is on the side of the "perceptible," of "matter"—to "ideas," in particular to ideas about herself, that are elaborated in/by a masculine logic, but so as to make "visible," by an effect of playful repetition, what was supposed to remain invisible: the cover up of a possible operation of the feminine in language.[42]

So perhaps here is the return of essentialism, in the notion of a "feminine in language"? And yet, she continues by suggesting that *miming* is that very operation of the feminine in language. To mime means to participate in precisely that which is mimed, and if the language mimed is the language of phallogocentrism, then this is only a specifically feminine language to the extent that the feminine is radically implicated in the very terms of a phallogocentrism it seeks to rework. The quotation continues, "[to play with mimesis means] 'to unveil' the fact that, if women are such good mimics, it is because they are not simply resorbed in this function. *They also remain elsewhere*: another case of the persistence of 'matter.' " They mime phallogocentrism, but they also expose what is covered over by the mimetic self-replication of that discourse. For Irigaray what is broken with and covered over is the linguistic operation of metonymy, a closeness and proximity that appears to be the linguistic residue of the initial proximity of mother and infant. It is this metonymic excess in every mime, indeed, in every metaphorical substitution, that is understood to disrupt the seamless repetition of the phallogocentric norm.

To claim, though, as Irigaray does, that the logic of identity is potentially disruptible by the insurgence of metonymy, and then to identify this metonymy with the repressed and insurgent feminine, is to consolidate the place of the feminine in and as the irruptive *chora*, that which cannot be figured, but which is necessary for any figuration. That is, of course, to figure this *chora* nevertheless, and in such a way, that the feminine is "always" the outside and the outside is "always" the feminine. This is a move that at once positions the feminine as the unthematizable, the nonfigurable, but that, in identifying the feminine with that position, thematizes and figures, and so makes use of the phallogocentric exercise to produce this identity that "is" the nonidentical.

There are good reasons, however, to reject the notion that the feminine monopolizes the sphere of the excluded here. Indeed, to enforce such a monopoly redoubles the effect of foreclosure performed by the phallogocentric discourse itself, one that "mimes" its founding violence in a way that works against the explicit claim to have found a linguistic site in metonymy that works as disruption. After all, Plato's scenography of intelligibility depends on the exclusion of women, slaves, children, and animals, where slaves are characterized as those who do not speak his language, and who, in not speaking his language, are considered diminished in their capacity for reason. This xenophobic exclusion operates through the production of racialized Others, and those whose "natures" are considered less rational by virtue of their appointed task in the process of laboring to reproduce the conditions of private life. This domain of the less than rational human bounds the figure of human reason, producing that "man" as one who is without a childhood; is not a primate, and so relieved of the necessity of eating, defecating, living and dying; one who is not a slave, but always a property holder; one whose language remains originary and untranslatable. This is a figure of disembodiment, but one that is nevertheless a figure of a body, a bodying forth of a masculinized rationality, the figure of a male body that is not a body, a figure in crisis, a figure that enacts a crisis it cannot fully control. This figuration of masculine reason as disembodied body is one whose imaginary morphology is crafted through the exclusion of other possible bodies. This is a materialization of reason that operates through the dematerialization of other bodies, for the feminine, strictly speaking, has no morphe, no morphology, no contour, for it is that which contributes to the contouring of things but is itself undifferentiated, without boundary. The body that is reason dematerializes the bodies that may not properly stand for reason or its replicas, and yet this is a figure in crisis, for this body of reason is itself the phantasmatic dematerialization of masculinity, one that requires that women and slaves, children and animals be the body, perform the bodily functions, that it will not perform.[43]

Irigaray does not always help matters here, for she fails to follow through the metonymic link between women and these other Others, idealizing and appropriating the "elsewhere" as the feminine. But what is the "elsewhere" of Irigaray's "elsewhere"? If the feminine is not the only or primary kind of being that is excluded from the economy of masculinist reason, what and who is excluded in the course of Irigaray's analysis?

Improper Entry: Protocols of Sexual Difference

The above analysis has considered not the materiality of sex but the sex of materiality. In other words, it has traced materiality as the site at which a certain drama of sexual difference plays itself out. The point of such an exposition is not only to warn against an easy return to the *materiality* of the body or the materiality of sex but to show that to invoke matter is to invoke a sedimented history of sexual hierarchy and sexual erasures, which should surely be an *object* of feminist inquiry but would be quite problematic as a *ground* of feminist theory. To return to matter requires that we return to matter as a *sign* that in its redoublings and contradictions enacts an inchoate drama of sexual difference.

Let us then return to the passage in the *Timaeus* in which matter redoubles itself as a proper and improper term, differentially sexed, thereby conceding itself as a site of ambivalence, as a body that is no body, in its masculine form, as a matter that is no body, in its feminine.

The receptacle, she, "always receives all things, she never departs at all from her own nature and, never, in any way or any time, assumes a form like that of any of the things that enter into her" (50b). What appears to be prohibited here is partially contained by the verb *eile-phen*—to assume, as in to assume a form—which is at once a continuous action, but also a kind of receptivity. The term means, among other possibilities, to gain or procure, to take, to receive hospitality, but also *to have a wife*, and *of a woman to conceive.*[44] The term suggests a procurement, but also both a capacity to conceive and to take a wife. These activities or endowments are prohibited in the passage above, thus setting limits on the kinds of "receptivity" that this receiving principle can undertake. The term for what she is never to do (i.e., "depart from her own nature") is *existatai dynameos.* This implies that she ought never to arise out of, become separated from, or be *displaced from* her own nature; as that which is contained in itself, she is that which, quite literally, ought not to be *disordered in displacement.* The *siempre*, the "never," and the "in no way" are insistent repetitions that give this "natural impossibility" the form of an imperative, a prohibition, a legislation and allocation of proper place. What would happen if she began to resemble that which is said only and always to enter into her? Clearly, a set of positions is being secured here through the exclusive allocation of penetration to the form, and penetrability to a feminized materiality, and a full dissociation of this figure of penetrable femininity from the being resulting from reproduction.[45]

Irigaray clearly reads the "assume a form/shape" in this passage as "to conceive," and understands Plato to be prohibiting the feminine from contributing to the process of reproduction in order to credit the masculine with giving birth. But it seems that we might consider another sense of "to assume" in Greek, namely, "to have or take a wife."[46] For she will never resemble—and so never enter into—another materiality. This means that he—remember the Forms are likened to the father in this triad—will never be entered by her or, in fact, by anything. For he is the impenetrable penetrator, and she, the invariably penetrated. And "he" would not be differentiated from her were it not for this prohibition on resemblance that establishes their positions as mutually exclusive and yet complementary. In fact, if she were to penetrate in return, or penetrate elsewhere, it is unclear whether she could remain a "she" and whether "he" could preserve his own differentially established identity. For the logic of noncontradiction that conditions this distribution of pronouns is one that establishes the "he" through this exclusive position as penetrator and the "she" through this exclusive position as penetrated. As a consequence, then, without this heterosexual *matrix*, as it were, it appears that the stability of these gendered positions would be called into question.

One might read this prohibition that secures the impenetrability of the masculine as a kind of panic, a panic over becoming "like" her, effeminized, or a panic over what might happen if a masculine penetration of the masculine were authorized, or a feminine penetration of the feminine, or a feminine penetration of the masculine or a reversibility of those positions—not to mention a full-scale confusion over what qualifies as "penetration" anyway. Would the terms "masculine" and "feminine" still signify in stable ways, or would the relaxing of the taboos against stray penetration destabilize these gendered positions in serious ways? If it were possible to have a relation of penetration between two ostensibly feminine gendered positions, would this be the kind of resemblance that must be prohibited in order for Western metaphysics to get going? And would that be considered something like a co-optation and displacement of phallic autonomy that would undermine the phallic assurance over its own exclusive rights?

Is this a reverse mime that Irigaray does not consider, but that is nevertheless compatible with her strategy of a critical mime? Can we read this taboo that mobilizes the speculative and phantasmatic beginnings of Western metaphysics in terms of the specter of sexual exchange that it produces through its own prohibition, as a panic over the lesbian or, perhaps more specifically, the phallicization of the lesbian? Or would this kind of resemblance so disturb the compulsory gendered matrix that supports the order of things that one could not claim that these sexual exchanges that occur outside or in the interstices of the phallic economy are simply "copies" of the heterosexual origin? For, clearly, this legislation of a particular version of heterosexuality attests full well to its nonoriginary status. Otherwise there would be no necessity to install a prohibition at the outset against rival possibilities for the organization of sexuality. In this sense those improper resemblances or imitations that Plato rules out of the domain of intelligibility do not resemble the

•
•   masculine, for that would be to privilege the masculine as origin. If a
resemblance is possible, it is because the "originality" of the masculine
is contestable; in other words, the miming of the masculine, which is
never resorbed into it, can expose the masculine's claim to originality as
suspect. Insofar as the masculine is founded here through a prohibition
that outlaws the specter of a lesbian resemblance, that masculinist institution—and the phallogocentric homophobia it encodes—is *not* an
origin but only the *effect* of that very prohibition, fundamentally dependent on that which it must exclude.[47]

Significantly, this prohibition emerges at the site where materiality is
being installed as a double instance, as the copy of the Form, and as the
noncontributing materiality in which and through which that self-
copying mechanism works. In this sense matter is either part of the
specular scenography of phallic inscription or that which cannot be
rendered intelligible within its terms. The very formulation of matter
takes place in the service of an organization and denial of sexual difference, so that we are confronted with an economy of sexual difference as
that which defines, instrumentalizes, and allocates matter in its own
service.

The regulation of sexuality at work in the articulation of the Forms
suggests that sexual difference operates in the very formulation of matter. But this is a matter that is defined not only against reason, where
reason is understood as that which acts on and through a countervail-
ing materiality, and masculine and feminine occupy these oppositional
positions. Sexual difference also operates in the formulation, the staging, of what will occupy the site of inscriptional space, that is, as what
must remain outside these oppositional positions as their supporting
condition. There is no singular outside, for the Forms require a number of exclusions; they are and replicate themselves through what they
exclude, through not being the animal, not being the woman, not being
the slave; whose propriety is purchased through property, national and
racial boundary, masculinism, and compulsory heterosexuality.

To the extent that a set of reverse mimes emerge from those quarters,
they will not be the same as each other; if there is an occupation and
reversal of the master's discourse, it will come from many quarters, and
those resignifying practices will converge in ways that scramble the self-
replicating presumptions of reason's mastery. For if the copies speak, or
if what is merely material begins to signify, the scenography of reason is
rocked by the crisis on which it was always built. And there will be no
way finally to delimit the elsewhere of Irigaray's elsewhere, for every
oppositional discourse will produce its outside, an outside that risks
becoming installed as its nonsignifying inscriptional space.

And whereas this can appear as the necessary and founding violence of any truth regime, it is important to resist that theoretical gesture of pathos in which exclusions are simply affirmed as sad necessities of signification. The task is to refigure this necessary "outside" as a future horizon, one in which the violence of exclusion is perpetually in the process of being overcome. But of equal importance is the preservation of the outside, the site where discourse meets its limits, where the opacity of what is not included in a given regime of truth acts as a disruptive site of linguistic impropriety and unrepresentability, illuminating the violent and contingent boundaries of that normative regime precisely through the inability of the regime to represent that which might pose a fundamental threat to its continuity. In this sense radical and inclusive representability is not precisely the goal: to include, to speak as, to bring in every marginal and excluded position within a given discourse is to claim that a singular discourse meets its limits nowhere, that it can and will domesticate all signs of difference. If there is a violence necessary to the language of politics, then the risk of that violation might well be followed by another in which we begin, without ending, without mastering, to own—and yet never fully to own—the exclusions by which we proceed.

Formless Femininity

Awkwardly, it seems, Plato's phantasmatic economy virtually deprives the feminine of a *morphe*, a shape, for, as the receptacle, the feminine is a permanent and, hence, nonliving, shapeless nonthing which cannot be named. And as nurse, mother, womb, the feminine is synecdochally collapsed into a set of figural functions. In this sense Plato's discourse on materiality (if we can take the discourse on the *hypodoche* to be that) is one that does not permit the notion of the female body as a human form.

How can we legitimate claims of bodily injury if we put into question the materiality of the body? What is here enacted through the Platonic text is a violation that founds the very concept of matter, a violation that mobilizes the concept and that the concept sustains. Moreover, within Plato there is a disjunction between a materiality that is feminine and formless and, hence, without a body, and bodies that are formed through—but not of—that feminine materiality. To what extent in invoking received notions of materiality, indeed, in insisting that those notions function as "irreducibles," do we secure and perpetuate a constitutive violation of the feminine? When we consider that the very concept of matter preserves and recirculates a violation, and

- then invoke that very concept in the service of a compensation for vio-
- lation, we run the risk of reproducing the very injury for which we seek
redress.

The *Timaeus* does not give us bodies but only a collapse and displacement of those figures of bodily position that secure a given fantasy of heterosexual intercourse and male autogenesis. For the receptacle
is not a woman, but it is the figure that women become within the
dream world of this metaphysical cosmogony, one that remains largely
inchoate in the constitution of matter. It may be, as Irigaray appears to
suggest, that the entire history of matter is bound up with the problematic of receptivity. Is there a way to dissociate these implicit and disfiguring figures from the "matter" they help to compose? And insofar as
we have barely begun to discern the history of sexual difference encod-
ed in the history of matter, it seems radically unclear whether a notion
of matter or the materiality of bodies can serve as the uncontested
ground of feminist practice. In this sense the Aristotelian pun still
works as a reminder of the doubleness of the matter of matter, which
means that there may not be a materiality of sex that is not already bur-
dened by the sex of materiality.

NOTES •

This essay was originally written for this volume, but appeared first in Bodies
That Matter: On the Discursive Matter of "Sex" *(New York: Routledge, 1993).
I thank Naomi Schor for her thoughtful and helpful comments on earlier drafts.*

1. Gianni Vattimo, "Au delà de la matière et du texte," in *Matière et
    philosophie* (Paris: Centre Georges Pompidou, 1989), p. 5.
2. For a further discussion on how to make use of poststructuralism to
    think about the material injuries suffered by women's bodies, see the
    final section of my "Contingent Foundations: Feminism and the Ques-
    tion of Postmodernism" in Judith Butler and Joan Scott, eds., *Feminists
    Theorize the Political* (New York: Routledge, 1992), pp. 17–19; see also,
    in that same volume, Sharon Marcus, "Fighting Bodies, Fighting Words:
    A Theory and Politics of Rape Prevention," pp. 385–403.
3. Jacques Derrida, *Positions*, Alan Bass, ed. (Chicago: University of Chica-
    go, 1978), p. 64. On the following page, he writes: "I will not say
    whether the concept of matter is metaphysical or nonmetaphysical. This
    depends upon the work to which it yields, and you know that I have
    unceasingly insisted, as concerns the nonideal exteriority of the writing,
    the gram, the trace, the text, etc., upon the necessity of never separating

them from *work*, a value itself to be thought outside its Hegelian affiliations"(p. 65).

4. For a compelling analysis of how the form/matter distinction becomes
essential to the articulation of a masculinist politics, see Wendy Brown's
discussion of Machiavelli in *Manhood and Politics* (Totowa, N.J.: Row-
man and Littlefield, 1988), pp. 87–91.

5. See Marx's first thesis on Feuerbach, in which he calls for a materialism
that can affirm the practical activity that structures and inheres in the
object as part of that object's objectivity and materiality: "The chief defect
of all previous materialism (including Feuerbach's) is that the object, actuality, sensuousness is conceived only in the form of the *object or perception*
(*Anschauung*), but not as *sensuous human activity, practice* (*Praxis*), not
subjectively" (Karl Marx, *Writings of the Young Marx on Philosophy and
Society*, trans. Lloyd D. Easton and Kurt H. Guddat [New York: Double-
day, 1967], p. 400). If materialism were to take account of praxis as that
which constitutes the very matter of objects, and praxis is understood as
socially transformative activity, then such activity is understood as constitutive of materiality itself. The activity proper to *praxis*, however, requires
the transformation of some object from a former state to a latter state,
usually understood as its transformation from a natural to a social state,
but also understood as a transformation of an alienated social state to a
nonalienated social state. In either case, according to this new kind of
materialism that Marx proposes, the object is not only transformed, but in
some significant sense, the object *is* transformative activity itself and, further, its materiality is established through this temporal movement from a
prior to a latter state. In other words, the object *materializes* to the extent
that it is a site of *temporal transformation*. The materiality of objects, then,
is in no sense static, spatial, or given, but is constituted in and as transformative activity. For a fuller elaboration of the temporality of matter, see
also Ernst Bloch, *The Principle of Hope*, trans. Neville Plaice, Stephen
Plaice, and Paul Knight (Cambridge: MIT Press, 1986); Jean-François
Lyotard, *The Inhuman: Reflections on Time*, trans. Geoffrey Bennington
and Rachel Bowlby, (Cambridge: Polity Press, 1991), pp. 8–23.

6. Aristotle, "De Anima," *The Basic Works of Aristotle*, trans. Richard
McKeon (New York: Random House, 1941), book 2, chapter 1,
412a10, p. 555. Subsequent citations from Aristotle will be from this
edition and to standard paragraph numbering only.

7. See Thomas Laqueur, *Making Sex: Body and Gender from the Greeks to
Freud* (Cambridge: Harvard University Press, 1990), p. 28; G.E.R. Lloyd,
Science, Folklore, Ideology, (Cambridge: Cambridge University Press,
1983). See also Evelyn Fox Keller, *Reflections on Gender and Science*
(New Haven: Yale University Press, 1985); Mary O'Brien, *The Politics of
Reproduction* (London: Routledge, 1981).

8. Aristotle, "De Anima," book 2, chapter 1, 412b7–8.

9. Foucault, *The History of Sexuality* (Harmondsworth: Penguin), volume 1,

•
•
    p. 152. Original: "Non pas donc 'histoire des mentalités' qui ne tiendrait compte des corps que par la manière dont on les a aperçus ou dont on leur a donné sens et valeur; mais 'histoire des corps' et de la manière dont on a *investi* ce qu'il y a de plus *matériel*, de plus vivant en eux." *Histoire de la sexualité 1: La volonté de savoir* (Paris: Gallimard, 1978), p. 200.

10. Foucault, *Discipline and Punish: The Birth of the Prison* (New York: Pantheon, 1977), p. 30. Original: "L'homme dont on nous parle et qu'on invite à libérer est déjà en lui-même l'effet d'un assujettissement bien plus profond que lui. Une 'âme' l'habite et le porte à l'existence, qui est elle-même une pièce dans la maîtrise que le pouvoir exerce sur le corps. L'âme, effet et instrument d'une anatomie politique; l'âme, prison du corps." Foucault, *Surveiller et punir* (Paris: Gallimard, 1975) p. 34.

11. "What was at issue was not whether the prison environment was too harsh or too aseptic, too primitive or too efficient, but its very materiality as an instrument and vector of power [c'était sa matérialité dans la mesure où elle est instrument et vecteur de pouvoir]," *Discipline and Punish*, p. 30 (*Surveiller et punir*, p. 35).

12. This is not to make "materiality" into the effect of a "discourse" that is its cause; rather it is to displace the causal relation through a reworking of the notion of "effect." Power is established in and through its effects, where these effects are the dissimulated workings of power itself. There is no "power," taken as a substantive, that has dissimulation as one of its attributes or modes. This dissimulation operates through the constitution and formation of an epistemic field and set of "knowers"; when this field and these subjects are taken for granted as prediscursive givens, the dissimulating effect of power has succeeded. Discourse designates the site at which power is installed as the historically contingent formative power of things within a given epistemic field. The production of material effects is the formative or constitutive workings of power, a production that cannot be construed as a unilateral movement from cause to effect. "Materiality" appears only when its status as contingently constituted through discourse is erased, concealed, covered over. Materiality is the dissimulated effect of power.

    Foucault's claim that power is materializing, that it is the production of material effects, is specified in *Discipline and Punish* in the materiality of the body. If "materiality" is an effect of power, a site of transfer between power relations, then insofar as this transfer is the subjection/subjectivation of the body, the principle of this *assujettissement* is "the soul." Taken as a normative/normalizing ideal, the "soul" functions as the formative and regulatory principle of this material body, the proximate instrumentality of its subordination. The soul renders the body uniform; disciplinary regimes train the body through a sustained repetition of rituals of cruelty that produce over time the gestural stylistics of the imprisoned body. In *The History of Sexuality*, volume 1, "sex" operates to produce a uniform body along different axes of power, but "sex" as well as "the soul" are understood to subjugate and subjectivate the body, produce an enslavement, as it were, as the very principle of the body's cultural formation. It is in this sense that materialization can be described as the sedimenting effect of a regulated iterability.

13. An ideology always exists in an apparatus, and its practice, or practices. This existence is material.

> Of course, the material existence of the ideology in an apparatus and its practices does not have the same modality as the material existence of a paving-stone or a rifle. But, at the risk of being taken for a Neo-Aristotelian (NB Marx had a very high regard for Aristotle), I shall say that "matter is discussed in many senses," or rather that it exists in different modalities, all rooted in the last instance in "physical" matter.

Louis Althusser, "Ideology and Ideological State Apparatuses (Notes Towards an Investigation)," in *Lenin and Philosophy and Other Essays* (New York: Monthly Review Press, 1971), p. 166; first published in *La Pensée*, 1970.

14. See Irigaray, *An Ethics of Sexual Difference*.

15. Bridget McDonald argues that for Irigaray "the *entre* is the site of difference where uniformity becomes divided . . . every *entre* is a shared space where differentiated poles are not only differentiated, but are also subject to meeting one another in order to exist as differentiated." "Between Envelopes," unpublished manuscript.

16. For a discussion of a notion of an "interval" that is neither exclusively space nor time, see Irigaray's reading of Aristotle's *Physics*, "Place, Interval," *Ethics*, pp. 34–55/"Le Lieu, l'intervalle," *Ethique*, pp. 41–62.

17. See Elizabeth Spelman, "Woman as Body: Ancient and Contemporary Views," *Feminist Studies* (1982), pp. 8(1):109–131.

18. See Elizabeth Weed's "The Question of Style," this volume; and Elizabeth Grosz, *Sexual Subversions* (London: Routledge, 1991).

19. This is my translation even though it is clear that Irigaray in the following uses the term for "being" [*être*] and not for "essence" [*essence*] based on the sense of the subsequent sentence, in which the notion of an "essence" remains foreign to the feminine, and the final sentence, in which the truth of that being is wrought through an oppositional logic: "Elle ne se constitue pas pour autant en *une*. Elle ne se referme pas sur ou dans une vérité ou une essence. L'essence d'une vérité lui reste étrangère. Elle n'a ni n'est un être. Et elle n'oppose pas, à la vérité masculine, une vérité féminine," Irigaray, *Amante marine*, p. 92; "She does not set herself up as the *one*, as a (single) female unit. She is not closed up or around one single truth or essence. The essence of a truth remains foreign to her. She neither has nor is a being. And she does not oppose a feminine truth to a masculine truth," Irigaray, *Marine Lover*, p. 86.

•
•   Given Naomi Schor's reading of "essence" as itself a catachresis, one
         might ask whether the discourse of essence cannot be redoubled outside
         of traditional metaphysical proprieties. Then the feminine could well
         enjoy an essence, but that enjoyment would be at the expense of meta-
         physics. Naomi Schor, "This Essentialism Which is Not One: Coming
         to Grips With Irigaray," this volume.
    20. Jane Gallop, *Thinking Through the Body* (New York: Columbia Universi-
         ty Press, 1988).
    21. Strictly speaking, matter as *hyle* does not figure centrally in the Platonic
         corpus. The term *hyle* is for the most part Aristotelian. In the *Metaphysics*
         (1036a), Aristotle claims that *hyle* can only be known through analogy. It
         is defined as potency (*dynamis*), and is isolated as one of the four causes; it
         is also described as the principle of individuation. In Aristotle it is some-
         times identified with the *hypokeimenon* (*Physics*, 1:192a), but it is not con-
         sidered a thing. Although Aristotle faults Plato for failing to differentiate
         between *hyle* and *steresis* (privation), he nevertheless identifies the Platonic
         notion of the receptacle (*hypodoche*) with *hyle* (*Physics*, 4:209b). Like Aris-
         totelian *hyle*, the *hypodoche* is indestructible, can only be known by means
         of "bastard reasoning" (*Timaeus*, 52a–b), and is that for which no defini-
         tion can be given ("there is no definition of matter, only of *eidos*" *[Meta-
         physics*, 1035b]). In Plato *hypodoche* takes on the meaning of place or
         chora. It is only once Aristotle supplies an explicit philosophical discourse
         on matter that Plotinus writes a reconstruction of the Platonic doctrine of
         matter. This then becomes the occasion for Irigaray's critical rereading of
         Plato/Plotinus in "Une Mère de glace" in *Speculum*, pp. 168–179.
    22. Derrida, *Positions*, p. 64.
    23. All citations will be to the standard paragraph number and to *Plato: The
         Collected Dialogues*, Edith Hamilton and Huntington Cairns eds., Bollin-
         gen Series 71 (Princeton: Princeton University Press, 1961).
    24. In the *Theatetus dechomenon* is described as a "bundle of wax," so Aristo-
         tle's choice of the "wax" image in "*De Anima*" to describe matter might
         be read as an explicit reworking of the Platonic *dechomenon*.
    25. Here *diaschematizomenon* brings together the senses of "to be modeled
         after a pattern" and "formation," suggesting the strong sense in which
         schemas are formative. Plato's language prefigures Aristotle's formulation
         in this specific respect.
    26. For a discussion on how *physis* or *phusis* meant genitals, see John J. Win-
         kler's discussion, "*Phusis* and *Natura* Meaning 'Genitals,' " in *The Con-
         straints of Desire: The Anthropology of Sex and Gender in Ancient Greece*
         (New York: Routledge, 1990), pp. 217–220.
    27. This very opposition insists upon the *materiality* of language; what some
         will call the materiality of the signifier is what Derrida proposes to do in
         "Chora," *Poikilia. Etudes offertes à Jean-Pierre Vernant* (Paris, EHESS,
         1987). To call attention, however, to that word's materiality would not
         be sufficient, for the point is to gesture toward that which is neither

material nor ideal, but, as the inscriptional space in which that distinction occurs, is neither/nor. It is the neither/nor that enables the logic of
either/or, which takes idealism and materialism as its two poles.

Derrida refers to this inscriptional space as a third gender or genre,
which he associates on page 280 of the above text with a "neutral space";
neutral because participating in neither pole of sexual difference, masculine, feminine. Here the receptacle is precisely what destabilizes the distinction between masculine and feminine. Consider the way that this inscriptional space is described, especially how the act of inscription works on it:
"in a third genre/gender and in the neuter space of a place without place, a
place where everything marks it, but which in itself is not marked." Later,
on p. 281, Socrates will be said to resemble Chora inasmuch as he is someone or something. "In every case, he takes his place, which is not a place
among others, but perhaps *place itself*, the irreplaceable. Irreplaceable, and
implacable place." (my translation).

The polarity of idealism/materialism has come under question.

But that is not to claim that there are no future questions. For what
do we make of Irigaray's claim that for Plato, the inscriptional space is a
way of figuring and disfiguring femininity, a way of muting the feminine, and recasting it as mute, passive surface. Recall that for Plato the
receptacle receives all things, is that through which a certain penetrative
generativity works, but that itself can neither penetrate or generate. In
this sense the receptacle can be read as a guarantee that there will be no
destabilizing mimesis of the masculine, and the feminine will be perma-
nently secured as the infinitely penetrable. This move is repeated in Derrida in his references to "the place without place where everything marks
it, but which in itself is not marked." Have we discovered here the
unmarked condition of all inscription, that which can have no mark of
its own, no proper mark, precisely because it is that which, excluded
from the proper, makes the proper possible? Or is this unmarked inscriptional space one whose mark has been erased, and is under compulsion
to remain under permanent erasure?

"She (is) nothing other than the sum or the process of that which
inscribes itself 'on' her, 'à son sujet, à même son sujet,' " but she is not
the *subject* or the *present support* of all these interpretations, and she does
not reduce to these interpretations. That which exceeds any interpretation, but which is itself not any interpretation. This description does not
explain, however, why there is this prohibition against interpretation
here? Is this not perhaps a virgin spot in or outside of the territory of
metaphysics?

Although here Derrida wants to claim that the receptacle cannot be
matter, in *Positions* he confirms that matter can be used "twice," and that
in its redoubled effect, it can be precisely that which *exceeds* the
form/matter distinction. But here, where matter and mater are linked,
where there is a question of a materiality invested with femininity, and

- then subjected to an erasure, the receptacle cannot be matter, for that
- would be to reinstall it in the binarism from which it is excluded.

28. See Julia Kristeva, "The Semiotic *Chora* Ordering the Drives," in *Revolution in Poetic Language* (New York: Columbia University Press, 1984); abridged and translated version of *La révolution du langage poétique* (Paris: Seuil, 1974).

29. For a very interesting discussion of the topography of reproduction in Plato and for a generally interesting comparison of psychoanalytic and classical thinking, see Page DuBois, *Sowing the Body* (Chicago: University of Chicago Press, 1988).

30. Irigaray makes a similar argument in "La Croyance même" ("Belief Itself") in the course of rereading the fort-da scene in Freud's *Beyond the Pleasure Principle.* In that text she offers a brilliant rereading of the action of imaginary mastery effected by the little boy in repeatedly throwing his spool into the crib and retrieving the spool as a way of rehearsing the departures and returns of his mother. Irigaray charts the scenography of this masterful play and locates the substitute for the maternal in the curtains, the folds of the bed linen that receive, hide, and return the spool. Like the *chora,* "she"—the dissimulated maternal support for the scene— is the absent but necessary condition for the play of presence and absence: "Elle y était et n'y était pas, elle donnait lieu mais n'avait pas lieu, sauf son ventre et encore. . . . Elle n'y était pas d'ailleurs, sauf dans cette incessante transfusion de vie entre elle et lui, par un fil creux. Elle donne la possibilité de l'entrée en présence mais n'y a pas lieu" (p. 31).

31. *Plotinus' Enneads*, trans. Stephen MacKenna, 2d ed. (London: Faber and Faber, 1956).

32. Irigaray, "Une Mère de glace," in *Speculum*, p. 179/224.

33. Irigaray makes a similar argument about the *cave* as inscriptional space in *Speculum*. She writes, "The cave is the representation of something always already there, of the original matrix/womb which these men cannot represent," p. 244/302.

34. My thanks to Jen Thomas for helping me to think this through.

35. Naomi Schor, "This Essentialism Which Is Not One: Coming to Grips with Irigaray," this volume.

36. Luce Irigaray, "When Our Lips Speak Together," *This Sex*, p. 216/*Ce sexe*, p. 215.

37. *This Sex*, p. 77/*Ce sexe*, p. 75.

38. For readings in feminist ethical philosophy that reformulate Irigaray's position in very interesting ways, see Drucilla Cornell, *Beyond Accomodation: Ethical Feminism, Deconstruction, and the Law* (New York: Routledge, 1991); and Gayatri Chakravorty Spivak, "French Feminism Revisited: Ethics and Politics," in *Feminists Theorize the Political*, pp. 54–85.

39. Contiguous relations disrupt the possibility of the enumeration of the sexes, i.e., the first and second sex. Figuring the feminine as/through the contiguous thus implicitly contests the hierarchical binarism of mascu-

line/feminine. This opposition to the quantification of the feminine is an implicit argument with Lacan's *Encore: Le séminaire Livre XX* (Paris: Seuil, 1975). It constitutes one sense in which the feminine "is not one." See Irigaray, *Marine Lover*, pp. 86–87/*Amante marine*, pp. 92–93.

40. Margaret Whitford, *Luce Irigaray: Philosophy in the Feminine* (London: Routledge, 1991), p. 177.

41. Ibid., pp. 180–181.

42. Irigaray, "The Power of Discourse" in *This Sex*, p. 76/ *Ce Sexe*, p. 74.

43. Donna Haraway, responding to an earlier draft of this paper in a hot tub in Santa Cruz, suggested that it is crucial to read Irigaray as reinforcing Plato as the origin of Western representation. Referring to the work of Martin Bernal, Haraway argues that the "West" and its "origins" are constructed through a suppression of cultural heterogeneity, in particular, the suppression of African cultural exchange and influence. Haraway may be right, but Irigaray's point is to expose the violent production of the European "origins" in Greece, and so is not incompatible with the view Haraway outlines. My suggestion is that this violence is remaindered within the Platonic doctrine as the "site" of representational inscription and that one way to read Plato and Irigaray for their founding exclusions is by asking what becomes stored in that receptacle.

44. H. G. Liddell and Robert Scott, *Greek-English Lexicon* (Oxford: Oxford University Press, 1957).

45. It is important to raise a cautionary note against too quickly reducing sexual positions of active penetration and passive receptivity with masculine and feminine positions within the ancient Greek context. For an important argument against such a conflation, see David Halperin, *One Hundred Years of Homosexuality* (New York: Routledge, 1990), p. 30.

46. What follows may be an overreading, as some of my classicist readers have suggested.

47. Diotima attempts to explain to an apparently witless Socrates that heterosexual procreation not only contains but produces the effects of immortality, thus linking heterosexual procreation with the production of timeless truths. See *The Symposium*, 206b-208b. Of course, this speech needs also to be read in the rhetorical context of the dialogue that might be said to assert this heterosexual norm only later in order to produce its male homosexual contestation.

· *Jean-Joseph Goux*

LUCE IRIGARAY

VERSUS THE

UTOPIA OF THE

NEUTRAL SEX

In a little-known utopia, written at the beginning of the twentieth century (and published in 1905), Anatole France imagines that his hero visits the Paris area in the year 2270. Everything is provided for, and amply: the "European Federation" has been installed for 220 years, the sky is crowded with "flying machines," money, of course, no longer exists, replaced by work "vouchers," the factories run more or less automatically, supervised by a few rare workers (who drink alcohol-free beer), towns have disappeared thanks to the rapidity of communications and the "wireless telephone," statistics have replaced history, food comes in tablet form (it has by now become common practice to have the large intestine removed)—in short, there has been a bloodless transition from capitalist anarchy to "collectivism," and only one soldier remains, since "one only has to press a button to destroy an army of 500,000 men," etc. . . . Thus, already in 1905, at a moment of decisive technological advance whose effects are still with us today, Anatole France looked into the new world of the future with a forebod-

•
•
ing prescience whose clairvoyance can still (or perhaps only now) be recognized.

Now the question of the difference between the sexes in this utopia is not without interest. One might even say, perhaps, that it is the most incisive and the most disturbing aspect of this imaginary society of the future. In the European Federation of 2270 equality between the sexes has been an undisputed achievement for a long time. It is no longer presented as a recent victory that still needs to be justified, as in Etienne Cabet's *Voyage en Icarie* (1840). But we seem to be heading toward a disquieting limit.

In the dreams of the slumbering hero how is this anticipated world represented? What does he discover about the difference between the sexes, about the relation between women and men, the family, love? Curiously, in this world of the future, we discover the dominance of what Luce Irigaray has called "the neutralization of sex,"[1] or "gender neutralization,"[2] which leads in fact to the "masculine neutral"[3] that she denounces as putting us, "individually and collectively, in danger of death."[4] In *Sur la pierre blanche* we find a very precise anticipation of the neutral sex.

In 2270 the difference between the sexes has almost disappeared. The narrator, visiting the banks of the Seine (whose course has changed), realizes only gradually that some of the "men" surrounding him are women. For they are all similarly dressed, and, on closer inspection, "the women are mostly androgynous in appearance."[5] What has happened over the last three hundred years? Just as it was necessary to explain patiently to Hippolyte Dufresne (the time traveler) how economic exchanges work in a society that has lost "even the memory of the circulation of money,"[6] he now has to be told how a society functions without a socially significant sexual difference. Comrade Perceval, the Diotima of the new era, provides the clinching information: "In order to show you how the sexual question is regulated in our society, Hippolyte, let me tell you that in many factories, the labor contractor does not even ask whether one is a man or a woman. A person's sex is of no concern to the collectivity."[7] This is the ruling principle of the new order. Contrary to all the rather barbaric, archaic, and prehistoric prejudices that characterized the "old order" now past, the progress of equality leads to this provision: "A person's sex is of no concern to the collectivity." But such a surprising declaration demands a longer explanation. The latter is provided by Comrade Chéron—another woman (somewhat neuter in appearance), with "an air of tranquil curiosity and casual amusement"—who is described later on by the narrator as looking like a young boy.[8]

As far as sexual character is concerned we have views which were unthinkable for the primitive simplicity of the men of the old order. From the fact that there are two sexes, and only two sexes, for a long time false consequences were drawn. It was concluded that a woman is a woman absolutely and a man is a man absolutely. Reality is not like this, there are women who are extremely feminine and women who are hardly feminine at all. These differences, which were formerly concealed by dress and lifestyle, and masked by prejudice, appear clearly in our society. That is not all; they become more marked and more apparent with each generation. Since women have been working like men, acting and thinking like men, we now see many women who look like men. *One day perhaps we will succeed in creating "workers" without sex,* just like the bees. It will be a great advantage: we will be able to increase the work force without increasing the population disproportionately in relation to needs.[9]

Is it not remarkable that the nuances of sexual difference and the egalitarian move to diminish the difference between the sexes should lead, in this imaginary future, to an evolution in the direction of a sexual neutralization? Which is, to be more precise, that of a masculine neuter? What is foreshadowed here is the direction of sexual egalitarianism. It is significant that feminization should never be truly envisaged in this imaginary future. And no doubt there are very deep-seated reasons for this, partly connected to the author of course, but connected far more to the inexorable logic of his extrapolation. The effect is that in this world of triumphant technology, of the so-called neutral sex, it is women who are destined to disappear, not men. If, in this society, "a person's sex is of no concern to the collectivity," and if as a result "the collectivity takes absolutely no cognizance of issues concerning the relation between the sexes,"[10] it is in the end only women who lose their distinctive characteristics and their difference. Most significantly, Anatole France is silent on the movement in the other direction. It is in the end women who wear men's "clothes," which makes them indistinguishable from their male comrades. Equality can be conceived in this historical imagination only as equality with men, in the evolution toward the hegemony of the masculine-neutral (and not as a genuine generalized androgyny).

No doubt it would be too simple (although not a priori ruled out, of course) to attribute this account to a secret or unconscious misogyny on the part of the author, or even (though this is a more likely explanation) to attribute it to the fact that it is more difficult to represent the feminization of men than the masculinization of women (the term *representation* is crucial here). The phenomenon the author foregrounds

•
•   (against an economic and technological background) is, in fact, the disappearance of women, their evolution toward neutralization, or more
precisely, their gradual metamorphosis into the masculine-neutral: this
is more than a prejudice, it is the immanent logic of modernity, or
rather of ultramodernity.

We should not read too much into this interpretation. It has no particular claim to authority as an account of reality. It is a futurist construction—a hypothesis about the future—and we could invent others.
However, the extent to which this hypothesis resonates with the contemporary conjuncture is striking. For this reason I did not think it was
a detour to approach the implications of Luce Irigaray's work via this
fiction; it seemed to me, rather, the best way of addressing the issue
directly. The fiction is an early illustration of an uneasiness, which,
until recently, might have been thought of as suspect (and taken for a
disguised objection to a legitimate trend toward equality) but nowadays
appears in quite a different light.

What is the genealogy of this uneasiness? How have we passed from
the age-old prejudices (with their structural mechanisms) that claim to
legitimate (and institute) patriarchal and male dominance, to modern
egalitarian claims (which, despite the difficulties, and the vagaries of
numerous local struggles, can be said, at least in principle, to be in the
process of winning), and from there to the horizon of the masculine-
neutral, which disturbs some men and women to such an extent that it
is becoming the target of a new assault? It is this process that I would
like to clarify here, in order to situate more clearly the contemporary
implications of Luce Irigaray's work.

To legitimate social domination through the immutable decrees of
nature, or through the dignity of an eternal essence, is perhaps the ideological gesture par excellence. There exists an unchanging order, willed
by God, or in conformity with the nature of things. Human beings, fee-
ble creatures or infinitesimal cogs in the machine of the world, can only
bow to this order, or succumb. There are great and small, rich and poor,
kings and subjects. One can find an unambiguous formulation of this
philosophy in Fénelon, who represents (if one takes account of the
more tolerant of his writings) the moderate wing:

> To violate the rights of established subordination is a crime against the
> divine right of kings; to desire to overthrow the superiority of rank, to
> reduce men to an imaginary equality, to envy the fortune and the dig-
> nity of others, not to resign oneself to the mediocrity and the lowliness
> of one's estate, is to blaspheme against Providence, and threaten the
> rights of the sovereign father and head of the family, who gives to each

of his children his allotted place. This is the certain and immutable foundation of all legitimate authority.[11]

This sums up in a nutshell the patriarchal philosophy of the political power of the Ancien Régime. The "established order" takes on here its strong, transcendental meaning, which is not simply a question of public authority but of theology. God, "sovereign father and head of the family," has willed the just order of the world, which it is criminal to aspire to change. Its subordinations, its principles of authority are justified by reference to a supreme authority that is manifest through them. For "there is only one original source of all authority, which is found in our natural dependence on God's sovereignty."[12] Fénelon does not mention women. He does not need to. A subject can become a king, a poor man can become rich. But a woman can do no more than remain a woman, which means, according to Saint Paul, accept a master.

Faced with the ancestral power of such a theological immobilism, which legitimates the established order with reference to the eternity of essences and the impenetrable mystery of God's decrees, one can understand the suspicion of everything that would seek to preserve the condition of men and women against change, and turn it into a destiny that neither initiative, choice, or freedom can affect. If this providential theology, which was opposed to any possibility of "overthrowing the superiority of rank" and "reducing men to an imaginary equality" was designed to put down in advance any insurrection, claim, or revolution, we can understand how the assertion of its opposite, which would free human beings from their subjection, can retain its enduring power of contestation. At the opposite historical pole from Fénelon, who posits that man "is neither his own master nor his own law,"[13] we could situate the work of Sartre, a kind of postrevolutionary end point of a long struggle for freedom and autonomy. In Sartre's exemplary work the human being, pure consciousness springing forth from nothing, has no preestablished definition: "There is no human nature, since there is no God to conceive it."[14]

The entire modernist claim for freedom and equality rebels—rightly—against essentialist theology. It is the specter of this medieval or (premodern) monarchical immutability, prescribing for everyone their rank, their condition, and their function in a hierarchical universe willed into being by God the Father, that still seems to haunt, sometimes unbeknownst to them, those who seek their subversive resources in an intransigent affirmation of equality. One might say that, as far as the question of the sexes is concerned, this modernist claim goes from

·   Poulain de la Barre, influenced by Cartesian rationalism in his *De l'égal-*
· *ité des deux sexes* (1673), to Simone de Beauvoir, influenced by existentialism, which is the logical end point of antiessentialism.

It may be that this modernist phase is today coming to a close. The
immense historical distance separating us from this world of fixed hierarchy, the speed of social transformations, the obsolescence of the concept of divinely ordained authority, all this reassures feminism that the
old order will not return (and, in fact, it lacks any basis in the social philosophy of liberal capitalism or the generalized market economy).
Instead of falling back on a claim that the rapid current of History has
rendered more and more obsolete, feminist demands now have the
chance to go deeper, become more refined, precisely address the real
danger that threatens women and sexuation. One might go so far as to
say: essentialism is no longer a danger, for it is no longer even thinkable.
What is taken to be essentialism has no longer anything in common
with what gave it its metaphysicosocial force. In a world dominated by
the market and the media, governed by a generalized equivalence (of
persons, signs, goods) and the inconvertibility of circulating values,
something completely different is at stake.

Thus, the conviction emanating more and more from Luce Irigaray's
texts is that we are now "at a different stage of History."[15] If there was a
time for egalitarian claims—whose achievements cannot be forgotten—it is now "the time of difference," to quote the title of her 1990
publication. What Irigaray reveals is that the egalitarian claim, which
seemed as though it ought to threaten the modern system of male domination, is no longer adequate to challenge it. Furthermore, without
intending it, egalitarian claims are complicit with the deep logic of this
domination. Nowadays it is the limits and the dangers of egalitarianism
(and not, of course, its achievements) that must be denounced:
woman's dispossession within a male unisex (or masculine-neutral)
order that destroys her, the mutilating and repressive "totalitarianism"
of egalitarian slogans, the deathly obliteration of sexuation, these are all
signs of the danger. In short, the freedom "to acquire rights within a
male, unisex order is merely a superficial freedom which has already
exiled woman from herself, and has already deprived her of any specific identity."[16] Hence a new feminism that is no longer just feminism.
This philosophy of sexuation has already taken note of the results and
the consequences of egalitarianism; it draws the conclusions, some of
which are negative—and even felt, in the long term, to be catastroph-
ic. The emancipatory universe of the equality of the sexes has become
an anti-utopia. We have gone from Cabet, Flora Tristan, and Engels to
Huxley and Orwell. What we see today is not a total failure (for certain

achievements remain as conditions of the next stage) but the other and
dangerous side of the egalitarian quest. Without wishing to exaggerate,
one might see the movement here as "dialectical" in a Hegelian sense,
and see in Luce Irigaray's recent explorations the *sublation* of the egalitarian phase of feminism by a differentialist phase. Egalitarianism is
now no more than a moment "conserved and overcome" by the following phase. For an "analysis of the claims to equality shows that at the
level of a superficial culture critique, they are well founded, but that as
a means of liberating women, they are utopian."[17] Without the succeeding phase there will be disaster. Irigaray becomes apocalyptic here.
Against the apostles of the "neutralization of sex" she proclaims unhesi-
tatingly that "to wish to suppress sexual difference is to call for a genocide more radical than any previous destruction in History."[18] The battle is urgent, decisive.

For Luce Irigaray, as we can see, the indisputable fact—simultaneously biological and cultural—of the division of the human species into
two kinds, feminine and masculine, is *not* the primitive and shameful
residue of humanity's animal origins, an ancient, prehistorical vestige, a
regressive prejudice from the days before the constitutional state, a
nominalist illusion, a repressive superstition imposed by a male conspiracy, or even a pre-68 misconception to be demolished. In this division lies the fate of the future of the world: either a totalitarian neutralization (in an asexual universe of human ants) or a different culture, in
which contradiction, the drama of sexual alterity, will be an
undreamed-of power of creation.

In short, Luce Irigaray clarifies two confusions in current discourses:
1. To overthrow patriarchal and phallocentric power does *not* mean
denying the difference between the sexes but living the relation between
them differently; 2. To assert the difference between the sexes is *not* at
all the same thing as positing an essential femininity (or masculinity).
Luce Irigaray's differentialism cannot be equated purely and simply
with an essentialism. What remains, and will continue to remain, is the
difference between the masculine and the feminine, but that is not to
draw any conclusions in advance about what that masculine and feminine might historically and culturally become. It is sexuation that is
"essential," not the content of dogmas fixing once and for all, in an
exhaustive and closed definition, what for eternity belongs to the masculine and what belongs to the feminine. Although this infinite, open
difference is necessarily supported by a dimorphism provided for us by
nature (and that cannot be denied or thwarted without danger), it is
also a constructed difference, which must be constantly constructed,
reconstructed, cultivated. The deconstruction of this difference does

•
•

    not dispense us from its permanent reconstruction in civil and civilized life. In this sense it is as if Luce Irigaray might also, in her own right, be subscribing to Simone de Beauvoir's famous dictum: "One is not born, but rather becomes, a woman."[19] But the voice is different. Woman's being is acquired, won, determined, invented, produced, created. Not by totally denying its biological preconditions (which would be both absurd and dangerous—not to say unjustified in its complicity with an ancient patriarchal ideology that has devalued in advance this natural substratum), but through an elaboration of the sexuate.

    Thus, for Luce Irigaray becoming-woman is a creative value, no longer a metaphysical or historical curse. In a strategic reversal it is now egalitarianism that is interpreted as the ultimate ruse of masculine supremacy.

    Not only is there something suicidal in the prospect of pure and simple disappearance of all sexual difference (a principle of death, chaos, entropy), but the prospect of such a disappearance is perhaps the extreme form of a kind of rationalizing utopia that is precisely the worst expression of the extravagance of masculine intellectualism. Such an idea can only find its driving force within the perspective of an exorbitant Cartesianism—which aspires to build everything from scratch, through force of intellect, by mastering, denying, doing violence to unknowable Nature, making her give up her secrets by force—and thus within the perspective of a masculine voluntarism carried to its most extreme and most sacrilegious presumption.

    For a woman to give up her sexuate identity "represents the greatest possible submission to masculine culture."[20] Unwittingly egalitarian claims belong to a project that can only ensure the perpetuation of subjection—not subordination to individuals but dispossession by masculine culture—by a structure, an order, a system. In this unisex world the overwhelming and, before long, exclusive genre would be the "masculine-neutral."

    The move made more and more clearly by Luce Irigaray, then, is to maintain (in spite of all the well-known and often-rehearsed risks of such a position) the assertion of an irreducible difference between the sexes. In opposition to the assumptions of egalitarianism she asserts that "woman does not belong to the same type of subjective identity as man,"[21] if only because the male subject is born from a being of a different sex from his own, while the female subject is born from a being of the same sex. It is this specific mother-daughter relationship that must first of all be disinterred, beginning with a rediscovery of "female genealogies" and the knowledge—of the body, language, the gods, ethical values—that they retain. Thus, against the utopia of indifferentiation, in which some people see a desirable end and solution to the battle of the sexes, and in which others see an inevitability inscribed in human technological history, Luce Irigaray deepens the axiom of sexuation. The ultimate aim of the "liberation of women" is not "equality with men,"[22] which is always a disguised submission to the masculine-neutral, but a more positive and innovative horizon, the emergence of new values that will allow us to live sexual difference, which means as well the difference of bodies, voices, languages, rights, genealogies, gods—the difference in subject-object and subject-subject relations. These are the differences that Luce Irigaray elaborates with greater clarity and depth.

In relation to the earlier work, which was primarily defensive, there is no contradiction, but the shift of emphasis is significant. The aim is no longer merely "to escape patriarchal culture" and learn to speak "among women";[23] it is now explicitly to denounce "egalitarian dreams about sexual difference."[24] Rather than the abstract postulation of equality, we need a more profound notion of what feminine identity is or might be. Further, between persons a new *we* is emerging, that of the relation between different sexes: a "we" that does not resemble an undifferentiated group of neutral subjects but depends on the irreducible difference between an "I" and a "you" who, ultimately, are a woman and a man. For Luce Irigaray writes, in a formulation both strong and enigmatic that admirably sums up what is now at issue: "The most intimate and universal, the most everyday and divine locus of this *we* is situated between woman and man."[25] Thus the claim that was initially only "feminist" becomes enlarged in the direction of an ethics of sexual alterity that gives a new lease of life to feminism. "In fact, the liberation of women goes well beyond the frame of feminist struggles which nowadays too often go no further than the critique of patriarchy, separatism, or the claim to equality with men, without putting forward new values to live sexual difference with justice, civility and spiritual fertility."[26]

The work of Luce Irigaray aspires to situate a dialectically new moment. Beyond egalitarian demands in which (at least in France) the first wave of feminism has exhausted itself, she has restored to the movement a prophetic vocation by thinking anew the subversive and creative possibilities of difference. It is true that the tension between egalitarian demands and the concern for women's difference has for a long time been a more or less divisive undercurrent in feminist discourse. It is the principal antinomy confronted by feminism, which that movement has attempted to resolve by different routes. "Women equal or different?"—this is the question Irigaray foregrounds in the title of an article that defines her position in relation to that of Simone de Beauvoir.[27] In fact, if one goes back to the book that has played such a major role in twentieth-century feminism, one observes that the polemical thrust of *The Second Sex* can be summarized in a chiasmatic *inversion* (to use a rhetorical term), which may seem subtle or rather thin, but nonetheless underpins the whole argument: it refuses the slogan "equality in difference"[28] in favor of "difference in equality."[29] For Simone de Beauvoir the whole issue resides in this apparently minimal distinction, whose rationale is not immediately obvious. The first slogan is refuted in the introduction; the second adopted in the conclusion. How are we to understand this inversion? Of what effects is it the vehicle? From the outset Simone de Beauvoir criticizes a formulation that she says has had considerable success and that, in the guise of an egalitarian concession, in fact serves merely to maintain or introduce the most extreme discrimination: equality, yes, but in difference. To this formulation she opposes her own philosophy, which is summed up on the last pages of her book, in this shift of emphasis: difference, yes, but in equality. This time it is equality that is the primary claim, to be demanded without any kind of compromise, and it is difference that is merely granted, as though conceded with the utmost reluctance. However, Luce Irigaray apparently returns to the first formulation Simone de Beauvoir had rejected at the outset. This is the move, this is the divergence. How can one think this new shift? What strategic advantage can Luce Irigaray hope to gain from it today?

Let us note straight away that the "equality, yes, but in difference" that Simone de Beauvoir attacks in the opening pages of her book is uttered by a male voice. It is the masculine but uneasy voice of those who concede certain of the superficial achievements of equality on condition that a deep disparity is retained at all costs. Simone de Beauvoir (perhaps justifiably) interprets this precaution as the indirect but persistent desire to perpetuate male dominance. In disparity segregation lies hidden, and in segregation, discrimination and hierarchy. Equality is conceded superficially, since the rationalistic bourgeois ethic, ultimately, is an ethic of equality, but only with the stipulation of a difference around which the well-defended bastion of male supremacy is soon consolidated.

Today, however, with Luce Irigaray, the statement is in a different voice. As in opera, where the same melody may be repeated in different registers, in deep or in soprano tones, we can hear the repetition of the same phrase, but its meaning has changed, for the subject of enunciation has changed sex. "Equality, yes, but in difference," uttered, proclaimed in the voice of Luce Irigaray, inaugurates a new moment in the history of feminism. The warning has now changed sides, and changed its tone. It signifies that egalitarianism works toward the disappearance of women, in the totalitarian order of the masculine-neutral.

Around the time of the bicentennial of the French Revolution two books, among others, appeared in France, both by women, both concerning the controversial problem of the difference between men and women. The opposition between these two books is striking. Their titles sum up the debate: Elisabeth Badinter, *L'Un est l'autre* (One is the other); Luce Irigaray, *Le Temps de la différence* (The time of difference). The first book comes close to arguing for complete identity or interchangeability between men and women (or at the very least, to foreseeing this as an imminent possibility). We are not far here from Anatole France's utopia. The other book proclaims that the difference between the sexes is irreducible, and seeks to imagine their new relations.

The unbudging position taken up by Luce Irigaray, her conviction that we are "at a different stage of History," enables us to see more clearly what is at stake in the passage from modernity to postmodernity. It forces us, perhaps, into seeking a more precise and more complex periodization of this passage, which remains so difficult to conceptualize in a coherent interpretation of History. Ultramodernist: this is how one might, I think, qualify the tendency toward neutralization of the sexes, which bases itself on a certain juridicism, a certain rationalism, a certain scienticity, radicalizing in this way the indisputable achievements of the modern age but, in a schematic utopian projection, extrapolating along a straight line. It is an ultramodernism that believes itself to be combating an intolerable archaism that goes under the name of sexual difference. The demands of equal opportunity at work and in everyday family life, the technical advances that abolish all the former necessities of a division of labor based on a sexual dimorphism, the economic and symbolic process of generalized equivalence (not to mention biological advances that would make the male superfluous or else allow him to give birth), all these things lead us toward a unisex human universe, a universe in which the war between male and female would disappear along with the fertility of their relationship. Even the idea of "complementarity" (which some women suspect of harboring secret reserves of domination)[30] would be replaced by similarity and identity, in an androgynous world that inevitably resembles the nightmares of science fiction or the uneasy forebodings of utopia.

It is against this ultramodernist utopianism (for which "one is the other" in a progressive abolition of difference) that Luce Irigaray takes a stand, marking an intervention that one would not hesitate this time to call postmodernist, if the term had not acquired a conceptual looseness affecting its ability to mark a rupture. However, there is no doubt that we are talking about a historical move that corresponds to at least *one* of the meanings of this still floating term, indicating not the acceleration that "dehumanizes" and "axiomatizes" in the indefinite play of permutations without anchorage (what I would prefer to call ultramodernism), but rather the more recent suspicion *against* what exceeds identity, dissolves the subject, or disorientates any possibility of biography. This is where I locate the appearance of this moment and its needs, *after* the ultramodernity of the utopias and the axiomatic arts, at the moment at which a new genealogy and a new subject is seeking itself.

If Luce Irigaray's position is postmodern, it is in the sense that this word has taken on, for example, in architecture from 1975 onwards, leaving no ambiguity about the turn that has been taken. It is no longer the combinatory play between abstract and decontextualized elements, no longer the pure axiomatics of forms, colors, and functions, detached from history and meaning (an ultramodern prospect that corresponds visibly to structuralism and poststructuralism in literature and philosophy), but the moment after, more uncertain, more uneasy, marked in a different way by the concern to think the collective memory, the constants of the imagination (if there are any), the problematic constitution of the social bond, the dimensions of living that are irreducible to the functional. It is this moment, at which a certain ultramodernism is put into question (the ultramodernism that disintegrates the subject and meaning to the point of absurdity, even in cases where it appeals to the toughest rationalism), for which we should no doubt reserve the name of postmodernity; and one can then see in what way the concern to go beyond neutralization, to think "the civil rights and duties for both sexes," or to disinter "the forgotten mystery of female genealogies,"[31] clearly inscribes itself in this moment.

For it is the fatal slope of ultramodernity that Anatole France foresaw in 1905 with remarkable perspicuity. It is in fact only today that the premonition of the "neutral sex" is beginning to seem likely, and may become the object of a disquiet that is no longer merely literary and speculative.

There is no utopian vision that does not examine, define, and regulate the relation between men and women. Either the subordination of women is accepted as ineluctable, requiring only a new regulation (in Fontenelle, for example), or else, especially in postrevolutionary utopias, women's position is seen as crucial to the project of universal liberation—in Fourier, first of all, who was able, on the basis of his theory of passional affinities, to state that in any given society the extent to which women are emancipated is an index of emancipation in general.[32]

However, in Anatole France Fourier's optimism seems to falter; France's image of the future is somewhat less rosy. An affable and skeptical writer, he lived at a time when utopian discourse (though not revolutionary energy) seems to have exhausted itself, and, worse still, when the inauguratory utopia (or rather a projection of the future like Mercier's *L'An 2440*) tends to tip over into a utopia marked by uneasiness. Perhaps one could even say that *Sur la pierre blanche* marks the precise moment at which utopia passes into dystopia, when what had earlier looked like a desirable achievement begins to turn into a discordant premonition. The enthusiasm of utopia is succeeded by the doubt of anticipation. Not that France is regressive in relation to the movement of emancipation dreamed of by Fourier, Flora Tristan, and others, which they (but especially the women) worked to bring about. But, despite his progressivism, Anatole France foresaw even in 1905 a strange conclusion, a disturbing limit, as if the vital issues of earlier revolutionary projects might reach (in the imagination at least) a sort of closure.

Sur la pierre blanche is not a utopia in the full, political sense, the construction (fictional in the first instance) of an ideal society, but rather in the weak sense of the forecast of a possible historical future, whether desired or feared. Unlike the greatest utopian thinkers of the previous two centuries, Anatole France's work does not seem to describe, in a major key, a perfect and wished-for society. It is more of an exercise in looking ahead, an "objective" extrapolation of a probable development. As a literary genre this writing would be better described as futurology (a futurist exercise) rather than as utopia or revolutionary anticipation. It could thus be said to indicate an inexorable evolution of the genre; it is not a coincidence that utopian optimism in this fiction turns into a sour and uneasy futurology in which "the equality of the sexes" is no longer a triumphant claim, bearing the hopes of subversion and justice, but a prospect of neutralization that perhaps contains within itself the risk of death. The logic of ultramodernity is at work here.

Nor is it just by chance that Anatole France should have foreseen (and feared) the neutralization of sex at the very moment when Cubist painting was emerging on the scene, when Saussure was founding structural linguistics, when Roussel was flinging himself into his metagrammatic games. Why does sexual neutralization become a possible horizon just at the moment at which we see emerging the aesthetic and theoretical avant-gardes, marking an acute crisis in representation and the appearance of pure structure for which the appeal to the referent is irrelevant? It is because this progressive neutralization is part of a sociosymbolic process of rapid denaturalization of general equivalents (gold, father, phallus, speech), the unraveling of their functions, and the increasing and soon radical hegemony of the function of exchange (of substitution) over every other function (such as that of measurement and that of treasure). It is that critical moment whose reverberations were amplified by the avant-gardes of the beginning of the century in their scandalous and iconoclastic rejection of figurative and representational requirements.[33] Sexual neutralization, as a horizon, would be one of the virtual consequences of this new "abstraction," of this dissolution of being into exchange value, of the domination of the pure symbolic (the inconvertible token) over any common measure or standard yardstick, or any actually existing treasure. The system would no longer be governed by a general equivalent, capable of being represented or embodied (in gold, in the father, in the phallus, in speech), ruling over what resists the regulatory common measure (identified by Auguste Comte ahead of his time as "proletarians, women, artists")[34] but would instead be a regime of generalized equivalence—incorporating everything, without residue—into the systemic play of a commutative (or synallagmatic) economy (which is not guaranteed, backed, or covered by any reserves). With this new structure of the sign and of value, homologous to banking and the stock exchange (instead of commodities), the "humanist" domination of the masculine over the feminine will disappear (insofar as it is locatable in terms of role, person, or function) and the structural and abstract reign of the masculine-neutral will emerge as a horizon, reducing value to an indefinite play of substitution and interchangeability.[35]

If Anatole France's anticipatory fiction is, as it were, the ultimate utopia, it is because abstract equality can still be inscribed in utopian and avant-gardist reason. It can be extrapolated to the point at which the sexes are neutralized. On the other hand their future difference cannot easily be imagined in advance. Of course it is possible to dream of that difference. But no utopian planification can say in advance, through a purely rational projection, what the world would be like if the feminine had "assumed its language, its speech, its style,"[36] or if the subject were to go on stage "in a scene in which it engaged with the other sex."[37] Here we have reached the limits of the utopian cycle and those of what modernism can foresee.

The real postmodernism would only begin beyond these limits. Like a cry of pain, a revolt, the protest of Antigone, but in different historical conditions and for a different tragedy. One can see the kinds of suspicion and misunderstanding that such a position will have to confront, and the guarantees it will need to offer if it is not simply to be confused with a return to premodern prejudices. Through its ethical stance and its internal economy it will need to demonstrate that it has pushed egalitarianism to its limits and measured itself against the deadly impasse of the neutral sex. It is then—against the mortal entropy that threatens us, against the chaos of a primitive and undifferentiated libido that knows nothing of Aphrodite (a necessarily female image of the "elevation of love to human and divine identity")[38]—it is then that "the access to a sexuate cultural and political ethics will be our contemporary hope for the future."[39]

Thus the periodization becomes clear. The essentialist and *premodern* presupposition of natural sexual inequality, whose self-evidence depended on its longevity, was succeeded by the *modern* claim to equality between men and women. This led inexorably to the *ultramodern* perspective of a sexual neutralization. The ultramodern moment, in turn, has been overcome by the *postmodern* concern with sexual difference, by the quest for a social and cultural sexuation whose eventual outcome one cannot, by definition, foresee, any more than one can invent overnight the characteristic forms and style of a civilization.

Translated by Margaret Whitford

NOTES •

1. Irigaray, *Je, tu, nous*, p. 12/p. 12.
2. Ibid., p. 80/p. 99.
3. Irigaray, *Le Temps de la différence*, p. 104.
4. Irigaray, *Je, tu, nous*, p. 80/p. 99.
5. Anatole France, *Sur la pierre blanche* (Paris: Calmann-Lévy, 1905), p. 253.
6. Ibid., p. 291.
7. Ibid., p. 300.
8. Ibid., p. 311.
9. Ibid., p. 301; my emphasis.
10. Ibid., p. 313.
11. Fénelon, *Essai philosophique sur le gouvernement civil* (1721), excerpt in Serge Baudiffier, *Textes politiques du XVIIIe siècle* (Paris: Hachette, 1980), p. 29.
12. Ibid., p. 28.
13. Ibid., p. 29.
14. Jean-Paul Sartre, *Existentialism and Humanism*, trans. Philip Mairet (London: Methuen, 1948), p. 28/ *L'Existentialisme est un humanisme* (Paris: Nagel, 1946, 1970), p. 22.
15. Irigaray, *J'aime à toi*, p. 72.
16. Irigaray, *Le Temps de la différence*, p. 120.
17. Irigaray, *Je, tu, nous*, p. 12/p. 12.

- 18. Ibid., p. 32/p. 13.
- 19. Simone de Beauvoir, *The Second Sex,* trans. H. M. Parshley (New York: Vintage, 1952, 1974), p. 301/ *Le Deuxième sexe,* 2 vols. (Paris: Gallimard, 1949, 1976), 2:13. This is the opening sentence of volume 2.
20. Irigaray, *Sexes et genres,* p. 13.
21. Irigaray, *Le Temps de la différence,* p. 36.
22. Ibid., p. 14.
23. Irigaray, *Ce Sexe,* back cover.
24. Irigaray, *Sexes et genres,* back cover.
25. Irigaray, *Je, tu, nous,* back cover.
26. Irigaray, *Le Temps de la différence,* p. 14.
27. Irigaray, *Je, tu, nous,* p. 9/p. 9.
28. Beauvoir, *The Second Sex,* p. xxvii/1:24.
29. Ibid.
30. Elisabeth Badinter, *Man/Woman: The One Is the Other,* trans. Barbara Wright (London: Collins Harvill, 1989)/*L'Un est l'autre* (Paris: Odile Jacob, Livre de poche, 1986).
31. *Le Temps de la différence,* pp. 101–123.
32. Charles Fourier, *Théorie des quatre mouvements* in *Oeuvres complètes* (Paris, 1841), 1:195–196.
33. Cf. Jean-Joseph Goux, *Symbolic Economies* (Ithaca: Cornell University Press, 1990), and *Les Monnayeurs du langage* (Paris: Galilée, 1984; translation forthcoming, Oklahoma University Press). See also Jean-Joseph Goux, "Banking on Signs" in *Diacritics* (Summer 1988), 18(2):15–25.
34. See Jean-Joseph Goux, "The Crisis of Modernity: Proletarians, Women, Artists" in ed. Mikkel Borch-Jacobsen, *The Social Bond* (Stanford University Press, forthcoming).
35. See ibid.
36. Irigaray, *Parler n'est jamais neutre,* p. 11.
37. Ibid., p. 11.
38. Irigaray, *Le Temps de la différence,* p. 107.
39. Ibid., p. 24.

· *Joanna Hodge*

IRIGARAY

READING

HEIDEGGER

1. Setting Up the Documents of Civilization

> There is no document of civilization which is not at the same time a document of misogyny. And just as such a document is not free of misogyny, so misogyny taints also the manner in which it was transmitted from one owner to another. A historical materialist therefore dissociates herself from it as far as possible. She regards it as her task to brush history against the grain.

This epigraph is taken, with a few apposite alterations, from Walter Benjamin's 1940 essay on the concept of history.[1] In place of the word *barbarism* I have substituted the word *misogyny*, and in place of the word *he* I have substituted the word *she*. I am using this transposed epigraph to illuminate the manner in which Irigaray rewrites philosophical and psychoanalytical texts, the "documents of civilization," preserved as authoritative in their respective canons. The results derived by Irigaray from this rewriting change between the earlier *Speculum of the Other Woman* (1974) and later *Ethics of Sexual Difference* (1984), and essays collected together in *Le Corps-à-corps avec la mère* ("The Bodily Encounter with the Mother," 1981). However, there is an unfolding trajectory that reveals concealed within those documents the residue of an originary matricide at the source of human self-interpretation. The term *originary* used here to qualify this conception of matricide is borrowed from Heidegger, and this essay seeks to show

•   how an interaction between Irigaray and Heidegger is key to a number
•   of crucial turns in Irigaray's thought.

For Heidegger an originary event does not take place at the beginning of some sequence of events, as a founding myth or source, from
which all human history then proceeds. The originary from which a
particular discursive formation emerges has to be repeatedly reenacted and reinscribed if the formation is to stay in place. There is no past
origin from which a clearly defined sequence of consequences can be
seen to flow, like a birth, from which date the development of a particular human individual can be traced. An originary event articulates
itself as an omnipresent and recurrently affirmed set of parameters
that open up certain lines of possibility while closing off others. Irigaray's readings of the philosophical tradition reveal a matricide as
continually reinscribed within the institutions and texts through
which the parameters of contemporary theoretical, supposedly progressive inquiry are set up. This matricide is the ground for the difficulties women experience in gaining authority within those institutions, and can be traced within the daily lives of women and mothers
throughout the contemporary world—probably no more and no less
in our supposedly "civilized" Western European democracies. Irigaray
demonstrates the matricide at work in the tradition called European
philosophy.

The aim of this essay is not to trace out shifts in focus in Irigaray's
reading of the tradition. My aim is to show how Irigaray makes use of
elements from the writings of Heidegger, and from Heidegger's
responses to Nietzsche and to Kant, to develop her diagnosis of a murder, actual and symbolic, of mothers and of women. I will show how
Irigaray twists elements from the work of Heidegger and Nietzsche into
a startling proximity to feminist critique. The essay in which the theme
of matricide emerges most forcefully is translated in *The Irigaray Reader* as "The Bodily Encounter with the Mother." There Irigaray suggests
that the death of the father, inscribed as the founding moment of psychoanalysis and, by extension, of civilization in general, serves to mask
this originary murder and annihilation of the body of the mother. The
death of Socrates becomes an emblematic event masking death and
masking the erasure of birth and of mothering.

Irigaray sets out the tragedies of Aeschylus, the *Oresteia*, as a text in
which this concealment is accomplished. She indicates that the repeated return to Sophocles' *Oedipus* by Hegel, Freud, and Heidegger continues that work of erasure, with the discreetly offstage suicides of Jocasta and Antigone. The women die, sacrificed to the exigencies of plot
and powerlessness, while the men achieve position and immortality. In

the *Oresteia* the Furies, pursuing the blood right arising out of the murder of Clytemnestra, become the Eumenides, the kindly ones, who are to preside over the welfare of citizens, the men, of Athens. The motherless Athena and her brother, Apollo, triumph over the chthonic gods and the relation between mother and daughter—between Clytemnestra and Iphigenia—is erased. What goes missing is mothering and the powerful symbolism of the mother/daughter relation as split femaleness, between Ceres and Proserpina, Demeter and Persephone, Gaia and Rhea. Irigaray sums all this up in "The Bodily Encounter with the Mother":

> What the *Oresteia* describes for us still take place. Here and there, regulation Athenas whose one begetter is the head of the Father-King still burst forth. Completely in his pay, in the pay of the men in power, they bury beneath their sanctuary women in struggle so that they will no longer disturb the new order of the home, the order of the polis, now the only order.[2]

This marks a split between the feminine woman, who is acceptable, indeed constructed in accordance with the requirements of male power, providing a subordinated complement to that masculinity, and the female woman, figure of self-regulating ambiguity, both mother and daughter, both fertile and sexual. This splitting between "woman" and "femininity" divides women from each other rather than permitting women to be internally divided between alternating stances. The woman/femininity split takes over from a split internal to individual women, within which a woman may grow, and is impacted on top of another theme, also stated in this essay: "All of western culture rests on the murder of the mother."

Speculum is a work of self-constitution that operates by retrieving moments in the philosophical and psychoanalytical tradition at which the silencing of women and murdering of mothers are both marked and repressed. This self-constitution requires an affirmation of maternity and of the body of the mother, as given in advance of subordination to any law of the father—through which a father's right over the child is established—in advance of any symbolic order privileging male power, in advance of the repression of sexual difference from philosophy. Irigaray's monographs on Nietzsche[3] and on Heidegger[4] reveal the possibility of a dialogue with the male authority figures, which opens up once the task of self-constitution has begun. I suggest that Irigaray's mode of work fits the following description of the historical materialist's task given by Benjamin, transposed in line with the changes in the epigraph:

- Historical materialism wishes to retain that image of the past which
- unexpectedly appears to women singled out by history at a moment of
  danger. The danger affects both the content of the tradition and its
  receivers. The same threat hangs over both: that of becoming a tool of
  the ruling classes. In every era the attempt must be made anew to wrest
  tradition away from a conformism that is about to overpower it. The
  Messiah comes not only as the redeemer, she comes as the subduer of
  Antichrist. Only that historian will have the gift of fanning the spark of
  hope in the past who is firmly convinced that even the dead will not be
  safe from the enemy if that enemy wins. And this enemy has not ceased
  to be victorious.[5]

The problem is: how to prevent women's writing being well received in
the short term only to fade out in the partial transmission of the tradition, like that of medieval nuns and obscure nineteenth-century
women poets. In each generation there is a contestation of the mechanisms of subordination by women, which in the transmission is lost,
such that each generation seems to start anew as though there had been
no predecessors. The return of the mother can be thematized to subvert
the appearance that these contestations spring up each time from
nowhere, like Athena; instead they can be grounded back in a labyrinth
of half-suppressed memories and struggles—a half-forgotten history of
feminist critique and women's struggle.

In *Speculum* Irigaray reads back into the heroic texts of the philosophical tradition a subversive femininity that is, at one and the same
time, made use of, contained, and expelled. This ambiguous treatment
makes it all the harder to disentangle the issues in play, especially granted the preference within philosophical analysis for the clear and distinct, the direct and unequivocal. Rather than disambiguate and argue
directly, conforming with this preference, Irigaray retains the mode of
articulation in which questions of sexual difference and of gender have
more usually been posed within philosophical texts: oblique, ambivalent, parodic. She does not look for an alternative tradition of forgotten
or undervalued texts, written by women. She looks for the silencing
gesture of these alternative voices in the heroic texts themselves, and
seeks by brushing these texts against the grain to empower that silenced
energy. Irigaray works within the parameters of phenomenology, revealing hidden conditions of possibility for what there appears to be. The
surface of reason and of lucid argument in philosophical texts turns out
under her reading to be held together at the cost of eliding an other; the
death and transfiguration of Socrates inscribed at the beginning of philosophy conceals the death of the mother. Irigaray uses the work of
other philosophers, particularly that of Heidegger and Nietzsche, to

reveal this concealment, but also reveals in that work a continuing silencing of women.

Themes from Nietzsche that are especially relevant to Irigaray's diagnosis of an originary matricide are his analysis of the value of forgetting for the affirmation of life and his explorations of temporality in the thematics of the eternal return of the same.[6] The main themes from Heidegger are his analysis of an originary concatenation of forces, out of which an order of things, a concept of truth, and an account of what there is arises. Also relevant is his diagnosis of the way in which this concatenation of forces or "transmissions of being," *Seinsgeschichte*, is prone to metaphysical reduction. In this reduction the historicality of that sending is erased, being is forgotten, and the emergent order of things takes on the image of timelessness. In the writings of both Nietzsche and Heidegger there is a twisting together of the themes of forgetting, enabling, and repetition. These themes play a role in their diagnoses of a culmination of European culture in nihilism, of an end to the philosophical project launched by Socrates, and of the advent of some new formation. Irigaray takes these thematics and frames them within a context of asking "openings and closures for whom?" Emphasizing the place of women within theory disrupts any unqualified declaration of an end of metaphysics and a closure of philosophy. For some, metaphysics and philosophy have not yet begun.

2. Common Readings

Irigaray transforms Heidegger's violent readings of the texts constituting the history of philosophy into an amorous discourse. The contrast between the readings of Nietzsche offered by Irigaray[7] and by Heidegger[8] respectively is just one example of this. Irigaray opens up a dialogue with Nietzsche, whereas Heidegger imposes a magisterial if self-subverting reading. The end of philosophy that Heidegger announces in his 1964 essay "The End of Philosophy and the Task of Thinking"[9] becomes for Irigaray the hoped-for return of the mother and the rebirth of women. The time of greatest danger, announced by Heidegger in connection with his readings of Hoelderlin,[10] becomes the present time, in which women confront a challenge of either rising above the determinations of complementing maleness and the masculine or continuing in this mode that generates rivalry between women, wasting the energies gathered together in the last thirty years of feminist agitation. The invocation of a time of need between departed and future gods, also located by Heidegger in his readings of Hoelderlin, becomes with Irigaray the invocation of an ideal, a divine for women.[11] Irigaray suggests that this ideal/divine is needed if women are to cease developing in self-destructive opposition to other women, as competing complements to a figure of masculinity grounded in the predominantly male and masculine images of the divine.

Irigaray rewrites Heidegger's ontological difference as sexual difference; the forgetting of being and of the earth becomes the forgetting of women and the death of the mother; and in place of Heidegger's technical term *Dasein* Irigaray's texts cumulatively establish the necessity of thinking the apparently paradoxical "sensible transcendental." Irigaray transforms Heidegger's originary emergence of meaning and order out of a self-concealing sending or history of being. She refers it back to the emergence of human individuals through a process of emancipation from the mother who gave birth to that individual. The distance from the point of origination, the erasure of the role of the mother, is at first enabling. But in the absence of a cycle of rebirth and retrieval, that distance turns into the rigidities of a metaphysics without history, a science without humanity, a concept without a world, a masculinity to which a figure of femininity is subordinated—not one that itself emerges out of an originary encounter between female and male. I am mainly concerned with Irigaray's rewriting of the end of philosophy as the return of the mother and the emergence of the term *sensible transcendental.* However, there will be remarks in passing indicating their relation to these other transcriptions.

In her transformation of Heidegger Irigaray's writings come into close proximity with the responses to Heidegger of Levinas and Foucault. Both use their readings of Heidegger to develop an affirmation of ethics as superior to metaphysical thinking, although both read Heidegger as neglecting ethical considerations. In *An Ethics of Sexual Difference* Irigaray affirms Heidegger's and Foucault's thought that there is something new in the structures of thinking containing our twentieth-century inquiries. They thematize a turning point within being and in the discursive formations within which being inscribes itself as absent. For Heidegger that turning point (*die Kehre*) is the deepening danger marked by the spread of technology, and the hoped-for healing (*die Heilige*) in a return of being. For Foucault a turning point is marked negatively by the erasure of the concept of man, which he anticipates in *The Order of Things* (1966). Irigaray insists that sexual difference, not Heidegger's preferred technology or Foucault's end of man and demise of the subject, is the formation distinctive of the modern epoch. The three agree that a new formation is in evidence; they disagree about its nature. Notoriously, Heidegger sought a new foundation in what he saw as the promise of an innovative thinking in Nazism. Disappointed

in this hope, he withdrew into ascetic acceptance. Foucault insists on
multiplicity as a defense against fascism,[12] but remains trapped within
an unthought masculinism. Irigaray construes an affirmation of sexual
difference as an enabling force, making available new possibilities,
which Heidegger and Foucault both look for but deny themselves
through their incapacity to recognize the truth and urgency of feminist
critique.

Yet the questions of sexual difference, of sexuality, and of the feminine can be posed in a way that simply closes them off again.[13] Irigaray's
texts, especially *Speculum* and *An Ethics of Sexual Difference*, make it
impossible to contain them in this way, and a resistance to leaving these
issues open underpins an inability to engage with those texts. Gender
blindness in the tradition is revealed as a powerful and corrupting
misogyny. The readiness to write about femininity and about sexual difference is shown to function, on occasion, as yet another powerful strategy to counteract the destabilizing influences that again disrupt the
supposed neutrality of the tradition's authority. In *An Ethics of Sexual
Difference* Irigaray recognizes a proximity between her own thinking
and that of Levinas's recuperation of the ethical, of femininity, of the
erotic. These are all inscribed at the beginning of the philosophical tradition in Plato's *Symposium*, but left to one side. The erotic is reduced
first to a love of God, and then rewritten by Nietzsche as a love of fate.
Irigaray reveals Levinas's retrieval of the erotic as yet another sign of crisis in the tradition, marking the urgency of a reversal from a celebration
of sameness into an exploration of difference. Levinas celebrates the
erotic in order to affirm the importance for self of the encounter with
another. He reintroduces touch, fecundity, and femininity as important
dimensions in human experience, which are more usually reduced and
denied in the construction of accounts of knowledge and of what it is
to be human. Levinas insists on the priority of ethics over metaphysics,
the good beyond being, but in so doing supposes himself to be criticizing Heidegger, since Levinas takes Heidegger's fundamental ontology
to be a cover for metaphysics.[14]

This reading is plausible only if *Being and Time* is taken in isolation
from Heidegger's subsequent thinking. However, in the critique of
metaphysics, launched in his inaugural lecture "What is Metaphysics?"
of 1928, Heidegger makes it clear that the critical distance taken up in
Being and Time with respect to the term *ethics* is a critique of the whole
European philosophical tradition as marked by a rigid opposition
between ethics and metaphysics. Thus, in contrast to Levinas, Irigaray
does not suppose herself to be in conflict with Heidegger when she
endorses Levinas's term "ethics" in the title of her recent book. For her,

all three, Heidegger, Levinas, and Irigaray, are exploring unrecognized and repressed dimensions of a tradition, which reproduces conceptions of sameness, by making these dimensions unrecognizable. All three, for their different reasons, have a disruptive stance with respect to the tradition. However, when Irigaray inserts her voice alongside Levinas's insistence on touch, fecundity, the feminine, she makes space for articulating the unease generated by yet another male appropriation of the feminine, without a saving critique of male power. Thus, having in *Speculum* acquired an autonomous philosophical voice, Irigaray uses it to open up reverberations within the texts of male, masculinist thinkers such as Nietzsche, Heidegger, Levinas, and Foucault to reveal their inability to register the issue of the mother.

As Irigaray remarks in the introduction to her collection of essays *Parler n'est jamais neutre* (1985), the philosophical tradition of Europe plays a leading role in articulating the ideals of universality, neutrality, and impartiality, while simultaneously showing them, over and again, to be untenable. Thus, the articulation has a double function. It investigates the problem, gives it an airing, and then neutralizes it. In the course of the nineteenth and twentieth centuries, however, it becomes increasingly difficult to contain it; and the tradition from Kant, through Hegel and Nietzsche, to Heidegger and Foucault shows an increasing precariousness in the strategies deployed to delay the disintegration of the ideals of the European philosophical tradition. It is in this tradition that Irigaray's texts function as a further marker in a process of destabilization. Where the tradition sets philosophy up as immaterial, gender neutral, and temporally invariant, Irigaray seeks to identify as internal to philosophical construction those forces that it seeks to place on the exterior. She reveals how materiality, gender, and time are internal to the tradition, exactly insofar as the claim is made that they are external. Irigaray works closely with the texts of Nietzsche and Heidegger because both intervene decisively to disrupt the supposed neutrality of European conceptions of rationality. In her reading of Nietzsche Irigaray explores the thought that there is no neutral discourse, only that which persuades its reader to think it neutral. This thought encourages in Irigaray a degree of intellectual transvestism, refusing the immediate gestures of feminist solidarity and of grieving for our silenced sisters in favor of a more frontal engagement with the textures in the tradition that exclude and silence. In *Marine Lover* Irigaray imitates Nietzsche's indirectness and uses his images to disrupt the fear and hatred of femininity that is evident in his texts. She uses similar strategies of mimicry and pastiche in her reading of Heidegger. Both monographs link back to her analyses in *Speculum* of a masquer-

ade involved in any authoritative language use, but especially in such
language use by women.

Indirectness is characteristic of Irigaray's writing. It is also characteristic of the writings of Nietzsche and Heidegger. This indirectness
makes possible a sustained ambiguity that is particularly productive in
the context of women engaging with philosophy, since it permits a discussion of the absence of women from the heroic tradition without
either affirming or rejecting that tradition. Marking a difference in the
texts of the tradition can work to conceal a residual sameness; while an
insistence on the unifications of reason masks a multiplicity of voices
within the tradition, whose differences are thereby elided and contained. Irigaray seeks, via an insistence on the question of sexual difference, to replace the same/other dichotomy, and its emphasis on identity, with a revival of a Parmenidean reflection on the many forms of
relating the one and the many, in which not identity but difference is
predominant. Thus she, like Heidegger and Nietzsche, mobilizes the
premetaphysical, presystematic thought of the pre-Socratics against the
rigidities of philosophical categories. Heidegger and Nietzsche turn to
the thought of Heraclitus, the theorist of strife, to the fragments of
Anaximander, and to Parmenides' reflections on the multiple emana-
tions of sameness. They stand apart from the tradition of eliding the
other, the unvoiced, the dissident, the presystematic. They seek to
retrieve resources from these neglected elements of the tradition to
make possible a response to the specificity of the present post-Christian
epoch.

It is a mark of their difference that readers often, rather than expend
the effort of trying to make sense of the writings of these disruptive
thinkers, resort to denouncing their politics, their affiliations, their
friendships. Irigaray's writings are also open to such denunciation, and
again this operates as a substitute for thinking through the challenge
they pose. Thus Nietzsche, Heidegger, and Irigaray are bound together by their insistence on, and transgression of, difference. Their texts
function as palimpsests, obscuring but preserving the traces of the
thinkers with whom they have engaged on the way to developing their
own thought. Like many of her contemporaries in France, Irigaray
makes use of the convention evident in the writings of Heidegger and
Nietzsche of refusing the Anglo-American scholarly apparatus. With
Irigaray references are not so much oblique as interiorized, in the very
movement of the thought, in the cadences of the language, in the
devices it refuses to employ: footnotes, explicit quotation, direct references. These devices permit a subversion of the boundary between
one's own text and text of the other, between theory and fiction,

between writing authoritatively in an established genre and speaking as a particular individual, with specific responsibilities to self and others. It permits a writing with explicit ethical intent, defying the canons of neutrality.

This continental convention has both a classical and a hermeneutical inflection, and it is important to distinguish between the two. The classical inflection, with a memorializing ethic of triumphalism, suggests that there simply is a shared culture, a body of texts and issues, to which reference may be made, implicitly, without belaboring the point. This inflection presumes a standard curriculum, with a canon of authorities and a clear method of becoming a recognized participant. It excludes the uninitiated and assumes the justice and adequacy of an existing system of education. It has the inevitable overtones of elitism and esoterism. The hermeneutical inflection by contrast results from the thought that references, quotations, and footnotes are strategic weapons in a game of persuasion; Nietzsche's "mobile army," not definitive proofs of correctness. The hermeneutical inflection is thus in direct conflict with the classical inflection. It suggests that authority and authorization are always contestable, however apparently well-documented. In the former there is not, whereas in the latter there is a questioning of what counts as authority; and it is in the latter strand that Irigaray's writing should be located.

The violent reading strategies of Heidegger[15] add another dimension to this conflict. His move is to read texts for their moment of rupture, for the moment at which they conceal their conditions of possibility. This is the form of his reading of Nietzsche's writings as bound to reaffirm the metaphysical structures they appear to subvert. This mode of reading violates the logic of the explicit text to reveal a hidden logic that Heidegger finds at work in all the major texts of the European philosophical tradition: he reads them all as flawed by an impasse at which what should be argued for has to be assumed; or worse, as culminating in a disproof of the very theme to be displayed. These texts set up a conceptual structure, and by so doing obscure the problem to which those structures are supposedly responding, obscuring their own process of production. It is a moment of revelation at which the gesture is hidden and what is revealed takes on the structure not of a momentary illumination but of a permanent fixture. At the moment of revelation what is revealed conceals the movement through which the revelation take place. This is the double movement of presencing and withdrawal, the event, *Ereignis*, which is also a taking away, an *Enteignis*. For this movement Heidegger finds many different forms of expression, none of which can remain uncontaminated by the problems surrounding the self-refuting attempt to name simultaneously both what is present and what makes it present. In this view the task of philosophy is the impossible attempt to name an unnameable unobservable process, of which only one part can be evident at any one time. This finds a place for the Platonic dialogues as paradigmatic of philosophical construction in their restless demonstration of the untenability of their own theoretical points of departure. Thus, for Heidegger, from the beginning, philosophical inquiry has acknowledged and held at arm's length the impossibility of its own aims.

3. Generic Writing

In *Speculum* Irigaray makes use of Heidegger's rewritings of Kant to license her own rewritings of Kant, of Heidegger, of Plato, of Freud, of Lacan. While *Speculum* provides ample evidence of Irigaray's familiarity with key themes in Heidegger's thinking and the centrality to his thinking of his views about the philosophical tradition, she also has a thorough, independent knowledge of that tradition, which enables her to keep a critical distance from his views. *Speculum* reveals both this knowledge of that tradition, from the pre-Socratics to the present day, and her further advantage of understanding, as do Nietzsche and Heidegger, the link between this tradition and Christianity. She demonstrates her knowledge of the tradition in the interleaved passages in the middle of *Speculum*, which carry the subtitle "Speculum." There she provides a sequence of tantalizing glimpses of what a history of philosophy beyond masculine privilege might look like. She also makes use of this understanding of Christianity in her invocation of angels in *An Ethics of Sexual Difference*. In her sketch of a history of philosophy she both parodies and makes use of Heidegger's reading of the differences between philosophical construction in different epochs as having a common set of thematics. Irigaray imitates Heidegger in construing philosophy as the affirmation of sameness and the repression or containment of difference.

Heidegger seeks to disrupt this affirmation, by writing of the forgetting of being[16] and insisting on ontological difference.[17] Irigaray seeks to place sexual difference at the center of attention. They both construct accounts of European philosophy as a unified structure, identifying it as a single repeated gesture of containment and silencing. They analyze distinctions basic to the development of particular philosophical texts and reveal a silenced third moment, which simultaneously makes the distinction possible and destabilizes it. The texts of the philosophical tradition thus consist in a tension between the explicitly stated argument and that which is assumed in order to let the argument go through but is often in conflict with the results to be produced. There are two levels in any text: an evident argument of rigorous conceptuality and other processes, only indirectly evident, that are the more concealed the closer the attention is fixed on the first level. To paraphrase Benjamin,[18] the more closely the text is inspected, the further away it draws back. By drawing back from the immediate argument, that argument can be shown to conceal its embeddedness in nonthematized levels of textuality.

Heidegger and Irigaray explore the dynamic of dependence and incompatibility between the philosophical ideal of rigorous conceptual structure and human experiences of time, difference, and incompleteness. Rigorous conceptual structure imposes sameness and strict simultaneity; historical process threatens to introduce irreducible difference and disruption, through the operations of delay and postponement. This suggests that if philosophy consists in rigorous conceptual construction, and history consists in processes of development, there can be no history in the history of European philosophy, merely the playing out of a determinate number of variations within a single structure. Thus Heidegger displays a form of historical process in which there is no development, but rather a sequence of disjointed structures succeeding one another, without any cumulative evolution from the one structure to the next. He supposes we deceive ourselves into believing in continuities when there are none by refusing to recognize that some sequences in time are disjunctive in this way. Thus, in place of history as process, Heidegger invites us to think of history, at least in the context of the history of philosophy, under the imprint of the eternal return of the same.

Heidegger and Irigaray reveal sameness inscribed at the heart of the theoretical constructs of Kant and of Plato, with an originary knowledge of sameness in the *Meno* repeated in the transcendental unity of apperception to be found, according to Kant's *First Critique*, in all bearers of reason. Irigaray reveals it again in the relation between Freud and Plato, showing in both an initial recognition of sexual difference that is contained by the subordination of one sex to the model provided by analysis of the other. Difference is thus theorized as accidental and derivative. In the present epoch, however, it lies within human capacity to impose sameness, by genocide, murdering bearers of the marks of difference, and by use of biotechnology, to reproduce sameness. Thus there is now a particular urgency to reveal what is concealed and elided when sameness is imposed in this way. Heidegger's concern, however, appears abstract and nebulous: he detects a groundlessness of human rationality that is concealed when philosophical inquiry is directed toward providing itself with foundations and legitimations. His attempt to disrupt the imposition of sameness by insisting on ontological difference remains abstract. Irigaray by contrast emphasizes a lived relation, that of sexual difference, and thus can identify what is missing from philosophical inquiry as women and femininity.

Irigaray's relation to Heidegger and to philosophy is then quite as unconventional as her relation to feminism. Philosophy is possible only on condition that the difference between women and men, and its role in reproducing the human species, is forgotten. But this forgetting is one with the direct consequence of excluding half the human race from the production of meaning and value. Irigaray suggests that the relation of the evident and the concealed in the texts of the philosophical tradition parallels that between the confident garrulousness of men and the silencing and hysterization of women. The textual and the social are in her texts inextricably connected. The silencing of women in the seminar room, the absence of women authorities within the canon of philosophical texts, the representation of women within those texts and the erasure of that representation, the importance assigned to the death of the father and, by implication, the irrelevance of the death of the mother, all function together to produce a set of multiple, mutually reinforcing effects within texts and lives. Irigaray, however, takes the opportunity to disrupt the repressive mechanisms that prevent this collusion being identifiable, and two of her major resources are the texts of Nietzsche and Heidegger.

In *Speculum* she takes up and develops the contrast set up by Heidegger between Kant's distinction between the empirical and the transcendental and Heidegger's own distinction between the ontical and the ontological. It is this intersection of themes that makes way for her insistence on a sensible transcendental. The distinction between the ontical and the ontological is introduced by Heidegger in *Being and Time* in opposition to the Kantian distinction. Roughly speaking, the ontical is the domain of actually existing entities, the ontological is the domain of possibility, the general structures within which actual existence occurs. Heidegger demonstrates in the course of *Being and Time* that the two cannot in the end be kept separate from each other. Kant's distinction by contrast is absolute; here the problem is to explain how the two can be in any way connected. Thus Irigaray's sensible transcendental can be seen to result from applying Heidegger's insistence on the inseparability of the ontical and the ontological to Kant's distinction between the material or sensible and the transcendental or intelligible domains. There is for Kant a distinction between knowledge of time-bound entities and circumstances, for which evidence may be acquired directly through experience, and knowledge of temporally uncondi- tioned structures and conditions of possibility, which do not themselves appear, but make the appearance of these direct evidences possible. Knowledge of these temporally unconditioned structures is restricted to those who are also temporally unconditioned. There is then no knowl- edge for human beings of transcendental conditions of possibility. They are matters for complex indirect reflection, tending to generate paradox if approached uncritically. Kant thus maintains the Platonic distinction between ephemeral knowledge of appearances and knowledge of eter- nal truths, but marks the latter with a Kafkaesque "not for us."

In *An Ethics of Sexual Difference* Irigaray suggests that in order to make sense of this Kant has to construe the relation between the unlim- ited and the finite as the relation posited in Christianity between God and Christ. She then suggests that such dependency on a Christian image subverts the rigorous conceptuality of Kant's argument. The Kantian system thus both is and is not an example of rigorous concep- tual construction, confirming Irigaray's and Heidegger's suggestion about its self-subverting nature. This links to Heidegger's insistence that there cannot be ontological inquiry without ontical specificity, which undercuts the possibility of an absolute view from nowhere and of a privileged stance, among those achievable by human beings, that could provide such a view. This is part of the point of the term *Dasein.* In *Speculum* Irigaray points out that what usually happens is that men appropriate to themselves the nontemporal nonpositional stance from which it is supposed to be possible to acquire unconditional knowledge, and assign to women the specificity and positionality that makes such knowledge impossible. Thus Heidegger's insistence on positionality for all observers subverts the traditional conceptual sexual division of labor. Irigaray accepts this move and takes it further by showing how the absolute stance of the masculine gaze is conditional on repressing the feminine as the bearer of positionality. The cave from which Plato's seekers for knowledge in the *Republic* emerge into the sunlight of knowledge is in Irigaray's reading both womb, mother, and woman.

Out of his distinction between the ontological and the ontical Hei- degger develops a contrast between analyzing what there is and analyz- ing how it comes to be like that. The first, the ontical domain, is that of scientific inquiry; the second, the domain of ontology, is the preserve of phenomenological description. Thus far Heidegger's phenomenolo- gy is in agreement with that of Husserl, who contrasted regional and general ontological inquiry. The difference is that Heidegger takes seri- ously the thought that at different epochs what there is appears in radically different ways. He rejects Husserl's implicit triumphalism, indeed Hegelianism, of supposing current knowledge to have preserved all previously discovered truths and to be on the way to perfection. He seeks to make room for the challenge to epistemological continuity posed by the startling shift from medieval European thinking to the modern global view. The discontinuity between Greek and medieval, between medieval and modern worldviews reveals the degree of possible change in question. In the one epoch the earth is flat and there are hierarchies of angels connecting the finite and mortal to the infinite and eternal. In the next the world is round, and rotating in a steadily expanding universe, with positive and negative matter held in precarious balance. In the one there is a hierarchy of increasingly unknowable and increasingly perfect spheres of existence. In the other there is a single time-space frame into which everything is ordered.

These changes in the how of what there is suggest to Heidegger that there are ruptures in human history, setting one epoch apart from another. These result from what Heidegger calls *Seinsgeschichte*, what I translated earlier as the "transmissions, history, or layerings of being." He supposes a new epoch to be dawning now, at the close of the epoch that began with the emergence of European philosophy. He reads the pre-Socratic texts to show that at some point in early Greek thinking an unparalleled initiative took place, and philosophy, in the form practiced in Europe for the past two millennia, appeared. Out of the pre-Socratic move of attempting to produce a theory of everything that there is, Heidegger supposes the powers of modern technical capacities to have gradually emerged, with their transformative effects on the world and on human experience. From an initial stance of merely contemplating what there is, there has been a shift into actively producing it through the interventions of advanced technology. The completeness of this shift is conditional on forgetting being and forgetting to pose the ontological question about how what there is comes to be as it is. For Irigaray this conditionality is the forgetting of sexual difference, of women, of mothering.

For Heidegger European philosophy is culminating in a change of what there is. What there is becomes the upshot of technological activity; and the distinction between what there is and human activity is eroded; the gap between what there is and what there is thought to be is an ever diminishing one. Such a collapse would make real the ancient philosophical hope that there should cease to be a difference between thinking and its object, making knowledge of the objects of thought complete. This could be accomplished only at the cost of abolishing the autonomous existence of the objects of thought;

putting what there is wholly at the disposal of human beings and our destructive urges. This poses the greatest danger of the current epoch. The gap, as Heidegger construes it in the paper "The Origin of the Art Work,"[19] is between the earth, external to us, and the world, as our construct. He seeks to protect the earth from the erosion imposed by the world. However, in *L'Oubli de l'air* Irigaray identifies Heidegger's construal of the earth as an unknowable starting point for human existence as a residual metaphysical reduction in Heidegger's thought, forgetting and repressing not being, but air, as the medium of alterability. The insistence on the earth imposes a basic image of fixed rigidity, not one of flux; it thus invites metaphysical recuperation. Irigaray thus reads Heidegger's texts for the moment at which they, in turn, impose a rigid sameness in place of an alterability, which might be held in play by insisting on a relation between earth and air, between matter and spirit. She uses Heidegger's reading of Nietzsche, as imposing will to power on a flux of interpretation, to reveal a similar repetition of metaphysical closure within Heidegger's attempt to break free.

In his postwar essays on technology Heidegger insists that it is now not metaphysics but historical process that threatens to reduce what there is to a projection of human activity. Because technological innovation threatens to destroy human beings and the world we create, the difference between earth and world is in danger of disappearing, in a different sense, and with it the earth on which we live. The impossible internal logic of technology is to destroy what there is and replace it with human activity and its products: to abolish difference and install nothing but a humanness which cannot survive without the earth, but all the same expresses itself by working toward the destruction of that earth. This diagnosis confirms the importance of Heidegger's insistence on respect for the earth; but Irigaray takes the analysis further. She disrupts the other side of the reduction by developing Heidegger's critique of humanism and anthropology in *The Letter on Humanism* (1947) into a critique of the conception of humanness underlying the human activity that results in technology. She does this not by further criticizing the underlying conception of humanism but by insisting on sexual difference. This leads to a disruption, not a displacement, of the concept of humanism. She thus disrupts both sides of the juxtaposition: earth and human activity. This might lead to a displacement of a rigid conception of earth in favor of a system of transformative flux, which would be human, lived relations to sexual difference. She reveals in this humanness not a philosophically required structure of sameness, but multiplicity; not a single set of aims with respect to the world we find ourselves in, but an irreducible multiplicity of conflicting aims, defying reduction to a single frame.

There is a wind of change blowing over the earth's surface, disturbing the logic of sameness that lies concealed in Heidegger's invocation of the earth. There is a productive duplicity within that earth: annually Persephone returns to her mother, Gaia, the earth, bringing fertility and assuring another cycle of growth. It is this relation between Persephone and Gaia, between daughter and mother, that gets elided in the rigidities of Nietzsche's eternal return of the same, in Heidegger's transmissions of being, and in the obsessional closures of metaphysics. By denying sexual difference, by erasing the body of the mother and the relation between mother and daughter, decadence and death are installed in place of life and growth. Preoccupation with the death of the father obscures the urgency of retrieving the mother. However, revealing a concealment within the text of philosophy poses the problem of what in that revealing process is in turn being concealed: the problem of the otherness revealed in the encounter with another. Irigaray reveals that there can be no female other for the male to encounter, if that female other does not have its own female other, most powerfully symbolized by the mother/daughter relation. However, once the figures of the other/woman and of the mother have ceased to be the hidden other, some further layer of concealment in the text of European culture can perhaps be uncovered: perhaps the questions of race, imperialism, neocolonialism, indeed of being European.[20] Certainly Irigaray's concerns seem to be shifting. There are the themes of the four elements of pre-Socratic thought, there is her attempt to develop a sense of the divine specific to women. At the moment when women can disrupt the exclusions of philosophy, the issues themselves are likely to shift. Philosophy itself has changed such that the exclusion of women can now be named and discussed; and the complaint about being excluded begins to lose purchase. Only for the conservers of an outmoded philosophical tradition can the exclusion of women from the text of philosophy continue to be an issue. Irigaray is no such conserver; she is moving on.

NOTES   •

1. See Walter Benjamin, "Theses on the Philosophy of History" in Hannah Arendt, ed., *Illuminations*, trans. Harry Zohn (Jonathan Cape: London, 1970), p. 258.

2. Irigaray, "The Bodily Encounter," *The Irigaray Reader*, p. 37.

3. Irigaray, *Marine Lover*.

- 4. Irigaray, *L'Oubli de l'air.*
- 5. Benjamin, "Theses," p. 257.
6. For the value of forgetting, see Nietzsche, *The Uses and Drawbacks of History for Living,* in *Untimely Meditations* [1872] (Cambridge: Cambridge University Press, 1990); for the eternal return of the same, see *Thus Spoke Zarathustra* [1876] (Harmondsworth: Penguin, 1961).
7. Irigaray, *Marine Lover.*
8. Martin Heidegger, *Nietzsche,* trans. David Farrell Krell, 2 vols. [1961] (New York: Harper and Row, 1979–1984).
9. See Heidegger, *Zur Sache des Denkens* (Tuebingen: Max Niemeyer, 1969)/*On Time and Being,* trans. Joan Stambaugh (New York: Harper and Row, 1972), pp. 55–73.
10. See Heidegger, *Erläuterungen zu Hölderlins Dichtung* (Frankfurt a.M.: Vittorio Klosterman, 1947, 1951).
11. See Elizabeth Grosz, "Irigaray and the Divine," *Selected Studies in Phenomenology and Existential Philosophy,* eds. Arleen Dalleng and Charles Scott (Albany: State University of New York, forthcoming).
12. See Foucault's introduction to the English translation of Gilles Deleuze and Félix Guattari, *Anti-Oedipus: Capitalism and Schizophrenia* (Minneapolis: University of Minnesota Press, 1983).
13. See Rosi Braidotti, "The Ethics of Sexual Difference: The Case of Foucault and Irigaray" *Australian Feminist Studies* (1986), 3:1–13. In her article Braidotti identifies Nietzsche and Derrida as reacting against the claim of women to be silenced within the tradition, with the effect of concealing the justice of that claim. See also her recently published *Patterns of Dissonance* (Oxford: Polity, 1991), in which these themes are treated at greater length and in more detail.
14. See Levinas, *Totality and Infinity* [1961], trans. Alphonso Lingis (Pittsburgh: Duquesne University Press, 1969).
15. For the difference between reading and interpretation with respect to Heidegger's practice of responding to the texts of philosophers see Andrzej Warminski, *Reading in Interpretation: Hoelderlin, Hegel, and Heidegger* (Minneapolis: University of Minnesota Press, 1987).
16. See *Being and Time* [1927], trans. John Macquarrie and Edward Robinson (Oxford: Basil Blackwell, 1962).
17. See his inaugural lecture as professor of Philosophy at Freiburg, given in 1928, "What is Metaphysics?" in Heidegger, *Wegmarken* (Frankfurt a.M.: Vittorio Klostermann, 1967, 1978); translated by David Farrell Krell in Heidegger, *Basic Writings* (London: Routledge, 1978).
18. See Benjamin, *Gesammelte Schriften,* Band 1.2 (Frankfurt a.M.: Suhrkamp, 1974). In a footnote to section 11 of "On Some Motifs in Baudelaire" Benjamin attributes this thought to Karl Kraus, in the remark "Je näher man ein Wort ansieht, je ferner es sieht zurück," from *Pro domo et mundo* (Munich 1912), p. 164. Benjamin also refers to it indirectly in his essay "The Work of Art in the Age of Mechanical

Reproduction" (in *Illuminations*), which he cites in the Baudelaire essay, as footnoted in the Tiedemann and Schweppenhauser edition of Benjamin's writings. There is a connection here to Nietzsche's preoccupation with the pathos of distance. The thought captures Benjamin's difficulties in discussing the auratic quality of art, which can exist only if art is not directly inspected. It also captures the more general problem of analyzing anything that is only indirectly experienced. Once it is made the focus of attention its quality of indirectness, which was to be analyzed, has disappeared.

19. In Heidegger, *Holzwege* (Frankfurt a.M.: Vittorio Klosterman, 1950); and *Poetry, Language, Thought*, trans. by Albert Hofstadter (New York: Harper and Row, 1971).
20. See Joanna Hodge, "Nietzsche, Heidegger, Europe," *Journal of Nietzsche Studies* (Spring 1992), 3:45–66.

· *Ellen Mortensen*

WOMAN'S (UN)TRUTH

AND LE FÉMININ:

READING

LUCE IRIGARAY WITH

FRIEDRICH NIETZSCHE

AND

MARTIN HEIDEGGER

In her poetico-philosophic work, *Marine Lover of Friedrich Nietzsche* (1980), Luce Irigaray not only launches a far-reaching attack on Nietzsche's limited understanding of woman but seriously challenges all traditional phenomenology as well.[1] By strategically inserting herself in the openings of Nietzsche's writings and by "listening" to the silent *mater-ial* "ground" upon which he erects his philosophy, Irigaray retrieves that which has been muted in his discourse. This "silence" then serves as a potentiality for her exploration of sexual difference, or, for what she refers to as *le féminin*.

The following inquiry will attempt to make resonate some of the major philosophical intertexts in *Marine Lover*, particularly Plato, Nietzsche, and Heidegger. And, by retracing Irigaray's meandering in the labyrinth of Nietzsche's thinking, it will explore Irigaray's projective anticipation of *le féminin*. Finally, this study will seek to reveal how Irigaray appropriates and critiques Martin Heidegger's thinking in her quest for sexual difference.[2]

Marine Lover can be read as a meditation on Nietzsche's philosophy of will to power, a philosophy that for Irigaray might prove fruitful in providing her with new paths of thinking in the quest of sexual difference. However, by unveiling Nietzsche's apparent complicity in Western metaphysics, Irigaray's deconstruction of his oeuvre also warns against premature and facile appropriations.

I will argue that it is illuminating to read Irigaray's meditation on Nietzsche in light of the nihilism problematic. Nietzsche defines nihilism as the historical movement whereby "all values hitherto have been devalued."[3] This means that man has lost the ground upon which his moral and reason-able universe had been erected. No longer can he be assured of the existence of "universal truth" or "absolute value." Nietzsche provides the answer to this unfortunate state of affairs through his conception of will to power, wherein man finds the imperative to shape his own existence and his universe through an act of transvaluation.[4] This transvaluation, which revalues all previous values, has no universal validity. However, Nietzsche's transvaluing subject has gained the power to define his own being as value, without being restrained by any universal (moral/epistemological) law. Man willfully inscribes the circumference of his own being through his perspectival perception of what *is*.

In *Marine Lover* Irigaray indicates obliquely the failure of Nietzsche's transvaluation to leave the circle of the same. In Nietzsche's concentric perspective "woman" remains "the other of the same," despite his claims to have overcome metaphysical oppositional thinking. As a value, "woman" is thought in terms of that which appears to and that which enhances the power of the subject. Irigaray rejects this Nietzschean-inspired phenomenology and its appropriating gesture, since it assumes that what appears to the subject constitutes the totality of what *is*.

Instead, Irigaray introduces her understanding of *le féminin*, which must be thought outside this phenomenological apparatus. *Le féminin* is different from traditionally conceived beings in that it does not have to *appear* in order to *be*. This presents the reader with a number of problems, not all of which are resolved by Irigaray. For instance, how does Irigaray gain access to *le féminin* if it, indeed, does not appear? And, how is *le féminin* affected by the nihilism problematic?

To approach these questions Irigaray turns to Heidegger's radicalization of phenomenology,[5] which argues that metaphysics is forgetful of the ground upon which beings rest. Heidegger claims that when Nietzsche privileges transvaluation, through which he seeks to overcome metaphysics, he acknowledges the principle of valuation. And, in so doing, he is thinking Being in terms of beings, as such, that is, as values. Consequently, instead of overcoming metaphysics, he solidifies it.

Her alignment with Heidegger's thinking is on the one hand

expressed in her indebtedness to his thinking on the question of the
ontological difference between Being and beings. In Irigaray's rewriting
le féminin is thought in terms of Being, that is, as that which appears as
other than what it is, or, as that which is *hidden from view*. *Le féminin*
can thus only appear in metaphysical language as that which it is *not*.
Consequently, Nietzsche's "woman," which is firmly lodged in metaphysics, remains trapped within its (t)autological circle. On the other
hand Irigaray also criticizes Heidegger in *L'Oubli de l'air*[6] for his privileging of the philosophical *logos*, which she interprets as a gesture on the
part of Heidegger to try to save philosophy.[7]

I believe that Irigaray's rereading of Nietzsche convincingly and elo-
quently argues for the shortcomings of his conception of "woman." A
problem arises, however, in Irigaray's vacillation. She sometimes fails to
acknowledge the workings of nihilism, and subsequently turns *le
féminin* into a transvalued value. In those cases Irigaray falls into the
same trap as does Nietzsche, and *le féminin* will consequently be perceived as another being. However, when she approaches *le féminin*
ontologically she pays heed to the Being question, and in those
instances *le féminin* has the potentiality to "speak" *difference*.

i

In *Beyond Good and Evil* Nietzsche speaks to the question of woman
and truth and argues that "from the beginning, nothing has been more
alien, repugnant, and hostile to woman than truth—her great art is the
lie, her highest concern is mere appearance and beauty."[8] When Irigaray
quotes this passage in her opening paragraph of "Lèvres voilées," she
vehemently disagrees with Nietzsche's fundamental presupposition in
making the remark, namely that "nothing has been more alien . . . to
woman than truth." To Irigaray the lie, appearance, and beauty are not
foreign to truth but are in fact proper to it. Their common denomina-
tor is the oppositional logic that creates these antithetical couples:
truth/lie, reality/appearance, beauty/imperfection, etc. Instead of
speaking of difference, these couples rather convey sameness; difference
understood as binary opposition can never speak of difference. One
term is opposite to but nevertheless determined by a *logic* of the *same*,
because one term will always be privileged over the other. And in an
effort to safeguard this term's propriety and integrity, an antithetical
term is established in order to differentiate it from that which it is *not*.
That which would be alien or foreign to truth would have to be found
"elsewhere." However, within Nietzsche's "economy" of truth this possibility for (sexual) difference has been forgotten.

Irigaray's deconstruction of the multiple figurations of woman in Nietzsche reveals his complicity in Western metaphysics, even as he seeks to reach beyond its limits. Pointing to Nietzsche's complicity in Platonic mimesis, Irigaray demonstrates how Nietzsche's understanding of woman remains confined within the paradigm of Echo and Narcissus,[9] in which Echo cannot be perceived as other than Narcissus's double. Echo's function in Ovid's mythical poem is to accompany the movement of Narcissus's self-reflection, to adorn and to deploy his self-representation, while keeping the integrity of the image intact. In this sense woman's femininity, defined within a narcissistic echo-nomy, ensures the smooth workings of the mimetic machinery.

Within the philosophic discourse of truth as we know it, from Plato onwards, woman has become the incarnation of that which is erroneous, deceitful, but nevertheless beautiful, like Helen of Troy. For Plato woman's proximity to materiality and her sensuousness constitute the cause of her imperfection, whereas man's self-image, generated within the principle of *eidos* as the idea(l) image of truth, accounts for his affinity with perfection.

Conversely, for Nietzsche woman's beauty exists precisely in her material imperfection and, as such, exemplifies the superior principle of illusion as opposed to truth. But femininity is still a necessary element for the economy to be operational. In Nietzsche as well as in Plato, Irigaray argues, woman's femininity has always already been appropriated as the negative counterpart to the masculine economy of truth. In fact the aphorism in question from *Beyond Good and Evil* seeks to ridicule woman's attempt to "find herself" within the scientific discourse of truth that Nietzsche so much despises. When Nietzsche claims that "nothing is more alien to woman than truth," we have to understand his statement within the context of his own position with regard to truth.

Nietzsche identifies a process as having taken place in the "History of an Error" that might be read as synonymous with the "History of Western metaphysics." In Nietzsche's stance against Platonism and Christianity, and the common pursuit of the "true world" obtainable through the virtuous endeavor of the sage/the pious man, he posits in his *Twilight of the Idols*: "Progress of the idea: it becomes more subtle, insidious, incomprehensible—*it becomes female*, it becomes Christian."[10] Nietzsche indicates with this pronouncement that if error becomes the "truth" of pleasure, then the "idea" becomes "woman." He thus aligns error, woman, and the Christian. What takes place in the Nietzschean transposition of the "idea" of woman is merely a change from one realm of representation to another. In the Platonic

scheme the "eternal feminine" must be devalued because of her primordial connection with temporal and sensuous nature. With Nietzsche the representation changes to a possibility of a "different" idea
as a new resource for a(n artistic) force, with remnants from the memory of Dionysus. It is in this sense that Irigaray reads his juxtaposition
of woman with Christian. With the advent of nihilism subjectivity
becomes perspectival and truth becomes by implication void of universal validity. The "idea" is transformed from eternal truth to
"woman," denoting the affirmation of will to power as art in all of its
fictive splendor. In the Nietzschean schema art is worth more than
truth. Consequently, when he aligns woman with art, woman is
worth more than truth. For Nietzsche she embodies the simulacrum,
the illusion, and everything he views as alien to this kind of reasoning
logic.

If woman, in a Socratic gesture, seeks to enlighten herself and others
about herself, her gesture becomes as futile and nihilistic as that of the
pedantic scientist so often ridiculed by Nietzsche. When woman likewise "puts on airs" of the philosopher, she becomes an easy target for
Nietzsche's ironic scrutiny. His position thus questions woman's ability
to actually *want* enlightenment about herself. If woman is "true" to her
"untrue" self (which is, of course, a paradox in itself), she cannot possibly desire to enlighten herself or anyone else about herself. In her
assigned function within this mimetic economy woman has had to
assume an identity of un-truth in order for the paradigm to uphold
itself. As such, her identity could not do without (*s'en passer*) this lie that
she herself is said to embody in order for her to pass herself off as (*passer pour*) the other of the same.

We keep forgetting, claims Irigaray, that these significations do not
speak of woman's (sexual) difference but instead result from a philosophical construct that has appropriated her (potential) being into an
assigned position within a paradigm that cannot tolerate (sexual) difference. Consequently for Irigaray it matters little that Nietzsche trans-
values woman's materiality and thus elevates her alleged affinity with
lying (as opposed to truth), appearance (as opposed to Platonic reality),
and beauty (as opposed to ugliness/imperfection) into the principle of
will to power as art.

The comic effect to which Nietzsche aspires in his ridiculing of
woman's scientific endeavor is, of course, aimed at undermining the
foundations of the "feminist movement." In the fashion of most civil
rights movements, the feminists of his time saw in the Enlightenment
the legitimation of their claims. Thus Nietzsche mockingly refers to the
Kantian aspect of their advocacy:

> •
> •   Woman wants to become self-reliant—and for that reason she is begin-
> ning to enlighten men about "woman as such": this is one of the worst
> developments of the general *uglification* of Europe. For what must these
> clumsy attempts of women at scientific self-exposure bring to light![11]

It is in light of these considerations that we must interpret the following provocative and ironic statement: "And I think it is a real friend of
women that counsels them today: *mulier taceat de muliere!* [woman
should be silent about woman]."[12]

When Nietzsche sees woman as the error of metaphysics, as that
which ironically appears to be something different than what it is—"she
gives herself out to be: what she is not"[13]—he then posits woman as
becoming and as perpetual change. But for Irigaray Nietzsche's positioning of woman as a counterpart to the Platonic scheme of truth cannot possibly let woman's *difference* emerge, since he remains firmly
lodged within the Platonic duality of truth/error, permanence/change,
and self-identity/nonidentity. Throughout history woman's "profundity"[14] has been alternately denigrated or valorized within this duality,
and Nietzsche's contribution does not radically diverge from that of his
previous fellow philosophers.

In *The Will to Power* Nietzsche defines nihilism in terms of the fact
"that the highest values devaluate themselves."[15] For example, "woman"
considered as value had attained the status of a devalued value in metaphysical thinking, until Nietzsche's philosophy opened up for a "transvaluation," thus making "woman" the emblem of his new "truth."

Moreover, the fact that Nietzsche puts the entire quotation from *The
Twilight of the Idols* in brackets, in a distancing gesture, signifies for Irigaray his attempt to enclose his newfound idea of woman. He further
elaborates on the importance of distance in another "rumination" on
the question in *The Gay Science*: "The magic and the most powerful
effect of women, is, in philosophical language, action at a distance, *actio
in distans*; but this requires first of all and above all—*distance*."[16] But
even Nietzsche's new, dressed-up version of the idea as woman remains
too coldly theoretical. And, in its resemblance to "being," it seems to
have become devoid of all sensuality. One might in fact say that Nietzsche has performed a biting critique of the history of metaphysics, but
that, in the process of transvaluation, he has managed to suck the blood
out of his newfound "idea." Irigaray chooses the following words to
describe the unfortunate bloodletting of woman that has taken place:
"Something red was lacking, a hint of blood and guts to revive the will,
and restore its strength. A wound. Which however will only be opened
up in its representation from within that extra setting: the brackets."[17]

Irigaray makes a link to the psychoanalytic theory of castration for-mulated by both Freud and Lacan, whereby the question of the (re)pre-sentation of woman moves from the possibility of present-ing herself (*se donner*) to that of giving herself *as* (*se donner pour*) something. Or else woman operates in an undecidable space between truth, "truth," and appearances, as in the Nietzschean schema. But in all cases the femi-ninity of woman will still remain the "other" of the same. Even when woman is elevated into a "new truth," the operation of castration remains intact. In this context Irigaray poses the following questions:

> Castration? Wasn't that, precisely, the gesture of repetition which gave the key to the whole stage set by the same? And therefore gave it some play, gave the game the possibility: to be played. In the second or third degree: the Apollonian dream, the Socratic truth, the simulacrum (both of them within a certain indifference, a repeat that suspends the gash between them, covers the [female] one and the other and yet never real-ly does so, still adhering to a belief in difference—if only to play with it). (*p. 80/86*)

Castration is but a simulacrum, claims Irigaray, and its main function is to set the operation into *play*, even if it has lost its power of differen-tiation. It is thus in the order of the sign that woman is subject to cas-tration and has to become the repository for absence, death, and lack. Since this is the "other," which the masculine subject fears above all, it robs him of his possibility of mastery, and must, for this reason, be shunned.

Nietzsche proclaims that art has the capacity to gather everything into itself, thinking included. But it will always appear *as something*, an appearance that emerges under the sway of Apollonian illusion. How-ever, for Nietzsche, the *illusion* inherent in signification can finally be acknowledged, which he does through his philosophy of nihilism with the phrase "God is dead."[18] The simulation necessary for the play of signs to unfold embraces the (simulated) castration that has taken place in relation to philosophy's power to speak totality. But Irigaray asks if this move, instead of undermining the position of mastery sought by the Socratic subject, does not in fact solidify the (illusion) of mastery by incorporating everything within its artistic play of the subjective will, thus reducing it all to a play of *sameness*.

> Perhaps by admitting the part played by illusion, by claiming it openly, airing it publicly, one is cleared of the burden of a secret, the guilt of concealment, of the pure and simple assurance of being adequate to mastery. Not by losing. Especially if the scenario is now presumed to be *general*. Including this residue: the other would threaten castration. The

> other? Of the same? If castration means the same thing as: kill him, if it
> is equivalent to death, then the other is equivalent to the same. Or else
> perpetuates the alternation of everything and nothing. Fulfilling the
> master's desire. Which he can dress up differently, according to the his-
> torical moment.   *(p. 81/87)*

Woman's only being within this representational theater is *as* the
nothing that resists representation. The symbolic murder of woman
through the category of femininity has found expression in a host of
roles in the course of the last centuries, Irigaray says: "Since several centuries of silence have taken on quite a number of roles: echo, place,
interval, abyss, thing, possibility of repetition, of articulation . . . mirror" (p. 85/91). However, this *nothing* that then has become the ground
upon which the masculine edifice has been erected—whether we think
of it in terms of the unconscious or as the silent primordial ground that
is essentially undecidable—nevertheless signals an outside or an elsewhere, outside of the enframing view of that which has hitherto been
thought.

ii

The major thrust of Irigaray's writing attempts to make a bridge to this
elsewhere that she refers to as *le féminin*. *Le féminin* differs from femininity in that it does not enter into the ec(h)onomy of mimesis other
than as that which defies representation, as absence or as silence. In Irigaray's writings it comes into play only within an economy that is *specific* to itself, but never *proper* to itself, and that attains its value from its
different "form(s)," based on the morphology of the female sexual
organs.

Despite Irigaray's convincing deconstruction of Nietzsche certain
questions remain to be asked. First, does Irigaray herself escape the
mimetic trap into which women have traditionally been forced in her
exploration of *le féminin*? Second, can she possibly overturn the state
of affairs that has reigned from Plato to Nietzsche and thus claim to be
capable of speaking *differently* about women? Furthermore, if every
theory of the subject has always already been appropriated by the masculine,[19] is it in fact possible for woman to speak? Will she not always
have to *pass for* a masculine subject in order to have a language at all,
and then in the process by necessity "lose herself"? Is this what Irigaray
attempts to allude to in the chapter in *Marine Lover* entitled "Lèvres
voilées"? If her lips are veiled/violated, does she thereby suggest that
women have no *different* language because their language/body have
thus been violated? Obviously, I can only tentatively deal with these

questions within the scope of this article. Since Irigaray herself never fully provides an answer to them, I believe that they need further exploration.

However, Irigaray's fragmented and multifaceted text speaks to some of these questions, without ever giving any affirmative answer postulated in propositional language. She questions and provisionally explores a morpho-logic of difference, based on the very form(s) of the female sexual organs. Its/their morphology defy the traditional notions of unity, sameness, and solidity and speak instead to the principle of multiplicity, difference, and fluidity. She describes the connection between the form(s) of the feminine sex and the traditional paradigm of thought in the following way:

> If the female sex takes place by embracing itself, by endlessly sharing and exchanging its lips, its edges, its borders, and their "content," as it ceaselessly becomes other, no stability of essence is proper to her. She has a place in the openness of a relation to the other whom she does not take into herself, like a whore, but to whom she continuously gives birth.
> *(p. 86/92)*

The/a woman can already sub-sist to be double in herself, that is, be both the one and the other. In this way she continuously exchanges herself in the other, without ever exercising any ownership over herself or over the other. Thus, *le féminin* is totally foreign to the possibility of unity, of possession in the sense of belonging (to someone/thing), even reflexively as belonging to herself.

At this juncture, Irigaray makes the startling pronouncement:

> The feminine goes beyond "phenomenology." Were it not for the demands of the economy of sameness. Because "she" affects herself already (within herself) without the appearance of a sensible sign. She has no overriding need to produce herself under any form whatever.
> *(p. 87/93)*

What emerges here is an indirect critique of phenomenology and its proclaimed philosophy of beings, including the "being" of the construction of the subject itself. With this pronouncement Irigaray separates her thinking from phenomenological thinkers. If we are to understand her as saying that all "beings" that emerge within the phenomenological optics are always already contaminated with the "ec(h)onomy" of (phallic) truth as it emerges from Plato and Aristotle onwards, then *le féminin* must be understood to reside outside the realm of these confines.

But *le féminin* may not have to appear at all, and must therefore not

be confined to the requirement of (a coherent, solid, unified) phenomenological form in order to be. Her being might consequently be found
in her lack of being, and this default of being might actually also reside
in her excess (*en plus*). What most clearly appears to be Irigaray's target
here is the Cartesian and later phenomenological obsession with cer-
tainty, first of the subject and subsequently of the object that the subject "understands and perceives."

Another question to Irigaray would be: If *le féminin* resides outside
the phenomenological framework, how does Irigaray herself gain
access to this "elsewhere"? What grants her power to reach inside this
domain and (poetically) speak (its being), if in fact it has no being?[20]
By the same token, how can it possibly be anything—even multiple,
fluid, without limits, without property, and free-flowing pleasure?
What is the status of Irigaray's language when she makes these pronouncements? Finally, how does the question of nihilism enter into
this problematic?

According to Irigaray *le féminin* exists prior to and is more primordial than the system of thought that has hitherto attempted to
contain woman, whether that be defined as "truth" or "error" in
philosophical language. *Le féminin's* functioning within itself remains
ludic in the most open-ended sense of that which is free and playful.
Irigaray refers to the workings of *le hasard* in the determination of
what woman will be. But woman will always give herself *as* something, in her words: "Chance—the deal. Can only be dealt out for
what he/she is not."[21]

This seemingly simple statement contains rather far-reaching implications if we interpret it to mean that chance determines how woman
is given in language, and she will appear only in terms of what "he"
is/"she" is not. What this suggests is that woman is forever subjected to
a phenomenological apparatus that is fundamentally foreign to her.
This phenomenology belongs instead to a masculine logic, which will
always attempt to appropriate woman within phenomenological forms
that will, in turn, negate and deny her existence. Within this framework
woman can therefore only "give herself for/as" something that she is
not, namely, as femininity.

Irigaray thus emphatically rejects phenomenology as a valid structure through which *le féminin* could be approached. Because *le féminin*
would yield nothing to be shown (i.e., Freud's notion of woman *as* a
castrated man without *one* visible sex) within this phenomenological
optics, and since it can only see what it has already seen, traditional phenomenology cannot possibly do justice to *le féminin's* potentiality for
being.

iii

Despite the fact that she denounces traditional phenomenology as an avenue to approach *le féminin*, Irigaray's statement, however, appropriates Martin Heidegger's radical phenomenology as outlined in *Being and Time*. Irigaray is of course no stranger to Heidegger's thinking on the *as-structure*, and, like Heidegger, she highlights the workings of "receptivity" (the gift) in regards to *le féminin*'s possibility for being.[22]

Heidegger emphasizes the ontological difference that exists between what he nominates the existential-hermeneutic "as" and the *apophantical* "as."[23] What this means is that whenever something is uttered, it appears *as* something in language. This *as*-structure makes something appear, that is, conceptual objects appear in everyday language as "ready-to-hand" objects for us to manipulate. But prior to this facilitative aspect of language, something more fundamental has happened and is forgotten: the "being-there"/*Dasein* of the subject that speaks has had to constitute itself existentially through the *existential-hermeneutic "as"*. Therefore, when the theoretical subject speaks, no matter how stringent its logic, it can only speak of the apophantical "as" of the "ready-to-hand," which is always derivative of the prior.[24] In Western metaphysics from Aristotle onward, Heidegger claims, there has been a forgetfulness of the primordial understanding provided in the existential-hermeneutic "as" and simultaneously a privileging of the apophantical "as," which obeys the ontic logic of the theoretical interpretation.

It seems to me that Irigaray accepts Heidegger's observation that the kind of interpretation that understands the world apophantically, that is, through theoretical or philosophical language, cannot pay heed to the Being question, and by implication cannot "perceive" *le féminin*. What the apophantical "as" forgets is that something is hidden from view in its metaphysical appropriation of what *is*. Thus, phenomenological beings are predominantly thought as "the present-at-hand," that is, they are conceived as that which appears to the I/eye.

Therefore, one might say that Irigaray uses a Heideggerian path of thinking in her exploration of *le féminin* in the sense that she reveals how it can only appear in metaphysical language as that which it is *not*. The "phenomenon" *le féminin*, in the Heideggerian sense, is destined to appear *as* "femininity," which again shows itself as the negative double of the logical categories that already exist. The "in-itself" of *le féminin* is what withdraws from view. Femininity thus becomes a difference, but a difference within the *same* to that which is privileged in the optical logic of the masculine, which is only capable of perceiving unity, solidity, and oneness. *Le féminin* is therefore caught within the "as" of the already existing theoretical paradigms of Western metaphysics. Chance, which rules the destiny of this history of Being as it has unfolded itself, has relegated woman to "ce qu'il est/elle n'est pas."

Irigaray opens up the question of the *as-structure* as Heidegger thought it in its relationship to the history of nihilism. Heidegger redefines nihilism as synonymous with the history of Being in Western metaphysics in the sense that there is "Nothing to Being" in our tradition of thinking what *is*. Nihilism is defined in the unfolding of the history of Western metaphysics as the withdrawal of Being in metaphysics. Heidegger understands them to be one and the same thing, and therefore inextricably linked.

For Heidegger as for Irigaray Nietzsche reverses Platonism through his valuative philosophy, in the sense that what had previously been devalued is now valued. As a transvalued value "woman" exemplifies this operation and comes to figure at the center of the nihilism problematic.

Heidegger's chapter entitled "Nihilism as Determined by the History of Being" in his fourth volume on Nietzsche, *Nihilism*,[25] seems to resonate in Irigaray's treatment of the possible profundity of woman as it is thought by metaphysics in general and by Nietzsche in particular. In an attempt to assess Nietzsche's position in relation to the metaphysical tradition and his alleged overcoming of nihilism through his valuative will to power, Heidegger points to the inability of Nietzsche to think the Being question. Heidegger claims that, like most of his predecessors, Nietzsche remains trapped within Western metaphysics and thus fails to see that metaphysics reaches deeper than it acknowledges. It reaches toward that which belongs to a different realm and can only appear as an enigma:

> According to its essence, nihilism is the history of the promise, in which Being itself saves itself in a mystery which is itself historical and which preserves the unconcealment of Being from that history in the form of metaphysics. The whole of the essence of nihilism, to the extent that— as the history of Being—it bestows itself as an abode for the essence of man, grants thinking everything that is to be thought. Consequently, what is given to thinking as to be thought we call *the enigma*.[26]

For Heidegger Being is what gives rise to thought, it "gives food for thought," and "Being, the promise of the unconcealment as the history of the secret, is itself the enigma."[27] It is therefore Being itself that gives rise to metaphysics, and it follows that metaphysics cannot possibly determine the enigma of Being. The implication of this is, for Heidegger, that the essence of nihilism in the history of Being is not something that can be willed by human beings. Nor can the essence of nihilism be produced in thought through theoretical philosophical categories. Rather, that which is *given* "reality" in metaphysics can only *be* on the basis of the essential history of Being itself, which allows beings to be, but only through the *default* of Being. The essence of nihilism *is the nothing in Being.*

Irigaray seems to rely on Heidegger's thinking in her attempt to question Nietzsche's reversed valuation of woman as becoming, as error, or as illusion when she posits: "Full awareness—dissimulation that hides (itself)" (p. 89/95). But, in addition, *le féminin* seems to speak of an ontological difference between that which emerges and that which *le féminin is* in its difference, that is, in its absence. If one were to apply a logic of analogy at this level, one might contend that Irigaray, even though she denounces traditional phenomenological structures, has partially appropriated Heidegger's radical phenomenology in her projected vision of *le féminin.* As that which in its absence is always already split and only appears *as* that which it is not, *le féminin* may be said to point to an as yet unspoken ontological (sexual) difference akin to Heidegger's differentiation between Being and beings.

What cannot be thought in traditional phenomenological representations of woman is that she is double or fragmented *en elle-même* ("in her-self"). In this sense the "being" of "woman" exceeds the boundaries of the unified phenomenon as it is understood in traditional phenomenological terms. But then, what is/are the possible meaning(s) of *en elle-même?* We have to assume that Irigaray is not talking about a Kantian notion of an "in itself," which even the most stringent phenomenology declares unattainable. What seems to be at stake is an attempted envisioning of a *material immediacy* that is not implicated in traditional representations determined by unity, self-sameness, and identity. Instead, what Irigaray attempts to project is rather *different* "being(s)":

> So, when she touches herself (again), who is "she"? And "herself"? Inseparable, "she" and "herself" are part the one of the other, endlessly. They cannot really be distinguished, though they are not for all that the female same, nor the male same. That can be reassembled within some whole. This is to say again, or further, that it would be impossible to decide definitively which "of the two" would be "she" and which "herself."
>
> (p. 90/97)

This means that discursively, the subject is not identifiable in its relationship to the object. The *se* cannot be read reflexively, since there is no true property of the self nor is there any identity to *elle. Elle* exists outside the masculine discourse founded upon the self-identity of the

- subject and its predicate. In the case of *le féminin* Irigaray projects a new
- algebra: "X is (to, in, . . .) y—which still allows passivity to have a place
in auto-affection, or else a suspension between activity and passivity in
the attribution of being—it will never be known who/what is y in the
female" (p. 91/97). Indecidability will thus replace certitude and calcu-
lability in the "there" of *le féminin*. *Elle* does not possess the instrument
that would give her access to her own "property," or that of the "other."

Both Irigaray and Heidegger emphasize the ontological difference
between Being and beings, or, in Irigaray's terminology, between *matière
première* (first matter) and *formes* (forms). The primordial nature of this
difference comes to light as that which is "prior" to all emergent (phenomenal) beings, as that which gives rise to them. Irigaray's discourse
pays heed to the figure of the *mater*-ial aspects of giving birth, whereas
in Heidegger's language emphasis is put on the "giving" as present-ing in
language. Both, however, insist on the *difference* inherent between the
gift giving and what is given, as well as the oblivion that enshrouds this
primordial operation. *Le féminin* is for Irigaray this oblivion of the primordial (sexual) difference that cannot be thought in Western metaphysics in general and in phenomenology in particular.

From the position of outsider woman nevertheless supports this representational economy. What is important to understand in this mechanism is that she can uphold the logic of predication without there
being anything proper to her in so doing. To reveal this would in effect
mean the death of the subject. The ground is taken away from the solidity of the subject's foundation, thus causing the collage of forms to subsequently crumble. But her function as death does not exhaust her
being. There is always that which exceeds death. Woman does not die
from death other than as a subject. In fact she remains unmarked by this
functioning, in her sub-sistence underlying all discursivity, which for
Irigaray gives her an ontological status as *matière première*:

> Out of the storehouse of matter all forms are born. She brings them into
> the world, she "produces." From between her lips comes every new fig-
> ure: a warm glowing heat comes out of that self-embrace and becomes
> "visible." But once, one single time, and one instant only: beauty. After-
> ward, or, by default and repetition, there are veils. Unless there be a
> divine reality.   *(p. 92/98)*

This status of *matière première* and the *visible* hearkens back to Heidegger's understanding of Being in its relationship to beings.[28] Heidegger's Being can never assume any identity, but, as it unfolds in the clearing of history, it will always be appropriated by tradition and thus always
appear as beings, *different* from Being. The "as-which" that appears,

belongs to and is determined by tradition, and its destiny is claimed in
Ereignis as the event of appropriation.[29] Likewise, *le féminin* will never
appear in discourse as that which it is, but always *as* that to which tradition subjects it. This is the reason why *le féminin* has appeared as truth,
abyss, death, untruth, art, interval, excess, etc. Tradition, ruled by
chance, in this sense determines the destiny of every being.

Irigaray's deconstruction of the privileged symbols of femininity has
furthermore shown how woman's being has ranged from connotations
such as death, abyss, interval, intermediary, truth, untruth, lie, art, etc.
However, what these connotations all have failed to confront is *le féminin*
as the total potential of woman, which cannot be appropriated into any
fixed form/idea. Nor can it be spoken in traditional metaphysical language. However, while she has appropriated the Heideggerian path of
inquiry in her attempt to deconstruct dominant modes of thinking about
women, Irigaray eventually rejects what she considers to be Heidegger's
privileging of the *logos*, or, as she formulates it, Heidegger's privileging of
philosophical language. In her view Heidegger as well as Nietzsche, like
all of their predecessors, cannot confront woman's *mater-iality*, but insist
on the translation of woman into some realm that deprives her of her fluidity and her multiplicity. The following quotation from *L'Oubli de l'air
chez Martin Heidegger* articulates Irigaray's quest for a sensible immediacy that has yet to be explored and that still seems to incite fear in those
who seek to unravel "l'essence profonde du dionysiaque":

> Does not being find its foundation in a sensible immediacy as yet unspo-
> ken? In a silence about that which secretly gives nourishment to think-
> ing? The forbidden/unspoken or the inexpressible in the relationship of
> man to a nature which escapes his *logos*. Which gives itself (to be) in the
> unnamed site where the organs' contribution to its/their meaning/sense
> gather(s). A given/gift which it reprojects in(to) a world and its objects.
> Thus recreating the whole, and making of everyone the whole, and of
> the whole everyone, without the secret of this production ever being
> apparent to it.[30]

Marine Lover of Friedrich Nietzsche can thus be read as an attempt at
invoking this dormant, silent, but still fecund reservoir of profound *difference, le féminin.*

NOTES •

1. In the introduction to his essay "Phenomenology," in *Encyclopaedia Bri-
   tannica*, trans. Christopher V. Salmon, 14th ed. (1927), 17:699–702,
   Edmund Husserl defines phenomenology in the following words:

.
.

> The term "phenomenology" designates two things: a new kind of descriptive method which made a breakthrough at the turn of the century, and an *a priori* science derived from it; a science which is intended to supply the basic instrument (*Organon*) for a rigorously scientific philosophy, and in its consequent application, to make possible a methodological reform of all the sciences.

In my use of the term, which is much broader than Husserl's definition, I include such "early" phenomenologists as Kant and Hegel, since the intertextual link to Husserl's thinking on transcendental phenomenology seems obvious, despite the fact that Husserl has been characterized as both anti-Kantian and anti-Hegelian in his rhetoric. Thus, *phenomenology*, in my use of the term, comes to stand for the philosophy that seeks to define the way in which beings are perceived and appear as such.

2. See also Ellen Mortensen, " 'Le féminin' and Nihilism: Reading Irigaray with Nietzsche and Heidegger," Ph.D. diss., University of Wisconsin-Madison, 1989.

3. See Friedrich Nietzsche, *The Will to Power*, trans. Walter Kaufmann (New York: Vintage, 1967), p. 9.

4. The concept of transvaluation in Nietzsche is perhaps best illuminated in *Thus Spoke Zarathustra*, trans. Walter Kaufmann in *The Portable Nietzsche* (New York: Viking, 1968), pp. 103–442.

5. Heidegger's radicalization of phenomenology consists of his attempt to bring the self-evidence of the maxim "To the things themselves" closer to view. In so doing he asks the question of Being, and of the Being of beings. "Phenomenology" usually refers to the *science of phenomena*. Heidegger, however, wants to take the preliminary conception of the maxim a step further, or, more accurately, a step back. By going back to the Greek roots of the words that form *phenomenology*, namely, *phenomenon* and *logos*, Heidegger attempts to retrieve that which has been lost in the modern appropriation of the words. *Phenomenon* in Greek signifies "to show itself in itself," or, the manifest. However, for Heidegger appearance, as different from phenomenon, is a *not-showing-itself* of that which-is-in-itself. In *Being and Time*, he elaborates on the term *phenomenology*, saying:

> What is it that phenomenology is "to let us see?" What is it that must be called a "phenomenon" in a distinctive sense? What is it that by its very essence is *necessarily* the theme whenever we exhibit something *explicitly*? Manifestly, it is something that proximally and for the most part does *not* show itself at all: it is something that lies *hidden*, in contrast to that which proximally and for the most part does show itself; but at the same time it is something that belongs to what thus shows itself, and it belongs to it so essentially as to constitute its meaning and its ground.

Martin Heidegger, *Being and Time*, trans. John Macquarrie and Edward Robinson (New York: Harper and Row, 1962), p. 59.

6. In Irigaray's *L'Oubli de l'air*, which constitutes the second volume of a series of deconstructive texts, *Marine Lover* being volume 1, Irigaray tries to speak from inside the Heideggerian discourse. While remaining "close" to Heidegger's texts, *L'Oubli* may nevertheless be read as a critique of Heidegger's forgetfulness of the invisible element, namely air. In her reading Heidegger privileges the earth, like Nietzsche privileges fire. He thus fails to acknowledge the conceptual implication of the *invisibility* of air, much like Nietzsche fails to acknowledge his fears of water.

7. In my view Irigaray's reading of Heidegger on this question does not adequately take into account his understanding of *logos*, which cannot be reduced to a synonym of "rationality," but "speaks" instead of the unconcealment of beings/concealment of Being inherent in that which appears in "saying."

8. Nietzsche, *Beyond Good and Evil: Prelude to a Philosophy of the Future*, trans. Walter Kaufmann (New York: Vintage Books, 1974), p. 163.

9. This argument is predominantly based on Ovid's mythical poem "The Story of Echo and Narcissus" in *Metamorphoses*, trans. Rolfe Humphries (Bloomington: Indiana University Press, 1955), pp. 68–69.

10. Nietzsche, *The Twilight of the Idols*, in *The Portable Nietzsche*, p. 485.

11. Nietzsche, *Beyond Good and Evil*, p. 162.

12. Ibid., p. 164.

13. Irigaray, *Marine Lover*, p. 79/*Amante marine*, p. 85.

14. However, when Irigaray speaks of *profondeur* in *Marine Lover*, she will always invoke the (unspoken) ground upon which the entire philosophical edifice rests and which continues to sub-sist, namely *le féminin* (cf. *Marine Lover*, p. 94/*Amante marine*, p. 88).

15. Nietzsche, *The Will to Power*, p. 124.

16. Nietzsche, *The Gay Science*, trans. Walter Kaufman (New York: Vintage Books, 1974), p. 124.

See Jacques Derrida's *Spurs: The Styles of Nietzsche*, trans. Barbara Harlow (Chicago: Chicago University Press, 1979), where he attempts to situate Nietzsche's conception of woman in terms of the Heideggerian "landscape." Derrida is on the whole more willing than Irigaray to play within the Nietzschean parameters of "woman." He thus stages a dialogue with the Heideggerian reading of Nietzsche's philosophy in *Nietzsche* (which Derrida incidently refers to as "the mighty tome") on the question of "woman" and "truth."

17. Irigaray, *Marine Lover*, p. 85/*Amante marine*, p. 79. All further parenthetical page references in this chapter refer to this work.

18. See Nietzsche, "Zarathustra's Prologue" in *Thus Spoke Zarathustra*: "But when Zarathustra was alone he spoke thus to his heart: 'Could it be possible? This old saint in the forest has not yet heard anything of this, that *God is dead!* '" (p. 124).

19. Irigaray, *Speculum*, p. 133/165.
20. Shoshana Felman has posed similar questions to Irigaray in her article entitled "The Critical Phallacy," *Diacritics* (Winter 1975), 5(4):2–10.
21. Irigaray, *Marine Lover*, p. 96/*Amante marine*, p. 90; translation modified.
22. Heidegger, *Being and Time*, pp. 200–201.
23. In *Being and Time* Heidegger defines the word *apophantical* in the following way: "Setting down the subject, setting down the predicate, and setting down the two together, are thoroughly 'apophantical' in the strict sense of the word" (p. 197).
24. Ibid., p. 210.
25. Heidegger, *Nihilism*, in *Nietzsche*, trans. David Farrell Krell, 4 vols. (New York: Harper and Row, 1982), 4:197–252.
26. Ibid., 4:228.
27. Ibid., 4:228.
28. Heidegger says in *Identity and Difference*:

> We speak of the *difference* between Being and beings. The step back goes from what is unthought, from the difference as such, into what gives us thought. That is the *oblivion* of the difference. The oblivion here to be thought is the veiling of the difference as such, thought in terms of concealment; this veiling has in turn withdrawn itself from the beginning. The oblivion belongs to the difference because the difference belongs to the oblivion. The oblivion does not happen to the difference only afterwards, in consequence of the forgetfulness of human thinking.

Identity and Difference, trans. Joan Stambaugh (New York: Harper and Row, 1969), pp. 50–51.

29. Heidegger's notion of *Ereignis* is usually translated as the "event of Appropriation." This term must be thought, Heidegger insists, absolutely negatively. What is here in *Ereignis* is already *not* here. In this sense it is useless to approach this guiding path of thinking through logic or through technological thinking. *Ereignis* therefore cannot be named, nor transposed into propositional thinking, but can only serve in the service of thought. See Heidegger, *On Time and Being*, trans. Joan Stambaugh (New York: Harper and Row, 1972), pp. 21–22.
30. Irigaray, *L'Oubli de l'air*, p. 130; my translation.

· *Philippa Berry*

THE BURNING GLASS:

PARADOXES OF

FEMINIST REVELATION

IN SPECULUM

In the nineteen years that have elapsed since the publication of her first major book, *Speculum of the Other Woman*, in 1974, the work of Luce Irigaray has gained increasing prestige and importance among English-speaking feminists. But although growing numbers of feminists are now engaging with the radical themes of Irigaray's more recent work, it seems that we have yet to comprehend fully the complex significance of *Speculum*, as the inaugural statement of a new feminist philosophy. The central preoccupation of the work is certainly clear enough: this presents an extended critique of the use of woman as a *speculum* or mirror of masculine resemblance within a patriarchal intellectual tradition that extends from Plato to Freud. Writing of the psychological construction of masculine identity as described by Freud, Irigaray points out:

> Now, if this ego is to be valuable, some "mirror" is needed to reassure it and re-insure it of its value. Woman will be the foundation of this specular duplication, giving man back "his" image and repeating it as the same. If an *other* image, an *other* mirror were to intervene, this inevitably

•
•

would entail the risk of mortal crisis. Woman, therefore, will be this sameness—or at least its mirror image—and, in her role of mother, she will facilitate the repetition of the same, in contempt for difference.[1]

In exposing this appropriation of woman (especially of woman as mother) as a mirror of masculine resemblance, Irigaray's concern is to free woman from her one-dimensional, reflexive position within phallocentric culture. But the wider philosophical implications of this move, and the subtle way in which it intersects with yet significantly *differs* from both the writings of earlier Western thinkers and also those of some of the central protagonists of postmodern thought have yet, I believe, to be properly understood. This essay is therefore an attempt to read *Speculum* more closely, and in particular to assess the ambiguous function of its central motif, which is not a mirror as such, but a *burning* or *fiery* mirror, a *miroir ardent* that sets *things on fire*.

In this book Irigaray's primary concern is to deconstruct that philosophical dualism which she suggests has resulted in a misunderstanding of the necessary interrelationship between the very terms dualistic thought typically opposes: spirit and matter. For *Speculum* is a daring attempt to investigate the buried and oblique connections between woman, in her figurative relationship with the forgotten, bodily, and material other of philosophy, and the fires of spirit. Irigaray allies what she sees as a philosophical distancing from and miscognition of spirit with philosophy's repression and entombment of that which is closely allied to matter: "the other woman." Through this endeavor she also opens the question of the hidden status of the "fires of spirit" in postmodern thought—a question Derrida has recently shown to be closely entangled in its powerful but politically extremely disturbing Heideggerian legacy. As Derrida asks, in *Of Spirit: Heidegger and the Question*, "Is it not remarkable that this theme, spirit, occupying . . . a major and obvious place in this line of thought, should have been disinherited? No one wants to do anything with it any more."[2] Well, it is very clear from her more recent work that Irigaray does want to address this theme. What is not yet properly recognized, however, is its centrality to *Speculum*. This may be due to the fact that here, in the book that was her doctoral dissertation, Irigaray approaches the problem from a deliberately oblique angle, tackling it in and through the tilted and burning glass of her new feminist philosophy. Yet my contention is that, in *Speculum*, there is an unacknowledged but extremely important dialogue with Heidegger on just this question—of spirit. This dialogue anticipates to a surprising degree several of the themes treated by Derrida in two works published in France in 1987: *Of Spirit* and *Cinders*.[3]

In *Le Corps-à-corps avec la mère* ("The Bodily Encounter with the
Mother"), published in 1981, Irigaray announced her intention of producing a tetralogy on the four elements: air, earth, fire, and water, in
each of which she would dialogue with a key male thinker whose work
had neglected one of these elements. Thus *L'Oubli de l'air* (Forgetting
air) critiqued Heidegger, and *Amante marine* (*Marine Lover*), Nietzsche
(although the identity of the addressee of the "earth" text, *Passions élémentaires* [Elementary passions], is never made explicit). But the fourth
text in this series—the volume intended to investigate the strange lack
of fire imagery in a political body of work, in the writings of Marx—
has never appeared, and Agnès Vincenot has recently suggested that fire
is consequently a "strange lack" in Irigaray's own work.[4] Vincenot is
mistaken, however. For it is clear from the centrality of the "burning
glass" to *Speculum* that fire—which for Irigaray is evidently the fire not
only of sexuality but also of *esprit*, or spirit—was fundamental to her
philosophical project as originally conceived. Indeed, we might even
argue that *Speculum* is the missing "fire book":[5] a work that anticipates
but also completes the tetralogy, and whose radical philosophical trajectory still has important implications for contemporary discourses of
ethics and politics (for, while until recently these were dominated by the
ghost of Marx, they might now be said to be haunted, albeit very differently, by Heidegger).

The specific meaning of *Speculum*'s fire imagery, however, can only
be understood with reference to the figurative *darkness* of Irigaray's new
philosophical perspective, which offers as its inaugural move an extended critique of that visual or "oculocentric" bias she shows to be implicit in patriarchal models of knowledge. The presence of this bias in modern or post-Renaissance Western thought has been much discussed in
recent years, in essays that often owe much to the influence of Heidegger, who criticized an "enframed, enframing" mode of vision (which
dominates by desiring total visibility and constant surveillance), and
who complained that "vision has degenerated into mere optics."[6] Yet,
as Heidegger himself pointed out, a scopic bias was in fact fundamental to the project of Western philosophy from its inception, since the
Greek word *theorein*, whence we derive our term *theory*, actually means
to contemplate.[7] By emphasizing that association between a privileged
model of knowledge and notions of clear vision which subtends Western thought, and by attempting to redirect and reform that "looking"
which is implicit in theoretical or philosophical activity, Irigaray seems
therefore to be working within a phenomenological tradition whose
complex influence upon deconstruction is only now beginning to be

understood. And she is certainly indebted to Heidegger here. But Irigaray gives an important, feminist difference to the phenomenological and Heideggerian themes in her work. While her central objective is not unlike that of the later Heidegger—to set philosophical speculation figuratively *on fire*—she stresses the instrumentality of a devalorized idea of woman to this process. Thus a vital preliminary to this move is her emphasis upon the *darkness* and *materiality* of that other woman which has eluded the gaze of oculocentrism.

Speculum stresses the horror of matter and the female body in particular that underlies philosophical dualism—together with the visually overdetermined, oedipal subjectivity it legitimates. It begins, therefore, by *reapplying* Freud's definition of sexual difference in visual terms (when he stressed the disturbing "nothing to see" of the female genitals) in order to show that, as Freud's "dark continent," woman actually eludes the lens of oculocentrism. In fact, Irigaray argues that, in order to assert his own subjectivity, man must forever distance himself from a feminine and corporeal reality, through a process of deliberate miscognition. Thus "mother-matter" must only be "apprehended by her mirage, not by her dazzling radiance," in other words, by an image of sameness rather than one of difference: an image that unproblematically *mirrors* masculine identity.[8] With such formulations Irigaray subverts the terminology of Lacanian as well as Freudian psychoanalysis.[9] Her declared intention in *Speculum* is to reveal the "blind spot" in phallocentric speculations and to see through it darkly, or otherwise; she compares this blind spot to the darkness of the pupil in the eye, a point whose designation as *kore* in Greek associates it with that feminine apprehension of subterranean depth represented by the myth of the Greek goddess Kore, the maiden (otherwise known as Persephone), whose identity was mysteriously divided between the roles of daughter (to the earth goddess Demeter) and bride (to Hades or Death). It is important to note in this connection that, for Irigaray, the blind spot is actually associated with a daughter rather than a mother figure; in the first section of *Speculum* Irigaray elaborates the feminist implications of Freud's theory of female psychic development, which stresses the little girl's loss of self-esteem and alienation from her first love object, the mother, when she discovers the mother's castration. Yet while Irigaray's implication is that this damaged relationship between daughter and mother must be repaired, it seems this should precisely prevent the daughter from taking the place of the mother (insofar as this place has been determined by phallocentric thought), since it is above all in her role of mother that woman facilitates "the repetition of the same." In its search for the "other woman," therefore, *Speculum* implicitly directs our attention to a fil(l)ial feminine alterity that is associated with the creative subversion of the process of maternal mirroring. In his rather earlier attempt to find a different philosophical blind spot—that of Hegelianism—Georges Bataille had opposed to the philosopher's panoptic vision another, pineal eye, that is positioned at the summit of the skull, and that metaphorically castrates the philosopher by exposing the blindness of his knowledge.[10] But Irigaray's different view is defined in terms of interiority—of the body as well as of the psyche. For she figures her feminist opposition to philosophical oculocentrism in terms of a feminine, genital eye, which looks inward rather than outward. Her attempt to formulate the potential of this figuration plays with considerable elegance upon the neglected but highly important relationship between mother and daughter.

When we read *Speculum* as the linear or diachronic elaboration of an argument, its overall chronological structure (which moves from Freud to Plato) appears to reject the future-oriented gaze of most Western thought in order to retrace its steps in a predominantly backwards direction—toward what seems in the first instance to be a maternal, as well as a Platonic, origin. Yet the backwards intellectual movement ostensibly traced by Irigaray in *Speculum* is also a figurative descent; a descent of woman in search of the forgotten other woman, which opposes and subtly parodies that "ascent of man" celebrated in Western philosophy but also anticipates, I think most suggestively, the imagery of subjectivity's crypt or tomb that was later to surface in the writings of Derrida, reminding us of the hidden, unacknowledged *la* in his *Glas* or death-knell (a text published in the same year as *Speculum*).[11] Irigaray writes in her opening chapter on Freud that as well as affording man the opportunity to sublimate and if possible master the work of death, woman "will also be the representative-representation (*Vorstellung-Repräsentanz*) . . . of the death drives that cannot (or theoretically could not) be perceived without horror, that the eye of consciousness refuses to recognize."[12] She uses the daughter to figure this relationship between the other woman and a crisis of vision associated with death, pointing to the pupil or *kore* as that point of darkness at the center of the eye (or I) that involuntarily mirrors another. Moreover, when the pupil is dilated or expanded, the dark eye becomes an enigmatic, nonrepresentable sign for those drives that undermine the sovereignty of consciousness, inviting us to look behind or beneath the eye/I. "A mirror untouched by any reflection [resembles] *a pupil—a kore*—dilated [*dilatée*] to encompass the whole field of vision, and *mirroring itself.* Reflecting nothing (but) its own void, that *hole* through which one looks."[13] What Irigaray attempts in *Speculum* is consequently to guide

.
    .

us *through* the dilated pupil or *kore*, to the other side of the convex surface of the eye/I, in order to construct an inverted, concave mirror that
can obliquely and darkly delineate the other side of philosophical oculocentrism. Hence, after its opening chapter on Freud, the rest of the
book uses a motif of descent into the darkness of the underworld or
death realms: regions that postmodern thought appears to be as much
fascinated by as was modernism.

Roland Barthes once characterized Orpheus, who descended to
Hades in search of his dead wife, Eurydice, as the natural hero of the
theoretical endeavor,[14] but the Greek myths of Kore/Persephone and
Antigone are seemingly of more interest to Irigaray. These virginal or
maiden figures, whose "marriages" to death give a new significance to
their former identity as daughters, are both evoked in the central section of *Speculum.* Yet Irigaray's objective in *Speculum* is not to bury her
dead (like Antigone), neither is it to establish feminine rule over this
other domain (like Kore/Persephone). Rather it is to force open, discursively (and specifically, through her rhetorical *dilation* or expansion
of key philosophical texts), the cryptic space in which the otherness of
woman has been interred. Her objective is seemingly not to bring to
light but rather to *enflame* (in the sense of reviving and motivating,
inspiring) what remains there, and so to dissolve a vital philosophical
boundary. The ambiguous, even ghostly, function of flame in this
process, as signifying both fire and something that is dead and gone (the
past?) can be usefully clarified, I think, with reference to a remark by
Derrida in *Cinders* (*Feu la cendre*) that: "the word *feu* alludes to 'the late
so and so,' the departed."[15]

The initial justification for Irigaray's philosophical metaphor of
descent, however, is the dependence of her feminist critique of oculocentrism upon Plato's parable of the cave, related by Socrates in book
7 of *The Republic,* where the philosopher is the man able to scramble
out of the womblike cave of origin into the light of true reason. The
specific implications of this fable are only interpreted in the last section of *Speculum,* "Plato's *Hystera,*" yet a remapping of its philosophical geography informs the entire project of the book. In this passage
Socrates described the condition of ordinary men as being like prison-
ers in a cave, forever chained with their backs to its entrance, and able
to see only the dim shadows that are cast by a fire behind them, in
front of which other men are moving back and forth. For Socrates the
philosopher is the one who is able to free himself, turn around, and
eventually leave the cave, to seek the light of day—that is, a true and
presumably rational mode of knowledge. But according to Irigaray

such thinkers "walk, without stopping, toward the 'sun,' taking no notice of the shadow that it still projects, *behind*."[16] Thereby she turns Socrates' extended metaphor on its head, reversing the exodus of the Platonic philosopher, and redirecting philosophical attention from an outer reality and exterior light to a mysteriously *empty* yet suggestive inner reality, which is represented by the darkness of the cave and its fire-cast shadows—the original, originary state that Socrates' philosopher was so swift to abandon:

> For the optics of Truth in its credibility no doubt, its unconditional certainty, its passion for reason, has veiled or else destroyed the gaze that remained mortal. With the result that it can no longer see anything of what had been before its conversion to the Father's law. That everything foreign, other, outside its present certainties no longer appears to the gaze. . . . Except—perhaps? sometimes?—the pain of being blinded in this way, of being no longer able to make out, imagine, feel, what is going on *behind* the screen of those/his ideal projections, divine knowledge. Which cut him off from his relations with the earth, the mother, and any other (female) by that ascent towards an all-powerful intelligibility.[17]

If for the philosopher described by Plato the commitment to knowledge as light means that there can be "no going back down toward the earth, or into the earth," the question for the feminist philosopher, according to Irigaray, is rather how to recover and reinterpret a buried feminine darkness, in those shadows upon which representation depends: "How . . . can one return into the cave, the den, the earth? Rediscover the darkness of all that has been left behind? Remember the forgotten mother ?"[18]

Through its interrelationship of the images of con*cave* mirror (a motif that appears in Plato's *Timaeus*) and fire, in the figure of the burning glass, *Speculum* stresses the obscurity, the invisibility, as well as the volatility of any idea of woman that escapes from the binary logic of patriarchy. Simultaneously, it directs our gaze away from the sun of patriarchal philosophy (a blazing spectacle that, as Irigaray points out, the impersonal philosophical gaze cannot really apprehend anyway) to what could be described as its internally refracted image, a barely smoldering fire that figures the source of worldly representations. This mysterious fiery phenomenon is made manifest precisely in the dark place where woman escapes from that specular logic that has denied her the freedom of alterity.

In the first stage of this process the *speculum* or mirror of the title serves as both mirror and gynecological instrument; thus the opening

up of this hitherto unexplored "crypt" or underworld for feminist
investigation is described as a process that is like and yet unlike a technique of masculine gynecology. Gynecology, Irigaray points out, inserts
the concave mirror of the speculum into the female vagina in order to
"*dilate* [*écarter*] the lips, the orifices, the walls, so that the eye can penetrate the interior."[19] It thereby concentrates and polarizes light for the
exploration of those "inner cavities" that, for Irigaray, figure woman's
bodily and psychic otherness. But although it has been abused by a
patriarchal culture, she suggests that the mirror of the speculum, like
philosophical speculation itself, need not be abandoned. What Irigaray
does to this mirror is suggested in the word that Gillian C. Gill here
translates as "dilate," *écarter*, which can signify both to part or divide
and also to deviate, to turn or move aside. In her separation of the other
woman, not from the mother but rather from the restricted place of the
mother allocated to woman in patriarchy, one of Irigaray's key moves in
Speculum is to turn the mirror that is "mother-matter" *in upon itself,* in
an act of self-examination that also wittily exaggerates the circular orbit
of the earth. This philosophical move, like a tilt of the earth's axis,
might be expected to make man lose his balance:

> If the earth turned and more especially turned upon herself, the erection
> of the [masculine] subject might thereby be disconcerted and risk losing
> its elevation and penetration. For what would there be to rise up from
> and exercise his power over? And in?[20]

Irigaray's emphasis upon a feminist *écart* or in-turning into a mysterious opening—an opening she implies to be the forgotten ground of
philosophical speculation—seems much indebted to Heidegger's
notion of "the turning" (*Kehre*), set out in his essay of that name published in 1950. In Heidegger's central preoccupation with the search for
Being (*das Sein*), the turning is a vital event, a kind of metaphysical
"homecoming" (*Heimkehr*). He wrote of an "in-turning" (*Einkehr*)
toward the hidden truth of Being, a truth the Western philosophical
tradition, according to Heidegger, had persistently overlooked:
"Toward where does in-turning bring itself to pass? Toward nowhere
except into Being itself, which is as yet coming to presence out of the
oblivion of its truth."[21] The in-turning was described by Heidegger as
entry into a particular and privileged space—a space in which philosophy could become otherwise. This space was called by him "the clearing" (*Lichtung*). Heidegger contended that "in this turning, the clearing belonging to the essence of Being suddenly clears itself and lights
up. This sudden self-lighting is the lightning-flash."[22] The revealed
radiance of this space or clearing asserts its status as truth or *aletheia*.

This was a formulation Heidegger derived from the thought of the pre-Socratic philosopher, Heraclitus, who was seemingly much preoccupied with the interrelationship of light and shadows, and who wrote of what he called "turnings of fire."[23]

As elaborated by Heidegger the clearing is somewhat oddly positioned between the humanist preoccupations of modern thought and the deconstructive tendencies of postmodern thought; its association with a concept of "Being," which Heidegger himself was later to place *sous rature* (under erasure), is the clearest indication of this contradictory character of the concept. Nonetheless, its influence upon postmodern thought has been surprisingly pervasive. I have written elsewhere of the simultaneous feminist appropriation and deconstruction of the Heideggerian *Lichtung*, by Irigaray as well as Julia Kristeva, both of whom relate it to a concept derived from another Platonic text: that of *chora*.[24] While retaining the uncanny combination of luminosity with hiddenness or concealment that characterizes Heidegger's *Lichtung*, both Kristeva and Irigaray accord a feminine materiality to this curious philosophical space, primarily by allying it with the preoedipal stage of psychic development. At the same time, both have at different times associated this feminine "turn" with a return, not to a moment of origin but to an in-between historical epoch—that of the late middle ages and Renaissance. Yet while Kristeva has described the mother who dominates *chora* as "almost no sight—a shadow that darkens, soaks me up or vanishes amid flashes,"[25] the feminine focus of Irigaray's "turning" inward is different. In her angling of the maternal mirror the dark place toward which she gestures, which the burning glass obliquely illuminates/inflames, is seemingly a location where woman might be asymmetrically "other" to the mother, as a daughter who does not have to occupy the maternal place.

In contrast to the strange impersonality of the luminous *Lichtung*, the fieriness of Irigaray's revisioning of Plato's cave—and the fieriness of the female body to which it figuratively alludes—locates philosophical transition in a specifically human and erotic experience, drawing out the more dynamic and transformative associations of Heraclitus's "world fire"—which, for all his fulminations about the "optics" of knowledge, Heidegger's account of the clearing seems to convert into a primarily visual spectacle. This fire of sexual desire is wholly absent from Heidegger's writings. But the fire of *Geist*, or spirit, does appear in his work, as Derrida has shown in *Of Spirit*, and often in contexts where the political results of Nazism—in the fires of the Holocaust—are tragically prefigured, for such references were often used to authorize his Nazi politics, in the celebration of a specifically German *Geist* against which Jews in particular were defined as other. Derrida's implicit conclusion in *Of Spirit* seems therefore to be twofold. The fires of spirit must be placed back on the agenda of Western thought. But, at the same time, the dangerous ambivalence of their political associations for that which is constituted as "other" must be interrogated, if we are seriously to avoid repeating Heidegger's terrible error. In her fiery reformulation of the Heideggerian clearing, Irigaray is consequently treading on dangerous ground. And, like other postmodern thinkers, she does not in my view entirely resolve the dilemma she has inherited from Heidegger—perhaps because she never addresses it explicitly. Nonetheless, in her association of fire with woman, Irigaray is initially allying it with the other rather than with the same, although, as I shall explain shortly, she also uses it as the temporary locus of a deconstruction of those very oppositions.

In her investigation of the other woman, Irigaray suggests, one must look not in but *through* the mirror, thereby rejecting woman's formerly passive reflexivity for an oblique and inflammatory application of her borrowed light. Due to its dramatic intensification of light, a calculated turning or angling of the concave mirror used in the gynecological speculum can set things on fire. The male, "scientific" investigation of woman, Irigaray suggests, is extremely wary of this attribute of its instrument and "defends itself phobically in/by this inner 'center' from the fires of the desire of/for woman."[26] Yet, when applied in the form of the investigative—or *speculative*—language of a feminist philosopher, the speculum can become a "burning glass," or *miroir ardent*, a concave textual as well as intellectual surface in which the mimicry adopted by the feminist philosopher angles and refracts the light of the sun of traditional philosophy, with the result that "the fires of desire of/for woman" are magnified rather than annulled.

> And if indeed it is a question of breaking with a certain mode of specula(riza)tion, this does not imply renouncing all mirrors or refraining from analysis of the hold this plane of representation maintains. . . . But perhaps through this specular surface which sustains discourse is found not the void of nothingness but the dazzle of multifaceted speleology. A scintillating and incandescent concavity, of language also, that threatens to set fire to fetish-objects and gilded eyes. The recasting of their truth-value is already at hand. We need only press on a little further, into that so-called dark cave which serves as hidden foundation to their speculations.[27]

As this passage suggests, Irigaray's feminist *dilation* of woman's body has implications for language as well as for vision, applying the rhetorical as well as the gynecological implications of that term in order to reveal a "scintillating and incandescent concavity" in words, which implicitly undermines their use in the service of masculine *speculation.* This discovery suggestively anticipates Derrida's reformulation of the trace as *cendre* or ember. Through this radical appropriation of the speculum of a phallocentric philosophy and science, Irigaray implies, the feminist philosopher can rekindle an inner fire that has long been forgotten:

> For there where we expect to find the opaque and silent matrix of a logos immutable in the certainty of its own light, fires and mirrors are beginning to radiate, sapping the evidence of reason at its base! Not so much by anything stored in the cave—which would still be a claim based on the notion of the closed volume—but again and yet again by their indefinitely rekindled hearths.[28]

The conversion of the speculum into a *miroir ardent* or burning glass is hence a vital device in the book's inflammatory, and ostensibly revelatory, procedure. Possibly Irigaray was familiar with the Renaissance literature of emblems, in which the concave mirror was held to represent, among other things, woman, beauty, the appearance of God or the holy spirit, the contemplative soul, one who is just or upright, but also a prostitute, a bad minister, an evil person.[29] Premodern interpretations of the burning glass are similarly contradictory: in Renaissance emblem literature its political associations are stressed, with a suggestion that this political "fire" could be directed for good or bad;[30] however, an epigraph to the chapter in *Speculum* called "*La Mystérique*" directs us to its most notable appearance in medieval literature, in the works of the fourteenth-century mystic Jan van Ruysbroeck. This use of the image stresses fire as spirit, although there is also a political—and sexual— dimension to Ruysbroeck's mystical application of the burning glass. Like Irigaray, Ruysbroeck was a native of what is now Belgium, but was then Flanders. And, interestingly, it was in a work whose title, *The Book of the Twelve Béguines,* acknowledged the existence in Flanders (as well as in Germany) of a contemporary feminine freedom of spiritual inquiry that he used the burning glass as an analogy to an inward-looking style of *theoria* or contemplation—one that differed significantly from that favored by traditional philosophy. Here, in an attempt to communicate the culmination of contemplative or mystical experience, Ruysbroeck wrote,

> Take a mirror curved like a basin, put in it dry and inflammable straws, and hold the mirror so as to catch the sun's rays. These dry straws, by

•
•

reason of the heat of the sun and the concavity of the mirror, will rapid-
ly catch fire. So within thyself, if thou hast an open heart, the light of his
pity, illumining this open soul, consumes all thy shortcomings in the fire
of divine love.[31]

Clearly, Irigaray is indebted to Ruysbroeck for her use of the figure
of the burning glass (as she may also be, in fact, for her meditation in
Ethique upon the two angels positioned opposite one another on the
Ark of the Covenant). Like him, she associates the burning glass with
the deconstruction of a limited model of knowledge, and with a consumption of egoism: hence of those selfish, solipsistic loves or desires
allied to the traditional association of the mirror with physical beauty.[32]
However, Irigaray's feminist application of this device is at odds not
only with Ruysbroeck's ascetic rejection of bodily pleasures but also
with his attack in the same work on the untrammeled expression of an
uncloistered, nomadic, and predominantly female expression of spirituality then manifesting itself in what was called the Béguine movement.[33] This is an attack he implicitly authorizes through his declared
knowledge of the mysteries of contemplation, as figured by the burning glass.

It is partly because of the prominent position it accords to the burning glass that I consider "*La Mystérique*" to be the pivotal chapter in
Speculum. But, significantly, this chapter is near the center rather than
at the end of the book, embedded in its middle section, which is itself
called "Speculum."[34] I think this should alert us to the ambiguous positionality of that locus of the other woman Irigaray's speculum reveals,
which, since it is illuminated by a "paternal" light angled by the maternal mirror, has a significantly oblique (*à l'écart*) relationship to both
these terms.[35] This is in fact the only chapter in the book where Irigaray
does not mimic the discourse of different male philosophers. It is also
the place where she evokes a pivotal and "in-between" historical
moment: *after* the classical era of Platonic and Neoplatonic dualism,
but *before* the advent of an equally—albeit differently—polarized modern subjectivity associated with Descartes (the subject of the previous
chapter). This is the time of the late middle ages and Renaissance, when
certain women dared to mimic, dilate, and angle another traditionally
masculine discourse: that of theology:

> This is the place where "she"—and in some cases he, if he follows "her"
> lead—speaks about the dazzling glare which comes from the source of
> light that has been logically repressed, about "subject" and "Other"
> flowing out into an embrace of fire that mingles one term into another,
> about contempt for form as such, about mistrust for understanding as

an obstacle along the path of jouissance and mistrust for the dry desola-
tion of reason. Also about a burning glass. This is the only place in the
history of the West in which woman speaks and acts so publicly.[36]

Hence one of the things that Irigaray appears to be doing in this
chapter is challenging the antifeminist stance of Ruysbroeck in *The
Twelve Béguines*, by claiming the right for woman to speak from the
place inflamed by the burning glass—and to speak of that locus and
state differently.

The speech evoked in this chapter is multiple: Irigaray seems indebted to the writings of several women mystics, including Angela of Folig-
no, Catherine of Siena, and Teresa of Avila. But there is one text in particular that she may have been thinking of when she wrote "*La Mystérique,*" a text that (together with its female authorship) had only
recently been rediscovered. This was a work whose title, as well as its
fiery subject matter, mirrored that of her own book, *Le Mirouer des sim-
ples âmes* (or *Speculum simpliciarum animarum*) of Marguerite Porete,
written sometime between 1296 and 1306.[37] Not only was the author
of this other "speculum" from Flanders, but many contemporary com-
mentators associated her with the Béguines, although she was most
closely connected with another unorthodox religious movement of the
late middle ages known as the Brethren of the Free Spirit.[38] Porete's
book was written in the tradition known as negative theology, which
placed "God" outside of all representations;[39] its most controversial
aspect, however, seems to have been its rejection of the body-spirit dualism that was fundamental to orthodox Christian theology as well as to
post-Platonic Western philosophy. By declaring that "a soul annihilat-
ed in the love of the Creator could, and should, grant to nature all that
it desires," it appeared to ally the achievement of divine love with the
rejection of moral law—a position usually seen as central to the Free
Spirit heresy. (This "freedom" of spirit was held to include, among
other things, a permissive freedom of sexual expression.) The book was
declared heretical, and Porete was burnt at the stake in Paris in 1310.

The emphasis by Porete upon the soul's transformation by the fire of
divine love has parallels in many other mystical texts, but several allusions to her text may, I think, be discerned in "*Mystérique.*" First, Irigaray's focus in this chapter is upon a feminine soul (*âme*) who transgresses and wanders randomly in darkness. Second, it emphasizes "this
'simplicity' stripped of all attributes," which characterizes *la mystérique,*
since, like the "God" she embraces, she is positioned outside or to the
side of straightforward representation. Third, Irigaray's description of
the union of *la mystérique* with her God stresses that this is also a

reunion of woman with herself, via a(nother) process of mirroring in
which the other woman is not lost but rediscovered. And there is also
an implicit focus upon feminine mirroring in Porete's treatise that per-
sonifies the divine love of which it speaks as a "Lady Amour."[40]
Although it seems at times that this figure is but an intermediary
between the soul and God, elsewhere she appears to represent that fiery
Holy Spirit upon which Porete and other unorthodox mystics of her
day placed so much importance. Lady Amour's feminine gender therefore compromises the supposed masculinity of the Trinity (just as does
the treatise as a whole, since it purports to describe the process whereby a female mystic becomes divine). Likewise, Porete's emphasis upon
the angelic or seraphic identity of one who has been transfigured in the
fire of divine love is paralleled in Irigaray's later work where she sometimes uses angels to figure the possibility of a new human identity that
might mediate the opposites of spirit and matter.

One of the things many readers of *Speculum* have seemingly found
problematic about "*La Mystérique*" is not just its poetic excesses but also
its use of the androcentric language of Christian theology and mysticism. But it is important to note, I think, that Irigaray is pointing here
to the need to read religious as well as philosophical discourse *otherwise*,
and above all in relation to those whom it has excluded, labeled heretical and "other." Irigaray is searching in *Speculum* for a new, nondual
mode of knowing that would be appropriate to a new philosophy: a
paradoxical dark vision that can be rooted in matter and the body rather
than simply using these degraded terms as a mirror. Irigaray writes of
the "other" woman in *Speculum*: "Something of her a-specificity might
be found in the *betweens* that occur in being, or beings."[41] And once
illuminated this other woman is situated on the borderland *between*
oppositions, in "the place where consciousness is no longer master,
where, to its extreme confusion, it sinks into a dark night that is also fire
and flames."[42] Through her burning glass the subject-object division of
seer and seen, masculine and feminine, spirit and matter, same and
other, objective knowledge and personal experience is momentarily
undone. Hence, while her preoccupation in *Speculum* with the imagery
of fire and flame seems to allude to the possibility of a radiant, even
explosive, revelation or unveiling (the Heideggerian term would be
"unconcealment") of that multiple otherness which Western philosophy has repressed, to see no further than this is to overlook Irigaray's
ironic undermining of the desire for formal truths—or for the truth of
Platonic forms. She resists unambiguously what Heidegger called
"enframing" (*das Ge-stell*): a historical trend toward the objectification

of reality, which, he argued, had produced a severe restriction of philosophical vision.[43] Her hidden feminine origin is empty rather than full, spacious rather than solid. Its eventual appearance, through the tilt of the burning glass, has the ghostly attributes of a spirit or *revenant*, as an elusive fiery image that seemingly can only be represented metonymically by the embers marking its extinction or disappearance.

Irigaray points out that

> woman is neither open nor closed. She is indefinite, in-finite, *form is never complete in her*. She is not infinite but neither is she a unit(y), such as letter, number, figure in a series, proper noun, unique object (in a) world of the senses, simple ideality in an intelligible whole, entity of a foundation, etc. This incompleteness in her form, her morphology, allows her continually to become something else, though this is not to say that she is ever univocally nothing. No metaphor completes her. Never is she this, then that, this and that. . . . But she is becoming that expansion that she neither is nor will be at any moment as definable universe.[44]

The achievement is seemingly of a dynamic state of *becoming* rather than the stasis of Heideggerian Being: a continuing transformation that seemingly aims to elude, nomadlike (Béguine-like), the fixed points and structures of patriarchal thought. Irigaray's other woman consequently serves not as the telos or goal of a feminist philosophy, but as its instrument in the elaboration of a radically new nondualistic mode of physical, metaphysical, and ethical speculation—a future toward which the feminist speculum only points the way.

NOTES •

1. Irigaray, *Speculum*, p. 54/63.
2. Jacques Derrida, *Of Spirit: Heidegger and the Question*, trans. Geoffrey Bennington and Rachel Bowlby (Chicago: University of Chicago Press, 1989), p. 3.
3. *Of Spirit* was published in France as *De l'esprit* (Paris: Galilée, 1987). *Feu la cendre*, which first appeared in *Anima* (December 1982), vol. 5, is the only text by Derrida to have been published by the feminist publishers Des femmes (Paris 1987). It was recently translated as *Cinders* by Ned Lukacher, who also wrote an important introduction to the text (Nebraska: University of Nebraska Press, 1991).
4. Vincenot, "Genèse," in Agnès Vincenot, Marion de Zanger, Heide Hinterthür, Anne-Claire Mulder, eds., *Renaissance: drie teksten van Luce Irigaray*, pp. 86–88 (The Hague: Uitgeverij Perdu, 1990). I am very grateful to Anne-Claire Mulder for making available her unpublished translation of Vincenot's article.

•
•   5. I owe this point to Margaret Whitford's most perceptive and helpful
          comments on an earlier version of this essay.
      6. Martin Heidegger, *Introduction to Metaphysics*, trans. Ralph Manheim
          (New York: Doubleday, 1961), p. 52. Among the more recent critics of
          oculocentrism are Martin Jay, in "Scopic Regimes of Modernity," in Hal
          Foster, ed., *Vision and Visuality* (Seattle: Bay Press, 1988), pp. 3–28, and
          David Michael Levin, *The Opening of Vision: Nihilism and the Postmod-
          ern Situation* (London: Routledge, 1988).
      7. See Levin, *The Opening of Vision*, pp. 99–104.
      8. Irigaray, *Speculum*, p. 150/186.
      9. The ambiguous status of Lacan in this text is discussed by Carolyn Burke
          in "Irigaray Through the Looking Glass," this volume and *Feminist Stud-
          ies* (Summer 1981), 7(2):288–306.
     10. Georges Bataille, *Visions of Excess: Selected Writings, 1927–1939*, trans. A.
          Stoekl (Minneapolis: University of Minnesota Press, 1985).
     11. See Geoffrey Hartmann, *Saving the Text: Literature/Derrida/Philosophy*
          (New York and London: Johns Hopkins University Press, 1981), p. 87.
     12. Irigaray, *Speculum*, p. 55/63. In this formulation Irigaray's debt to
          Bataille is apparent.
     13. Irigaray, *Speculum* p. 328/410. For a brilliant feminist investigation of
          the rhetorical term of *dilatio*, see Patricia Parker, *Literary Fat Ladies:
          Rhetoric, Gender, Property* (London: Methuen, 1987). Irigaray invests the
          term with a subtle visual as well as verbal significance, however, through
          its association with the dilated pupil in addition to the feminist angling
          or *écartement* of mother/matter/mirror.
     14. See Michael Holland, "Barthes, Orpheus . . . " *Paragraph* (July 1988),
          11(2):143–174.
     15. Derrida, *Cinders*, p. 35.
     16. Irigaray, *Speculum*, p. 314/392.
     17. Ibid., p. 362/454.
     18. Ibid., p. 345/433.
     19. Ibid., p. 144/180.
     20. Ibid., p. 133/165.
     21. Heidegger, "The Turning," in *The Question Concerning Technology and
          Other Essays*, trans. William Lovitt (New York: Harper and Row, 1977),
          p. 44.
     22. Ibid.
     23. Heraclitus, Fragment 38. For a good discussion of this fragment, see
          Charles H. Kahn *The Art and Thought of Heraclitus: An Edition of the
          Fragments with Translation and Commentary* (Cambridge: Cambridge
          University Press, 1979). See also Levin, *The Opening of Vision*, p. 362.
     24. Philippa Berry, "Woman and Space According to Kristeva and Irigaray,"
          in Philippa Berry and Andrew Wernick, eds., *Shadow of Spirit: Postmod-
          ernism and Religion* (London: Routledge, 1993), pp. 250–264.

25. Kristeva, "Stabat Mater," in Toril Moi, ed., *The Kristeva Reader* (Oxford: Basil Blackwell, 1986), p. 180.
26. Irigaray, *Speculum,* p. 144/179.
27. Ibid., pp. 143–144/178–179.
28. Ibid., p. 144/179.
29. See Filippo Picinelli, *Mundus Symbolicus,* vol. 2, index, ed. A. Erath (Cologne: H. Demen, 1694; reprinted New York and London: Garland, 1976).
30. Arthur Henkl and Albrecht Schöne, eds., *Emblemata: Handbuch zur Sinnbildkunst des 16. und 17. Jahrhunderts* (Stuttgart: J. B. Metzlersche Verlagsbuchhandlung, 1967).
31. Jan van Ruysbroeck, *The Book of the Twelve Béguines,* chapter 10, cited in A. Wautier d'Aygalliers, *Ruysbroeck the Admirable,* 2d ed. (Port Washington: Kennikat Press, 1969), p. 195.
32. It might be argued that the middle ages and the early Renaissance were especially interested in the use of an angled or oblique vision in order to reveal the limitations of a worldly existence. See, for example, Hans Holbein's famous painting of *The Ambassadors* (1533), whose anamorphic skull, perceptible only from the side of the painting, has been much discussed.
33. See Robert E. Lerner, *The Heresy of the Free Spirit in the Later Middle Ages* (Berkeley: University of California Press, 1972), chapter 2.
34. Here I disagree with Toril Moi, who, in her important reading of *Speculum* in *Sexual/Textual Politics* (London: Methuen, 1985), which points out that the unifying metaphor of the speculum directs our attention to the center rather than the end of the text, thinks that the chapter thereby privileged is the discussion of Descartes, " . . . And If, Taking the Eye of a Man Recently Dead." I would rather contend, as does Elizabeth Grosz in *Sexual Subversions: Three French Feminists* (Sydney: Allen and Unwin, 1989)—although for different reasons—that Irigaray's speculum points to the medieval, premodern context of *"La Mystérique."*
35. The importance of *écart* in recent French thought seems primarily to be indebted to Merleau-Ponty's usage. See for example his remark that "it is that *separation (écart)* first of all that is the perceptual *meaning"* (*The Visible and the Invisible,* ed. C. Lefort [Evanston: Northwestern University Press, 1968], p. 197). In *The Irigaray Reader,* p. 29, Margaret Whitford has noted Irigaray's play on *écart, écarter, écarteler,* and their cognates in the chapter of *Speculum* entitled "Volume-fluidity." (In fact, the macabre association of *écarteler* with an act of capital punishment—the quartering of the criminal—should alert the reader to the additional association of the term with a body designated as "other" by the dominant culture.) Rosi Braidotti has commented on the feminist use of *écarts,* by Hélène Cixous, to signify successive and systematic shifts of perspective (*Patterns of Dissonance* [Oxford: Polity Press, 1990], p. 242). Yet Irigaray's rather

• different application of the concept, in connection with the angled mir-
• ror (as well as with a creative differentiation between mother and daugh-
    ter), resonates more closely with a comment made by Geoffrey Hart-
    mann in a discussion of Mallarmé's *Les Mots anglais*: "And is not *Elle* a
    mot anglé?" (*Saving the Text*, p. 87).

36. Irigaray, *Speculum*, p. 191/238.

37. While the rediscovery of this text, and of its authorship, was announced
    by Romana Guarnieri in 1946, the text itself was not published until
    1965, in *Archivio Italiano per la storia della pieta* (1965), 4:513–635. Yet
    its impact upon a European intelligentsia recently fascinated by Norman
    Cohn's highly romantic description of the Free Spirit heresy in *The Pur-
    suit of the Millennium* (London: Temple Smith; first published in 1957,
    with editions in 1961 and 1970), is likely to have been considerable. Sig-
    nificantly, Derrida mentions both Cohn's book and Marguerite Porete in
    Of Spirit, p. 116.

38. See Lerner, *The Heresy of the Free Spirit*.

39. The striking parallels between negative theology and aspects of decon-
    struction, poststructuralism, and postmodern thought have now been
    widely discussed. See in particular Kevin Hart, *The Trespass of the Sign:
    Deconstruction, Theology, and Philosophy* (Cambridge: Cambridge Uni-
    versity Press, 1990), passim; Harold Coward and Toby Foshay, eds.,
    Derrida and Negative Theology (Albany: SUNY Press, 1992); and Derri-
    da, "Comment ne pas parler? Dénégations," in *Psyché* (Paris: Galilée,
    1987). A key figure in the late medieval tradition of negative theology
    was Meister Eckhart, who was actively supportive of the Béguines, and
    whose work has been thought to bear a marked resemblance to the
    heresy of the Free Spirit (see Lerner, *The Heresy of the Free Spirit*, pp.
    1–3, 182–186). His influence upon Heidegger has been analyzed by
    John D. Caputo in *The Mystical Element in Heidegger's Thought* (Athens:
    University of Ohio Press, 1978).

40. See Peter Dronke, *Women Writers of the Middle Ages: A Critical Study of
    Texts from Perpetua to Marguerite Porete* (Cambridge: Cambridge Univer-
    sity Press, 1984), pp. 275–278.

41. Irigaray, *Speculum*, p. 166/207.

42. Ibid.

43. See Heidegger, "The Question Concerning Technology," in *The Ques-
    tion*.

44. Irigaray, *Speculum*, p. 229/284.

PART 3

.
.
.

*Toward
a New
Symbolic
Order*

· *Carolyn Burke*

TRANSLATION

MODIFIED:

IRIGARAY

IN ENGLISH

While it is obvious that one translates into
a cultural context as well as into a language, the effects of this truism on the
reception of particular thinkers is not
always recognized. When English translations of the "French Feminists" appeared
in piecemeal fashion starting in the 1970s, many English-speaking feminists found it difficult to overcome their concern that such writing was
not only elitist but deeply contaminated by the theories it sought to
demystify. In the case of Irigaray such readers responded to her work
with expressions of bafflement, exclusion, or antagonism, since even in
translation, it seemed as foreign to their ways of thinking as if it had
remained in French. Moreover, some of her most sympathetic interpreters took up only those aspects of her work that corresponded to our
cultural contexts at the time: consequently, more attention was paid to
the idea of an *écriture féminine* than to Irigaray's attempts to enact or
perform what she called, rather differently, a *parler-femme*.

By 1985, when *Speculum* and *This Sex Which Is Not One* appeared in
English, roughly a decade after their original publication, even readers

who had responded enthusiastically to their massive rethinking of the conditions of theory making found it hard to take an interest in the "new," as yet untranslated Irigaray—the one who was writing about the elements, angels, and female spirituality in such books as *Amante marine* (*Marine Lover*), *Passions élémentaires* (*Elemental Passions*), and *L'Oubli de l'air*. What, they asked, had become of the savagely witty thinker who deconstructed Freud and Lacan, who practiced Derridean turns on the (non)articulation of sexual difference? Since only those texts that corresponded to particular stages in feminist debate were known to a larger readership, many prematurely concluded that Irigaray's scope was limited to critiques of psychoanalytic tradition and the positing of a special language peculiar to women. In this context, when *This Sex* appeared, it was too soon to rethink the implications of her "speaking (as) woman" (the phrase Catherine Porter and I chose to retain the pun in *parler-femme*). Moreover, it went largely unnoticed that Irigaray had already gone beyond this notion, to emphasize "the sexuation of discourse."[1]

In other words, rather than encouraging readers to focus on the *manner* of Irigaray's interventions into the possibility of representing sexual difference, the history of her work's reception tended to limit discussion to what was seen as its *matter*—the lips as rhetorical figure, mimicry and masquerade as theories, "speaking (as) woman" as concept. As a result of such readings discussions of her work became mired in the antiessentialism debates of the eighties, while her subtly performative strategies were reified rather than experienced as phases of a work on and in language—whose aim was to transform our modes of understanding.[2]

At the same time two things were occurring to make it possible for English-speaking readers to catch up with her work, both in the sense of being able to grasp its range and learning to respond to its strangeness. First, by the end of the decade, appropriate, wide-ranging, and sympathetic interpretations were enabling readers to go beyond the antiessentialism debates that had circumscribed discussion. Judith Butler, Elizabeth Grosz, Naomi Schor, and Margaret Whitford, among others, had begun to situate her writing in broader and deeper intellectual contexts, where her rethinking of philosophy could be seen as the ground of her other forms of critique. Once this body of interpretative material was available, it became possible to move back and forth (to use one of Irigaray's favorite figures)—to effect a passage between theory and practice, commentary and translation.

Second, following upon this renewal of interest, Irigaray's most recent work has begun to appear in English: as of this writing, transla-

tions of all but one of her books have been commissioned or are forthcoming.[3] As this double process of translation—linguistic and cultural—takes place, however belatedly, it becomes increasingly clear that
readers should pay close attention to her writing itself, to its mobilization of syntax, figuration, spacing, and other textual features. In other
words, we should read it not only as thought *about* sexual difference but
an attempt to bring that difference *into* language.

For when readers refocus on the material aspect of Irigaray's work—
its way of returning theory to an awareness of its implication in the
physical world—they experience most intimately what she is "saying."
Indeed, in my view, some translations may have been worse than none
at all, particularly when they tried to smoothe out, naturalize, or nor-
malize her idiosyncracies. As in the case of Derrida, those aspects of her
prose that are the most opaque and consequently the most untranslatable are also the moments of greatest intervention into the process of
signification. Which means that the translator's lot is not a happy one.
As Barbara Johnson observes, the transference of such work into the
English-speaking context is nearly always "an exercise in violent
approximation."[4]

From the outset, to be sure, Irigaray urged readers to "*overthrow syntax* by suspending its eternally teleological order." Given the power of
the "signifying order," she preferred *not* to make sense, rather, "to speak
only in riddles, allusions, hints, parables. . . . Until the ear tunes into
another music."[5] I find myself wishing that all English-language readers could diagram Irigaray's syntax, parse her riddles, and feel the
provocative exasperation that accompanies this retuning of the ear in
the process of translation. It is in such exercises that one experiences the
extent to which, for Irigaray, grammar plays its part as an agent of
change.

The history of a particular translation may give the feel of this process,
which Johnson calls—in a different context but in intriguingly gendered terms—a renewal of "our love-hate intimacy with our mother
tongue," in which "we tear at her syntactic joints and semantic flesh" in
the effort to render a textuality that "displaces the very notion of *how* a
text means."[6] A decade ago, when I first translated Irigaray's "Fécondité
de la caresse," her revisionary reading of Emmanuel Levinas, *An Ethics
of Sexual Difference* had not been published, nor was it apparent that
this essay would form its conclusion.[7] Irigaray's response to Levinas had
to be grasped on and in her own terms—especially those that translated his vocabulary into her project. Although sympathetic to Levinas's
attempt to posit the other *as* other, she was critical of what she saw as

•
•
•   his failure to posit this other as a sexuate being: for her his meditation
     on the erotics of the caress allocates the subject position to the mascu-
     line and the object position to the feminine.

     Seeking to redistribute this grammar, Irigaray distinguishes Levinas's
term for the woman as loved one, *l'aimée,* from her own for the woman
as desiring subject, *l'amante.* (Although *amante* exists in French as the
feminine of *amant,* lover, it is an older form, generally used as a synonym of *maîtresse,* mistress.) Working from the context of her dialogue
with Levinas, I initially translated *amante* as "beloved," to echo the term
as used in the King James version of the Song of Solomon, that
"amorous" writing whose music can be heard in counterpoint to Irigaray's essay: as she later observed, in this Biblical text the identities of
the male and female beloveds are blurred, and both become mutually
desiring subjects.

     Once "Fécondité de la caresse" was reprinted as the conclusion of
Ethique de la différence sexuelle, however, it became clear that Irigaray's
project was broader, and more urgently focused upon ethical issues,
than was first apparent.[8] The *amante* appears in other sections of
Ethique, which posits the paradigm of "amorous exchange" as a mode
combining dialogue and the responsible recognition of sexual difference. In an implicit critique of Levinas her terms for the lovers revise
both positionality and agency; for this reason, however much it might
tear at the syntactic joints of English, this "sexuation" of grammar had
to be rendered literally. Thus, in preparing the essay for *An Ethics of Sexual Difference,* Gillian Gill and I translated *amant* as "male lover" and
amante as "female lover," to retain Irigaray's emphasis on the woman as
a desiring subject; similarly, we translated *aimée* as "beloved woman"
and *aimé,* where it occurred, as "beloved man," to underscore the point
that both subject and object positions may be gendered. However awkward, such a rendering underscores the ethical force of her work by
marking its central distinction between the woman as active subject and
the woman as passive object.

     If nouns, which in principle are more readily translatable, can call
into question the protocols of syntax, what of verbs and their morphological hold on the articulation of movement? *Devenir,* a recurrent
Irigarayan term, usually translated as "becoming," suggests the effort
implicit in her verb choices to stress not completed actions but the very
process of acting and being present in one's action: this *devenir* is not
an evolution toward some higher state but an ongoing flow, a (self)
generation of being.[9] Similarly, statements in the indicative that seemingly observe the rules of predication are often followed by question
marks, such that the translator feels obliged to add a "perhaps" or

another term to indicate that what is being said is posited in a mode other than the declarative—a realm of possibility closer to an "as if" or an optative.

Working on (and in) the text at this level, it was clear to me that Irigaray's linguistic interventions seek to unsettle the conceptual modes in which language imagines the shape of actions. In the section of *Ethics* entitled "Love of Self," for example, Irigaray thinks her way through the obstacles inherent in language when one tries to comprehend this reflexive:

> *Love of self* creates a particular movement, a kind of play between active and passive, in which, between me and me, there takes place this double relationship. . . . A liaison takes place which corresponds to no other coded or codable operation: neither active nor passive nor middle-passive, even if this operation is the closest.[10]

This "liaison" upsets our notions of space-time: where women are concerned, self-love would occur "without the involvement of anything that passes from one place to another, but only a place of passage, and its movement."[11]

Similarly, the verbal forms through which we voice our understanding of agency—active, passive, and the surviving forms of the middle-passive, used to convey the subject's performance of an action in which she or he is implicated—do not suffice to convey the possibilities that Irigaray imagines, were our languages more supple, flexible, and mobile. That different kind of movement would be "ceaselessly engaged in seeking its rhythm, its measure . . . its shortcuts toward itself, toward the other, others." Its verbs would be as unfamiliar as its nouns because it is "a speech that is always at risk, stable and unstable, like a step that is discovering itself, inventing itself at each instant."[12] In her view we pay a price—usually unacknowledged—by acceding to the familiar order of the sentence, that teleological structure that makes it possible to get to the point.

With the alteration of our assumptions about nouns and verbs, the possibility of dialogue—long one of Irigaray's concerns—is similarly disrupted and, provided her linguistic in(ter)ventions achieve their ends, translated into another realm. The psychoanalytic model of dialogic exchange between subjects has, to some extent, been deemphasized in Irigaray's more recent work, which increasingly stresses the "amorous exchange" between the sexes as a cultural paradigm. In the case of her "exchanges" with (male) philosophers, her practice has always been to situate herself as a female speaker in order to force the question of sexual difference—the sexual subtext or "the fantasmatic

· organization underlying the surface rationality" which philosophy
· ignores.[13]

Readers of Irigaray's work in English-speaking countries have often
been vexed by one way in which her writing mimes this exchange with
the imaginary of philosophy—its tendency to mingle her voice with
that of the philosophical text she is rereading rather than follow the
scholarly conventions for citation. From the outset, however, it was
clear that her challenge to such codes was deliberate, as Irigaray indicated in the endnote to *Speculum*:

> Precise references in the form of notes of punctuation indicating quota-
> tion have often been omitted. Because in relation to the working of the-
> ory, the/a woman fulfills a twofold function—as the mute outside that
> sustains all systematicity; as a maternal and still silent ground that nour-
> ishes all foundations—she does not have to conform to the codes theo-
> ry has set up for itself.

Furthermore, she wagered, any challenge to codes like those that have
just been enacted (subordinating the quotation through changes in
alignment and spacing) gives rise not only to discomfort but also to a
situation in which "something of the difference of the sexes would have
taken place."[14] Thus, by flouting the conventions that underpin scholarly systematicity, her writing would make visible its presuppositions
and requirements—for example, the scholar's demonstration of "mastery" through the use of the standard citational apparatus, as well as the
punctuation and spacing that subordinate the quotation to the "main"
argument.

The translator, then, grapples with the fact that Irigaray's frustrations
of convention must be rendered as significant—and not as idiosyncratic lapses from "standard" practice. In *An Ethics of Sexual Difference*, for
example, she uses a differently eccentric citationality, in which both the
nonindentation of the "quoted" passages and the unusual typogra-
phy—in this case, "quotations" are italicized—signal that these readings of Plato, Aristotle, Descartes, and others are a series of active dialogues with philosophical partners.[15] In other words, the italicized passages that give voice to Irigaray's interlocutors are intended to function
dialogically, and, as such, claim equal status with the main text. If this
strategy is effective, we understand in a more immediate and situated
way that we are, in a sense, reading her readings—a form of engagement
that is somewhat less discomforting than that set up by her earlier practice of weaving her own voice in and out of others' texts.[16]

Similarly, Irigaray's typographical and conceptual use of spacing suggests still another way in which writing draws attention to the condi-

tions of its existence. Again, like Derrida, Irigaray underscores the functions of spaces, pauses, and the white of the page in the act of reading
by stressing their roles as "figures" in signifying practice. But when Irigaray adapts one of Derrida's favorite terms, the *entre* that figures both
fusion and separation, she does so not only to suggest a third term
between binaries like subject and object, masculine and feminine, or
inside and outside, but also to posit an economy where "desire occupies
or designates the space of the *interval*."[17] As Whitford observes, the
between is a way of rethinking the traditional dispositions of space-time,
since "it" urges us to refigure this problematic from a gendered perspective, bringing to consciousness the ways in which the presuppositions of Western thought assign the woman to materiality while denying man awareness of his embodiment.[18] Such writing solicits the reader's response: it requests not commentary but a reply to its questions
about the possibility and conditions of dialogue, whether something
can take place in the *entre-nous*.[19]

For it is in the recognition of the *entre-deux* of human relations, genres, and styles of being that Irigaray places her hope for the future.
Whether this "between" figures as the "interval," "intermediary," "third
term," or by some other name, its function is the same—to designate
the space for a respectful, admiring, evolving encounter between the
sexes, but also between other pairs of opposites that tend to collapse
into one term's dominance over the other. Thus, when Irigaray rereads
Plato's Symposium in *Ethics*, she teases out the strands of Diotima's lesson that point in a direction Plato never considered: this Diotima
emphasizes not the disjunction between idea and reality but rather "that
which stands *between*, that which makes possible the passage between
ignorance and knowledge."[20] In this view, what Plato, and the subsequent tradition of Western philosophy, ignored in Diotima's lesson is
the role of love as mediator—or that which allows a meeting between
equals who respect and admire each other in their difference.

In a general way this figure for spacing is one of the keys to the "new"
Irigaray, whose voice emerges most clearly in *Ethics*. It is present in her
reminder that philosophical language is backed by the materiality that
lies "behind" the words—hence her call for "the unceasing practice of
openness between signs" or "letting the flesh appear between sign and
sign."[21] It is also at work in her attempts to forge a prose that corresponds to this vision of language's neglected relation to embodiment:
like Diotima's, her own style " *entwines with* what she says without *tying
the knot*," particularly when she evokes the role of love "as an intermediate terrain, a mediator, a space-time of permanent *passage* between
mortal and immortal."[22]

•
•
•

It is as if Irigaray imagined another idiom, one where the spaces between, and within, words opened of their own accord. This is especially true of the abstractions of philosophical language, which, in Irigaray's usage, permit a glimpse through their transparent surfaces into their opaque, material backing or source. And because many of these key terms bear within them their etymological and philosophical histories, reopening them involves a double translation—from French to "Irigarayan," then from this idiosyncratic tongue to English. For example, in her attempt to reorient ideas of transcendence to experience in the here and now, *Ethics* uses the term "instance" in its radical sense: as a reembodied standing within the self that is the opposite of "ecstasy," a standing outside the self. Since this usage resembles Heidegger's,[23] we followed the practice of some of Heidegger's translators by translating "instance" as "in-stance," thereby signaling its Latin root (*instare*) by means of the hyphen. Thus, when Diotima tells Socrates that "he is incapable of grasping the existence or the in-stance of that which stands *between*,"[24] the letter of the text strains to imitate the spirit.

Similarly, in "L'Admiration," the section of *Ethics* in which Irigaray rereads Descartes on this primary "passion of the soul," *admiration* could have been handled in the same way as "in-stance," by opening the term to its etymological past. But, in this case, an alternative was available: it may also be translated as "wonder," which carries greater immediacy due to its Germanic root. We decided to render *admiration* as "wonder," chiefly because in English the Latinate term felt too heavy to evoke the sense of awe, mystery, and enchantment that Irigaray intends.[25] As in *This Sex Which Is Not One*, where she adopted the persona of a quizzical Alice tracing her steps back through a philosophical Wonderland, so in this section of *Ethics* she reads her way back to Descartes's pre-Freudian psychology, and to wonder, as "the passion that Freud forgot."[26] For, in a general way, this voyage back through philosophical language into its material past illustrates in miniature Irigaray's large-scale retraversals of Western thought—whether the classic texts of philosophy, their popular versions in myth and fairy tale, or the explanatory models that underlie our modern sciences.

Ethics was, however, a turning point where Irigaray's stylistic innovation is concerned. Following its publication, she summarized her thoughts on style as that aspect of writing which "resists coding, summary, counting, cataloguing, programming" and insisted that "it cannot be brought down to the level of such oppositions as sense/mind, poetry/ideas . . . masculine/feminine, as these dichotomies have been presented to us so

far." Furthermore, she explained, what she had said in *Ethics* "moves
through a double style: a style of loving relationships, [and] a style of
thought, of exegesis, of writing. The two are consciously or uncon-
sciously linked, with a more immediately corporeal and affective side in
one case, a more socially developed side in the other." Moreover, Irigaray
reiterated her belief that both kinds of language work, "the analysis of
the formal structures of discourse . . . and the creation of a new style"
were necessary "for setting up different norms for life."[27]

In books published since that date, however (*Parler n'est jamais
neutre, Sexes et parentés, Le Temps de la différence, Je, tu, nous,* and *Sexes
et genres à travers les langues*—which could be said to voice the
"newest" Irigaray), one-half of this language work—the analysis of the
formal structures of discourse—is carried out at the expense of what
seemed her most radical endeavor, her gestures toward a different
style, or styles. The enigmatic tone of her earlier prose has given way
to a prophetic voice, one that spells out its vision rather than trying
to enact it; and Irigaray runs the risk of seeming more accessible, but
at the expense of the subtlety of the analyses that preceded these
recent books—on which their "lucidity" depends. Yet, as Whitford
observes, her later writing "is in some ways as difficult to understand
as her earlier work, for the simplified statements cannot simply be
taken at face value."[28] It now seems as if Irigaray has won her way to
greater simplicity via the stylistic experiments that made her so hard
to read (and translate), yet for the reader who has not followed her
trajectory—that "passing from one to the other"—her thought may
appear deceptively straight-forward.[29] Ironically, with this shift, the
translator's work also becomes more straightforward, yet I am tempted to conclude that Irigaray's message is best served when both aspects
of her style are present and engaged in dialogue with each other—and
with the reader.

What is this message, the urgency of which (particularly since Chernobyl) has caused Irigaray to set aside her work *in* language to speak
about language, in the hope of reaching a wider audience? It is that sexual difference—or "sexuation"—as the primordial, irreducible difference has been forgotten, suppressed, annulled in language, law, philosophy, and science, and that these cultural forms prize the masculine
under the guise of the so-called universal or impersonal, associate transcendence with this sex alone, and consequently devalue those aspects
of culture and nature construed as feminine. The current technological
and spiritual impasses of our civilization would result from this "dereliction" of the female "genre"[30]—and whatever is associated with it—to
the status of the material, the less than human. In this view, a radical

•
•
•

and salutary shift in our modes of thinking can come only from our mutual recognition as "sexuate" beings, as sexually differentiated, with the concomitant possibility of woman's access to subject status.

To be sure, becoming the subject of discourse—rather than its object or unspoken, unvoiced pre-condition—has been at the heart of Irigaray's work from the beginning. But what was first enacted as a work on, in, and through language, or a rescue project carried out via a grammatical terrorism, is now being voiced as a linguistic myth—a syntactical counterpart of the fall from Eden. Of her use of the term *amante*, Irigaray has said that she "wanted to signify that the woman can be a subject in love": this, she felt, would counter the old story in which "the woman's pleasure is alienated to that of the man, according to the most traditional of scenarios of temptation and fall." She locates this fall "in the reduction of the feminine to the passive, to the past tense and to the object of man's pleasure," and identifies the remedy to this sexual economy in the assumption of subjecthood by both sexes: "here would lie the way out from the fall, for in this case, love can become spiritual and divine."[31] Indeed, our current situation "is, then, only an exile, a waiting to return. The ban on the flesh, the obligation to work and to suffer, are the reverse image, the failure of our first birth." Her work on language would, then, be part of a reclamation project whose aim is to undo our "*exile* from this garden." "But all the while he is bound here and now by a *fault* he can never be free of, and for which he can never substitute a third party such as love, grace, the jubilation of the flesh and the share these have in language too."[32]

To dismiss this counter-myth as utopian or poetic is to fail to register the importance of mythology for Irigaray, who calls it "one of the principal expressions of what orders society at any given time."[33] And given her assumption—that language work is one of the principal ways to undo the damage, "the cultural injustices perpetrated by language"— Irigaray's analyses of linguistic structures may be another face of the same project. However technical these studies seem, they can be read in the broader context of her overall program, since—as she says again and again in recent books—Irigaray believes that women will only attain full subject status when the female gender is revalorized: because grammar is coded on the basis of social realities, sexual liberation can come about only through radical shifts and changes in language.[34]

How, then, does one feel when translating work that is engaged in a struggle to bring about such shifts in our modes of understanding and expression? Translator Helen Lane observes of the translation process itself, "One is constantly trying one's best to 'bring over' meanings from one language to another. The *primary activity* of translation thus takes place somewhere *between* the source language and the target language."[35] If this is the case for translation in general, one's sense of floating in the "between" is enhanced, intensified, and taken to the next power in the case of Irigaray. Indeed, in my experience, her translators find themselves in multiple "betweens"—between the rules of French grammar and Irigaray's idiosyncratic practice, between Irigarayan as the source language and standard English as the target, and between this straightforward target and the strangeness of what one eventually "brings over" as/in translation. For it is in this time afloat, or in linguistic free fall, that one "discovers those elements that constitute the dynamic process of how a text might come to mean."[36]

But as well as knowing how to stay afloat in linguistic ether, one also needs the ability to slow down to a meditative trance in order to follow Irigaray's voyages through the process of "coming to meaning." In fact, the slow-motion reading that takes place while one is translating offers a privileged, albeit peculiar, way into the rhythms of her thought. Figuratively speaking, this work tries our patience by asking us to stay up all night with it—as Gertrude Stein did with her own investigations into grammar—for in such a space we elude the constraints of syntax, and words float free of their usual moorings. Yet in the light of day (or under the pressure of completing a translation), one emerges from this suspended state, steps back from the text, and makes choices. For if "translation is based on the dissolution of the self," it also "creates a specific kind of distance."[37] In this same space—the middle distance opened up in the process of translation—other choices can, and will, occur, as new translations modify the realm of possibility and are, in turn, modified. Finally, the allure and the impossibility of translating Irigaray both reside in the suspension she conjures, that undecidable between where we need not make the distinctions required in the clear light of daytime logic.

NOTES •

1. Margaret Whitford makes this point in *The Irigaray Reader*, p. 78.
2. On the antiessentialism debates, see Schor's and Whitford's introductions to this volume.
3. See bibliography, this volume.
4. Johnson, "Translator's Introduction," Derrida, *Dissemination*, (Chicago: University of Chicago Press, 1981), p. xviii. For a critique of the Derridean aspects of Irigaray's work, see Schor, "This Essentialism Which Is Not One," this volume.

5. Irigaray, *Speculum*, pp. 142, 143/177, 178.

6. Johnson, "Taking Fidelity Philosophically," in Joseph F. Graham, ed., *Difference in Translation* (Ithaca: Cornell University Press, 1985), pp. 143, 145.

7. "Fécondité de la caresse" appeared first in excerpted form in *Land* (1982), 2:37–39, then in full in *Exercices de la patience* (1983), 5:119–137. The essay was translated as "The Fecundity of the Caress," in Richard A. Cohen, ed., *Face to Face with Levinas* (Albany: SUNY Press, 1986), pp. 231–256.

8. It should be noted that the publication of *Ethique* in 1984 anticipated and influenced the recent focus on ethics in feminist theory: see the sections on Irigaray in Drucilla Cornell, *Beyond Accommodation: Ethical Feminism, Deconstruction, and the Law* (New York and London: Routledge, 1991); and Gayatri Chakravorty Spivak, "French Feminisms Revisited: Ethics and Politics," in Joan Scott and Judith Butler, eds., *Feminists Theorize the Political* (New York: Routledge: 1992).

9. On the relations between Irigaray's and Deleuze's somewhat different notions of "becoming," see Rosi Braidotti, this volume.

10. Irigaray, *Ethics*, p. 62/*Ethique*, p. 63.

11. Ibid., p. 72/74.

12. Ibid., p. 166/197.

13. See Whitford, *The Irigaray Reader*, pp. 7, 8, 78.

14. Irigaray, *Speculum*, p. 365/458. The English edition supplies the references lacking in the original, thus reinscribing the conventions.

15. See Burke, "Romancing the Philosophers: Luce Irigaray," in Dianne Hunter, ed., *Seduction and Theory* (Urbana: University of Illinois Press, 1989), pp. 226–240, for a slightly different discussion of this aspect of her work.

16. It is still the case in *Ethics*, however, that another intellectual partner, Lacan, is referred to only within the confines of a parenthesis, as if to contain the charged valence of this particular thinker.

17. Irigaray, *Ethics*, p. 4/*Ethique*, p. 15.

18. Whitford, *Luce Irigaray: Philosophy in the Feminine* (Routledge, 1991), p. 163. For another discussion of Irigaray's figures of mediation, see Gail Schwab, this volume.

19. See Irigaray, *Sexes and Genealogies*, p. 178/*Sexes et parentés*, p. 192.

20. Irigaray, *Ethics*, p. 21/*Ethique*, p. 28.

21. Ibid., p. 157/184.

22. Ibid., p. 29/34.

23. On some aspects of Irigaray's relation to Heidegger, see the essays of Joanna Hodge and Ellen Mortensen, this volume.

24. Irigaray, *Ethics*, p. 21/*Ethique*, p. 28.

25. In so doing we also followed the example of the standard translation, *The Passions of the Soul*, trans. E. S. Haldane and G. R. T. Ross, *The Philosophical Works of Descartes*, vol. 1 (Cambridge: Cambridge University Press, 1931).

26. Irigaray, *Ethics*, p. 82/*Ethique*, p. 87.

27. Irigaray, *Sexes and Genealogies* pp. 177–178/*Sexes et parentés*, pp. 191–192. For another view of Irigaray's style(s), see Elizabeth Weed, this volume.

28. Whitford, *The Irigaray Reader*, p. 11.

29. Commenting on *Sexes et parentés* (1987), one of Irigaray's most sympathetic readers observed that because this book consists of lectures, its style is at once more accessible and less sustained than in her earlier work (Roger-Pol Droit, *Le Monde*, September 25, 1987, p. 21).

30. In French *genre* suggests both "gender" and "genre": on this point see Irigaray, "The Three Genders," *Sexes and Genealogies*, pp. 169–181/"Les Trois genres," *Sexes et parentés*, pp. 183–196.

31. Irigaray, "Questions to Emmanuel Levinas," *The Irigaray Reader*, pp. 185, 186.

32. Irigaray, *Sexes and genealogies*, pp. 178–179/*Sexes et parentés*, p. 193.

33. Irigaray, *Je, tu, nous*, p. 24/28.

34. Ibid., p. 68/84. More generally, on the need to repair these linguistic "injustices," see Irigaray, "Linguistic Sexes and Genders"/"Sexes et genres linguistiques," *Je, tu, nous*, pp. 67–74/83–91.

35. Lane, cited by Nancy Kline, "Writing as Translation: The Great Between," *Translation Review* (1991), 36(36):7. Kline's account of her translation process in this suggestive article resembles my own experience.

36. Rainer Schulte, "Translation and Literary Criticism," *Translation Review* (1982), 9:3–4; cited in Kline, "Writing as Translation," p. 5.

37. Eliot Weinberger, "Translating," *Sulfur* (1992), no. 30, p. 227.

· *Dianne Chisholm*
·
·

IRIGARAY'S

HYSTERIA

> As for woman, one may wonder why she submits so readily to this make-believe, why she "mimics" so perfectly as to forget she is acting out man's contraphobic projects, projections, and productions of her desire. . . . And why does she comply so readily? Because she is suggestible? Hysterical? But now we begin to be aware of the vicious circle.
> —Luce Irigaray
> *Speculum of the Other Woman*

Her feminist readers, especially the readers of *Speculum of the Other Woman*, may well ask of Irigaray: why does *she* mime so perfectly those projects, projections, productions, contraphobias of phallogocentric discourse, why does she mirror so readily the "woman" of philosophy and of psychoanalysis, why does she lend her writing to the re-production of theory in seeming complicity with masculine desire? Is *she* suggestible? Hysterical? Does *she herself* not entertain a *vicious circle* when *as a woman* she enters the circles of philosophy and psychoanalysis where "woman" (if Irigaray is correct) functions as a trope of female absence and negation to constitute the figurative illusion of male presence and autonomy? In entering these circles, does Irigaray not, like the philosopher/analyst, take this "woman" too literally to be the universal—symbolic, ontological, historical—(non)representative of women, and, consequently, like the hysteric, resign herself to being spoken for, to a mutism of miming an imposed femininity? *In other words, does Irigaray not mime the philosopher/analyst as a woman who has been displaced by the discourse that she speaks, forget-*

.
.
. *ting that this "woman" is also a mime?* When does Irigaray's "make-
believe" switch from histrionics to hysterics, from playacting the
woman among philosophers, or miming the philosopher as a woman,
to serious acting out as "she" who has been excluded from coauthoring
the history of representation in which she must continue to represent
herself though it so thoroughly abuses her image?[1]

The reader of *Speculum*'s extensive criticism will be familiar with the
skepticism and outrage over Irigaray's apparent reduction of historical
woman to hysterical mime—to the "woman" of philosophical and psychoanalytic discourse.[2] What I want to know is, *Is there a method to her
madness*, one that breaks through philosophy's phallogocentrism and
that the feminist producer/reader of texts might learn as a critical strategy of production and/or reception?

If Irigaray cannot speak outside the circle of phallogocentrism, since,
accordingly, the symbolic order encompasses/constitutes all possible
discursive positions, then what are the most enabling positions for her,
as woman, as hysteric, to mime? "She" could speak *con*centrically, *as if*
the sex which is not one, *as if* voicing the *con* (Fr. cunt, female orifice,
"hole") of sexual difference, exaggerating her dis/avowal of phallic lack
and thereby exposing the structural abyss that man *con*ceals with fetish
projections, erecting his imaginary and symbolizable phallic presence.
Or, "she" could speak as *ex*-centric, *as if* she were outside, or *as if* she
could stage her exit from the man-made male-dominated discursive
universe. Does Irigaray then speak as a *con*-artist, an artful histrionic
miming the discursive blankness or bleakness of *being* the woman of
theory? Or does she speak as *ex*-centric, outside phallogocentric discourse but signifying allusively to an other order, a woman's symbolic
realm, reserved in cultural latency? Does she shift from speaking as an
ex-centric to speaking as a *con*-artist and vice versa—and to what effect?
Does she not run the risk of speaking as an *ex-con*, as a woman who
comes to *believe* in her incarceration in an alien language and who must
blast her way out of it? When this happens does she not run the risk of
resorting to a terrorism that destroys her "self" along with the language
that imprisons/excludes her—like the hysteric in her cataleptic crisis?

When Irigaray poses this question of woman is she aware of the
vicious circles in which she circulates and of the risks she takes, the risks
of turning histrionics into hysterics and of taking her reader with her,
of hystericizing her reader by persuading her to make the same hysterical identifications? In the discussion that follows I inquire further into
Irigaray's use (and possible abuse) of hysterical mimicry as a strategy of
cultural subversion and counterproduction. To determine the critical

efficacy of this strategy, *as a feminist strategy*, I will examine its limits,
and the risks it entails for both author and reader.

vicious circles and hysterical eLucedation

The "vicious circle" to which Irigaray refers when she asks of woman
why she "mimics" and "complies" so easily is the logical possibility that
woman is made hysterical, suggestible, by the discourse that she is
forced to mime in patriarchal institutions. She reminds us that the hysteric pantomimes sexual pleasure in contractions and seizures, a tortu-
ous display/displacement of a feminine jouissance that cannot be
admitted or even articulated in the symbolic order of the masculine.
"What is played out in the body," echoes Monique David-Ménard,
"takes the place of a discourse that cannot be uttered."[3] The hysteric's
exaggerated "miming" of sexual pleasure in bodily contortion, in broken speech and/or aphasia, signifies her inability to cope with the discursive norms of desire and femininity. Moreover, for Irigaray, the hysteric exposes the normal masquerade of femininity, its poses and its
silences, its (apparently unsymptomatic) complicity with discursive
norms.

Woman's hysterical mimicry is a symptom of the way discourse functions differentially for the sexes, and not just a telltale sign of her repudiation of femininity: that women must mime discourse rather than
speak it directly is the logical and structural condition of a language system affording only one sex positive representation. Psychoanalysis, it is
true, pays attention to hysteria, offering an audience and enabling rapport, conducting it (back) into language, where it enacts its own "talking cure." But in the process of treating and theorizing hysteria it
(re)imposes the norms of patriarchal discourse in the guise of a cure. In
Speculum Irigaray accuses Freud of using analysis to "achieve a lasting
seduction on the hysteric" (p. 38/41). In *This Sex Which Is Not One* she
re-poses the question of woman's complicity in terms of the *duplicity* of
psychoanalysis:

> There again, one may raise the question whether psychoanalysis has not
> superimposed on the hysterical symptom a code, a system of interpreta-
> tion(s) which fails to correspond to the desire fixed in somatizations and
> in silence. In other words, does psychoanalysis offer any "cure" to hys-
> terics beyond a surfeit of suggestions intended to adapt them, if only a
> little better, to masculine society?   *(p. 137/135)*

Is the vicious circle of hysteria generated by psychoanalysis itself?
Lacan seems to suggest so. In *The Four Fundamental Concepts of Psycho-*

- *analysis* he acknowledges that while "the point at issue [in analysis] is to
- *get her* [the daughter/hysteric] *to speak* . . . to overcom[e] the barrier of
- silence," psychoanalysis does not even aim to uncover the motive of her
speech. If she speaks, she is cured of her silence, but this does not tell us
anything about why she began to speak.[4] In prompting the hysteric to
speak, Lacan clarifies, the analyst facilitates *the constitution* (not merely
the revelation) of her desire (p. 12), and Freud, accordingly, possessed
the "genius" to realize the "relation of desire to language." But, he
admits, "this is not to say that the relation was fully elucidated" (p. 12);
in fact what Freud discovered is that "in order to cure the hysteric of all
her symptoms, the best way is to satisfy the hysteric's desire—which is
for her to posit her desire in relation to us as an unsatisfied desire."
While this "cure" affords the hysteric the opportunity to verbalize, and
thereby recognize, the source of her hysterical symptoms—forbidden
desire—it does not afford her even the minimal satisfaction of knowing
why this desire must remain unsatisfied: such a cure "leaves entirely to
one side the specific question of *why* she can sustain her desire only as
an unsatisfied desire" (p. 12).

Lacan acknowledges that in getting the hysteric to speak, in having
her constitute her desire in language, analysis also has her constitute the
impossibility of that desire—a "cure" that keeps the hysteric in analysis
as the only place where she can spell out the desire she can never satisfy. "So hysteria places us," Lacan confesses, "on the track of some kind
of original sin in analysis" (p. 12). Furthermore, while Freud understood that the hysteric constituted her desire in analysis, "the desire of
Freud himself . . . was never analyzed" (p. 12).

Irigaray intervenes in psychoanalysis precisely where psychoanalysis
continues to perpetuate this "original sin" of facilitating the reproduction of hysterical desire. The first section of *Speculum*, "The Blind Spot
of an Old Dream of Symmetry," exposes Freud's desire, the desire of the
father, demonstrating the vicious logic structuring psychoanalytic theory and treatment:

> How could [the little girl, the woman] be anything but suggestible and
> hysterical when . . . the father [Freud/the analyst] forces her to accept
> that, while he alone can satisfy her and give her access to pleasure, he
> prefers the added enjoyment to be derived from laying down the law,
> and therefore penalizes her for her (or his own?) "seduction fantasies."
> *(p. 60/70)*

Though it may have been her tactic of exposure that led to her expulsion from Lacan's Ecole freudienne, submitting the father to analysis is
not the primary object of Irigaray's reading. She would elucidate further

what Freud hesitated to uncover about the hysterical "relation of desire
to language," asking impertinent questions such as the hysterical
daughter might ask of the father of psychoanalysis: for instance, whose
desire is it that cannot be satisfied, that cannot even be spoken except
as a desire the father would/would not hear? What is the relation of this
desire to the Law (of discourse) that constitutes it? (Normal and yet
taboo?) Is this desire that is constituted in the language of analysis the
desire of the father, which the father wants to affirm but that, by Law,
he must refuse to satisfy, OR, is it a more renegade desire, a desire of the
mother that is a negation of this Law, that inhabits the woman's imaginary outside the scope of paternal fantasy and is thus beyond the scope
of Freudian transference, and/or therapy? Irigaray agrees with Lacan
that not all has been elucidated about hysteria, but she also proposes a
further elucidation, which would mean privileging female sexuality in
an analysis that would necessarily extend *beyond Freud*:

> Although hysteria gives rise to the inaugural scene of analysis and indeed
> to its discourse . . . and although Freud's earliest patients are hysterics,
> an exhaustive analysis of the symptoms involved in hysteria and the
> establishment of their relation to the development of female sexuality
> would extend beyond the framework of . . . Freudian positions; as it
> happens, moreover, no systematic regrouping of the various phases of
> the investigation of hysteria is to be found in Freud's work.[5]

To go beyond. I suggest that Irigaray elucidates a symptomatology
and/or strategy of hysterical mimicry for woman-as-speaking-subject
with the purpose of transforming the conditions of her speaking. In posing
the question of why women mime—as if all women were hysterics—
Irigaray asks her feminist reader to analyze her investment in whichev-
er masquerade of sex she has chosen (femininity? masculinity? lesbianism? heterosexuality? maternity? a chimera of these?) In posing the
question of woman's complicity, she prompts women to ask how their
sexual masquerade serves as a strategic response to discursive coercions
and seductions imposed on them by patriarchal institutions—how
compliant, how resistant, and at what cost to themselves as women.

Like her contemporaries Hélène Cixous and Juliet Mitchell, Irigaray
affirms the subversiveness of hysteria, but unlike either Cixous or
Mitchell, she does not celebrate the hysteric as cultural revolutionary.[6]
Instead, she derives a *method* of subversive mimicry from the hysteric's
charade of suffering. She learns from the hysteric to "assume the feminine role deliberately" in order to "convert a form of subordination into
an affirmation, and thus to begin to thwart it."[7] It is the hysteric's *strategic* mimicry, her feminine art of miming discourse, not her psychic

- ambivalence or bisexuality, that Irigaray elucidates for a radical analyt-
- ic practice:

> To play with mimesis is . . . , for a woman, to try to recover the place of
> her exploitation by discourse, without allowing herself to be simply
> reduced to it. It means to resubmit herself . . . to "ideas," in particular
> to ideas about herself, that are elaborated in/by a masculine logic, but so
> as to make "visible," by an effect of playful repetition, what was sup-
> posed to remain invisible: the cover-up of a possible operation of the
> feminine in language.   *(p. 76/74)*

The problem that Irigaray faces as analyst is the problem of transforming the hysteric's symptomatic inarticulateness into subversive discourse and, finally, into women's speech. She regards hysterical mimicry as an initial break from the vicious circle of women's complicity ("an
initial phase" in women's history [p. 76/74]) but also as signifying
woman's repressed potential to speak for herself (" 'to unveil' the fact
that, if women are such good mimics, it is because they are not simply
resorbed in this function" [p. 76/74]). Hysterical mimicry implies that
woman could produce an other mimesis, could speak not from the
compromised positions as patriarchy's feminized or masculinized
"woman" but as woman's woman, whatever that might be, moving from
speaking as patriarchy's mimic, that is, as more or less hysterical, to
speaking as woman's mimic: from speaking (as) hysteric to speaking (as)
woman.

> Does the hysteric speak? Isn't hysteria a privileged place for preserving—
> but "in latency," "in sufferance"—that which does not speak? And in
> particular (even according to Freud . . .), that which is not expressed in
> woman's relation to her mother, to herself, to other women? . . . mim-
> ing/reproducing a language that is not [her] own, masculine language, it
> caricatures and deforms that language: it "lies," it "deceives," as women
> have always been reputed to do.
>   The problem of "speaking (as) woman" is precisely that of finding a
> possible continuity between that gestural expression or that speech of
> desire—which at present can only be identified in the form of symp-
> toms and pathology—and a language, including a verbal language.
>   *(pp. 136–37/134–35)*

To speak as woman among women to women means speaking to
women directly, but not speaking without mimesis, a form of self-representation: Irigaray foresees replacing a production of speech that is
intended for male audiences with one that engages women in articulating the desire of the "other" woman, imagining and symbolizing what
the other woman, mother, daughter, lover, or companion, wants:

"There may be a speaking-among-women that is still a speaking (as) man but that may also be the place where a speaking (as) woman may dare to express itself. . . . That said, by *speaking (as) woman*, one may attempt to provide a place for the 'other' as feminine" (p. 135/133).

subversive mimeses

Irigaray points to two different mimeses, or to two different phases in one subversive process: a symptomatic mimicry of patriarchy's fetishes and projections, which is potentially both terroristic and terrorized, *and* a utopian mimesis of woman's fantasy, mimesis without man as interlocutor, allowing for production, representation, and cultivation of women's auto- and homoeroticism, of women's non"hom(m)osexualized" fantasies. Since this utopian mimesis would be the mimicry of "perversion" (of non-normative desire), must it not be distinguished from the hysterical mimicry of desire so alienated, so repressed by patriarchy's discursive constraints that it cannot be uttered except in self-destructive compliance?

Ironically, she finds support in Plato for this distinction of mimeses:

> In Plato, there are two *mimeses . . . mimesis* as production, which would lie more in the realm of music, and there is the *mimesis* that would be already caught up in a process of *imitation, specularization, adequation,* and *reproduction*. It is the second form that is privileged throughout the history of philosophy and whose effects/symptoms, such as latency, suffering, paralysis of desire, are encountered in hysteria.
>
> *(p. 131/129–130)*

Irigaray uses Plato,[8] whose "masculine hysteria" is submitted to analysis in the last section of *Speculum*, to formulate the double scene of subversive mimicry: her utopian mimesis corresponds to Plato's mimesis of *production* ("postures and melodies connected with the goodness of soul or body, whether with such goodness itself or with some image of it . . . which exhibit an intrinsic rightness,")[9] while her hysterical mimesis corresponds to his mimesis of *reproduction* ("the art of contradiction making, descended from an insincere kind of conceited mimicry [demagoguery/dissimulation], of the semblance-making breed . . . of production . . . assigned to the Sophist").[10] The "musical" form of mimesis suggests a kind of primary (productive/active) imaginary fixed or framed by a highly standardized, or stylized, "sophisticated" mimesis: "the first form seems always to have been repressed, if only because it was constituted as an enclave within a 'dominant' discourse" (p. 131/130). Yet, it is the first mimesis that gives rise to women's cultural productions: "It is doubtless in the direction of, and on the basis of, that

- first *mimesis* that the possibility of a woman's writing may come about"
- (p. 131/130).

A productive mimesis might, Irigaray supposes, be initiated if women could find a collective space within the patriarchal linguistic community where they could enact/speak what they are forbidden in public; *parler-femme* would then be a matter of women's imaging, symbolizing, performing, playing with, acting upon, speaking out—in the languages available—other parts of the oedipal drama already taken up by women, though marginalized and muted by the dominance of patriarchal norms in mixed society.

> It is certain that with women-among-themselves (and this is one of the stakes of liberation movements, when they are not organized along the lines of masculine power, and when they are not focused on demands for the seizure or the overthrow of "power"), in these places of women-among-themselves, something of a speaking (as) woman is heard. This accounts for the desire or the necessity of sexual nonintegration: the dominant language is so powerful that women do not dare to speak (as) woman outside the context of nonintegration.   *(p. 135/133)*

This productive mimicry, *parler-entre-femmes*, would not enact a hysterical mimicry, a miming of discourse to expose the impossibility of speaking (as) woman, but instead facilitate the production of speaking (as) woman; yet Irigaray chooses in *Speculum* to employ the hysterical mimicries of the *ex*-centric and of the *con*-artist. Why? Must she write this book before she can write *This Sex*, perform a (w)rite of passage from a "politics of despair" to a politics of cultural counterproduction?[11] Does enacting hysteria allow Irigaray to forge a break from the vicious circle of psychoanalytic phallogocentrism? It would seem that for Irigaray it is not possible for woman, for herself *as* philosopher/analyst, to imagine a radical discursive practice until she has acted the part of cultural terrorist, or until she feels so terrorized that she introduces hysterical mimicry into psychoanalytic/philosophical discourse itself. Such mimicry would systematically "unspeak" that discourse by performing a risky de(con)struction so as to clear the ground for other, less reactively *re*productive, more actively productive strategies of mimesis. The problem Irigaray must confront is how to liberate the first mimesis (the productive/active mimesis) through the second (reproductive/reactive mimesis)—how to open a space for countercultural production by overblown histrionic effects of hysterical reproduction without destroying that enclave in the process.

Is, then, Irigaray's text a hysterical text set among patriarchy's master discourses? (How) does it induce hysteria in the reader and to what

effect? What does a method of hysterical mimicry offer feminism apart
from its dis-ease and its risks?

hysterical Irigaray?

> The hysterical use of metaphor perhaps . . . accounts, at least in part,
> for a common feminine attitude that consists in adopting the rigor
> and demands of philosophy only to shed them at certain discursive
> moments by using stylistic figures that organize the mockery of these
> features, figures whose syntax and semantics merit study. Hysterical
> theatricalization, the conversion of the conceptual into a display by
> way of a linguistic pirouette that suddenly subjectivizes the "rigor" of
> a development, would be one version of hysterical metaphor, in the
> field of discursive practices.[12]

Since Shoshana Felman first posed the question of "who" does the speaking in *Speculum of the Other Woman*,[13] (Anglophone) feminist critics
have been perplexed and/or irritated by Irigaray's mimetic "voice," by its
refusal to identify itself (as woman's voice) and to locate itself in a
woman's literary or textual tradition. Irigaray speaks at great length "on"
woman "through" carefully selected passages of philosophical and psychoanalytic discourse. Why these discourses? She tells us in *This Sex* that
"it is indeed precisely philosophical discourse that . . . sets forth the law
for all others, inasmuch as it constitutes the discourse on discourse" (p.
74/72) and that "psychoanalytic discourse on female sexuality is the discourse of truth. A discourse that tells the truth about the logic of truth"
(p. 86/85). If this is so, is it not *most* strategic for a woman to voice herself here? But the truth psychoanalysis tells us about the logic of truth,
and thus about philosophy, is "that *the feminine occurs only within models and laws devised by male subjects*," that this model "is a *phallic* one,
[which] shares the values promulgated by patriarchal society and culture,
values inscribed in the philosophical corpus: property, production,
order, form, unity, visibility . . . and erection" (p. 86/85). How could this
body of language be an appropriate model for women to voice?

According to Irigaray a woman cannot speak (as) woman when she
delivers a theoretical discourse on woman, even if she painstakingly
appropriates that theory *for* women, for feminism:

> When she submits to (such a) theory, woman fails to realize that she is
> renouncing the specificity of her symbolic relationship to the imaginary.
> Subjecting herself to objectivization in discourse—to being "female."
> Re-objectivizing her own self whenever she claims to identify herself
> "as" a masculine subject. A "subject" that re-searches itself as lost (mater-
> nal-feminine) "object."   *(p. 133/165)*

•
•
•   When she, Irigaray, addresses the problem of theorizing woman *as* woman, she speaks directly neither as a man nor as a woman but *as* a mimic, deliberately theatricalizing and parodying—hystericizing— men's discourses on woman, exposing their oppressive inadequacy.[14]

Rather than identify the hysteric's "voice" as woman's masculine-theoretical voice, or as the masquerading "voice" of the absent Other, I read this voice as a trope, a parody-mime, that voices woman's silencing or exposes woman's being overspoken by men's logic of the Same. Such a "voice" does not emanate directly from the repressed female body but functions as a metaphorical disease in a body of male discourse, riddling it with hints, allusions, parables of women's sexual difference.[15] Hysteria, Irigaray diagnoses, is a display of that which cannot be articulated, not for *lack* of a language but because of the imposition of a linguistic code that subjects every language user to the same phallic norms, denying woman all but phallic or negative sexual self-representation:

> The nonsymbolization of her desire for origin, of her relationship to her mother, and of her libido acts as a constant appeal to polymorphic regressions (be they melancholic, maniacal, schizophrenic, paranoiac . . .). She functions as a *hole* . . . in the elaboration of imaginary and symbolic processes. But this fault, this deficiency, this "hole," inevitably affords woman too few figurations, images, or representations by which to represent herself. It is not that she lacks some "master signifier" or that none is imposed upon her, but rather that . . . the coining of signifiers . . . is difficult or even impossible for her. . . . She borrows signifiers but cannot make her mark, or re-mark upon them. . . . *Hysteria is all she has left.*[16]

Irigaray is not the first to point out that hysteria is a dis-ease with the symbolic order; Breuer and Freud were the first to testify that "it consists only in what might be called a 'symbolic' relation between the precipitating cause and the pathological phenomenon."[17] But, while they were relieved to discover that hysteria is *only* a disorder of the symbolic relation, not an organic degeneracy and therefore treatable, Irigaray demonstrates that psychoanalysis proceeded to treat the wrong subject, the woman, her repressed (recuperable) desire, as if "she," not the symbolic relation, were the locus of illness. Freud, Irigaray tells us, stopped listening to the hysteric. While he once gave the hysteric a sound audience and helped facilitate her translation of bodily symptoms into liberating narrative, he later conducted analysis to ensure her "aping" of theory. Today's hysteric is

> stripped even of the words that are expected of her upon that stage invented to listen to her. . . . [H]ysteria, or at least the hysteria that is the

privileged lot of the "female," *now has nothing to say*. . . . Unless it be by making her enter, in contempt of her sex, into 'masculine' games of tropes and tropisms. By converting her to a discourse that denies the specificity of her pleasure by inscribing it as the hollow, the intaglio, the negative, even as the censured other of its phallic assertions. By hom(m)osexualizing her.[18]

As it developed theoretically, psychoanalysis grew more deaf to hysteria, and more intrusive, eventually denying it its talking cure. "If psychoanalysis started with the hysterics," Irigaray observes, "one sees Freud change his position toward them between his studies of hysteria where he listened to them for he had everything to hear, and the case of Dora, where, having constructed his system, he bent Dora to his interpretations."[19] In her reproduction of psychoanalytic theory Irigaray mimics the original scene of hysteria, prompting the Freudian reader to listen once again, to learn from the "hysteric" the repressiveness of the psychoanalytic system. She reappropriates Anna O.'s hysterical strategy of speaking, transforming it into deconstructive practice. It is instructive to read the following passage from *Speculum* ("Any Theory of the 'Subject' . . . ") alongside Breuer's description of Anna O.'s hysterical body (of) contorted language as both explanation and an advocation of hysterical mimicry:[20]

> Then . . . turn everything upside down, inside out, back to front. *Rack it with radical convulsions*, carry back, reimport, those crises that her "body" suffers in her impotence to say what disturbs her. Insist also and deliberately upon those *blanks* in discourse which recall the places of her exclusion. . . . Reinscribe them hither and thither as *divergencies*, otherwise and elsewhere than they are expected, in *ellipses* and *eclipses* that deconstruct the logical grid of the reader-writer. . . . *Overthrow syntax.*[21]

Irigaray believes that is not possible for a woman to critique the discourses on woman in the *same* discourse (e.g., psychoanalysis) that negates the feminine, since her dispute can easily be dismissed as the desire to "speak as a man" in the misprision of phallogocentric misunderstanding. Yet a critique of discourse must be in *some* way discursive. It is therefore necessary for women to resort to such oblique tactics of discursive and linguistic attack as performed by psychoanalysis's first hysterics, "and even to accept the condition of silence, of aphasia as a symptom—historico-hysterical, hysterico-historical—so that something of the feminine as the limit of the philosophical might finally be heard" (p. 150/146).

But is Irigaray not advocating the use of strategies for/by the hysteric who has been persuaded by male theorists to identify the entire range

> of women's discursive possibility throughout history with the "eidetic structure" and "predicative mechanism" of idealizing, anthropomorphizing philosophy (p. 149/145), with the "eulogistic or denigratory metaphors" of psychoanalysis?[22] Is not the "destitution in language"[23] she feels due to her own phantasmatic investment in the master discourses? Does she not advocate hysteria as a strategy for the seduced?[24]

Irigaray mimes, advocates miming, the hysterical models of psychoanalysis's two most famous hysterics, Anna O. and her explosive, anarchic speech, Dora and her gynecophilic desire. Her ultimate aim, I would agree with Grosz, "is to say what has up to now remained unspoken of women's pleasures, experiences and perspectives,"[25] but first she must break the censorious silence imposed on women's narcissism, on her primary love for the mother and those derivative desires for the other woman. Irigaray reads Freud's "Femininity" with Dora's ears, overhearing the prohibiting passages, repeating them excessively—with hysteric cunning—to dramatize the despair of the psychoanalyzed "woman"/women, pressed to revolt in the disruptive style of Anna O. But does this hysterical hyperbole not encircle both writer and reader in antitheory and/or antitherapy ("Deconstruct the logical grid of the reader-writer, drive him [her?] out of his [her?] mind")? Who/how does this dramatization effectively affect?

affecting hysterical resistance: a risky method

> [Freud's] first interest was hysteria. . . . He spent a lot of time listening. . . . It was while listening to hysterics that he *read* that there was an unconscious. That is, something he could only construct and in which he himself was implicated; he was implicated in it in the sense that, to his great astonishment, he noticed that he could not avoid participating in what the hysteric was telling him, and that he felt affected by it. Naturally, everything in the resulting rules through which he established the practice of psychoanalysis is designed to counteract this consequence, to conduct things in such a way as to avoid being affected.[26]

Irigaray mimes hysteria with the intent of profoundly affecting her audience. She mimes the hysteric's "defiance through excess, *through overcompliance,*"[27] staging a re-representation of Freudian discourse that foregrounds, through parody, hyperbole, repetition, metonymy, those speculative passages that, in the service of a "dream of symmetry" between the sexes, negate, fetishize, and repress the *representability* of female sexual difference. Irigaray exaggerates the melancholic spectacle of Freud's woman manquée, the portrait of a wasted life that is the normal, expected image of a properly oedipalized woman.[28] Irigaray mirrors Freud's most frequent female patient, the one who comes to him at midlife to be treated for her incurable depression, which she expresses as frigidity or as penis envy, or in any case as the suffering of an unrepresentable loss of libido (an indistinguishably narcissistic and sexual libido, since this loss derives from the tabooed and ruptured attachment to the preoedipal mother, her primary imaginary).[29] But in miming this theoretical/analytical spectacle, Irigaray gives this woman manquée the power of the hysteric to affect her analytic audience, calculated, I would argue, to prompt a critical reaction to psychoanalysis in the Freudian reader.[30]

By affecting hysteria Irigaray would affect any woman reader who *"has yet to feel the need to get free of the fabric [of discourse], reveal her nakedness, her destitution in language, explode in the face of them all, words too."*[31] As analyst Irigaray would transfer every woman out of her indifference, objectivity, including her critical or theoretical distance, into the discursive *asylum* or *misprision* of phallogocentrism where she might feel what Anna/Dora felt when overpowered by the father's seductions/prohibitions or by the equally seducing/forbidding "dialogue" of countertransference.[32] In short, she would effect a radically negative transference between the woman, who would seduce, or who is seduced by, psychoanalysis, and the father of psychoanalysis, his authoritative text.[33]

To *demonstrate* rather than merely conceptualize what she means by hysterical mimesis, Irigaray reconstructs the scene of analysis in "The Blind Spot of an Old Dream of Symmetry." Acting as both psychoanalytic critic *and* feminist therapist, she stages and mediates a transference between Freud's (the "analyst's") desire to interpret the "problem" of sexual difference and the woman reader's (the "analysand's") desire to articulate her own feminine desire. In *re*citing lengthy passages from Freud's discourses on female sexuality, she strategically *overstates* or *overhears* his injunctions to the woman reader (analysand/training analyst) to resign herself to her essential or necessary lack of symbolic (phallic) means with which to constitute her difference and autonomy. It is this *hyperbole* that, I believe, is intended to facilitate the negative transference between text and reader. In being "told" so forcefully that she lacks the means to signify the loss of her mother, that she is "castrated" without the symbolic compensation reserved for men (the valorized representation of maleness, of his desire for a mother substitute, for a genealogy and place in history), without even the possibility of mourning (since this "lack" is not the loss of any "thing" and therefore not repre-

- sentable), the reader-analysand hears in mute pain that what she and
- her sex amount to in the symbolic/cultural order is no more than a
- black "hole" or blank space for man to fill with his narrative fantasies, his theoretical fetishes, his master signifier of phallic sovereignty.

Irigaray's mimicry of Freud uncovers the patriarchal interest invested in the rhetoric and logic of discursive speculation on the "symmetry" of sexual difference. Moreover, it allows the woman reader to see and to reflect that the "hole" her sex is taken to be is not a lack in her so much as a "gap" in theory where her otherness might have been positively represented. In short, the text acts as a feminist speculum inserted into the body of Freud's writings on woman.

But in reproducing, without poetic relief,[34] the oppressiveness of psychoanalytic discourse in her simulated transference, Irigaray risks reproducing the scene of hysteria, of prompting "hysteria"—a frustrated, muted or even "mad" response—in the reader, who, at every stage of this lengthy analysis, is prohibited from interpreting for herself the critical moments of her sexual history, and who is made to suffer communicative impotence, having been denied a theory, a discourse, a language with which to make her remark. Freud's discourse is felt to censor every stage it opens to inquiry and to foreclose every theoretical aporia in the formulation of sexual difference. The *effect* of this scenography is to provoke a mediated form of hysterical resistance, to prompt the reader to know what Dora felt in direct confrontation with Freud and to identify with Dora's refusal to be "the feminine" of psychoanalysis and of patriarchy (and thus to comprehend her feelings of sexual ambivalence, of not knowing whether she was a man or a woman or how to name her desire). Irigaray's *purpose* is to press the reader to her limits of disinterested acceptance of Freudian theory. By subjecting her to the symbolic violence of discursive mastery while showing her the "blind spots" in theoretical speculation, by prompting a negative transference to the "father of psychoanalysis," the text puts the woman reader/analysand "in touch" with her own, unrepresented, unacknowledged sense of difference so that she is in the best possible position to resist that violence and to speak out for herself.[35]

"Sickness is instructive," Nietzsche observed, "even more instructive than health—*those who make sick* seem even more necessary to us today than any medicine men or 'saviours.' "[36] Irigaray would transfer her disease with Freud, with the discourses of "femininity," onto her reader, to prompt critical and negative reaction. It is not healing that she is after but a return of dis-ease, which Freud's subsequent treatment rehabilitated without curing. In a sense she reenacts a *symptomatic* therapy in imitation of Freud's original treatment of hysteria, when treatment con-

sisted of simulating hysteria. The cathartic method of treatment was
invented in lieu of a theory/therapy of effective causes; it was designed
to *provoke* hysteria in hope of affecting *rapport* or even *resistance*.[37]

Irigaray's textual treatment of hysteria is not "effective causally,"[38]
but it does affect the reader's capacity to resist. It is staged to provoke
the reserve of power with which Dora resisted Freud when, in lieu of a
therapy, he attempted to treat her with a theory—a theory through
which he voiced the norm of compulsory heterosexuality while becoming blind to his own countertransference. In aiming to systematically
provoke the reader's hysterical resistance, Irigaray mobilizes the first
steps in cultural transformation, pressing women on to feel the need to
explode in the face of discursive limitations, to begin coining different
metaphors of self-representation collectively. "There is always, in hysteria," she insists, "both a reserve power and a paralyzed power . . . the
possibility of another mode of 'production' notably gestural and lingual; but this is maintained in latency. Perhaps as a cultural reserve yet
to come?" (p. 138/136).

Is this "reserve of power" that "enclave" of mimesis which would
found a women's culture, but only after it has been mobilized by hysterical resistance, prompted by Irigaray's risky simulation of transference neuroses?

a cultural reserve?

A reserve of culture, based on a reserve of power, "a power that is always
repressed, by virtue of the *subordination* of feminine desire to phal-
locratism; a power constrained to silence and mimicry."[39] A reserve of
power that if *collectively* activated and cultivated, and not merely acted
out in the asylums of the individual,[40] could forge a cultural break-
through for women. Irigaray takes the first step, a negative one, reviving hysterical resistance that was and perhaps is still the object of psychoanalysis's therapeutic and theoretical recuperation. Mobilizing an
affective break with the vicious circles of its discourse, she risks her own
"death" as theorist/analyst[41] in the same instance that she risks the withdrawal or the "madness" of her readers. This radical textual practice is
not without its dangers, and only collective feminist action, which
knows the difference between strategic and symptomatic reproductions
of hysteria, protects against an otherwise real risk of hysterical paralysis
or psychosis.

Channeled into cultural production of symbolic systems that articulate woman's difference and represent her autonomous desire, hysteria's "reserve of power" could, Irigaray prognosticates, effect a healing

change in society as well as in the individual. After having made an
affective break with men's tautological system of self-representation,
women's collective recovery of the latent imaginary capacity to figure
female difference will discover the most satisfying expression and "the
most historically curative" in direct, lingual as well as gestural, articulation. In the fabrication of "two syntaxes . . . coming out of different
times, places, logics, 'representations,' and economies . . . . [a speak-
ing] of the 'other' in a language already systematized by/for the same."[42]

To answer the question with which I opened this discussion: Irigaray's mimesis of phallogocentric discourse deploys hysterical resistance as a counterdiscursive strategy. In acting the hysteric, speaking
as hysteric in the circles of philosophy and psychoanalysis, Irigaray is
not herself hysterical nor does she advocate hysteria as an idealized,
alternative "discourse." Instead she reproduces the vicious and mad-
dening logic of master discourses to prompt necessary and sufficient
disenchantment with the masquerade to open a reserve of productive
mimesis.

NOTES •

1. I derive these questions from my reading of Jacques Derrida's *Spurs:
   Nietzsche's Styles/Eperons: les styles de Nietzsche,* trans. Barbara Harlow
   (Chicago: Chicago University Press, 1979), that is, from Derrida's reading of Nietzsche's figure of woman as histrionic-hysteric with the double
   critical capacity for *active* and *reactive dissimulation.* But since I do not
   develop this paper along Nietzschean or Derridean "lines," I reserve this
   brief commentary to the footnotes. The pertinent passages from
   Spurs/Eperons are as follows:

   > It . . . is the "man" who has decided to believe that his discourse
   > on woman or truth might possibly be any *concern* to [the
   > woman]. . . . She plays at dissimulation, at ornamentation,
   > deceit, artifice, at an artist's philosophy. Hers is an affirmative
   > power. And if she continues to be condemned, it is only from the
   > man's point of view. . . . If we consider the whole history of
   > women [that history which oscillates between histrionics and
   > hysterics . . .], are they not *obliged* first of all, and above all to be
   > actresses?   *(pp. 63, 67, 69)*

   My question for Irigaray's readers unacquainted with Nietzsche/Der-
   rida is this: is her mime, her dissimulation of philosophy, of psychoanalysis, active or reactive? Histrionic-artistic or histrionic-hysterical?
   And if it is the latter, how does she *as a woman* redeem hysteria?

2. Monique Plaza was one of the first to protest this apparent reduction, crit-

icizing in particular what she reads as Irigaray's structural equation,
women = hysterical = mimic:

> But does this amount to saying that the hysterical *structure*
> (assumed thus to define a woman) comes under the aegis of
> "mime"? The hysteric would then be defined as "pretence": for
> woman it would consist in doing what man expects, in full. . . .
> Thanks to this concept of hysteria, woman can be completely
> defined by the discourse of Freud, for example, it is enough to
> allow that woman—empty thing—fills herself with the role that
> man gives her. How has Luce Irigaray managed to reduce woman
> to this automaton?

Plaza, " 'Phallomorphic power' and the Psychology of 'Woman,' "
Ideology and Consciousness (Autumn 1978), 4:5–36, 17–18.

3. Monique David-Ménard, *Hysteria From Freud To Lacan: Body and Language in Psychoanalysis*, trans. Catherine Porter (Ithaca: Cornell University Press, 1989), p. 3. David-Ménard traces Freud's evolving interpretation of hysteria, starting with the idea of "conversion" and moving towards an idea of "pantomime," though not entirely. "The notion of pantomime, if it were developed," she writes, "would perhaps make it possible to escape from the psychical and somatic categories to which . . . the notion of conversion rivets us. But Freud in fact never goes so far as to attempt such an elucidation" (p. 10).

4. Jacques Lacan, *The Four Fundamental Concepts of Psycho-Analysis*, trans. Alan Sheridan (Harmondsworth: Penguin, 1977), p. 11.

5. Irigaray, *This Sex*, pp. 45–46/ *Ce Sexe*, p. 45.

6. See Hélène Cixous, *Portrait of Dora*, trans. Sarah Burd, *Diacritics* (Spring 1983), 13(1):2–32, a dramatization of the case history, which she also narrativizes in her novel *Portrait du soleil* (1973) and theorizes in *The Newly Born Woman*, written in collaboration with Catherine Clément, trans. Betsy Wing (1975; Minneapolis: University of Minnesota Press, 1986); Juliet Mitchell, "Femininity, Narrative and Psychoanalysis" and "The Question of Femininity and the Theory of Psychoanalysis" in *Women: The Longest Revolution* (London: Virago, 1984), pp. 287–294 and 295–313. Cixous and Mitchell are not the only other psychoanalytic feminists to theorize woman's hysteria as cultural subversion (see also Charles Bernheimer and Claire Kahane, eds., *In Dora's Case: Freud, Hysteria, Feminism* [London: Virago, 1985; New York: Columbia University Press, 1985; 2d ed., 1990]), but they present the most positive reading of hysteria as a kind of revolutionary activity.

7. Irigaray, *This Sex*, p. 76/ *Ce Sexe*, pp. 73–74. All further parenthetical references in this chapter refer to *This Sex*.

8. Kant formulates a similar distinction between mimesis as the repetition of production and mimesis as the repetition of the product. See Jacques Derrida, "Economimesis," *Diacritics* (1981), 11:3–25, 9–13.

9. Plato, "Laws," trans. A. E. Taylor, in Edith Hamilton and Huntingon Cairns, eds., *Plato: The Collected Dialogues* (Princeton: Princeton University Press, 1961), 2.655b-657b.

10. Plato, "Sophist," trans. F. M. Cornford, in *The Collected Dialogues*, 268c-d. I am supposing that these are the two Platonic mimeses Irigaray alludes to. Plato actually approves of the "musical" kind, the kind he witnesses in choric art and would preserve through legislation restricting innovative reproduction, while he despises "conceited mimicry," the rhetorical art of imitating and distorting the logos of wise men and statesmen to the speaker's advantage. Just as Plato detects the effects/symptoms of this second mimesis in the sophist and the demagogue, so does Irigaray detect effects/symptoms in the hysteric (the female sophist?).

11. I borrow the phrase "politics of despair" from Judith Butler, *Gender Trouble: Feminism and the Subversion of Identity* (New York: Routledge, 1990), p. 146.

12. David-Ménard, *Hysteria From Freud to Lacan*, p. 166.

13. If "woman" is precisely the Other of any conceivable Western theoretical locus of speech, how can the woman as such be speaking in this book? Who is speaking her, and who is asserting the otherness of the woman? . . . From what theoretical locus is Luce Irigaray herself speaking in order to develop her own theoretical discourse about the woman's exclusion? Is she speaking the language of men, or the silence of women?
    Shoshana Felman, "Women and Madness: The Critical Phallacy," *Diacritics* (Winter 1975), 5(4):2–10.

14. Carolyn Burke refers to Irigaray's "mimicry" of philosophy as a "strategy"—"the deliberate assumption of the feminine posture assigned to her within the realm of discourse in order to uncover the mechanisms by which it represses her." Though she does not link this strategy directly to hysterical mimicry, she notes Stephen Heath's clarification of it as "a kind of strategic reduplication of masquerade," that is, a deliberate appropriation of hysteria's symptomatic duplication of femininity. See her essay, "Romancing the Philosophers: Luce Irigaray," in *Seduction and Theory*, ed. Dianne Hunter (Urbana: University of Illinois, 1989), pp. 226–240, 228, 237, note 8.

15. Irigaray, *Speculum*, p. 143/178.

16. Ibid., p. 71/85.

17. Breuer, Josef, and Sigmund Freud, *Studies on Hysteria*, trans. James and Alix Strachey (Harmondsworth: Penguin, 1974), p. 55.

18. Irigaray, *Speculum*, pp. 140–141/174.

19. Irigaray, "Luce Irigaray," pp. 149–164, 163. See also Elaine Showalter's historical and material study of this shift in Freud's treatment of hysteria in *The Female Malady: Women, Madness and English Culture, 1830–1980* (London: Virago, 1987), pp. 158–159.

20. "Alongside of the development of the contractures," Breuer writes,

> there appeared a deep-going functional disorganization of her speech. It first became noticeable that she was at a loss to find words, and this difficulty gradually increased. Later she lost her command of grammar and syntax; she no longer conjugated verbs, and eventually she used only infinitives, for the most part incorrectly formed from weak past participles; and she omitted both the definite and indefinite article. In the process of time she became almost completely deprived of words. (Breuer and Freud, *Studies on Hysteria*, p. 77)

21. Irigaray, *Speculum*, p. 142/176.
22. Ibid., pp. 142–143/177.
23. Ibid., p. 143/177.
24. Elizabeth Grosz would say this is the case. But Grosz argues that Irigaray's seduction by "phallocentric philosophies and theoretical paradigms" is a "violation" that warrants exposure by counterseduction through the calculated ploys of hysterical mimicry. Grosz insists that Irigaray is not hysterical: "She imitates/parodies women's hysterical positions in discourse. . . . [She] mimics the hysteric's mimicry. She mimes mime itself." Grosz, *Sexual Subversions: Three French Feminists* (Sydney: Allen and Unwin, 1989), pp. 136–137.
25. Ibid., p. 138.
26. Transcribed from a recording of Lacan's talk at the "Kanzer Seminar" (Yale University, Nov. 24, 1975), translated by Barbara Johnson, and cited in Shoshana Felman, "Turning the Screw of Interpretation," in Shoshana Felman, ed., *Literature and Psychoanalysis, The Question of Reading: Otherwise* (Baltimore: Johns Hopkins University Press, 1982), pp. 94–207, 118.
27. "The hysteric's defiance through excess, *through overcompliance*," Grosz writes, "is a parody of the expected. . . . Irigaray shares the hysteric's *excessive* mimicry . . . by taking on . . . what is expected, but to such an extreme . . . that it . . . unsettles the system by throwing back to it what it cannot accept about its own operations" (Grosz, *Sexual Subversions*, pp. 135, 138).
28. "A woman [of about thirty] . . . often frightens [*erschreckt*] us by her psychical rigidity [*Starrheit*] and unchangeability," Freud writes in "Femininity," *New Introductory Lectures on Psychoanalysis*, trans. James Strachey (Harmondsworth: Penguin, 1973), pp. 145–169, 169. See also Sarah Kofman's discussion of Freud's "zombie" in *The Enigma of Woman: Woman in Freud's Writings*, trans. Catherine Porter (Ithaca: Cornell University Press, 1985), p. 223.
29. Irigaray, *Speculum*, pp. 66–72/78–87.
30. Sarah Kofman's *The Enigma of Woman* is a deconstructive critique of Freud's discourse on femininity, written, in part, in response to Irigaray's provocation (see chapter 1).

31. Irigaray, *Speculum,* p. 143/177; emphasis added.
32. Margaret Whitford emphasizes the effect Irigaray has on her readers. "In that she desires to 'speak as a woman,' " Whitford writes,

> [Irigaray] *needs* the other, the interlocutor, as the analysand needs the analyst. . . . For if her readers simply agreed with her work, with no affect, then something vital would be missing, that is to say, the engagement without which no change could possibly take place. . . . The "transference" of the reader is not a more or less accidental, "emotional" or subjective response which can be set aside to get at the "theory," but in fact gives a clue to what is at stake.

> Whitford, "Speaking as a Woman: Luce Irigaray and the Female Imaginary," *Radical Philosophy* (Summer 1986), 43:3–8.

33. Transference emerges in analysis in two forms: negative *and/or* positive. Jane Gallop emphasizes Irigaray's textual facilitation of the reader's positive transference onto the "author/analyst," while I emphasize its facilitation of the reader's negative transference onto "Freud." See Gallop, *Feminism and Psychoanalysis: The Daughter's Seduction* (London: Macmillan, 1982), pp. 56–79.
34. Jane Gallop criticizes Irigaray for re-presenting Freud's/Lacan's discourse as far less poetically playful than it is. See ibid., p. 38.
35. "If, as a reader, you 'resist,' " Whitford observes,

> then this resistance itself is worth analyzing and exploring further. It is not in itself a guarantee of the theoretical "correctness" of Irigaray's work . . . but it does indicate that you are not left indifferent, that your "resistance" is produced by something. If, in the interaction which takes place between you and Irigaray's work, you do not withdraw, to that extent she has succeeded and the scene is set for a possible exchange.

> Whitford, "Speaking as a Woman," p. 8.

36. Friedrich Nietzsche, *The Genealogy of Morals,* trans. Walter Kaufmann and R. J. Hollingdale (New York: Random House, 1989), p. 113.
37. Where it is a question of hysterias which run a chronic course, accompanied by a moderate but constant production of hysterical symptoms, we find the strongest reason for regretting our lack of a therapy which is effective causally, but we also have most ground for the appreciation of the value of the cathartic procedure as a *symptomatic* therapy. . . . Everything depends on reinforcing the patient's . . . capacity to resist.
Breuer and Freud, *Studies on Hysteria,* p. 348.
38. Ibid.
39. Irigaray, *This Sex,* p. 138/ *Ce Sexe,* p. 136.
40. Irigaray analyzes/mimics the deadly limits of this asylum of the lone resister in her chapter, *"La Mystérique"* (*Speculum,* pp. 191–202/pp. 238–252). While the female mystic's exemplary imitation of patriarchy's

onto-theological "woman" affords her the most public stage enjoyed by
women in the history of the West (p. 191/238), it also costs her her
"self" as historical agency. The mystic-hysteric or *mystérique*, as Irigaray
coins her, practices an extremist form of mime, reproducing the mutism,
subjection, and abjection expected of the Godly woman; in part, her
mimicry is a strategy to seduce the (Church) Father, but it is also a strategy of mimetic excess intended to annihilate patrocentric desire in the
"burning mirror" of her jouissance. Her ecstasy presents more than the
mirror/mere face of the unworldly, unpowerful, faithful submissiveness
of the Christian woman in which the Patriarch sees his own omnipo-
tence; it shatters her mirroring capacity altogether, divests herself of the
desire to have/to be a "self," including the desire to reflect patriarchy's
projections. In the madness of her extremism she purges herself of ego,
satisfies her soul (super-ego) with the nihilism of abjection, and glories in
self-dissolution, which she fantasizes as unmediated communion with the
Almighty—bypassing "man" and absolutely abandoning any struggle for
autonomy. Mysteria dramatizes woman's hysterical delusion, the seductions of asylum, of a wholly reactive power she affirms through "her
remoteness in ecstasy."

41. "It is in the nature of the [transferential] exchange, that Irigaray's own
    'theoretical' position is thereby put at risk and that, *qua* analyst/theorist,
    she herself risks 'death' " (Whitford, "Speaking as a Woman," p. 8).

42. Irigaray, *Speculum*, p. 139/172.

· *Elizabeth Hirsh*

BACK IN

ANALYSIS:

HOW TO

DO THINGS

WITH IRIGARAY

The *praticable*, or "setting," of psychoanalytic psychotherapy—what Freud called
the "technical rules of analysis"—includes
both mechanical and procedural elements
conditioning the therapeutic encounter,
and has been a subject of the professional
literature of psychoanalysis virtually since its inception. This essay considers the special pertinence of psychoanalytic technique to the work of
Irigaray, arguing that the therapeutic *praticable* of psychoanalysis constitutes a privileged frame of reference for understanding Irigaray. A
number of her essays and talks are explicitly concerned with reinterpreting the *praticable* from a double perspective of clinical experience
and theoretical inquiry. Drawing out the revolutionary potential that
she sees in the *praticable*, Irigaray transforms it into a special kind of
technique, or instrument, capable, like her more famous speculum, not
only of critique and subversion but also of feminine healing and transformation. Indeed, she deems *Speculum of the Other Woman*, her mon-
umental intervention into Western theoretical tradition, a "*praticable.*"[1]
Irigaray's *praticable* invites an approach to her writing, and more

> •
> •   generally to the projects of feminism, that is at once pragmatic and
> •   utopian. It solicits women to use her words critically, as a means to dis-
> engage themselves from the reproduction, reflection, and sustenance of
> man, as well as constructively, as a means to gain access to and trans-
> form the symbolic order as female subjects of history, psychoanalysis,
> literature, politics, philosophy—bearing in mind that these enterprises
> must themselves be transformed by the advent of sexual difference. In
> so doing, the *praticable* suggests a way of (re)opening psychoanalysis to
> the historical and material specificity of its subjects, and indicates that
> only by remaining open (on)to history can psychoanalysis stop repeat-
> ing itself and recover both theoretical interest (which among U.S. fem-
> inists has recently much diminished) and the power it once potentially
> had to help produce a future for women.

Crucial to the efficacy of Irigaray's *praticable* is her insistence on the
preeminently *dramatic* character of psychoanalytic therapy, as distinct
from whatever role might be played in the therapeutic process by narrative reconstruction or anamnesis, and from those dimensions of psychoanalysis that can be articulated in a(ny) theoretical metalanguage
ostensibly discrete from that which it "describes." It is no accident that
in French the term *praticable* is also used to designate the physical apparatus of a stage set, and particularly the kind that is not wholly one-
dimensional or illusionistic but that actually functions as "practicable"
in the action of a drama—for example, as a means of entering or exit-
ing a scene. For Irigaray the scene of psychoanalysis in a special way
recapitulates the total "drama of enunciation" (*le drame de l'énonciation*)
that enframes all representation, and it therefore has the potential to
(re)act upon this framework, particularly as the latter serves to engen-
der human subjectivity.

Irigaray's *praticable* reflects, among other things, an attempt to
rethink the relation of the philosophical categories of the empirical and
the theoretical, and of the a priori and the a posteriori. It attempts to
demonstrate how analysis itself reconnects such opposites in a relation
of perpetual, if unrecognized, exchange. In this interest it also seeks to
transvalue the value of presence, specifically with reference to the hic et
nunc of analysis, and to reorient the spatiotemporal coordinates that in
Irigaray's view govern the (non)representation of sexual difference within the current symbolic order—"the geography," as she puts it, "of auto-
affection."[2] While this revalidation of presence is something that marks
Irigaray's divergence from both Lacan and Derrida, it does not spell a
return either to the "therapeutic alliance" of American ego psychology
or to an unanalyzed metaphysics of presence. Irigaray has long recognized a need "to shake discourse away from its mooring in the value of

'presence' "[3] as key to the projects of feminism, and like Derrida she
repeatedly emphasizes that "[t]here is no simple . . . way to leap to the
outside of phallogocentrism, *nor any possible way to situate oneself there,
that would result from the simple fact of being a woman.*"[4] Nor does she
suggest, in the manner of ego psychology, that the hic et nunc of the
psychoanalytic session is simply given to perception or cognition as
such, engaging some kind of "conflict-free" zone in the ego that remains
exempt from the influence of the unconscious.

To the contrary, for Irigaray the analytic hic et nunc must be understood as *produced*—very much as a dramatic scene is produced—
through the dynamic interaction of the physical apparatus or props, the
gestures or bodily posture(s) of the actors, and the verbal and nonverbal exchanges of speaker(s) and auditor(s) that make up the analytic
praticable. It is important and powerful above all as a site where women
(can) meet and reproduce themselves in dialogue with one another.
Linking the analytic hic et nunc to the receptivity initially shown by
Freud and the early analysts first to the specificity of "each analysis" and
"each analysand," Irigaray argues that this receptivity was lost as psychoanalysis sought to establish itself as "universal law," stopped listening to its *analysant(e)s*, and instead objectified their words as examples
of an a priori truth. But initially "Freud and the first analysts did not
act quite like this, or at least not for some time," she writes. Instead,

> For them, every analysis was an opportunity to uncover some new facet
> of a practice and a theory. Each analysand was listened to as though he
> or she had some new contribution to make to that practice and that the-
> ory. But once psychoanalytic "science" begins to claim to have discov-
> ered the universal law of the workings of the unconscious, and once
> every analysis is no more than an application or a practical demonstra-
> tion of that law, the only status the now complete "science" can possi-
> bly have is that of an era of knowledge already over.   *(p. 83).*[5]

What Irigaray implicitly urges is a "return" not so much to Freud as theoretical lawgiver as to the dialogue of analyst and analysand, speaker
and listener, as this was played out in the first analyses. Reasserting the
importance of the hic et nunc to psychoanalytic practice, she rethinks
its "present" as an essential passageway, or copula, between apparent
opposites: between memory and utopia, between (a) past and (a) future
that differs from it, between the reproduction of the same and the
*re*production of the feminine.[6] This reworking of the analytic present
has cognates and consequences that are at once philosophical, cosmic,
and political. Ultimately the *praticable* does not deconstruct or displace
the oppositions it engages; its effect is rather to *connect*, and thereby

·
· ·
·   reconstitute, these oppositions, no longer as symmetrical reflections
that can never touch but as useable, useful distinctions on the feminine
side. In this way Irigaray's feminine *praticable* suggests a theoretical
basis for a feminist politics of specificity, which in her words can speak
to—because it listens to—"each woman, right where she is."[7]

My own interpretation of the *praticable* is elaborated in dialogue
with those who have contributed to a growing recognition of the
sophistication of Irigaray's reconstructive, as well as her deconstructive,
project: Rosi Braidotti, Carolyn Burke, Diana Fuss, Jane Gallop, Elizabeth Grosz, Anne Herrmann, Naomi Schor, Margaret Whitford, and
others, whose pioneering work (re)opens the always unorthodox text of
Irigaray (to those with ears to hear). Like Whitford, I approach Irigaray
as a theorist and enabler of change (and I think it fair to say, a deliberate *provocatrice*). "The importance of Irigaray's work," Whitford
writes, "does not lie primarily in its theoretical 'correctness' . . . [but in
creating] the conditions of possibility for dynamic cultural shifts."[8]
Exploring the importance of the psychoanalytic dialogue to Irigaray,
Whitford observes that within this framework "for change to occur, you
have to put yourself into play."[9] Irigaray's *praticable* reworks the politics
of the subject, showing that "dynamic cultural shifts" of a feminist kind
must, like psychoanalysis, be *both* personal *and* collective.

I will consider first Irigaray's reinterpretation of the specific con-
trivances that comprise the psychoanalytic *praticable*; next, some implications of this distinctive mode of intervention for feminist theory as
well as psychoanalytic practice; finally, its value for using Irigaray's text
as feminine *praticable*—for, in Elizabeth Grosz's words, the elusive task
of "reading Irigaray in an Irigarayan mode."[10]

I

The transformative powers of Irigaray's *praticable* are predicated partly on its powers as an instrument of deconstruction. In fact, deconstructive effects proceed from the analytic situation as a whole, which
she describes in one essay as "a technique for the subversion of the
énoncé"[11] and in another as "a *praticable* that baffles, confounds, destabilizes, the scene of representation."[12] "This method would come to
question certain a priori [assumptions] that govern the scene of theoretical representation," she writes, noting specifically "the divorce of
those oppositions finding themselves confounded there [in the analytic *praticable*]."[13]

But just as Irigaray's psychoanalysis is not Lacan's, her deconstruction is not precisely Derrida's. When she speaks (citing René Char) of

destroying "with nuptial tools,"[14] something of the difference is
expressed. Unlike Derrida, Irigaray is a matchmaker—or perhaps
more accurately, a couples therapist—concerned to make possible the
now universally "impracticable . . . sexual relation."[15] The deconstructive confounding of oppositions within the scene of analysis is
neither an end in itself nor does it set the stage for the eruption of
some new term or concept meant to displace the old opposition.
Instead, the *praticable* as interpreted by Irigaray (re)mediates the
"divorce" of the oppositions that silently govern the production of
theory—silently, because they occupy the place of the a priori that
stands outside and above any possibility of interrogation. Like a *praticable* connecting two spaces (one onstage and one off, for example),
the psychoanalytic *praticable* does not, ultimately, confound or
destroy the identity of the two but depends upon preserving them *as*
distinct even as it effects their connection.

While memory plays its part in the drama of analysis, "memory as
such is not the object of analysis." Rather, its proper "object" (marking
the term, Irigaray distances herself from the language of "objectivity")
is "the very framework of all representation."[16] In a sense the technique
of analysis effects a quasi-phenomenological reduction that makes
available the unrecognized *cadrage*, or framework, of representation
itself—"le derrière lui-même," in another formulation—independent
of any particular semantic or psychic "content." This is not, however, a
solitary meditative or cognitive operation, but a dialogic and psycho-
dynamic one, produced with the indispensable participation of two
actors and the material "props" of the scene of analysis. In effect the
actors in this scene construct a surrogate frame that they necessarily
continue to inhabit. "The frame, or the window, determine the form of
what appears [*l'apparition*]; they do not appear, no more do they exist
outside the session,"[17] Irigaray writes. The *cadrage* of representation
becomes available, then, not as a self-evident datum of transcendental
knowledge but in the sense that, like the physical apparatus which it
partly is, it becomes accessible to and for practical alteration(s).

Three technical rules of psychoanalysis figure in Irigaray's reworking
of the *praticable*: the configuration or "geography" of analysand and
analyst, the analysand's "fundamental rule" of free association and its
corollary, the special mode of "listening" sustained by the analyst, and
the nature of the transference, which Irigaray treats according to the
logic of the *praticable*, as at once an artifact of the *praticable*, the ground
of its efficacy, and a particular part of it. Some themes sounded by Irigaray in relation to therapeutic technique echo those of Freud or Lacan,
some differ subtly but importantly from theirs, and some pointedly

.
.   divcrgc from the masters. While these rules are interconnected, and in
.   fact comprise the *praticable* only by that virtue, each will first be con-
       sidered as if distinct.

(1) The Geography of Analysis In classical analysis the analysand lies on
her back unable to see the analyst, who sits behind and facing only partially toward her: "behind, back turned or at an angle," is Irigaray's
description of the analyst's position.[18] The analysand is thus deprived
of perception, the dialectic of the gaze is broken, and the two participants encounter one another not, as in the usual situation of representation, face-to-face, but obliquely—almost, as Irigaray not altogether
playfully hints, behind-to-behind.[19] "The behind is the failure of the
gaze," she writes, using the term widely associated with woman's putative lack—"nothing to be seen"—to denote the analysand's immersion
"into blindness."[20]

    This curious configuration has both epistemological and ethical
effects, she argues. Skewing the usual "vis-à-vis" of communication
into a kind of "corps-à-corps," it foregrounds the material circumstances that condition the production of meaning(s). It feminizes the
analysand, who is thus deprived of his or her "right" relation to the
world. "The subject of representation has a front, a back, a top, a bottom. He is thus assumed standing, forming a right angle with the plane
that supports him," Irigaray suggests. In analysis, however, "the right
angle is, at least temporarily, lost for the subject."[21] No longer does a
world of phenomena appear as if "before" the subject, nor can she or
he imagine herself or himself as "the axis of the world's ordering."[22] In
Irigaray's account of the Kantian subject in the essay "Sexual Difference," the traditional subject of knowledge encounters the world as
(his) horizon within an a priori or transcendental frame constituted by
the intersecting axes of space (the horizontal axis) and time (the vertical one). In this scheme the subject himself constitutes both the temporal axis and, since the two axes meet within his gaze, their source *and*
point of intersection.
    But when the subject reclines as analysand he *becomes* the horizon,
according to Irigaray, and must imagine the analyst "as maintaining the
vertical axis."[23] Habitually, for the speaking subject, "the relation
between the production of linguistic signs and the choice and constitution of their sense is orthogonal," but supine in the scene of analysis the
analysand is "deprived of the power *in the present* of producing *rational*
speech."[24] (Here Irigaray's French puns on the double meaning of *sens*
as both "sense" and "direction.") In language reminiscent of Lacan the

analytic situation is described as a scene of "*in-communication*," with "the speaking subject not being able to explain what he means, and his interlocutor not being able to understand what the *énoncé* expresses [*traduit*]."[25] By the same token it is no longer possible to imagine the speaking subject as the singular source or locus of his own world or discourse. "The junction-point of the two axes is therefore not *in* the one who speaks,"[26] she writes. It is, rather, "between [the] two [*entre deux*]."

The juxtaposition of bodies in analysis also destroys the symmetrical opposition and relation of correspondence that normally marks the face-to-face encounter:

> The analyst's body is lacking to the analysand's gaze. And the landmarks reverse themselves: from being face-to-face, right corresponding to left and left to right, there they are one behind the other: left corresponding to left, right to right. As if the analyst and the analysand were looking at themselves in the same mirror?[27]

The other as analyst no longer appears over against or as the mirror image of the subject, untouchable, impracticable in its virtual sameness. Removed from the scope of vision, both the subject and the other take on volume, corporeal and spiritual. This simultaneous derangement of the epistemological relation—the subject before the world/object—and of the ethical relation—the subject face-to-face with the other—at once exposes their common geography and (re)draws the latter, ambiguously creating a new site *between* analyst and analysand that connects them and/or reveals their ineluctable connectedness. "The source"—of speech, representation, the human and phenomenal world—"is no longer simple," Irigaray writes. "It is, in the scene of analysis, at least double."[28] This dealignment not only destroys the usual *praticable* of representation or communication but also precipitates a new site of production, which is precisely the site of *its own* production in the hic et nunc of analysis.

(2) The «Tout Dire» That the analysand should be deprived of the power "in the present" to produce meaningful discourse is nonetheless prerequisite to this reworking of the underlying framework. Such deprivation results not only from the geography of analysis but also from the "fundamental rule" of free association, which for Irigaray effectively suspends the economy of truth (the adequation of cause to effect, copy to original, outside to inside, etc.) that normally regulates representation. Freud wrote that the analysand was bound "to communicate everything that occurs to him without criticism or selection," the corollary of this technical rule being the special mode of "listening" that the analyst is

obliged to sustain during their encounter. In 1912 he described analytic listening as an "evenly-hovering attention" or "calm, quiet attentiveness" on the part of the analyst, and related it to the role in therapy of the analyst's unconscious as "a receptive organ" comparable to a telephone receiver: the analyst "must bend his own unconscious like a receptive organ to the emerging unconscious of the [analysand]."[29]

This double rule governing the production of discourse within analysis results in a dramatic staging of the interdependence of analyst and analysand. Without the special receptivity of the analyst, the fundamental rule of free association (*le «tout dire»*) cannot operate, nor can the analyst "receive" what the analysand does not produce. Here one might recall Lacan's precept that "there is no speech without a reply, even if it is met only with silence, provided that it has an auditor."[30] Like Lacan's account of the dialectic of speech in analysis, Irigaray's reading of the analytic dialogue implies among other things that, as Lacan says, the "ethic [of psychoanalysis] is not an individualist one."[31] But however dynamic, however resourceful in displaying the perpetual deferral of closure in human discourse, Lacan's dialectic remains for Irigaray a theoretically closed system, fully "axiomized" and constitutionally incapable of producing anything new.

Indeed, Lacan and Freud alike stand charged with failing to listen to their analysands in part (and especially in the case of Lacan) because analytic listening entails putting oneself into play, and at risk, in the scene of analysis. If Lacan justly warned against the coercion inherent in the notion of a "therapeutic alliance,"[32] Irigaray protests the symmetrical opposite of such a doctrine in Lacanian dogma, "the imperialism of an Unconscious of/to which all men and women have to become subject(s)."[33] And, she demands of Lacanian analysts, "listen to what the unconscious still has to say":

> Now, either the unconscious is no more than something you have already heard—and is therefore never "that" [*ça*: id]: what men or women may say that has never been heard before—or the unconscious is desire which is trying to speak of/to itself and, being analysts, you have to listen without excluding anything, even if listening to everything does call *your* desire into question, even if it does mean that *you* risk death.[34]

While Irigaray's respect for Freud is greater (she calls him "an honest scientist"), he too, at a certain point, turned from the implications of the *praticable* he and his analysands had devised:

> In seeking the conditions that might allow everything to be said without hierarchical judgment, without adequation nor a priori truth, Freud

deconstructed the framework of the proper, of a supposedly objective
reality. . . . But then why does he resubmit [this discovery] to the traditional logic of representation?[35]

As again with Lacan, the unconscious was effectively "sent to school"
(*l'inconscient fait Ecole*), and its *analysant(e)s*—most often marked feminine—stopped being heard in their specificity and came instead to
serve as "demonstrations" of a theory that thus became, in more senses
than one, finished ("reduced to a preestablished corpus, a preexisting
knowledge, a predetermined law").[36] And also as with Lacan, it was
Freud's desire that *la psychanalyse* should "submit" (*se soumettre*), as she
puts it, "to *a* theory or *a* science" that prematurely foreclosed the
processes of discovery it had inaugurated. In both cases this gesture of
self-totalization expressed a masculine desire for the self-as-same, while
precluding the understanding of female sexuality: it constituted the latter as enigma, the "dark continent," the outside or ground of its own
truth.[37]

Despite Freud's own use of the telephone analogy to describe therapeutic listening, Lacan dismissed attempts like that of Theodor Reik to
interpret Freud's analytic rules as permitting "a direct transaudition of
the unconscious by the unconscious,"[38] just as he dismissed therapeutic techniques designed to strengthen the ego or ground the analysand
more securely in the hic et nunc; for him, the hic et nunc was rather the
privileged site of the analysand's defensive evasions. I have indicated
that in rethinking the analytic *praticable* Irigaray construes the hic et
nunc not as a simple, passive place or moment but instead as a produced and productive site, one precipitated by and in the geography of
analysis. Its production is also vitally tied to the practice of analytic listening. This Irigaray describes as the particular "attentiveness" in which
the analyst functions at once as actor and audience, "[making] herself,
as far as she can, an available support for the inscription of the
analysand's traces for as long as the analytic drama unfolds, in order to
be unfitted to any actual presence, to any edict of common sense, to the
certification of some truth, etc."[39] As this language suggests, Irigaray
preserves a Lacanian emphasis on the trace in analysis, on the latter's
inherent antagonism to any "presence" conceived as real in the sense of
given "to common sense"—especially to the extent that such a present
could act as a standard of truth against which the word of the analysand
would be measured. But she is equally insistent that during analysis the
analyst must listen *without reference to* "a pre-scripted text," without
"submitting, comparing or evaluating" the analysand's traces with reference to any a priori whatsoever.[40] She or he must act as a kind of appa-

ratus similar to Freud's telephone receiver, or as Irigaray puts it, like *un répondant matériel*—a function implicitly inseparable from her corporeal attendance in/at the scene of analysis. In effect Irigaray again exposes a pernicious symmetry between Lacanian analysis and ego psychology: displacing the supposed hic et nunc of cognition with notions of textuality, Lacan's theory does not escape the normativity of its American foe, but merely substitutes one a priori—"the *a prioris* of the sign"—for another.[41]

Irigaray's analytic hic et nunc should then be contrasted not to the "other scene" of the unconscious but to the category of the a priori as traditionally construed, that is, to any naturalized framework of law within which the *parole* of the analysand is always already recuperated to a certain model of interpretation that (pre)judges it crazy or sane, full or empty, according to an economy of truth. Tacitly accepting the philosophical opposition between the a priori and the a posteriori as the necessary ground of scientific validity, psychoanalysis has suffered from a massive misrecognition of the latter for the former, specifically with regard to female sexuality. "The need for the phallus that has been attributed to women is an a posteriori justification for the obligation laid on women to become legal wives and mothers," Irigaray insists.[42] Such confusion of one thing for another—specifically, for the "thing" or category of thing construed as its "opposite"—is the probable result of a masculine imaginary passing for a universal symbolic, that is, an economy of truth that adjudicates the world in terms of specular opposites. (This is a point that Irigaray's discourse makes, implicitly or explicitly, over and over again.) What Freud and company failed to grasp was that their *praticable* potentially rendered this opposition *as such* obsolete, because psychoanalysis connected the a priori and the a posteriori; it precipitated a new, material/transcendental passageway between the "frame" of representation and its so-called content, permitting the one to (re)act upon the other.

If it is not memory as such but rather the *cadrage* of all representation that is the true "object" of therapy, access to the *cadrage* still requires that the subject be deprived of the power to produce meaningful discourse in the present, Irigaray says. Thus "memory imposes itself . . . as a privileged mode of articulation owing to the supine position [and] to the absence of immediate perception."[43] But while in this sense the scene of analysis "is set for *remembering*,"[44] Irigaray cautions that such associations may themselves signify a mode of defense, a stay against change as such: "inertia, filler for an imperceptible frame of representation with those contents that the subject thinks are proper to him."[45]

Analysis takes effect as a force for change only when past, present, and future are no longer preserved as discrete and impracticable categories, all modeled on a *metaphysics* of presence within the *cadre du propre*. Otherwise it merely replicates what Irigaray critiques, in discussing René Girard, as a fashion for the past, for "forget[ting] what remains to be discovered, especially the future in the past."[46] In the work of readers like Girard, she suggests, "myths and stories . . . sacred texts are analyzed, sometimes with nostalgia but rarely with a mind to change the social order."[47] By contrast, in the drama of psychoanalysis "attentiveness to the present"—an interpretive posture endorsed by Irigaray in contrast to methods like Girard's—implies listening to the *parole* of the analysand not in relation to "a prescripted text" but in order to hear "what is still to be discovered of the future in the past." Indeed, no phrase could more aptly summarize Irigaray's sense of what is most (im)properly the work of analysis as well as the unique virtue of its *praticable*.[48]

Thus if the hallmark of historicism is the preservation of the past for its own sake, the ahistoricism with which Irigaray has been charged might more accurately be termed antihistoricism. "[W]omen are more interested in the present, or the future, whereas men are interested in the past," she asserts in a statement apt to raise the hackles of some antiessentialists.[49] Irigaray's historical sense is that of an activist; change, not preservation, is her interest. The specificity of the past (and in this sense only, its preservation) is crucial—just as the analyst must provisionally act "to insure the care" of the analysand's mnemonic inscriptions—but not for its own sake: only for what it can contribute to a future of difference. And since the necessary locus of change is the present, equally crucial is the posture of "attentiveness to the present" epitomized by psychoanalytic listening—to "each analysis" and "each analysand" to "each woman, right where she is," to "society at present," and also to the "cosmic" specificities that are the stuff of myth. Irigaray's universe is at once continuous and heterogeneous; it is more like a liquid than a solid.[50] "Winter is not summer, night is not day, every part of the universe is not equivalent to every other,"[51] she observes. It is perhaps for this reason that Irigaray indicates by place and date, in many published collections of her papers, interviews, and talks, the particular dramatic setting of each—"their initial context of delivery," as she writes in the introduction to *Sexes et parentés*.

(3) The Transference The productive reintegration of time(s) by the *praticable* is also related to the last of the technical "rules" I will discuss,

the analytic transference. Irigaray describes the transference as "the projection onto the analyst of that which causes [the analysand's] *parole* or
the desire to reappropriate its frame."[52] It entails a confounding of the
positions of speaker and auditor, of the *«moi»* and the *«lui»*, which
effectively returns the subject to the real or imaginary scene of her first
entry into the symbolic (or, what comes to the same thing, returns that
scene in the hic et nunc of the scene of analysis). Here again the confounding of oppositions functions to open a dialogue between women,
of woman with herself, and potentially, between two sexes.

What Irigaray calls the "seesawing" of the scene of representation
within and by the analytic *praticable* fundamentally disorients the
subject and his world: up/down, in(side)/out(side), before/after,
before/behind, left/right all lose distinction, as do past and present,
memory and perception, memory and fantasy, even, potentially, perception and hallucination. "The scene of representation dissolves in
the confusion," she writes; and out of this confusion emerges the
transference.

> [The scene of representation] empties and at the same time loses its mas-
> tery in an *énonciation* more and more profuse. The subject no longer
> knows where to begin, which word to choose, what type of *énoncé* or
> *énonciation* to pronounce here, now. That which maintains what is said,
> what speaks itself—But in what time? what confusion of times?—it is
> the transference, the projection onto the analyst of what causes that
> parole or the desire to reappropriate its frame.[53]

Evoking the problematic of the transference apparently from the perspective of the analysand, she continues: "How to distinguish 'me' from
'him'? me as myself from him? All the more so since he gives few indi-
cations of himself as such. One would have to introject the analyst completely? The same question remains. Who, *I*? Who, *you*?"[54] Through
its multiple disorientations, analysis effects an *enfantinage*, or regression
to infancy, that is most potently expressed in this confusion of the positions of speaker and auditor, self and other. Freud's folly was to have
held back from such confusion, to have held fast to *one*, fixed position.
"Freud held only the position of the analyst and not that of the
analysand."[55] Her remark refers both to the fact that (placing himself
outside the institution of analysis as its origin/ator) Freud was and
remains the only self-analyzed analyst and, more generally, to his
avowed posture as dispassionate "scientist."

For Irigaray dialogue at once requires and consists in "connection
between the two positions."[56] Such rapport becomes possible only
when there are, in fact, two positions, not just one—a possibility his-

torically precluded by the monopoly of the phallic economy. To put the
same thing in different terms, Irigaray suggests that the specific symptomatology of the (female) hysteric is to lack an(y) "I," and of the
(male) paranoiac, to lack a "you"; Dora and Schreber are cited as paradigms. Their pathologies express in hyperbolic form the impoverishment suffered by all within the phallic monopoly. "To the extent that
men are themselves deprived of their first female interlocutrice, the
maternal one, and they are without a 'you' who is woman and sexual-
ized, they are by the same token deprived of a certain type of
exchange."[57] This comment alludes in part to Freud's vastly influential
account, in *Beyond the Pleasure Principle*, of his grandson's entry into the
symbolic via the game of *fort-da*, in which he contrives symbolically to
master his mother's absence by substituting for her a primitive toy, a
wooden bobbin or spool.[58]

Women are also deprived of "their first 'you,' their first interlocutrice," but in part because that one is "a person of the same sex as
themselves," the consequences of this deprivation are different and
potentially more dire: "women lose the possibility of relating *to themselves* as feminine, of communicating *among themselves*," and so of constituting themselves either as individual subjects or as a "feminine plural gender."[59] Elsewhere Irigaray claims that "girls do not enter into language in the same way as boys"[60]—apparently assuming an "essential,"
presymbolic difference between the two. (The status of this pronouncement, and others like it, will be considered in the last part of my
essay.) The "girl-subject" rather

> does not exert mastery . . . [she] does not have objects as the boy has. It
> splits into two in a different way and the object or the goal is to reunite
> the two by a gesture, to touch both perhaps so that birth is repeated, so
> that no unconsidered regression occurs, so that the self is kept whole or,
> sometimes, upright. Women do not try to master the other but to give
> birth to themselves. They only stoop to mastering the other (the child,
> for example, insofar as they have the power) when they are unable to
> engender their own axis.[61]

In the looking glass geography of analysis the site of intersection
between the two axes of the framework that supports the subject's *parole*
is displaced from its imaginary position "in" the subject-as-source to a
position *between* analysand and analyst, externalizing or objectifying
the representational function, and so exposing it as a transsubjective
construct. Similarly, the rapport (from OF *raporter*: re-, back, again, +
aporter, to bring) that characterizes the specific *enfantinage* of the transference temporarily bankrupts the phallic monopoly by re-turning the

subject to the scene of her first entry into the *praticable* of representation, in order to seek "what is still to be discovered of the future in the past." For the female analysand this affords an invaluable opportunity to reencounter her "mother-interlocutor" in the flesh as well as symbolically, and so to reconstitute a relation with herself and her kind within the alternative *praticable* of analysis.

For this to happen, however, it must be understood that the analyst, if female, brings to analysis not only corporeality but specifically her sexuate *female* body. Because the transference (re-)connects the hic et nunc of the analytic scene with the infantile scene, the two are enacted, and must be thought (of), not sequentially but *with* one another. Irigaray thus argues that, contrary to received wisdom, *enfantinage* does not "neuter" the subject or deliver him to an unsexed (because "preoedipal") condition, *and* that within the hic et nunc of analysis the relation of transference will always be conditioned by the biological sex of the participants. It will be conditioned, that is, by the similarity or difference between their necessarily sexuate—because material—bodies, and by the cultural elaborations of this materiality brought to analysis by its participants. For example, "lying down does not have the same sexual connotation for a man and a woman."[62] The scene of analysis, strange as it is, exists in a state of continual exchange with scene(s) outside it.

Finally, feminine passions attend the sexuate female body and build the feminine *praticable.* "Women are much more interested in others in general [than are men]," Irigaray announces.[63] Consider also her comment—"Dora and Schreber, in their respective sufferings, can help us to see the reasons for their illness and give us some part of what they, and we, need to recover."[64] The words bear remarking for several reasons. They suggest an "attentiveness to the present," a reading in detail, akin to analytic listening; they may also raise the possibility of recasting the "case study method" whose empiricism (which in a different sense mistakes the a priori for the a posteriori) has dominated American training in analysis. They also express a substantive difference between Irigaray and Lacan, Irigaray and Derrida: namely, her deliberately feminine concern for passion and affect as well as structure, her refusal to recognize the divorce of the two in their symmetrical opposition, and her own implied responsiveness at the level of pathos to that of her analysands. "The patient has come into analysis because he or she is in pain,"[65] Irigaray notes. The repeated term (*souffrir, souffrances*) underlines the point.

In rapport with her analysand the analyst is moved to com-passion; such figures of speech—to be moved, to be touched—are no accident, and may be contrasted with Lacan's description of analysis as "a relation which, by its very rules, excludes all real contact."[66] Here he probably refers to the same rules of analysis considered in the present essay, and Irigaray's interpretation of the geography of analysis suggests that she too would accept the Freudian prohibitions against perceptible contact in the therapeutic encounter. Her analytic compassion nonetheless affectively "supports" the suffering analysand, much as her role as "vertical axis" structurally supports her *parole*. At issue is not, however, the samaritanism at which Lacan sneered, but the difference between an economy of scarcity, embodied in Lacan's and Freud's insistence on deprivation, absence, and abstinence as therapeutic absolutes, and a feminine economy based on sustaining the hic et nunc as the ground of the future. For Irigaray the "rules" as *praticable* do not exclude real contact but provide the conditions for its possibility in providing the conditions for symbolic exchange.

The female analyst who is moved also potentially moves—restores to movement—her analysand. Ultimately, the ethico-epistemological axis now resituated between speaker and auditor may become an axis around which they move together. "Woman always speaks *with* the mother; man speaks in her absence," Irigaray asserts, challenging the universality of the fort/da. "This *with her*, obviously, assumes different types of presence, and it must tend to put speech *between* (them), lest they remain woven together, in an indissociable fusion." Presence need not and should not denote either the return of metaphysics or imaginary con-fusion. "This *with* has to try to become a *with self*."[67] The construction of a female subjectivity is inseparable from the construction of a mode of female sociality.

II

Irigaray's reinterpretation of the psychoanalytic *praticable* constitutes a kind of manual for radical analysts. But its implications also extend, via the theory of analysis, to the field of feminist theory in general. "The analytic *praticable* has no secret except that which psychoanalysis—or its readers, including those outside psychoanalysis—have neglected to interpret in the theoretical impact it can have," she writes,[68] inviting analysts and nonanalysts alike to join her in drawing out this (potential) theoretical impact. Irigaray emphasizes that the implications of the *praticable* represent an inherent *potential* rather than an intrinsic value or automatic effect, for they depend upon the specific chemistry and (pre)dispositions of those who enter, or remain aloof from, the scene of analysis.

.
.
.

Irigaray's reading of the *praticable* proposes a new relation between theory and practice, and between theory and history, that can help feminists negotiate some recurring impasses of feminist theory—perhaps most important, the impasse between essentialism and constructionism.[69] It does this not simply by displacing the question of theoretical legitimacy onto the field of practice or history, nor by a substitution of therapeutic for theoretical "force," but by proposing new and different criteria of *theoretical* legitimacy derived from an understanding of the relation between theory and therapy in psychoanalysis. These criteria are equally applicable to Irigaray's own text considered as a kind of *praticable*. I am not suggesting, though, that the scene of analysis presents an analogue or "model" of her text, let alone a model for feminist reading, writing, or practice. The *praticable* instead constructs a *means* and a *mode*—of theorizing, interpretating, writing, speaking—usable by and for diverse women because it is characterized by what I will call (after Irigaray) "coherent-incoherence." This mode is potentially common to both feminist theory and psychoanalysis. In attempting to theorize the mode of coherent-incoherence more explicitly, this section of my text is meant to serve as a kind of *praticable*, or passage, linking the discussion of therapeutic technique in part 1 with a reading of Irigaray's "style" in part 3.

Irigaray's discussions of analytic technique repeatedly suggest that only a new mode, as distinct from a new theoretical model, is capable of effecting change on the feminine side. "Models" as such remain within the scope of the totalizable, their virtue or legitimacy typically invested in that which is most unfeminine about them: their ability to reproduce the same.[70] The mode of the *praticable* recasts the question of Irigaray's theoretical "correctness" in basic terms, not so much situating the value of her interventions outside or beyond theory as calling into question the very criteria normally used to discriminate the theoretical as such—already a theoretical decision, and one that necessarily precedes any determination as to a particular theory's relative correctness. In effect the *praticable* embodies theoretical criteria that cannot be expressed in terms of a model, and to invoke the *praticable* is neither to abandon the term *theory* to its traditional expressions nor to cede the prerogative to theorize but rather to challenge the traditional self-constitution of theoretical discourse according to standards of mathematical formalization: discreteness, adequacy, self-sufficiency.

As I have suggested, for Irigaray psychoanalysis is an *unfinished* discourse in more senses than one. First, psychoanalysis resists closure on account of its dialogic nature. The dialogue in question is itself of two related kinds: the dialogue achieved by analyst and analysand in the

therapeutic encounter, and the dialogue between theory and practice
that constitutes the unique mode of coherence characteristic of psychoanalytic discourse, the latter both an historical and a theoretical
relation.

Irigaray distinguishes sharply between *texte* and *pratique* in psychoanalysis; strategically privileging the latter, she remarks, "Isn't the *theory* of sexuality, paradoxically, Freud's most regressive contribution?"[71]
This is not the simple antitheoreticism of the "pseudo-Irigaray" (Whitford's phrase) who haunts the texts of her detractors. Neither is it an
appeal for direct access to the voice and experience of women as repos-
itories of truth. It does, however, seek to (re)validate the experience and
parole of women in terms of a fully contemporary theoretical perspective, including a reconstruction of the category of the empirical.
Because psychoanalysis lost sight of the specific, dynamic relation of its
theory with its practice, the most radical implications it raised have as
yet gone uninterpreted:

> To refer only to the text of psychoanalysis . . . is perhaps already to have
> left out of account the *praticable* that vexes representation in analysis,
> and also its theoretical text, determining *its incoherence or its other theo-
> retical coherence*, the fact that Freud's text no longer responds to the
> same criteria of systematicity as a philosophical, scientific, or even a lit-
> erary text. This does not mean that it does not convey certain postulates,
> certain fragments, certain sequences . . . but without any possible
> anchorage in a domain, a method, a system.[72]

The therapeutic dialogue constitutes one part of the *praticable* that Irigaray here describes as vexing the scene of representation not only within the therapeutic encounter but also within the theoretical *texte* of psychoanalysis. Only when read in reference to, in dialogue with, or perhaps most accurately "within" the framework of that *praticable* does the
"other" coherence of psychoanalytic *theory* become available. By the
same virtue, as theory psychoanalysis remains necessarily unfinished,
incoherent, in the sense that it depends upon the continuing, changing,
and diverse discourses of what Irigaray repeatedly calls "each
analysand." The openness of psychoanalysis to history exists in the
most concrete sense as a receptivity to its analysands "heard" as material subjects of history and not of a symbolic order, to their words apprehended not as instantiations of an a priori law or *langue* that exhaustively interprets them, but as necessarily in excess of any theory to
which they might contribute.

What Irigaray says of Freud's text applies equally to her own: that
it does not "respond" to the same criteria of systematicity as a philo-

sophical, scientific, or literary text, but challenges us to read it in terms of "its incoherence or its *other* theoretical coherence." It is only with reference to the *praticable de la scène* that this alternative theoretical legitimacy can be appreciated. Lacan, reacting to the eclecticism of many post-Freudian therapies, insisted that the technique of psychoanalysis be anchored in a rigorous theory, and cited clinical experience, in turn, as the proof of this theory. Irigaray, on the other hand, proposes to reopen converse between theory and technique, insisting that neither one *can* be anchored in any single place or discourse—except, perhaps, in the interminable vicissitudes of the subject they work to produce. "For Irigaray, the metamorphoses of the female self can occur only in an open structure," Carolyn Burke observes.[73]

Anne Herrmann, placing Irigaray in oblique dialogue with Bakhtin, calls dialogue "a form of discourse whose contradictions are decided not in the text but in history."[74] History *enters* psychoanalysis by means of what Whitford explains as "that powerful *parole* which can imprison or set free, the word addressed to someone by someone."[75] To paraphrase Herrmann with Whitford, for Irigaray the force of psychoanalysis is (yet) to be produced in a future, both symbolic and institutional, made by and for women. Thus the psychoanalytic *praticable* stands in relation to the *texte* of psychoanalysis as something like a Derridean "supplement," something that both precludes and constitutes its coherence. Unlike the Derridean supplement, Irigaray's *praticable* acts not so much to suspend the production of meaning, or to aestheticize discourse, as to (re-)open a passageway between history and representation, for it is in the "other coherence" supplied by the *praticable* that the productive potential of psychoanalysis inheres.

Unfortunately, in the ways I have already indicated, the dialogic openness of psychoanalysis has been practically negated by its institutional past. To this extent the history of psychoanalysis mirrors what Irigaray identifies in the history of physics as a "lag in elaborating a 'theory' of fluids" because of a systematic priority granted to the mechanics of solids. This lag, she suggests, was the result of science's commitment to "mathematical formalization" as the sine qua non of "true" science, true "theory."[76] After all, the philosophical oppositions called into question by the psychoanalytic *praticable* are also those that function to regulate the discourses of science/knowledge in general.[77]

We have seen that the term *praticable* may designate not only the naturalized *cadrage*, or scene, of representation but also its potential nemesis, the conspicuously artificial scene of analysis. In addition, Irigaray uses the term *praticable* to designate the discursive framework that governs a particular scientific discourse at a particular stage of its development. This *scientific praticable* is not so much a positive paradigm in the Kuhnian sense as a functioning a priori, a network of tacit assumptions that determine, within the purview of that science, both what can(not) be thought and what can(not) appear in/as "the empirical" (just as what the analysand can and cannot say is determined by the framework within which she is heard). Irigaray emphasizes the restrictive force of the scientific *praticable* insofar as it erects a barrier between "causal modalities that dominate current discourses considered normal" and "the modalities of *the conditional* and *the unreal, the restricted*, etc."[78] To do so is to "fix the 'praticable,' limiting the freedom of the speaking subject that would not obey certain criteria of normality." In a question which is not one, Irigaray remarks, "do not these causal and restrictive modalities (the two are linked) introduce the intradiscursive brakes that preclude the possibility of a qualitatively different utterance?"[79]

When psychoanalysis legitimized itself as normal science, it closed itself "within its own field,"[80] losing the unique intercourse between theory and history that might have inaugurated a new epistemology along with a new ethic. On the other hand it might equally be said that psychoanalysis *failed* to stay "within" the coherent-incoherence of its own newly discovered or contrived *praticable*, reverting instead to established criteria of normal science. In either view psychoanalysis thereby lost the ability to "question . . . its own historical determinants."[81] From this delayed conformity to the "causal modalities" of normal science (even in the face of that which scandalously confounded them) followed the misrecognitions for which it is justly infamous.

But Irigaray is not precisely concerned with localizing a *true* prior cause—in the economic order, for example—of the (historical) obligations that psychoanalysis misrecognizes as intrapsychic givens. Rather, she suggests the following. This mistaking of (sociopolitical) *effects*— for example, the obligation to mother—for a priori *causes*—the putative need for the phallus—proceeds from a historical blindness, and blindness to history, that is itself the product, in part, of a theoretical capitulation. The historical and the theoretical are always connected, and to say so is more than a strategy. The modality of unilateral cause and effect cannot express this imbrication; the challenge, then, is to devise a new *praticable*, a new epistemological and expressive modality, that will do for women what the existing *praticable* has done for men, that is, be more productive than constraining. This the "other coherence" of Irigaray's own text attempts to do.

III

To suggest how the "other coherence" of the *praticable* operates in the text of Irigaray it seems fitting to end with a dramatic reading. That is, what I would like to do is enter a scene of analysis with Irigaray and allow the *praticable* to function, rather than provide something like a methodical account of how to "apply" the three analytic "rules" into which I have provisionally analyzed the analytic *praticable*. Admittedly the results of my effort probably lie somewhere in between a tradition- al "account" and a feminine dialogue.

Already partially quoted in part 1, the passage I have selected is one that might provide grist for the mill of either friend or foe.

> Girls do not enter language in the same way as boys. . . . The *fort-da* is not their move into language. It is too linear, too analogous with the to- and-fro of the penile thrust or its manual equivalent [*son substitut manuel*], with the mastery of the other by means of an object, it is too angular also. Girls enter into language without taking anything inside themselves (except perhaps the void?) [*(sauf le vide?)*]. They do not speak about an introjected him or introjected her, but talk *with* (sometimes in) a silence and with the other-mother in any case. Girls can find no sub- stitutes for the mother except in the whole of nature, the call to the divine or to do likewise. Woman always speaks *with* the mother, man speaks in her absence. This *with her* [*avec elle*], obviously takes different shapes and it must seek to place speech *between* [*mettre la parole entre*], not to remain in an indissociable fusion, with the women woven togeth- er. This *with* has to try to become a *with self* [*avec soi*].[82]

A critic might cite the passage as evidence of Irigaray's essentialism, positing as it apparently does an unmediated, ahistorical, and biologi- cally given difference between male and female modes of speech. A Lacanian might deride the seemingly naive isomorphism between the body and language; a Marxist, the reification of "language" and lack of reference to historical contingency. Admirers may receive the same words differently. As several readers have argued, the difference between a friendly and a hostile reading of Irigaray may itself turn on the differ- ence between *what* Irigaray is understood to say and *how* one appre- hends other more elusive or ephemeral aspects of her discourse: its tone, mode of enunciation, and pragmatics, for example.

In fact, it is not self-evident how one is to understand the force of the sentence "Girls enter language without taking in anything (except empty space?)." Certainly not in Irigaray's French, where the sentence concludes with the parenthetical *(sauf le vide?)*. This double or triple ending—?).—marking a question, an interpolation, and a declaration,

turns back on and interrogates the utterance that precedes it. It is the
sort of device that is wholly typical of Irigaray's style,[83] and one that
enacts in the grammatical register a reorientation of the spatial and temporal coordinates that for Irigaray govern not only theoretical discourse
but all that that discourse, in turn, governs: most especially, the
(non)representation of sexual difference. It is striking to note how
much the dynamics of the sentence correspond to the kind of writing
strategy endorsed by Irigaray in a much earlier remark:

> We need to proceed in such a way that linear reading is no longer pos-
> sible: that is, the retroactive impact of the end of each word, utterance,
> or sentence upon its beginning must be taken into consideration in
> order to undo the power of its teleological effect, including its deferred
> action. That would hold good also for the opposition between structures
> of horizontality and verticality that are at work in language.[84]

Such grammatical disorientation or reorientation within the text of Irigaray is homologous to that which characterizes the psychoanalytic
praticable.

In the case of my specimen sentence, insofar as it assumes the indicative mode as declaration or statement, it refers by definition (whether
truly or falsely) to a state of affairs as given, as an extralinguistic fact that
ostensibly precedes it; in this sense its temporal orientation is toward
the past, its spatial orientation toward a site outside itself. On the other
hand insofar as the concluding interpolation transforms the sentence
into a question, it instead anticipates an uncertain future, whether real
or hypothetical, actualizable or utopian, gesturing toward a site that is
not so much somewhere else as elsewhere, yet to be; it relays a speculative impulse akin to what Carolyn Burke early characterized as Irigaray's
"optative mode."[85] And, finally, within the semantic context of the passage, to conclude with a parenthetical interpolation might be said to
internally dialogize the form of the sentence itself, enacting in the present site of its own self-production a mode of feminine reciprocity suggested by Irigaray's "placing the *parole* between": the mode that is itself
deemed the precondition of (a women's) speaking "with herself"—that
is, *as* a woman.[86]

Of course there are other questions one might raise in examining the
sentence "Girls enter language without taking in anything (except
empty space?)."[87] Many of Irigaray's "indicative questions" are not
"true" questions opening onto a future, but rather, in the ordinary
sense, purely rhetorical, even sarcastic: for example, most of the inter-
polated pseudo questions with which she peppers Freud's "Femininity"
essay in "The Blind Spot of an Old Dream of Symmetry."[88] And not all

⋮

declarative sentences purport to refer to the world as already given, nor to the extralinguistic; performatives produce the state of affairs they express (although chiefly by recourse to time-honored formulae), and statements may refer to fictions or to themselves as linguistic operations. In the previous paragraph my reading of the dialogizing action and spatiotemporal derangement effected by a particular sentence— and particularly by *(sauf le vide?).*—is perhaps best described as a reading of *possible* and selected effects whose performative force depends as much on my own interest as a woman in so reading them as on the formal properties of Irigaray's writing practice. But here, once again, I would suggest, just as in the doubleness of its spatiotemporal articulation this utterance epitomizes the *praticable* of Irigaray's writing practice as a whole, particularly in that, as Braidotti and others have noted, *parler-femme* must be heard as implying *par-les-femmes.* Whether *(sauf le vide?).* should be taken as concluding a statement of fact (indicative mode), opening a speculative dialogue (optative mode), or performing an intervention designed to precipitate the condition it designates (performative mode) is arguable, but what is clear is that a reader's openness to entertaining these possibilities will participate in determining Irigaray's impact—indeed, her identity.

I suggest that the specimen sentence embodies, in a kind of dynamic interaction and interdependence, all three of the modes named above: indicative, with its orientation toward the past/outside, optative or speculative, with its orientation toward the future/elsewhere, and performative or productive, with its orientation toward the hic et nunc.[89] In other words, the internal dialogue formally enacted by the sentence as prelude to a feminine "with her" (implying the advent of an "other" woman) already implies and depends upon two things: on the empirical participation of another woman as interlocutor (thus, a speaking *avec elle*) and on a state of affairs that the specimen sentence takes as given, namely, a preexisting difference between girls and boys, women and men, that can be referred to in the sentence, and that is indispensable to the difference that can in turn be "formally" produced *by* it. At the same time it suggests, in the dynamic interaction of these different but mutually constitutive modes, something of Irigaray's "other syntax" and what she calls "the properties of *real* fluids—internal frictions, pressures, movements, and so on."[90]

In addition, when read in these terms this specimen sentence also exhibits in dynamic interdependence precisely those elements that several of Irigaray's most perceptive readers have singled out for attention: for example, Whitford, Fuss, and Braidotti's emphasis on the role of the interlocutor, so that, as Braidotti says, "my subjectivity is attached to the presence of the other woman";[91] Fuss's point about the "strategic essentialism" of Irigaray's language, in which "Irigaray seems to imply . . . that women both already have an identity on which to base a politics and that they are striving to secure an identity through the practice of politics,"[92] or Gallop's precocious observation about the importance of "the gesture of a troubled but nonetheless insistent referentiality" in the text of Irigaray;[93] and Whitford's and Grosz's attempts to explicate how Irigaray's writings "perform what they announce."[94] It is only *because* "there will always remain some part of 'woman' which resists masculine imprinting and socialization"[95]—in other words, because, Lacan to the contrary notwithstanding, woman *does* exist—that women can hope to produce (an identity for) themselves.[96]

It is this excess, in its stubborn material and historical facticity, this irreducible residue of representation to which Irigaray's indicative mode as such "refers." Such "essentialist" assertions are not therefore "purely" strategic, but neither should they be isolated from the optative and performative/productive modes with which they are imbricated—they should not, that is, be referred (back) to an economy of truth-as-correspondence within which their value could be adjudicated.[97] While it is possible to identify the effects of three distinct grammatical modes whose interaction constitutes the text of Irigaray as dynamically open, it is also apparent that in the imbrication of these modes no definitive line can be drawn between sexual difference as given and sexual difference as produced. It is precisely the regulation of representation by a phallic economy of truth-as-correspondence that has prevented women from recognizing themselves, except in the fleeting failures that at once undergird and undermine the symbolic.

Seemingly categorical pronouncements such as "Girls do not enter language in the same way as boys" (or, "women are much more interested in others in general," or, "women are more attentive in transmitting a message than men," etc.)—utterances that, considered as freestanding units, do not overtly exhibit the formal idiosyncrasies of my specimen sentence—are not then purely strategic or contestatory, but neither should they be isolated from the immediate context of their enunciation or from Irigaray's writing practice as a whole. Already, in another "technical" essay of 1969, "L'Enoncé en analyse," Irigaray had questioned the validity, the possibility, of isolating *un énoncé*, at least within a psychoanalytic context:

> Psychoanalysis insists at once on the division of the text and on its intrication in a network, in networks, of *énoncés* . . . from which it cannot be

•
•   isolated. Its unity always contested as unitary, there the *énoncé* finds
•   itself again and again referred back to its polyvalence, its ambiguity, its
     plurality.[98]

The double gesture that simultaneously isolates textual fragments for
intense formal scrutiny and insists upon the imbrication of these fragments within an inherently illimitable network of significations at once
describes the method of psychoanalysis as understood by Irigaray and
suggests an approach to the coherent-incoherence of Irigaray's growing
corpus. It is to this corpus as a whole and equally to the work of her
interlocutors that the many "parts" of Irigaray's project should be
referred. By the same token Irigaray emphasizes that it remains not only
for psychoanalysis but also for its "readers," including nonanalysts, to
adequately decipher the powers of the *praticable*. The suggestion, once
again, is that the *praticable* be recognized as an instrument of theoretical discovery, not merely the practical application or instantiation of a
(long) finished theory. This potential is the corollary of its effectiveness
as an instrument of personal and social transformation, of resistance,
not adaptation, to the symbolic status quo.[99]

NOTES   •

1. Referring to (her) *Speculum*, Irigaray writes in the jacket notes to the
    Minuit paperback edition, "this *praticable* [thwarts] the scenography of
    representation according to masculine parameters." My discussion of the
    praticable will focus mainly on the following pieces from *Parler n'est jamais
    neutre*: "L'Enoncé en analyse," pp. 117–133 (originally published in *Lan-
    gages*, 1969), "Le Praticable de la scène," "The Poverty of Psychoanalysis"
    (extract), "Is the Subject of Science Sexed?" (extract); and from *Sexes et par-
    entés*: "The Gesture in Psychoanalysis" (extract). Where available, I use
    already published English translations; other translations are my own.
2. Irigaray, "Le Praticable de la scène," p. 248.
3. Irigaray, *This Sex*, p. 75/*Ce Sexe*, p. 73.
4. Ibid., p. 162/157.
5. Irigaray, "The Poverty of Psychoanalysis," p. 83/*Parler n'est jamais
    neutre*, p. 257–258.
        Charcot's famous exhibitions of "his" hysterics might well come to
    mind here. While Freud as psychoanalyst no longer touches or publicly
    exhibits his analysands, he may be said to revert to the order of the spec-
    ular/spectacle to the extent that their discourse is reduced to the status of
    evidence for/of an established truth. The ear can also be an organ of
    vision, Irigaray suggests, so long as it only listens for the well-formed,
    i.e., that which con-forms to a certain a priori.
6. My reading of the hic et nunc and of the *praticable* develops a particular

perspective on themes also treated by other readers of Irigaray. For example, with somewhat different emphases, Rosi Braidotti, Elizabeth Grosz, and Margaret Whitford have all written about the importance of "the present" in Irigaray's writing, and Whitford links the hic et nunc of analysis with the idea of divine presence or Parousia (see *Luce Irigaray: Philosophy in the Feminine* [New York: Routledge, 1991], especially pp. 35–36, 146ff.). Whitford also discusses the importance of the "model" of the psychoanalytic session for understanding the nature of Irigaray's interventions. As I will argue further in the body of my essay, I do not regard the *praticable* as a "model," however, and I see myself as following Irigaray in an attempt to dispense with the language of models and analogies, in favor of a *means* and a *mode* of understanding not based on the privilege of such metalanguage. (Indeed, as Whitford also argues, the psychoanalytic session should be such a means.) On the other hand I also think it important to emphasize that the *praticable*, though not a "model," *is* a kind of apparatus, tool, or instrument, which at once literalizes and opens/forges the "intermediate space," "excluded middle," or "between" that figures so importantly in Irigaray's writing as an alternative to the world of specular oppositions—to the current "symbolic." Like the ongoing reproduction of the existing order of representation, the (re)production of the feminine depends upon material supports, although unlike the existing order it flaunts rather than attempting to conceal this dependence. The *praticable* is such a support, but it is also more than that.

7. "I think the most important thing to do is to expose the exploitation common to all women and to find the struggles that are appropriate for each woman, right where she is, depending upon her nationality, her job, her social class, her sexual experience, that is, upon the form of oppression that is for her the most immediately unbearable" (Irigaray, *This Sex*, pp. 166–167/*Ce Sexe*, p. 161). Incidentally, Irigaray has said that she dislikes the term *feminist* and prefers to speak of "the struggles of women" in order to emphasize the "plural and polymorphous character" of these struggles as well as avoid recuperation by the dominant order. Within the present context it does not seem to me important to mark this distinction; both terms connote political activism, which has been a salient feature of Irigaray's career. For Irigaray's comments on the term *feminist* see Elaine Hoffman Baruch and Lucienne J. Serrano, eds., *Women Analyze Women: In France, England, and the United States* (New York: New York University Press, 1988).

8. Whitford, *Luce Irigaray*, p. 36.

9. Ibid., p. 24.

10. Grosz, *Sexual Subversions: Three French Feminists* (Sydney: Allen and Unwin, 1989), p. 102.

11. Irigaray, "L'Enoncé en analyse," p. 117.

     I have adopted from Margaret Whitford the practice of keeping Irigaray's term *énoncé* in French. Whitford defines *énoncé* as "the content of

- · ·   the statement" made by the speaking subject, as distinguished from *énon-*
- ·   *ciation*, the position of the speaking subject in the discourse or statement
       (*Luce Irigaray*, p. 42).
12. Irigaray, "Le Praticable de la scène," p. 239.
13. Ibid., p. 251.
14. Irigaray, *This Sex*, p. 150/*Ce Sexe*, p. 147.
15. Ibid., p. 161/156.
16. Irigaray, "Le Praticable de la scène," pp. 242–243.
17. Ibid., p. 243.
18. Irigaray, *Sexes and Genealogies*, p. 92/*Sexes et parentés*, p. 106. The trans-
    lation actually quoted here is a more literal one, taken from "The Ges-
    ture in Psychoanalysis," trans. Elizabeth Guild, in Teresa Brennan, ed.,
    Between Feminism and Psychoanalysis (London: Routledge, 1989), p. 128.
19. Irigaray's play on the face-to-face relation alludes to the writings of
    Emmanuel Levinas, whose well-known work on ethics has been impor-
    tant to her. For several perspectives on Irigaray's relation to Levinas, see
    Grosz (*Sexual Subversions*, especially pp. 140–183); Carolyn Burke
    ("Romancing the Philosophers: Luce Irigaray," in Dianne Hunter, ed.,
    Seduction and Theory: Readings of Gender, Representation and Rhetoric, pp.
    226–40 [Urbana: University of Illinois Press, 1989]); and Whitford
    (*Luce Irigaray*, especially pp. 149–168).
20. Irigaray, "Le Praticable de la scène," p. 249.
21. Ibid., p. 241–242.
22. Irigaray, "Sexual Difference," *Ethics*, p. 7/*Ethique*, p. 15.
23. Irigaray, "Le Praticable de la scène," p. 242.
    In this context the scene of psychoanalysis as *praticable* might be said
    to embody or dramatize Irigaray's notion of a "*sensible* transcendental."
    For discussion of this difficult concept see Whitford, *Luce Irigaray*, pp.
    47–49, 112–113ff., 144ff. [Also discussed in Hodge, this volume.—Eds.]
24. Irigaray, *Sexes and Genealogies*, p. 93/*Sexes et parentés*, p. 107.
25. Irigaray, *Parler n'est jamais neutre*, pp. 117–118.
26. Irigaray, "Le Praticable de la scène," p. 242.
27. Ibid.
28. Ibid., p. 241.
29. Sigmund Freud, *Therapy and Technique*, ed. Philip Rieff (New York:
    Collier, 1963), pp. 118–122.
30. Jacques Lacan, *Ecrits: A Selection*, trans. Alan Sheridan (New York and
    London: Norton, 1977).
31. Ibid., p. 127.
32. American ego psychology generally conceives the task of psychotherapy
    to be one of "strengthening" the analysand's ego by, in Freud's formula,
    "making the unconscious, conscious." It proposed, where appropriate, a
    form of therapy based on a so-called therapeutic alliance (the language is
    Heinz Hartmann's) between the analyst and the "healthy part" of the
    analysand's ego. Lacan comments, "the subject, transformed into a *cela,*

has to conform to an *ego* in which the analyst will have little trouble in recognizing his ally, since in actual fact it is to the analyst's *ego* that the subject is expected to conform" (*Ecrits*, p. 91). Irigaray suggests that in Lacanian analysis it is to the analyst's (masculine) unconscious that the "unconscious" of the analysand-subject is "expected to conform."

33. Irigaray, "The Poverty of Psychoanalysis," p. 81/*Parler n'est jamais neutre*, p. 255.

34. Ibid.

35. Irigaray, "Le Praticable de la scène," p. 251; text slightly adapted.

36. Irigaray, "The Poverty of Psychoanalysis," p. 83/*Parler n'est jamais neutre*, p. 258.

   The charge that Freud stopped listening to his analysands should be distinguished from the charge, associated with Jeffrey Masson, that he stopped *believing* them when he abandoned the so-called seduction theory of the etiology of hysteria. Irigaray's revalidation of the *parole* of women and her reconstruction of the category of the empirical should not be mistaken for an argument in favor of a return to the theory of seduction or trauma, especially when such a claim discounts the priority of the unconscious in the determination of sexual identity—nothing could be further from her intent. But it might be valuable to explore the relation between these two different critiques of the institutional development of psychoanalysis.

37. *Speculum*'s "The Blind Spot of An Old Dream of Symmetry" provides an exhaustive analysis of this operation in the text of Freud.

38. Lacan, *Ecrits*, p. 45.

39. Irigaray, "Le Praticable de la scène," p. 246.

40. Ibid.

41. Ibid., p. 252.

42. Irigaray, *Sexes and Genealogies*, p. 100/*Sexes et parentés*, p. 114.

43. Irigaray, "Le Praticable de la scène," p. 242.

44. Irigaray, *Sexes and Genealogies*, p. 92/*Sexes et parentés*, p. 106.

45. Irigaray, "Le Praticable de la scène," pp. 242–243.

46. Irigaray, *Sexes and Genealogies*, p. 86/*Sexes et parentés*, pp. 100–101.

47. Ibid., p. 101/86.

48. The uses of the *praticable* as hic et nunc connecting past and future also seem related to Irigaray's interest in angels, figures she appropriates from orthodox Christian symbolism as heralds of the/a future of sexual difference. Where Jean-Joseph Goux and others suggest that the future can only be figured as a monstrous breach with the known, Irigaray's more benign figure embodies the possibility of both transformation *and* grace or continuity.

   Between God, as the perfectly immobile act, man, who is surrounded and enclosed by the world of his work, and woman, whose task would be to take care of nature and procreation,

•
•   *angels* would circulate as mediators of that which has not yet hap-
•   pened, of what is still going to happen. . . . Angels destroy the
         monstruous, that which hampers the possibility of a new age;
         they come to herald the arrival of a new birth, a new morning.

         Irigaray, *Ethics*, p. 15/*Ethique*, p. 22.

49. Irigaray, "Interview," p. 77.
50. Compare Naomi Schor's provocative remark, "The real in Irigaray is nei-
    ther impossible, nor unknowable: it is the fluid," in "This Essentialism
    Which Is Not One: Coming To Grips with Irigaray," p. 69 this volume.
51. Irigaray, *Sexes and Genealogies*, p. 88/*Sexes et parentés*, p. 102.
52. Irigaray, "Le Praticable de la scène," p. 243.
53. Ibid.
54. Ibid., p. 244.
55. Ibid., p. 251.
56. Ibid.
57. Irigaray, "Interview," p. 75.
58. Famously, the boy in Freud's account uses a wooden spool to substitute
    for his mother (Freud's beloved daughter), mastering her absence by
    symbolically placing himself in control of it. Casting the symbolic bob-
    bin away from himself he exclaims *fort!* (most often translated as
    "gone!"), and pulling it back again, *da!* ("there!"). In (post)structuralist
    terms, this alternation between the two opposites, presence/absence,
    becomes, in effect, a symbolic a priori, the master opposition that makes
    all others possible and upon which all the boy's future structures of
    meaning will be elaborated.
59. Irigaray, "Interview," pp. 74–75; my emphasis.
60. Irigaray, *Sexes and Genealogies*, p. 99/*Sexes et parentés*, p. 113.
61. Ibid., p. 99/114.
62. Ibid., p. 93/107.
63. Irigary, "Interview," p. 77.
64. Irigaray, *Sexes and Genealogies*, p. 104/*Sexes et parentés*, p. 118.
65. Ibid., p. 93/107.
66. Lacan, *Ecrits*, p. 44.
67. Irigaray, *Sexes and Genealogies*, p. 99/*Sexes et parentés*, p. 113.
68. Irigaray, "Le Praticable de la scène," p. 239.
69. This impasse is also addressed, with great resourcefulness, by Diana Fuss,
    Essentially Speaking: Feminism, Nature, and Difference (New York and
    London: Routledge, 1989), and by Schor, in her essay "This Essential-
    ism," for example.
70. Burke makes a similar point concerning the distinction between mode
    and model in relation to the figure of Irigaray's "lips," which, as she
    explains, "should not be reduced to a literally anatomical specification,
    for the figure suggests another mode rather than another model" (Burke,
    "Irigaray Through the Looking Glass," p. 51 this volume).
71. Irigaray, "Le Praticable de la scène," p. 251.

72. Ibid, p. 239.
73. Burke, "Looking Glass," p. 49 this volume.
74. *The Dialogic and Difference: "An/Other Woman" in Virginia Woolf and Christa Wolf* (New York: Columbia University Press, 1989), p. 5.
75. Whitford, *Luce Irigaray*, p. 35.
76. Irigaray, *This Sex*, p. 106/ *Ce Sexe*, p. 105.
77. This point is further developed in "Is the Subject of Science Sexed?" See Schor, "This Essentialism," for more on Irigaray's relation to the discourses of modern science, especially physics, and particularly Prigogine's model of "dissipating structures." Schor's discussion indicates to me that Irigaray considers herself a kind of physicist, but I believe that when Irigaray evokes scientific models as such she does so with reluctance and in the hope of moving science beyond them.
78. Irigaray, "Is the Subject of Science Sexed?" p. 65/ *Parler n'est jamais neutre*, p. 317.
79. Ibid.
80. Irigaray, *This Sex*, p. 125/ *Ce Sexe*, p. 124.
81. Ibid.
82. Irigaray, *Sexes and Genealogies*, p. 99/ *Sexes et parentés*, p. 113. I have modified Gillian Gill's translation of this passage very slightly, inserting certain phrases of Irigaray's French that are referred to in the body of my essay.
83. Thus in their translation of "Women, the Sacred, and Money," Diana Knight and Margaret Whitford choose to retain every instance of the "type of interrogative statement—in the indicative, with a question mark at the end—[that] is so characteristic of Irigaray's style" (p. 17n).
84. Irigaray, *This Sex*, p. 80/ *Ce Sexe*, p. 77.
85. " 'When Our Lips Speak Together' may be described as . . . a fable of female relations in the optative mode: it is written 'as if' we could forget the logical and emotional requirements of the phallic economy," Burke writes ("Looking Glass," p. 48 this volume).
86. This *avec soi* seems a deliberate echo of and alternative to the *pour-soi/en-soi* opposition adopted by Simone de Beauvoir, neither half of which can evoke the mode of identity that Irigaray deems feminine.
87. Margaret Whitford points out that an indicative reading of *(sauf le vide?)*. might say that it is the girl's place in the symbolic structure that is missing.
88. Still, in the text of Irigaray's *Speculum*, these rhetorical questions effectively puncture the seeming monolith of Freud's discourse, opening a space for real, not just pseudo, dialogue with "Messieurs les psychanalystes." For a fuller discussion of Irigaray's postfactum dialogizing of the "Femininity" essay, and of *Speculum of the Other Women* considered as *praticable*, see chapter 1 of my forthcoming book, *Re-Producing Modernism: Irigaray, Formalism, and the Place of the Woman-Writer*.
89. I prefer the term *productive* to *performative* as emphasizing the power of Irigaray's discourse to enable novel utterances and change in the symbol-

-
-
-

ic order, rather than to "perform" primarily actions previously authorized by the symbolic, which is the prevailing sense of "performative" in J. L. Austin's well-known account.

90. Irigaray, *This Sex*, p. 109/ *Ce Sexe*, pp. 107–108.

91. Rosi Braidotti, "Envy; or, With My Brains and Your Looks," in Alice Jardine and Paul Smith, eds., *Men in Feminism* (New York and London: Methuen, 1987), pp. 233–241.

Compare Fuss's remark: "*Parler femme* appears to be defined not so much by what one says, or even by how one says it, but from whence and to whom one speaks. Locus and audience distinguish a speaking (as) woman from a speaking (as) man . . . for a woman to speak, she must establish a locus from which to be heard, and to articulate such a space, she must speak" (Fuss, *Essentially Speaking*, p. 63). I am suggesting that What, How, *and* Whence/to Whom one speaks all must work together to constitute *parler-femme.*

92. Fuss, *Essentially Speaking*, p. 69.

93. Jane Gallop, "*Quand Nos Lèvres S'Ecrivent*: Irigaray's Body Politic," *Romanic Review* (1983), 74:83.

94. Grosz, *Sexual Subversions*, p. 102.

My sense of the essential imbrication of all three of these modes in Irigaray's writings may respond in part to Burke's interest in determining whether Irigaray's figurative language "is mimetic or referential, whether it hovers or shifts back and forth between these two types of signification, and whether it is used consistently" (Burke, "Looking Glass," pp. 51–52 this volume). I am uncertain about whether "mimetic" here corresponds either to "optative" or to what I am calling "performative/productive," but in any case my (partial) response to Burke's questions is that Irigaray's discourse does indeed shift back and forth between not two but three types of signification.

95. Fuss, *Essentially Speaking*, p. 61.

96. "How can I say it? That we are women from the start," Irigaray writes in "When Our Lips Speak Together" (*This Sex*, p. 212/ *Ce Sexe*, p. 211). Here her formulation implicitly contradicts Freud's belief that "it is necessary to *become* a woman, a 'normal' one at that, whereas a man is a man from the outset" (ibid., p. 134/132). At the same time it seems a deliberate repudiation of Simone de Beauvoir's famous dictum, "One is not born, but rather becomes, a woman." But, on the other hand, Irigaray's gesture of a "troubled but nonetheless insistent referentiality," her insistence that woman exists outside all representations of her, can be seen as a revised or post(post)structuralist version of Beauvoir's insistence that while Man "demands play-acting" of woman, wanting her "to be the *Other*," nonetheless "all existents remain subjects, try as they will to deny themselves" (*The Second Sex*, trans. and ed. H. M. Parshley [New York: Bantam, 1952], p. 579). For Beauvoir women, though represented as absolute Other, are always already subjects who must strive to realize

themselves as such; for Irigaray women, though (un)represented within
the order of the Same, are always already women who must strive to represent themselves as subjects. As Naomi Schor suggests, in "This Essentialism Which Is Not One," the relation of Irigaray's and Beauvoir's discourses may be more complementary than contradictory.

97. The "Plato's *Hystera*" section of *Speculum* provides an exhaustive analysis
of the mechanics of the economy of truth, and *Speculum* as a whole in
effect traces the dominance of the economy of truth throughout Western
theoretical tradition. For a more detailed discussion of this essential part
of Irigaray's critique, see Whitford, *Luce Irigaray*, especially pp. 101–122.
See also my discussion of "Plato's *Hystera*" in *Re-producing Modernism*.

98. Irigaray, "L'Enoncé en analyse," p. 117.

99. This essay is inscribed to Jane James, Interlocutrice (May 1992).

• *Luisa Muraro*
•
•

FEMALE

GENEALOGIES

The development of Luce Irigaray's thought has influenced, and been influenced by, women's politics. Her treatment of the theme of female genealogies provides a particularly good example of this relationship of exchange.

There are various ways to approach this theme. One way is to start from our personal relationship with the mother, which is often an area of devastation. The mother-daughter relationship is always present in Irigaray's work, from *Speculum* onward, even before the appearance of the theme that interests us, with which it will always be associated. In 1989 Irigaray wrote: "One of the lost crossroads of our becoming-women is situated in the blurring and erasure of the relations with our mother, and in our obligation to submit to the laws of the world of men-amongst-themselves."[1]

In our discussion of female genealogies we can also start with a readily observable social reality, for example, education. "Education," says Irigaray, "the social world of men-amongst-themselves, and patriarchal culture act on little girls like Hades on Kore-Persephone," that is, like

an infernal power that steals the daughter from the mother and rapes
her.

She continues: "The justifications given to explain this state of affairs
are imprecise. We can learn more from the traces of the history of the
relation between Demeter and Kore-Persephone."[2]

Both personal experience and social reality show signs of a suffering
and a puzzling disorder that suggests something very violent has taken
place. This violence, according to Irigaray, corresponds to the destruction, by patriarchy, of the genealogical relation between mother and
daughter.

To illustrate this issue I once used a woman's letter to the editor of a
newspaper. It was a very ordinary letter, in which the origins of patriarchy could be discerned in their contemporary reenactment, causing
women renewed suffering and confusion. This is what the woman
wrote:

To the Editor:
My parents had four children, two boys and two girls. The girls are mar-
ried now, but not the boys. My father always favored the two boys: he
gave them larger allowances, greater freedom, more nutritious food;
they had meat twice a day, we girls had cheese. He was convinced that
men were superior in every way and were entitled to privileged treatment in every domain, so that they would be better prepared for life; he
persuaded my mother to believe it too. When my brothers grew up, he
used all his retirement bonus and all his savings to build a large and
beautiful house for them in the center of our town, and gave them legal
ownership. When he died, there was a terrible quarrel. The outcome was
that my sister and I were ordered never to set foot in their house again
(although our mother was living there), and we were denied any contact
with her; they threatened to prosecute us for housebreaking if we dis-
obeyed. In this atmosphere of tremendous tension, I was unable to see
my mother for almost nine years; I couldn't spend a few minutes with
her, or ask her advice: all the things one remembers with such tenderness when times are difficult. I couldn't even wish her a Merry Christmas or a Happy Easter, even though I lived five minutes' walk away
from her house!

I ask myself sadly: so, does brute force always win, in spite of the
bonds of affection between mother and daughter? Are all the laws on
equal rights flouted, then? Do they submit to violence? To the strongest?
I hope this sad story of mine will enlighten those parents who still discriminate between their sons and daughters, so that this may never happen again.

Antonietta X

In my comments I showed the letter's similarities and differences with
the myth of Demeter and Kore,[3] taking my inspiration from Luce Irigaray both in the way I used myths as a clue to history and in my interpretation of the Demeter myth.

In addition to personal experience and social reality, historical documents can also provide us with a good introduction to our theme. From
the many possible examples Joan of Arc comes to mind. Joan of Arc's
trial can be regarded as a renewed attack on the ancient female genealogies (which still survived underground) by the triumphant religion of
the father. At the first public hearing Joan says: "Everything I know, I
know from my mother." It is very interesting for us today to notice that
although she distanced herself from her godmother who believed in
fairies—that is, she dissociated herself from the ancient female genealogies—she did not disown them. On the contrary, she reproduced them
in the context of the official religion. In fact, her whole life was guided
by St. Catherine and St. Margaret. They gave her advice, comforted her,
strengthened her, and spoke to her in God's name.

Greco-Roman mythology provides another approach (the one Luce
Irigaray prefers) to our theme. Still others are certainly possible, for
example, Ellen Moers's approach via literature in *Literary Women.*
Clearly, these different approaches do not exclude one another, but can,
on the contrary, be combined.

In listing the various approaches I wanted to formulate an initial definition of the concept of female genealogies. It is obviously not a classic kind of definition, but rather a contextual one, or, to be more precise, an indexical one (to use the term that Peirce introduces for cases
when someone points their finger and says, "It's that").

Why haven't I given a classic definition? Because it is impossible.
This theme lies on the border between the speakable and the unspeakable, like much—we do not know how much—of women's experience.
When, as in this case, we must make an uncodified reality speakable,
the semantic field must open, like the Red Sea, to let things (experience) pass through, and the only valid definitions are those based on
indexical signs.

Luce Irigaray gives no conventional definitions of female genealogies, and, as a general rule, gives very few definitions of the conventional type.

Her work is divided between two registers, the written (*Speculum,
Marine Lover, Elemental Passions,* and *L'Oubli de l'air* [Forgetting air]
belong to this group) and the spoken, mostly lectures, which were later
put into written form. The theme of female genealogies is only found

in the second kind of work. It appears for the first time in the 1980
Montreal lecture called "Le Corps-à-corps avec la mère"/"Body Against
Body: In Relation to the Mother."[4] It is, therefore, a theme that appears
relatively late, connected with the practice of oral teaching, a nonacad-
emic form of teaching almost always requested and often organized by
women for women.

In my opinion these circumstances are significant. They show how
this theme appears and develops through Luce Irigaray's direct encounters with women's politics. Irigaray's principal political practice is teaching, and I think that female genealogies are the most successful fruits of
this practice. I consider them of fundamental importance, in fact, in the
process of women's consciousness-raising.

In the Montreal lecture the genealogical relation between women
first appears as something that is denied, a denial represented in the
mythological figures of Electra and the goddess Athena in Aeschylus's
Oresteia. This trilogy recounts the story of King Agamemnon, who,
returning home after the Trojan War, is murdered by Queen
Clytemnestra, his wife. Their son, Orestes, murders his mother, with
the help of his sister Electra, to avenge their father. Orestes is then pur-
sued by the Furies until he escapes to Delphi, where Apollo and Athena
save him from the punishment for matricide. In *The Eumenides*, the
third play in the trilogy, Apollo defends Orestes, with this argument:

> Not the true parent is the woman's womb
> That bears the child; she doth but nurse the seed
> New-sown: the male is parent; she for him,
> As stranger for a stranger, hoards the germ
> Of life, unless the god its promise blight.
> And proof hereof before you will I set.
> Birth may from fathers, without mothers, be:
> See at your side a witness of the same,
> Athena, daughter of Olympian Zeus,
> Never within the darkness of the womb
> Fostered nor fashioned[5]

Luce Irigaray perceives the violent beginnings of patriarchal society in
the *Oresteia*. According to her, myths have a historical value: "Mythical
stories are not independent of History, but express it in narratives which
illustrate the major lines of development of a given period."[6] This thesis is implicitly critical of the Freudian transhistorical interpretation of
the Oedipus myth. But Irigaray is less interested in critique than in
finding a positive use for myths. She maintains that ancient mythology
proves that a gynecocratic society existed before patriarchy, thus giving

a new lease of life to Bachofen's famous theory. The mythological mode of narrating history, she explains, depends on the fact that at that time word and image (*parole et art*) were not separate. There was another relationship with space-time then. She concludes that "the mythical expression of History is more akin to female and matrilineal traditions."[7]

It is necessary, however, to keep in mind that the myths that have come down to us are a scenario already "staged" by patriarchy, which aims more at hiding than revealing, more at instructing than narrating. Irigaray talks about the masking operation of patriarchal culture. On this point, at a series of lectures held in Southern Italy recently, she made a more explicit, if somewhat debatable statement. "This patriarchal culture has erased—unwittingly or through ignorance perhaps—the traces of a culture which was anterior to it, or contemporaneous with it."[8] This hypothesis of ignorance or lack of awareness is incompatible with what Irigaray herself had said in Montreal in 1980, to the effect that an unpunished matricide lay at the foundation of our present civilization. "Orestes kills his mother because the empire of the God-Father, who has seized and taken for his own the ancient powers (*puissances*) of the earth-mother, demands it."[9] If this is in some way true (and for Irigaray myths are true in a historically determined way), the ignorance and unawareness of patriarchy seem to me a cover-up.

It is not a question of inconsistency on Irigaray's part but of the progression of her thought. That this specific point is unsettled derives, I think, from a contradiction, revealed in a paradoxical fact, namely, that in patriarchal society, sons have a far better relationship with their mothers than do daughters. When Irigaray moderates her polemics against patriarchy, she does it, I think, in reaction to this unresolved contradiction.

In the Montreal lecture she alludes to the unsolved enigma of our relationship with the mother when she says that Clytemnestra's murder drives both Orestes and Electra to madness, but that Orestes recovers with the help of Apollo while Electra remains mad.[10] Further on, however, she asks her listeners to "leave a world of madness which is not our own."[11] She goes on to make a veiled allusion to *our* madness: we women must be careful "not again to kill the mother who was immolated at the birth of our culture."[12] Sacrificed, of course, by the son on behalf of the father. Were we involved, it would be more as accomplices or imitators of men rather than as directly responsible for this murder.

So Irigaray points out the contradiction but does not scrutinize it. This is reflected in the structure of the lecture, which consisted of a first, theoretical part, mainly of interest to men, and a second, exhortatory part, particularly directed at women. In this second part we find phrases like the following throughout: "It is urgent for us to refuse. . . . It is also necessary for us to . . . we must be on the watch for something else." This form of discourse seems to indicate that there is nothing to be understood, nothing to explain about our relationship with the mother—there is only something to be improved. The problem almost exclusively regards men.

At a certain point in this final stream of exhortations (all, it is clear, morally and politically valuable) the concept of a genealogical relation among women takes positive form in these words: "If we are not to be accomplices in the murder of the mother, we also need to assert that there is a genealogy of women."[13]

This is a double genealogy. There is a genealogy based on procreation, which binds us to the mother, to her mother, and so on, maternity functioning as the structure of a female continuum that links us to the origins of life. Let us put it into words, says Irigaray. "We must also find, rediscover, invent the words, the sentences that speak of the most ancient and most current relationship to the mother's body."[14] These three verbs, *find, rediscover,* and *invent,* have a different meaning and are grouped together for a precise effect on the sense of the sentence. Irigaray frequently uses semantic constellations of this kind to attain a calculated effect in meaning; here, she wants to illuminate our relationship with a reality that is both very close and remote.

The other genealogy is based on words. "Let us not forget, moreover, that we already have a history, that certain women, despite all the cultural obstacles, have made their mark upon history and all too often have been forgotten by us,"[15] says Irigaray, making one of her infrequent references to the work of other women. The first "genealogical" practice of feminism consisted precisely in learning about the women who have affected either our biographical or historical past. Luce Irigaray therefore suggests the following interpretation of the extraordinary flourishing of historical research that has accompanied feminism: it was inspired by the love of the maternal genealogy and by the desire to give the mother's life, symbolically, back to her.

The Montreal lecture ends with an image that attempts to express the new idea in an intuitive way: "If a woman were to celebrate the Eucharist with her mother, giving her a share of the fruits of the earth blessed by them both, she might be freed from all hatred or ingratitude toward her maternal genealogy."[16] I find this image artificial, but it deserves our attention. It shows Irigaray's present political and philosophical effort to signify something that our culture has rendered inconceivable. It also reveals how much effort is involved in overcoming the barrier of this inconceivability, a barrier that is also made up of "hate" and "ingratitude" between women.

In 1986, talking to the leaders of an Italian political party, Irigaray suggested one way of overcoming these barriers; she proposed that images (photographs, paintings, sculptures, etc.) showing mothers and daughters together should be put in public places.[17] This concern for finding ways to translate theory into practice is an important aspect of Irigaray's thought.

Her image of the mother and daughter celebrating the Eucharist together seems to have a double origin, on the one hand in the fantasy of one of her patients,[18] on the other in the mythological couple Demeter-Kore. These two divinities, mother and daughter, who are at the origin of the Eleusinian mysteries, have become Irigaray's favorite representation of female genealogy.

In 1982 Irigaray again takes up this theme, in a series of lectures at the University of Rotterdam that were published two years later under the title *Ethique de la différence sexuelle.*

In Irigaray's thought "ethics" means something close to Hegel's ethicality (*Sittlichkeit*), although she makes a few corrections to the Hegelian conception.[19] Thus understood, ethics goes beyond morality and includes rights, customs, written and unwritten law, religion. . . . In an American book catalogue I found Irigaray's name associated with two exponents of French "poststructuralism" (who at one stage had simply been considered structuralists). Such an approach is fashionable, perhaps, but misleading. The deconstruction of received cultural forms is never one of Irigaray's aims. She is a political thinker at least as much as Hegel was in his context, the culture of the rising bourgeoisie after the 1789 revolution. This parallel does not mean that there is a close similarity between the two; Luce Irigaray differs a great deal from Hegel; she is poles apart from him on some points.

For Irigaray the existence of female genealogies constitutes a necessity of an ethical nature. This position begins to emerge in *An Ethics of Sexual Difference.* Irigaray says there that, to avoid a recurrence of the fate of Antigone in Sophocles' tragedy, the world of women must generate an ethical order of its own. Previously, she had said that women are prevented from acting ethically; she means that they are prevented from participating in the life of the polis in an autonomous, effective way. The absence of a sexuate language corresponding to women is the first impediment to their participation.

It is necessary, therefore, to create an ethical order among women that will have at least two dimensions: a vertical one, the genealogical

mother-daughter axis, and a horizontal one, the well-known axis of
sisterhood.[20]

These lines are few, but of great import. They indicate what I think
is the main characteristic of our present situation, in contrast to the
feminism of the sixties and seventies. At that time relations among
women were understood and practiced under the sign of sisterhood.
We were sisters in the fight against patriarchal oppression. Mothers and
daughters, of course, but actually sisters against everything denying us:
these are the words used by a great feminist writer portraying her relationship with her daughter. We did not know what place to attribute to
the mother. I will quote a lengthy passage from Adrienne Rich, which
nicely expresses the limits of sisterhood as understood in the 1970s:

> It was too simple, early in the new twentieth-century wave of feminism,
> for us to analyze our mothers' oppression, to understand "rationally"—
> and correctly—why our mothers did not teach us to be Amazons, why
> they bound our feet or simply left us. It was accurate and even radical,
> that analysis; and yet, like all politics narrowly interpreted, it assumed
> that consciousness knows everything. There was, is, in most of us, a girl-
> child still longing for a woman's nurture, tenderness and approval, a
> woman's power exerted in our defense. . . . When we can confront and
> unravel this paradox, this contradiction, face to the utmost in ourselves
> the groping passion of that little girl lost, we can begin to transmute it,
> and the blind anger and bitterness that have repetitiously erupted
> among women trying to build a movement together can be alchemized.
> Before sisterhood, there was the knowledge, transitory, fragmented, per-
> haps, but original and crucial—of mother-and-daughterhood.[21]

Irigaray says that verticality is a dimension that is denied in the
process of becoming a woman in our culture. "The bond between mother and daughter, daughter and mother has to be broken for the daughter to become a woman."[22] This is, notoriously, Freud's position in Lecture 33 of the *Introductory Lectures on Psychoanalysis*, where he made an
absolute truth out of what we now know to be a historically determined
culture datum. "Female genealogy"—this is Irigaray's name for the cultural datum—"must be suppressed in favor of the son-Father relation
and of the idealization of the father and husband as patriarchs."[23]

The lack of symbolic expression for the disparity between mother
and daughter is not only the cause of unhappiness in their relationship,
but it is also cause, as Adrienne Rich senses, of the bitterest conflicts
among women. According to Irigaray, the genealogical link serves to
symbolize what takes place between mother and daughter, allowing us
to overcome the patriarchal regime of lack of differentiation and rivalry between women.[24]

The theme of female genealogies has to do with our present. Its relevance is confirmed by a publication from those years entitled *The
Mothers of Us All* (1982; alluding to the name Gertrude Stein gave
Susan B. Anthony in her play *The Mother of Us All*). The authors of this
publication claim that the introduction of the word *mother* into our
political discourse has revolutionized our relationships with one another and with the world.[25]

Irigaray expresses herself along these lines in a 1984 lecture, "Divine
Women," calling genealogy "our generic incarnation," our incarnation
in the female gender.[26] Of all Irigaray's essays, this is the one I like best.
It has enormous political relevance, although this is not immediately
obvious. She begins by reiterating the idea that a vertical dimension is
necessary for female freedom, and that this dimension is made up of the
genealogical relation and, at the same time, of woman's relation to the
divine. Later, in an essay called "The Universal as Mediation,"[27] Irigaray introduces a distinction between these two reference points, the
divine and the genealogical, a distinction between god and ancestors.
Ancestors, she says, reveal a genealogy, a history, not an infinite.[28] I
think this distinction, however, characterizes the state of male culture
more than women's politics.

"Divine Women" was addressed to an audience of women only. Taking Feuerbach's *The Essence of Christianity* as her starting point, Irigaray
asserts that in order to attain freedom and grow in it, we must imagine
our god, a god "that we should incarnate . . . within us and in our sex:
daughter-woman-mother?"[29] Indeed rebelling against oppression is not
enough to make us free; we must have an end (telos, goal or purpose)
and one or more laws. She concludes that "a *female* god is still to
come."[30]

I do not agree with Irigaray on this last point. Since female freedom
exists, I think this means that the god she speaks of has come. I cannot
linger over the reasons for my disagreement with Luce Irigaray's
thought, and I cannot express them briefly, for I have been nourished
by her thought. I simply mention them, however, since they touch on
the subject at issue. Luce Irigaray interweaves the theme of female
genealogies with that of the relation between man and woman. I recognize and rejoice that the existence of female genealogies is conducive
to freedom, even in the relation between the sexes, but I consider it an
effect, not an end; I assign the dignity of being an end only to female
freedom and whatever is indispensable to attain it.

The theme of female genealogies is placed in a wider setting in the
1986 lecture, "The Universal as Mediation." This essay (which was first
presented at the Sixteenth International Hegel Congress, and has since

been presented several times) is Irigaray's most significant in its philosophical and political commitment. It can be likened to a medieval fresco of the end of the world. In this case not of the end itself, but of a possible transition to a new world. The idea expressed in the title brings
together many of the issues that can be found scattered throughout her
other lectures. According to Irigaray, the limits of our civilization now
are beginning to be acknowledged. It is a civilization incapable of preserving life, dominated by the problems of growth and material production. It is hard to improve it, however, partly because of our rigid
and arbitrary idea of the universal. She proposes an alternative way of
conceiving of the universal: the form of mediation.[31]

For Irigaray the imbalance in our social order derives from the "separation between the genders."[32] This is a historical separation as well,
since an early gynecocratic age was followed by a patriarchal one; consequently, the encounter between the two genders never really took
place. This clarifies the meaning of mediation, which must take place
between the sexes first of all. In addition, we are warned that the theme
of female genealogies will henceforth be considered in relation to the
setting up of an ethical world of men and women together, whereas
before it concerned the world of women-among-themselves.

Irigaray's theoretical and practical commitment to the construction
of an ethical world of women and men together will be unwavering. In
this new framework the theme of female genealogies is enriched in particular by being connected to themes like law, language, and religion,
which are the subjects that Irigaray explores most closely at this time.
Almost all of the essays that followed "The Universal as Mediation"
contain references to female genealogies, evidence that Luce Irigaray
continues to consider them important. She explicitly affirms this
importance when she says, for example, "It is necessary to reinsert into
History the interpretation of the oblivion into which female genealogies have fallen, and to re-establish their economy."[33] Other works
where this is particularly stressed are "A Chance for Life"[34] and "Le
Mystère oublié des généalogies féminines" (The forgotten mystery of
female genealogies),[35] from which the preceding quotation was taken.

In this last-mentioned essay Irigaray raises a question that could lead
to interesting developments. Why, she asks, were female genealogies
destroyed? Her answer is evasively brief: "To establish an *order* that man
needed, but which does *not yet* correspond to that of respect for sexual
difference and its fertility" (my emphasis).[36] It seems as if the writer
wants to attenuate the reality of sexist domination by rationalizing the
past and raising expectations for the future. Irigaray here hypothesizes
that patriarchy eliminated the culture based on female genealogies

through ignorance or incomprehension. Whereas in this essay she says that patriarchy "is based on the theft and violation of the virginity of the daughter and her use for commerce among men,"[37]—referring to the myth of Kore and to Lévi-Strauss's theory of the exchange of women—in the Montreal lecture, where she first spoke of female genealogies, Irigaray asserts that patriarchy was founded on the murder of the mother, which was committed to safeguard the power of the father and the husband.

As I mentioned earlier, these oscillations seem attributable to a contradiction that has not been resolved by women's politics, evident in the paradoxical fact that, in this society that we call patriarchal, sons have a better relationship with the mother than do daughters. Feminism has furnished explanations of this fact, but they are rationalizations, as Adrienne Rich pointed out in the passage quoted above. In any case the fact remains, and the paradox is a flaw at the very roots of our cause. In fact, it can be demonstrated that part of the virulence, the "anger" with which feminists attack male power, is nothing but the displacement of an unresolved aversion toward the mother, an aversion that is latent and ever ready to be directed against themselves or other women, especially against those who embody some aspect of the mother image.

The political value of the theme of female genealogies is related to this contradiction—and to overcoming it. The question arises as to what happens to this value when we pass from the first formulation— to create an ethical order among women—to the more recent one—to create an ethical order of women and men together. Is this value preserved? Lost? Changed?

Luce Irigaray's changing series of interpretations of the image of Antigone offers us an interesting clue to this problem.

Let us briefly review the outlines of the story of Antigone, eponymous heroine of Sophocles' tragedy and the daughter of Oedipus and Jocasta. After first caring for her blind and desperate father, she rebelled against Jocasta's brother, Creon, the tyrant of Thebes. Creon had forbidden the burial of Antigone's brother, after he was killed in an attempt to take his uncle's power. When Antigone buries her brother Creon condemns her to be buried alive in a cave, where she takes her own life and hangs herself.

At first, contrary to the male tradition, Irigaray did not consider Antigone to be a heroic figure. She thought Antigone seemed ambiguous, in a literal sense, that is, discordant and subject to contradictory interpretations, and therefore in need of a female interpretation to free her from her imprisonment inside men's symbolic order. In *An Ethics of Sexual Difference* Irigaray says, "So let me return to the character of

Antigone, though I shall not identify with it. Antigone, the antiwoman, is still a production of a culture that has been written by men alone." But, she adds, she must be released from night, shadow, and stone.[38]

Irigaray had already written about Antigone in the chapter on Hegel in *Speculum*. There Antigone is portrayed as a silent woman, roused to action by the mother's desire, a desire embodied in their brother-son who died in the war. "Thus the sister will strangle herself in order to save at least the mother's son. She will cut off her breath, her voice, her air, blood, life— . . . so that her brother, *her mother's desire*, may have eternal life."[39] In *Ethics*, as well, Antigone symbolizes the imprisonment of woman in a symbolic order that is not her own and the paralysis of the world of women that is a consequence of this. It will be recalled that Irigaray then introduces the principle of the double dimension, vertical and horizontal, of relationships among women, and adds, "If we are not to relive Antigone's fate."[40]

In a lecture in Rotterdam called "Le Genre féminin"/"The Female Gender" (1985),[41] Irigaray resolved Antigone's ambiguity, presenting her as the image of the woman who shows no signs of belonging to her sex or to the mother's genealogy. According to Irigaray, Antigone belongs to the world of men; she is not divine, she does not fulfill her duty as someone "belonging to the female race." She is already at the service of the male god, and of the state. She helps men in their struggles for power; her opposition to the State is more apparent than real.[42] "Antigone is already the desexualized representative of *the other of the same*,"[43] which means, the image of the female made to man's measure.

The Rotterdam lecture preceded and anticipated many aspects of the essay entitled "The Universal as Mediation," but differed from it in not making a synthesis; the emphasis was rather on contradictions. Its one positive point, which is the crux of the discussion, is the concept of belonging to the female gender. Irigaray's view of Antigone—a woman alone who struggles to act, even unto death, in a world of men—follows as a logical consequence.

"The Universal as Mediation" is a turning point from this point of view, too.[44] After this essay, in fact, Irigaray's interpretation of Antigone changes completely. In 1988, before a huge audience of men and women at the Unità Festival, Irigaray praised Antigone unreservedly. Antigone, she said, defended the community (*la convivenza civile*) on several fundamental counts, including respect for the cosmic order and respect for maternal genealogy. Her tragic death can only be blamed on the tyrant who failed to respect the most elementary laws of social order. Antigone's example is worth meditating on today, Irigaray said, and went on to speak of civil rights (the theme of the conference),

which ought to be reflected on again "in the light of Antigone's
truth."[45] She linked the recovery of Antigone with the theme of maternal genealogies, and said that Antigone was the woman whose "faith" in
and "fidelity" to maternal genealogies are punished by death on the
orders of a tyrant who wants to consolidate his political power.

Irigaray asserts that myths are not univocal; they have various versions.[46] Granted, but to this extent? To this extent we could hardly use
them to learn about the past, as she proposes.

However, we must consider that such a radical reinterpretation is
made only in Antigone's case. Hers is an exceptional case. So let us
return to the question we asked previously. What is the effect of the
shift in "The Universal as Mediation" on the theme of female genealogies? Along with this question I would ask another, simpler one: why
does Irigaray's assessment of Antigone change when we pass from the
first context, the ethical order among women, to the second one, the
ethical order of men and women together?

Sophocles' Antigone is a political heroine. The change in Irigaray's
view of her is obviously a sign of a change that has to do with politics.
This change does not directly concern either the theme of female
genealogies or the political practice of relations among women, the
validity of which Irigaray reaffirms, for example, in 1988 when she discusses the linguistic forms that are an obstacle to the feminine discovering a meaning for itself in language. "Another equally necessary solution [is] that of restoring to women female genealogies and women's
communities."[47]

Antigone, on the other hand, is the heroine of political demonstration and witnessing. She does not ask herself if her action will be effective. Irigaray insists on this aspect when she says that Antigone is the
female representative "of the other of the same," that is, a woman made
to man's measure. Woman as man imagines her, says Irigaray, is
deprived of the effectiveness of her woman's being, she is substance
deprived of actuality (quoting an American philosopher[48] who called it
"metaphysical vampirism").[49] To Antigone and her "apparent opposition," Irigaray opposes the female gender that

> according to the order of its ethical duty, struggles with itself, between
> light and shadow, in order to become what it is individually and collec-
> tively. This growth, which is partly polemical, between consciousness
> and unconscious, immediacy and mediations, mother and women, has
> to remain open and infinite for and in the female gender.[50]

There is no trace of this subject of efficacy or effectiveness (the
ancient philosophers spoke of *energeia*) in the praise of Antigone that

- comes later: it is neither attributed to her (as is fidelity to the maternal
- genealogy) nor denied her. Thus ethical action is tacitly detached from
  efficacious action.

It is "The Universal as Mediation," I think, that marks this transition in Irigaray's political thought. It seems as though feminine mediation is not an adequate politics within the horizon of the universal, where women's politics would become witnessing; efficacy at the universal level, then, would be something either produced by the power of men or by men and women together.

But it must be added that when Irigaray was speaking of the efficacy of the female gender, it was not as a reality experienced by herself, but as a missing reality, just as in "Divine Women" she says that the female god is yet to come. As I mentioned before, my position differs from Irigaray's on this point. Therefore what I call a turning point in Irigaray's thought must seem less important from her point of view than from mine. When she turns from the politics of women-among-themselves to a politics of men and women together, she is not abandoning an effectiveness that she has actually experienced; whereas I have experienced the power for change of the practice of the genealogical relation. I must not underestimate this difference.

These considerations bring to mind the most important problem, the enigma of women's hate and ingratitude toward the mother (Melanie Klein worked on this enigma before we did).

The responsibility for this enigma has been attributed to patriarchy by mainstream feminism. To this end it has acted in two ways. There has been an overt operation of *rationalization* so that we say, patriarchy has made slaves of our mothers, thus making them odious to (us) their daughters, who are lovers of freedom. There has also been a less openly admitted, more important operation of *displacement*, whereby negative feelings originally directed against the mother are turned against patriarchy and against man.

Luce Irigaray does not take this path. As she said when speaking of Antigone in 1985 (before the "turning point"), this would be an "apparent opposition" that distracts us from the "possibility of acting in affirmation."[51] Instead she proposes solving the enigma of hate and ingratitude with genealogical practice. Feminist history is an instance of genealogical practice for her. Her first proposal, as I mentioned, had been to celebrate the Eucharist with the mother. Later, she put forward the idea of exhibiting in public places images of the mother and daughter together.

But at a certain point the enigma of hate and ingratitude disappears from Irigaray's work. It is evoked no longer. Her favorite genealogical image becomes the Demeter-Kore couple, which represents the mother-daughter relation characterized by natural harmony and spiritual fruitfulness.

Its disappearance from her work does not mean the enigma is solved. She does not say that it is; if anything, she leads us to believe just the opposite. She simply does not talk about it any longer. At the same time she softens her polemical tone when talking about patriarchy. Her view of patriarchy has not changed, I think. She simply wants to pass over in silence *our* madness—that enigma of hate and ingratitude the ready feminist rage against patriarchy risks evoking, and certainly does evoke, when the listener is an experienced psychoanalyst like Irigaray.

The disappearance of this contradiction, which, more than any other, is an obstacle to women's effective action, allows Irigaray to widen the horizon of our politics and imagine a female presence on a cosmic scale. She is willing to pay for this expansion with a politics that takes the form of witnessing. Thus she modifies her view of Antigone. When her politics took the form of changing women's condition by changing the *mother*-daughter relation, Antigone seemed to be on the wrong track. When the scene expands to include all contradictions except the one that attacks us from inside, then politics takes on the characteristics of direct action and witnessing, as it did for Antigone.

For me the heart of politics remains the genealogical relation as portrayed by Irigaray in the section of "The Female Gender" where she talks about effective action. I think we are witnesses and protagonists of a change that has to do with women's relation to the figure of the mother, and, consequently, with the meaning of sexual difference. Knowing how to love the mother is the basis of our liberation. What we know, on a superficial level, as feminism, is the manifestation, I think, of a change in our civilization on a structural level—that level Braudel calls long-term history.[52] I am not referring to the feminism of rights and equality, but to the movement that has led us to choose to stay among women, to choose to act in accordance with the judgment of our fellow women, to accept the authority of women, and to seek the nourishment of female thought for our minds.[53]

Translated by Patricia Cicogna
Translation revised by Margaret Whitford

NOTES •

1. Irigaray, *Le Temps de la différence*, p. 111.
2. Ibid., p. 122.

3. Luisa Muraro, *Il concetto di genealogia femminile* (Rome: Centro culturale Virginia Woolf, 1988), pp. 24–28.
4. Irigaray, *Sexes and Genealogies*, pp. 7–21/*Sexes et parentés*, pp. 19–33.
5. Aeschylus, *The Eumenides*, lines 658–666.
6. Irigaray, *Le Temps de la différence*, p. 112.
7. Ibid., p. 113.
8. Ibid.
9. Irigaray, *Sexes and Genealogies*, p. 12/*Sexes et parentés*, p. 24.
10. Ibid.
11. Ibid., p. 18/30.
12. Ibid.
13. Ibid., p. 19/31.
14. Ibid., p. 18/31.
15. Ibid., p. 19/31.
16. Ibid., p. 21/33.
17. Cf. Irigaray, *Sexes and Genealogies*, p. 191/*Sexes et parentés*, p. 205; and *Le Temps de la différence*, pp. 27–28.
18. Irigaray, *Sexes and Genealogies*, pp. 25–26/*Sexes et parentés*, pp. 37–38.
19. Cf. Ibid., p. 127/141, note 1.
20. Irigaray, *Ethics*, p. 108/*Ethique*, p. 106.
21. Adrienne Rich, *Of Woman Born*, 10th anniversary ed. (New York: Norton, 1986), pp. 225–226.
22. Irigaray, *Ethics*, p. 108/*Ethique*, p. 106.
23. Ibid.
24. Ibid., pp. 101–104/pp. 100–102.
25. The Milan Women's Bookstore Collective, *Sexual Difference: A Theory of Social-Symbolic Practice*, trans. Patricia Cicogna and Teresa de Lauretis (Bloomington: Indiana University Press, 1990), p. 127ff.
26. Irigaray, *Sexes and Genealogies*, p. 71/*Sexes et parentés*, p. 83.
27. Ibid., pp. 125–149/139–164.
28. Ibid., p. 133/147.
29. Ibid., p. 71/84.
30. Ibid., p. 67/79.
31. Ibid., pp. 128–129/142–143.
32. Ibid., p. 129/143.
33. Irigaray, *Le Temps de la différence*, p. 121.
34. Irigaray, *Sexes and Genealogies*, pp. 183–206/*Sexes et parentés*, pp. 197–222; and *Le Temps de la différence*, pp. 19–52.
35. Irigaray, *Le Temps de la différence*, pp. 101–123.
36. Ibid., p. 120.
37. Ibid., p. 123.
38. Irigaray, *Ethics*, p. 119/*Ethique*, p. 115.
39. Irigaray, *Speculum*, p. 219/272.
40. Irigaray, *Ethics*, p. 108/*Ethique*, p. 106.

41. Irigaray, *Sexes and Genealogies,* pp. 105–123/*Sexes et parentés,* pp. 119–138.

42. Cf. Irigaray, *Sexes and Genealogies,* pp. 110–111/*Sexes et parentés,* pp. 124–125.

43. Ibid., p. 111/125.

44. This essay does not discuss Antigone—Eds.

45. Irigaray, *Le Temps de la différence,* pp. 82–85.

46. Ibid., pp. 106, 112.

47. Ibid., p. 60.

48. The American philosopher quoted is Ti-Grace Atkinson—Eds.

49. Irigaray, *Sexes and Genealogies,* p. 120/*Sexes et parentés,* pp. 134–135.

50. Ibid., p. 120/134.

51. Ibid.

52. Fernand Braudel, "Histoire et sciences sociales: La Longue durée," *Annales E.S.C.* (1958), 4:725–753.

53. When I wrote this paper I hadn't seen Margaret Whitford's "Rereading Irigaray," in Teresa Brennan, ed., *Between Feminism and Psychoanalysis* (London: Routledge, 1989), pp. 106–126, which addresses the issue that concerns me, the mother-daughter relationship.

· *Elizabeth Grosz*
·
·

THE HETERO AND

THE HOMO:

THE SEXUAL

ETHICS OF

LUCE IRIGARAY

Luce Irigaray is often regarded as a theorist and advocate of lesbian politics and sexual relations. Perhaps more than any other French feminist she affirms the necessity of women exploring their sexualities, bodies, and desires through their corporeal and affective relations with other women. Yet to describe her as a lesbian theorist is a misleading description of her interests, if one also takes into account published works other than *Speculum of the Other Woman* and *This Sex Which Is Not One*. Her position is much less straightforward than it seems, and indeed could be described as a theory of the *hetero-sexual* rather than the homo-sexual. Instead of seeing her work as a confirmation of lesbian and gay sexualities, it is important to see the critical distance she maintains from all existing modes of sexual relation. Irigaray considers female homosexuality to be a form of radical rupture in heterosexism and male domination, and, at the same time, believes that all sexual practices represented in our culture, whether "deviant" or "normal," are effects of an underlying phallocentrism that renders women socially and representationally subordinate.

•
•
•   I intend here to discuss Irigaray's view of the relations between the hetero and the homo. I will look, in the first section, at her earlier works, in
which her major concern is to create modes of representation of women
and femininity that resist attempts to define them only in relation to
men. This may explain how and why many readers conceive of Irigaray's
work as a positive espousal of homosexual love between women. In the
second section I will discuss the concept of the homo-sexual in her earlier works, and its strategic position in the context of her work on sexual
difference. This may render ambiguous her notion of the hetero-sexual,
and enable the concept of the homosexual to be rendered both a respite
from yet also a reproduction of the structure of patriarchy. In the third
section I will outline her position up to what might now be understood
as her middle period, particularly *L'Ethique de la différence sexuelle* (*An
Ethics of Sexual Difference*) and *Divine Women*.[1] These and other texts[2]
make explicit her aim of analyzing or articulating structures of exchange
between *sexually different* subjects. In the final section I will look at the
implications of her work for lesbian and feminist theory and politics.

1. Sameness and Difference

Irigaray's early works must be positioned in the context of her reading
and critique of Freudian/Lacanian psychoanalytic theory. Her relation
to it remains extremely significant in all of her works, whether or not
they specifically address psychoanalytic terms and concepts, providing
a paradigm of the ways in which her position is always ambiguous,
always tenuously internal to the discipline or theory she challenges. At
the same time, these works position themselves at those points outside
of the founding terms of theories or knowledges in those places, intolerable to and expelled by them—their vulnerable underbelly.

Irigaray intervenes into psychoanalytic theory at the level of the core
presumptions of Freud and Lacan, presumptions all related to the centrality of the oedipus complex. This complex marks the distinction
between the sexes, repression, and the distinction between consciousness and the unconscious. The oedipal model is a necessary commitment of psychoanalysis as a whole, theory and practice. She remains
ambivalent about the value of psychoanalysis; nevertheless, the problems posed by psychoanalysis are not resolved if one simply abandons
the theory. The problems it raises are symptomatic of a broader social
malaise—the insidious, oppressive functioning of patriarchal power.
Freud's theory at least has the advantage of recognizing and explaining
the continued operations of patriarchal psychosocial relations.

Her dilemma is the same as that facing all feminists working with

psychoanalysis: to reject Freud's work is to reject valuable tools in the
analysis of patriarchy that are extremely useful for effectively transforming it. Yet to accept it is to affirm the inevitability of current sexual roles. Without the luxury of a better or more useful theory, one however is not forced into a de facto acceptance of the theory: there remains
the possibility of a critical reversal or a strategic displacement of its
framework. To displace or deconstruct psychoanalysis is to use it against
itself. To overthrow it provisionally, without competing or alternative
theories, is to use its own "repressed" or disavowed subtext against its
overt pronouncements. If no text is able to be definitively fixed to a stable series of meanings, and always eludes one's rational or conceptual
grasp, the text may be seen as a psychoanalytic "symptom," with a consciousness and an unconscious. The unconscious and consciousness
can be seen as modes of discourse, textual products. This deconstructive gesture, moreover, enables Irigaray to deconstruct Lacan's intervention into Freudian theory as well: if the unconscious is structured like a
language, to and for whom does it speak? To and for what sex? How is
the position of enunciation sexually coded?

In psychoanalysis women are definitionally reduced to a necessary
dependence on men. Women's castration is sociohistorical and significatory rather than anatomical and physiological. It needs to be seen as
changeable, not given. More particularly, this sociolinguistic inscription of women's bodies must be seen as the unspoken condition of the
attribution of men's phallic status: it is only if women's bodies *lack* that
men's bodies can be seen to *have*.

In its male and female variants the oedipal model structures both
sexes according to the libidinal economy modeled on the law of the
same. This is the law of the phallus, the term that renders others capable of comparison or equivalence. To produce the same the law must
ensure that the archaic homosexual bond between mother and daughter is severed in order to subject the daughter to the phallic rule. The
phallus is not, as Lacan implies, a neutral term or signifier organizing
sexual identity per se, but is implicated in forms of male domination
that have reduced women's oppression to an invisible and unspoken
form. The girl must give up the mother in order to submit herself to the
laws of culture and sexual interactions.

> It would certainly be very interesting to raise the question of the "phal-
> lus" and its power in these terms: it would not be the privileged signifi-
> er of the penis or even of power and sexual pleasure were it not to be
> interpreted as *an appropriation of the relation to origin and of the desire for
> and as origin.* The tropism, as well as the rivalry, is in fact between the

- man and his mother. And woman is well and truly castrated from the
- viewpoint of this economy.[3]

While the mother is the corporeal and psychic source of the child's existence, she remains unacknowledged as such, subsumed under the father's name and law. The mother is designated as the "phallic mother" in Freud's representation of her preoedipal position. After the resolution of the oedipus complex (insofar as this is possible), both sexes regard her as castrated, and, consequently, as inferior to the father. The mother is either construed as, in the preoedipal period, phallic or, in the oedipal period, castrated. In both cases she is defined only by the presence or absence of the male term.

The daughter is "trapped" in her relation to the mother, insofar as she is incomplete, castrated, yet the mother is the basis of the daughter's subsequent attachments to the father and other men. Her identificatory model is inadequate, secondary, and subordinate. The daughter can have no viable, autonomous identity insofar as this primal attachment is based on a concept of the mother as phallic/castrated. This primary relation is sacrificed to found her heterosexual attachment to the father.

Irigaray advocates a *tactical homosexuality* modeled on the corporeal relations of the preoedipal daughter to her mother, aimed at exploring, and reclaiming, pleasures, knowledges, bodily contacts that the oedipus complex and repression attempt to eradicate from her consciousness and memory. Irigaray celebrates a concept of femininity that is capable of representing women in more adequate terms than has been possible within patriarchy. She evokes another mode of sexuality, identification, and pleasure than those made available to women in oedipal structures. She advocates a pleasure without distinct identity, boundaries, loss, a similarity with and difference from the other: mother and daughter rewriting their relations in order to affirm a morphology, body, narcissism, and desire that is woman's.

The attachment of mother and daughter, if it can be seen as a relation *between two women*, provides a homosexuality that is both autoerotic and "other"-directed. It provides a model of homosexuality not as a *substitute for* heterosexuality but as its disavowed prerequisite. It makes explicit the intolerable threat of *women's desire* within a culture founded on its denial. Women's identities as women, whether self- or other-defined, and their desires, date from this attachment. Yet it is an identity and desire that cannot be articulated in the discourses and frameworks currently available. Entry into the social systems of representation is possible only on condition that this archaic relation is given up. It remains the unsaid, certainly by women, in the constitutive conditions of patriarchy. Yet, women's submerged desire *can* be articulated, in some way represented, outside of phallic norms.

It makes perfect sense, then, that Irigaray's work could be read as threshold texts in the development of a positive identity, for women in general and lesbians in particular. More forcefully and convincingly than most, she shows the intolerable threat to a phallocentric, heterosexual economy posed by female desire. She affirms a lesbian reexploration of the maternal continent and an active affirmation of the specificities of women's bodies. It would be a mistake, however, to conclude that she wishes to abandon the hetero in favor of the homo. On the contrary, she stresses that the withdrawal from heterosexual commerce is a *provisional* maneuver, one whose function is tactical and temporary, remedial—one step in a long series of struggles necessary to establish an autonomous identity for women. She is quite open about the temporary status she accords lesbianism as it exists today as a political strategy in achieving women's autonomy. She is explicit in claiming that a *prescriptive* homosexuality is as closed to women's desire as any male-centered privilege. The concept of autonomy implies the *right to choose for oneself*, whatever this may entail. It implies women's access to the bodies of other women, but also women's access to men's bodies as well, if they so desire. At the point where she argues most forcefully for a lesbian exploration of women's corporeality, she also continually insists that this is not an attempt to eliminate or even undermine heterosexuality in itself: "Might not the renunciation of heterosexual pleasure correspond once again to the disconnection from power that is traditionally [women's]? Would it not involve a new prison, a new cloister, built of their own accord?"[4]

Her position, then, is far more complex than the lesbian separatism that is sometimes attributed to her. On the contrary, as an advocate of the concept of autonomy and sexual difference, she remains committed to women's "right" to the sexual relations they desire. The question of a sexual "ethics" for women is raised by her as a counter to prevailing moralisms, whether heterosexual (in the broader social context) or homosexual (as sometimes occurs in feminist circles). For her the problem is how to avoid these dichotomous choices—heterosexual or lesbian—without taking the noncommittal path of "bisexuality." Rather, hers is an attempt to undermine the system of binary choices imposed on women by occupying the impossible middle ground between them: new and exploratory forms of homo- and heterosexual intimacy. This implies, at the least, the possibility of women loving each other as women, not as male substitutes, heterosexual relations no longer dom-

.
. inated by the phallus and male desire, and relations between beings who
. recognize and respect the otherness of the other.

2. The Hom(m)osexual and the Homosexual

It is important to distinguish Irigaray's project of the analysis of sexual
difference from the analysis of homosexuality she develops in her writings. The operation of homosexual circuits of amorous exchange need
not coincide with the affirmation of difference—indeed that operation
can be the effect of its profound disavowal. In particular, in certain forms
of male homosexuality, there exists a high degree of contempt and
aggression toward women, including, or especially, directed toward the
mother. In Freud's model there are two quite distinct paths of development for male homosexuality, both of which are governed by the boy's
attempts to resolve the oedipus complex. In the first case the boy refuses the father's demand to give up the mother by refusing (or foreclosing)
the castration threat. As long as the mother can remain phallic in his
image of her, he can forestall recognition of the immense threat to his
narcissism that castration entails. Her phallic status acts as a guarantee of
his own. Grown to manhood, he may seek men on the model of the
phallic mother, men both "feminine" and phallic. Alternately, in the second path of development the boy maintains a passive, "feminine" attitude to the father, symbolically accepting his castration as a precondition
for passive sexual relations with the father or his substitute. Freud
describes this as the "negative oedipus complex." In neither case is there
any acceptance or affirmation of a mode of femininity or maternity
unrelated to the phallus. The phallus remains central, its value is unquestioned, and, as such, there can be no recognition of sexual difference.

Male homosexuality, Irigaray claims, may suffer the stigma of social
oppression, but this is not really because it is a forbidden, intolerable,
or threatening deviation from the norm. On the contrary, the oppression of gay men may well be a consequence of the male homosexual
openly avowing what is in fact implicit, and a social norm, for all patriarchal forms of exchange. The male homosexual says and does what
remains unspoken, a disavowed condition of social functioning. This is
Irigaray's object of investigation in the two texts "Women on the Market" and "Commodities Among Themselves" (both in *This Sex*). Here,
she argues that the whole of our culture is founded on exchanges (of all
kinds) between only men: "Women, signs, commodities, and currency
always pass from one man to another; if it were otherwise, we are told,
the social order would fall back upon the incestuous and exclusively
endogamous ties that would paralyse all commerce."[5]

Such networks of exchange are thus homosexual in nature: they are networks governed and regulated according to a libidinal economy appropriate only to male sexuality. Women are the objects of exchange between male partners. Irigaray has in mind here economic, sexual, and, most particularly, linguistic exchange. The problem of this fundamentally "closeted" dominance of the homosexual within our culture, as far as Irigaray is concerned, is that it accords no position to women as women. This is, once again, made clear in Freud's pronouncements about female homosexuality.

For Freud and in our culture in general, female homosexuality can only be understood on the model, and as an imitation, of the masculine. The female homosexual in Freud's "The Psychogenesis of a Case of Homosexuality in a Woman" (1918)[6] is seen to be under the sway of the "masculinity complex," in which the girl refuses to accept her castrated, secondary, "feminine" status. She desires "her lady" only *as a man would:* "*It is only as a man that the female homosexual can desire a woman who reminds her of a man.* That is why women in homosexual relationships can play the role of mother and child or husband and wife, without distinction."[7]

Freud describes her love object as a displacement of a girl's libidinal attachment to her brother: "Her lady's slender figure, severe beauty and downright manner reminded her of the brother who was a little older than herself."[8] He represents love between women as a love of one woman, mimicking phallic, masculine behavior, for another, who is the fantasized substitution or imitation of a man. Lesbian love as the peculiar twisting of male homosexual desire: a woman, acting like a man, loving another woman who reminds her of her brother!

Irigaray distinguishes forms of homosexuality ordered and sanctioned by phallocentrism from other forms it may take somehow "beyond the phallus" by punning on the interrelations between man (*homme*) and homosexual in the neologism *hom(m)osexual.* The hom(m)osexual order is the order of the phallic appropriation of sexual norms. "Hom(m)osexual" evokes the male dominance, the *homme* of a hom(m)osexual culture, economy, and exchange.

This hom(m)osexuality is the basis of the girl's relation to the phallic/castrated mother, the mother as patriarchal object. The sociocultural system itself is a product of this hom(m)osexuality: "The passage from nature to culture thus amounts to the institution of the reign of hom(m)osexuality. Not in an 'immediate practice,' but in 'social' mediation. From this point on, patriarchal societies must be interpreted as societies functioning in the mode of 'semblance.' "[9]

The logic of the "hom(m)o" is the logic of masculine sameness. This

•
•
•   sameness that is proliferated everywhere and on everyone is the sameness of phallic identity. Within this logic women are reduced to the
position of a mere semblance of difference. Difference is reduced to a
form of *distinction* or opposition. Oppositions always presuppose the
same key term: A and not-A. There is no space within such an economy for the "homo-," the sameness or integrity of *women* as lovers. The
mother and daughter remain inscribed within the structure of the patriarchal family and culture.

The daughter needs to remain in touch, corporeally, linguistically,
and in terms of desire, with her homosexual attachment to the mother,
if she is to create any positive self-representations, productive rather
than rivalrous relations with other women, relations of pleasure, narcissism, and autoeroticism. And even fertile creative relations with men.
She needs to remain in touch with the corporeality and subjectivity that
produced and nurtured her, and to which she remains similar as well as
different. Grounded as the mother/daughter relation must be within
patriarchy—in the law of the father—nevertheless, this provides,
through a psychoanalytic reading, the basis of understanding what is
intolerable to patriarchal operations, even if it is spawned by them.

> What we have to do . . . is to discover our sexual identity, that is, the sin-
> gularity of our auto-eroticism, of our narcissism, the singularity of our
> homosexuality . . . since the first body women relate to, the first love we
> relate to, is a maternal woman's body, women are, always, short of
> renouncing their desire, in an archaic and primal relation to what is
> called homosexuality. . . .
>   Let us also try to discover the singularity of our love for other women.
> What could be called (but I don't like these labels) in lots of inverted com-
> mas "'secondary homosexuality.'" Here I am simply trying to indicate a
> difference between the archaic love for the mother and the love for other
> women-sisters. This love is necessary in order not to remain servants of the
> phallic cult, or the objects of use and exchange between men, rival objects
> on the market, a situation in which we have all been placed.[10]

Her affirmation of lesbianism as practice and lifestyle is tempered by
her understanding of sexual difference. She remains critical of stereotyped forms of lesbianism that appear simply as imitations by women
of roles, mannerisms, gestures, movements, etc., either designated as
men's, or designated by men as women's. Presumably neither so-called
butch nor femme stereotypes provide alternatives to modes of sexual
identity governed by the phallus. By implication the kinds of sexual
relations that can be forged between and as women, outside phallocentric representations, need to be explored, experienced, and analyzed. A
homosexuality between a mother who is neither phallic nor castrated

and a daughter who is also, consequently, unaffected by the patriarchal
ascription of the (presence or absence of the) phallus is yet to be known.
If and when it is, it may form the basis of a homosexual bond between
women that takes only itself as a model. Freud privileges a model based
on the structure of the mother/child or husband/wife relation.
Women's seizure or creation of a sexuality that is theirs may provide the
basis for a very different understanding of female homosexuality, one
no longer modeled on pathology, failure, and victimization—that is, on
masculine values, even if they are expressed by women—but rather on
positive desire and choice for women as women. This is not in any way
to cast aspersions on more thoroughgoing challenges posed by other
forms of lesbianism; but Irigaray does recognize, as many separatists do
not, that insofar as lesbian sexual relations are posited as an alternative
to patriarchal power, they (and all sexual relations here and now), are
implicated in, and not pure from, patriarchy's complex functioning. Irigaray is not searching for a pure position uncontaminated by patriarchal values. This is naive, and involves disavowal of our histories. There
is no position outside its orbit—not in our culture. But there are possibilities of transformation, historical change. It is for this reason that
those recalcitrant "symptoms" of a culture, its excessive "deviations"—
like female homosexuality—may provide models, in their modes of
resistance, to be explored as a challenge to patriarchy.

3. Heterosexuality and Sexual Difference

It is not surprising that many feminists and lesbians read Irigaray as
advocating lesbianism. If this is understood as a self-conscious political
strategy ("political lesbianism"—something many "hard-core" lesbians
find repugnant and profoundly disturbing: there is something, after all,
worrying about having a sexual intimacy with someone for political
rather than sexual reasons!), that is, as provisional and temporary, or
perhaps even metaphorical—along the lines of the "lesbian continuum"
posited by Adrienne Rich—this seems a fair reading. But if it is regarded as an ontological commitment, a fundamental "truth" about
women's desire, then her work has been misread. Irigaray clearly refuses to moralize about the question of whether women *should* engage in
hetero- and homosexual relations. She believes that women individually and collectively must choose for themselves. Her position is an
attempt to move beyond the strictures of patriarchal definitions while
nevertheless recognizing their social and historical force and effects. It
is an attempt to locate the "blind spots" of knowledge—representations
of women and the feminine in phallocentric and patriarchal discours-

•
•
•

es—so as to be able to use, and subvert, these historically dominant discourses, and create new ones more appropriate to the exploration and
articulation of women's identities.

She understands difference as "pure difference"—not between two
independent or positive terms, but as negative differential. The relation
between terms is what establishes the possibility of identity for each.
Saussurian "pure difference" is transposed onto the terrain of the psychological and/or morphological. When one examines the "pure difference" governing the terms of sexual relations, up to now our history has
overwhelmingly reduced one to a variant of the other, thus in effect
obliterating any *relation* between them in favor of a homogeneity, an
absorption of one into the (image of) the other.

Irigaray's commitment to the project of speaking of/as sexual difference entails reexamining this reduction of one sex to the terms of the
other. It entails examining how sexual difference, a difference between
two or more terms, has been reduced to a "relation" between one and
its double, inversion, or counterpart. It entails reasserting the necessity
of *two positions* (not identities) in any relation. In short, it entails a commitment to examining relations of possible exchange between these two
terms. Exchange relations, under a hom(m)osexual commerce, reduce
women to the position of objects of exchange. Irigaray's more recent
works are an attempt to establish models under which the exchanges
engendered by pure difference, that is, "genuine" exchanges between
the sexes, can be understood (this is not unlike Saussure's definition of
linguistic exchange).[11]

This is the aim governing the collection of lectures on ethics, and her
work on the elemental. After reading these works, with their open affirmation of new modes of *heterosexual exchange*, exchanges between sexually different terms, one can see her earlier affirmations of lesbianism
as strategies aimed toward constituting the identity of women and the
feminine so as to position women as terms in relations of difference.
Strategic, perhaps even therapeutic, relations to women, are prerequisite to viable, ongoing relations between the two sexes.

This is an extremely difficult and complex project. It involves the
problem of relations of equivalence, reciprocity, and interaction
between two beings (or groups of beings) who recognize the differences
between them. How can we create relations of exchange between beings
who are different? So far, our exchange relations have been posited on a
fundamental universality or sameness between the agents within the
circuits of exchange, which renders the objects exchanged comparable
or equivalent. If we refuse the phallocentrism of these hitherto pervasive models of economic, social, and sexual exchange and put in their

place models based on a recognition of difference, in what ways will exchange be different? What can be produced from such exchanges between the sexes? In what ways can two sexually different types of being share and produce together? These are among the concerns Irigaray voices in her more recent work.

Although these texts are avowedly concerned with the hetero to the exclusion of the homo, they must at the same time be understood as a continuation of her project of deconstructing phallocentric discourses and systems of representation. The very question of exchange between the sexes must be seen in the context of a cultural and representational system that resolutely presents exchange modeled on relations between one sex, with the other as its object of exchange. It is her attempt to bring the question of sexual difference and women's autonomy to bear on the question of *whose* perspectives economics, anthropology, linguistics, communications, and other forms of knowledge analyzing exchange relations represent. It is her attempt to develop a perspective that speaks woman's point of view as well.

She aims to create some of the theoretical prerequisites for understanding the productivity that may result from the meeting or encounter of two sexually different beings. An understanding of this kind has been made difficult if not impossible in a system where women have no time and space. In an intellectual tradition that posits man, in the guise of the Divine lawgiver, constituting space as what governs the exterior of the subject and time as his interior,[12] woman has no space and time of her own by which to occupy position(s) within culture and knowledge. This in turn implies reconceptualizing the coefficients of space (matter-form) and time (interval-intermediary) so that they can include women's specificity:

> The transition to a new age requires a change in our perception and conception of *space-time*, the *inhabiting of places*, and of *containers*, or *envelopes of identity*. It assumes and entails an evolution or a transformation of forms, of the relations of *matter* and *form* and of the interval *between*: the trilogy of the constitution of place. Each age inscribes a limit to this trinitary configuration: *matter, form, interval*, or *power* [*puissance*], *act, intermediary-interval.* (p. 7–8/p. 15)

In *Ethics* she considers the problematic of space-time, hitherto represented patriarchally, within the framework of the question of sexual difference. If space and time are considered modes of male autorepresentation, Irigaray seeks out what is repressed or unacknowledged, yet necessary for the space-time problematic to function: its residues or remains (*les restes*), the interval between them. She considers this a "dynamic reserve," a space-time needed to mediate between space and time. While Western culture, until the modern era, represented this interval by God—for it is God who creates space and time in the world, according to the history of philosophy—she names this enigmatic economy of the interval "desire":

> *Desire* occupies or designates the place of the *interval*. . . . Desire demands a sense of attraction: a change in the interval, the displacement of the subject or of the object in their relations of nearness or distance. . . .
>
> Our age will have failed to realize the full dynamic reserve signified by desire if it is referred back to the economy of the *interval*, if it is situated in the attractions, tensions, and actions ocurring between *form* and *matter*, but also in the *remainder* that subsists after each creation or work, *between* what has already been identified and what has still to be identified, and so on.   (p. 8/pp. 15–16)

Woman has traditionally taken on the role of space or place for man, background, context, setting, or location against which he can distinguish his autonomous identity. As mother, she is corporeal *horizon* for the boy's identity: the space which he must abandon as a primal "home," a territory *not* or *no longer* his to explore or conquer. Insofar as she remains only in the position of horizon for man, she will have no place of her own. This excision of maternal and feminine space has the effect of leaving women's bodies unrepresented, or represented only as weakness, disability, or lack. Not granted positions from which to speak or write as women, and lacking representations in which to speak desire, women's desire cannot be said or satisfied. In making woman the condition of his own ability to be located in space, positioned as a speaking subject and able to represent and act out his desires, man makes her into the unlimited horizon of his existence.

Only when women take (up) a space and a time that are capable of mapping their unique morphologies, desires, and discourses can there be an encounter between, or touching of, the two sexes. Until then, we exist within a hom(m)osexuality that regards women only as objects, not partners, and that persecutes those (homosexuals) who make explicit and perhaps retain the potential to subvert phallocentric sexual circuits. The liberation from persecution and oppression for homosexual men, at least for those who are prepared to relinquish some of their investments in phallic performance, can in this way strategically relate to women's struggles for liberation from male domination and definition. Both, although in very different ways, pay for the cost of heterosexual, male-dominated social organization with the loss of the pleasures of the materiality of their whole bodies, not to mention their social misrepresentation and scapegoating.

(The AIDS crisis provides a perfect metaphor for a pervasive social conception of the plaguelike contaminatory effects of perverse sexual practices and proclivities of homosexuals and women—a sure index of straight men's conception of sexuality, their own included.)

When women have a place or space in which to live their bodies, sexualities, and identities, the false duality or symmetry of phallic domination—where woman is seen as man's negative double, modeled on an *economy of the same*—can be shattered. When women can represent themselves, and the world, from the perspectives or spaces of women, the two sexes may be able to encounter each other: "To do this requires time. Perhaps we are passing through an era when *time must redeploy space?* . . . A remaking of immanence and transcendence, notably through this *threshold* which has never been examined as such: the female sex" (p. 18/p. 24).

In place of the hostility and contempt with which women's bodies and desires are held in patriarchy, Irigaray would wish to position a Cartesian concept of wonder, astonishment, admiration: *"When the first encounter with some object surprises us and we judge it to be new, or very different from what we supposed that it ought to be, that causes us to wonder and be surprised"* (p. 13/p. 20). Irigaray's texts are thus directed toward establishing a conceptual system in which women as well as men can be represented as distinct, separate, different beings. When such beings accept and respect their own and their partner's specific features, their meeting will be marked by this wonder and surprise. When the two sexes, as autonomous categories—reciprocally positioned—encounter each other, each must marvel and be surprised at the other's difference. It is a wonder that means that "the two sexes [are] unable to be substituted, one for the other, in the status of their difference" (p. 13/p. 21). Each is awed by the other's irreducible difference; each may be able to give to or to take from the other in the recognition of what each specifically has to offer. Neither a universalism or sameness nor an opposition or otherness is capable of representing the *awesome* productivity of the meeting of the two sexes. This productivity or fecundity, usually represented in the form of the child, has yet to be thought.

In an interview Irigaray spells out some of the positive possibilities of this encounter:

> I think that man and woman is the most mysterious and creative couple. That isn't to say that other couples may not have a lot in them, but that man and woman is the most mysterious and creative. . . .
>
> What I regret is that our society operates too much in alternatives. Either you love a man or a woman. . . . On the basis of some texts peo-

•
•
•

ple say that I only love women. And sometimes I'm accused of loving
men. Why does society pose that alternative? I believe that you can love
the difference, but only if you're also able to love those who are the same
as yourself.[13]

She does not make it clear whether she believes that an encounter
between two subjects of the same sex also contains the potential for this
immense creativity. This omission has provoked justified anxiety on the
part of gay and lesbian theorists for its refusal to accord a place to gay
and lesbian relations, as it were, beyond the phallus.

4. The Hetero and the Homo

If Irigaray's recent texts advocate the creative, mysterious interchange
between woman and man, this does not imply that her work is irrelevant to gay and lesbian politics. These texts problematize our culture's
understanding of *both* homosexuality and heterosexuality in their present forms. Sexual relations between women or between men are both
implicated in the phallocentrism involved in all discourse, representation, and desire. To this extent they offer no alternative, no outside, to
phallocentrism. This is not to say that political struggles waged over the
right to "freedom of sexual choice" have unsuccessfully challenged male
and heterosexist domination. Neither (male) homosexuality or heterosexuality, nor lesbianism modeled on these relations, is able to focus on
the question of whose models these are, and whose positions they are.
All, in short, represent the primacy of a sexuality conceived in phallic
terms. This list, however, is by no means exhaustive; there still remains
the possibility of both heterosexual and homosexual relations based on
an acceptance and acknowledgment of women's pleasure.

Both men and women are judged according to norms appropriate
only to men. Irigaray's critique of phallocentrism, and her commitment
to the construction of a positive, autonomous identity for women, may
enable lesbians, and those male homosexuals prepared to put at risk
their privileged relation to the phallus, to reexamine and transform
their own practices and desires to develop different relations, models,
practices—to think and perform their desires. Each sex must reclaim its
own body and identity, its place and perfection for itself. In this process
homosexuality is clearly instrumental in, and a necessary part of, the
exploration of one's autoeroticism and narcissism—and particularly in
the exploration of relations of sexual reciprocity. Yet if these practices
are wholeheartedly and uncritically accepted as revolutionary, subversive, or socially provocative, they are also complicit in the maintenance
of men's privileged right to speak for women.

The exploration by women of their (lost) maternal relations, their connections to the bodies and lives of other women, is thus a kind of counterforce or check against women's subsumption under the father's phallus and law. Irigaray is not prescribing what women ought to do. She posits homosexuality—a homosexuality that may or may not involve sexual intimacy—as a political and personal necessity insofar as women are committed to challenging their social definitions. This implies that women, whether hetero- or homosexual, need to examine their sexual histories and desires: homo- and heterosexual orientations are the consequence of women's lives, histories, and the psychic meanings associated with them. If these are all problematized, it is no longer clear what women's various object choices would be. Neither heterosexual nor homosexual love objects are primordial, natural, innate, or given. Both heterosexual and homosexual women are produced by and in a history of woman hatred. What occurs as a result of sexualities that are not posited as adversaries (in heterosexual otherness) or counterparts (in homosexual sameness) remains an open possibility. Irigaray's critique of phallocentrism is a challenge to the hom(m)osexual reduction of woman to a sexual sameness with men. She introduces a *hetero* (= other) sexuality, a sexuality different from its phallic homo (= same) sexual definition. In this sense the female homosexual's—the daughter's—attachments to the mother enable a heterosexuality, a sexuality or sexualities other than, different from, men's, to be possible. And the heterosexual prescription of women's destiny as the material, emotional, and sexual supports for men will be opened up to the intervention of what is unexpressed and disowned—women's specificity. It is this that will provoke wonder, astonishment.

NOTES •

This is a slightly modified version of a paper first published in Gay Information: Journal of Gay Studies *(1987), 17–18:37–44.*

1. Her earlier works included *Speculum* and *This Sex*, the middle period, her works on the elemental and the divine, and the later texts are those centered on linguistics and language.
2. See also *Marine Lover of Friedrich Nietzsche, Elemental Passions, L'Oubli de l'air* (The forgetting of air), *La Croyance même* ("Belief Itself"), "Où et comment habiter?" (Where and how to live?), and "An Interview with Luce Irigaray ["For Centures We've Been Living in the Mother-Son Relation . . . "]."

3. Irigaray, *Speculum*, pp. 33/35–36.
4. Irigaray, *This Sex*, p. 32–33/ *Ce Sexe*, p. 31.
5. Ibid., p. 192/189.
6. Sigmund Freud, "The Psychogenesis of a Case of Homosexuality in a Woman," in James Strachey, ed. and trans., *The Standard Edition of the Complete Psychological Works of Sigmund Freud*, 24 vols. (London: Hogarth Press, 1955) 18:154. Hereafter SE.
7. Irigaray, *This Sex*, p. 194/ *Ce Sexe*, pp. 190–191; emphasis added.
8. Freud, "Psychogenesis," p. 156.
9. Irigaray, *This Sex*, p. 171/ *Ce Sexe*, p. 168.
10. *Le corps-à-corps avec la mère*, pp. 30–31. For a slightly different version, see *Sexes and Genealogies*, pp. 19–20/ *Sexes et parentès*, pp. 31–32.
11. Ferdinand de Saussure, *The Course in General Linguistics* (London: Pantheon Press, 1974).
12. Irigaray, *Ethics*, p. 7/ *Ethique*, p. 15. All further parenthetical references in this chapter refer to this work.
13. Irigaray, "An Interview with Luce Irigaray," pp. 199–201.

· *Gail M. Schwab*

MOTHER'S BODY,

FATHER'S TONGUE:

MEDIATION AND THE

SYMBOLIC ORDER

In postmodern psychoanalytic theory language and subjectivity have been the realms of the masculine. As feminists we knew we were in trouble when the only signifier with privilege was labeled the phallus. Lacan, who can hardly be said to have acted out of naïveté, did not call the privileged signifier *x*, or *y*, or Fred; as Jane Gallop points out, "Phallus/Penis, same difference"[1]—despite all affirmations to the contrary. Whether we are Lacanians or anti-Lacanians, our imaginary has come to relate the cultural order to the male body. It is virtually impossible to separate the phallus from the penis.[a] Theorizing women's exile in discourse has been a sticky problem for all postmodern feminists, and our struggles with the symbolic order owe a particular debt to Julia Kristeva and to Luce Irigaray. For this reason I hope to create a space for a continuum structurally linking these two thinkers, who are often paradoxically either lumped together in some sort of supposedly homogeneous category, "French theory," or else treated as a binary pair, one valorized, the other denigrated, thus canceling each other out. The work of both Kristeva and Irigaray has led us to examine the rela-

.
: tionship of the symbolic order, Father's Tongue, to identity and subjec-
: tivity, through the preoedipal attachment to the mother, Mother's Body.

Julia Kristeva: Is There Life Before Oedipus?

Preoedipal Triangles

Despite Kristeva's in many ways excessively orthodox adherence to the principles and praxis of Freudian psychoanalysis, she has consistently brought both theory and empirical evidence gained in her day-to-day dealings with patients to bear on what I might call the "pressure points" of Freudian and Lacanian theory—those areas most sharply in need of development, nuancing, or clarification. For example, it was Kristeva who thought out the "thetic phase" as a transitional moment, thus

---

[a] "The subject that knows cannot be separated from the subject that can mistake the phallus for a penis (with its 'turgidity' and its fluids that participate in 'generation'). After all even . . . the good guys know something rather equivocal" (Jane Gallop, *Reading Lacan* [Ithaca: Cornell University Press, 1985], p. 156). Meaning that even the "best" of us, that is, those of us who read Lacan and know that the phallus is not a penis, only "know" something ambiguous.

That the phallus is *not just* the penis is obvious for me. However, claims for its "neutrality," like those of Ellie Ragland-Sullivan, are far more difficult to accept (Ellie Ragland-Sullivan, *Jacques Lacan and the Philosophy of Psychoanalysis* [Urbana: University of Illinois Press, 1986], p. 273). Readers of Irigaray have come to mistrust "neutrality," knowing that its smooth surface is actually the mirror of masculinity.

Elizabeth Grosz writes, "In spite of Lacan's claims, the phallus is not a 'neutral' term functioning equally for both sexes, positioning them both in the symbolic order. As the word suggests, it is a term privileging masculinity, or rather, the penis" (Elizabeth Grosz, *Jacques Lacan: A Feminist Introduction* [New York and London: Routledge, 1990], p. 122). Grosz articulates what I believe is the "gut" position of many feminists, while providing a sound philosophical argument in support. She writes of the phallic signifier: "In relations governed by pure difference, *each* term is defined by all the others; there can be no privileged term which somehow dispenses with its (constitutive) structuring and value in relations to other terms. Distinctions, binary oppositions, are relations based on one rather than many terms, the one term generating a non-reciprocal definition of the other as its negative" (ibid., p. 124). So much for the "neutrality" of the phallus.

This debate is far too extensive for me to mention the positions of all critics. I would note, for those drawn to conservative, "no-nonsense" arguments based on classical logic, Patrick Hogan's point by point refutation of Lacan's position on phallic privilege. Hogan is a formidable reader of Lacan. Unfortunately a large part of his article is based on outdated and regressive readings of Irigaray (Patrick Hogan, *The Politics of Interpretation* [New York: Oxford University Press, 1990], pp. 108–110.)

fleshing out the rather abstract rupture between the imaginary and the
symbolic, and stressing the developmental aspect of movement into the
symbolic order. And it was of course Kristeva who targeted the preoedipal mother-child relation as an area for particular exploration, and
"discovered" there the semiotic, the presymbolic foundation of language in the rhythms, sensations, and spasms of infantile experience.[2]

Since Kristeva's work on the semiotic is well-known, and since much
fine critical work has been done on the semiotic disposition,[3] I do not
intend to re-present the principles here. It is important to point out,
however, that many feminists have come to criticize Kristeva's theory of
the semiotic. Elizabeth Grosz shows how the semiotic might almost
come to be read as just another phallic privilege. According to Kristeva
it is only certain males, to be precise avant-garde artists like Joyce, Mallarmé, Lautréamont, and Céline, who are fully able to recuperate the
semiotic through the symbolic. As men they have a masterful grasp on
the symbolic, a grasp that ultimately eludes women, who have "never
fully resolved their oedipus complex," and who are consequently unable
to use the symbolic for access to the maternal semiotic.[4] Truly a vicious
circle . . . Judith Butler's deconstruction of the semiotic is even more
radical. She shows how the "vicious circle" lies at the heart of Kristeva's
thought, and that the semiotic itself, far from being the expression of a
lost feminine maternal, is a product of the symbolic, of the discourse of
the law. Butler writes: "Kristeva, safeguarding that law of a bio-logical-
ly necessitated maternity as a subversive operation that preexists the
paternal law itself, aids in the systematic production of its invisibility
and, consequently, the illusion of its inevitability."[5]

Lacan ironically recommended that women look beyond the phallus
for another jouissance,[b] and I would argue that despite this ambiguity,
or even contradiction, we have observed in Kristeva's thought, her theorization of the semiotic was the first step toward language's liberation
from the power of the phallus. She demonstrated quite clearly that the
symbolic order does not spring fully formed from the—head—of Zeus.
Just as repression could not function without a prior structure of repression,[6] phallic difference could not come into play without an anticipatory structure. Distinctions and differences, discretenesses, can be
traced back to rhythms, to a digital-type encoding of needs and partial
gratifications, ultimately making "castration" and the resolution of the
oedipus complex possible. Positioning in sexual difference, having or
not having the penis, might be thought as another digital code overlay-
ing the earlier semiotic pulsing rhythms.

The concept of prephallic difference is central to Kristeva's theories
of primary narcissism and of the abject. As her psychoanalytic work has

led her to the love relation as the source of psychic stability, and to the transference as a paradigm for all love relations, Kristeva has come increasingly to focus on primary narcissism. She writes:

> Freud has described the One with whom I fulfill the identification (this "most primitive aspect of affective binding to an object") as a father. . . . He made it clear that this father is a "father of individual pre-history." A strange father if ever there was one, since for Freud, because there is no awareness of sexual dif-ference during that period (more accurately: with-in that disposition), such a "father" is the same as "both parents."[7]

The irruption of this father of individual prehistory, or imaginary father, into the premirror stage mother-child "dyad" creates a ternary structure that anticipates the oedipal triangle.[8] In other words, the structure of discursive subjectivity, the positioning of the individual in the signifying chain of the symbolic, identity itself—that "symbolic matrix sheltering emptiness"[9]—are shaken loose from absolute dependence upon castration and the phallus. Indeed, Kristeva even calls the relation to the imaginary father the "primer of the symbolic function,"[10] and relates it directly to "the bar separating signifier from signified" and "the arbitrariness of the sign," as well as to the "gaping of the mirror."[11] The acquisition of language and of identity both depend on the structures put in place during the individual's "pre-history," prior even to the mirror stage.

The imaginary father, like his symbolic counterpart, is not necessar-

---

[b] Ragland-Sullivan, *Jacques Lacan*, p. 269. While I admire Ellie Ragland-Sullivan's work on Lacan, and am in fact highly indebted to it, I find certain aspects of her final chapter, "Beyond the Phallus?" very troubling, notably her interpretation of Irigaray. It is based on inadequate readings and common misconceptions of the early eighties. Ragland-Sullivan, who understands that the "pressing global need to change the social, linguistic order depends, ultimately, on the need to restructure the myths attached to the humble experiences that create the human subject as a structure of Desire and Law" (p. 307), does not seem to grasp that this vast enterprise is Irigaray's own, and sees her work as some sort of biologically based throwback. I would speculate that this "blind spot" is due to Ragland-Sullivan's devotion to "getting Lacan 'right' " (p. 275), a goal I would call into question as unrealizable, and whose realization would be undesirable in any case. Ragland-Sullivan's own multivalent, diverse, and ultimately open interpretations of Lacan's "beyond the phallus" show that Lacan cannot be "got right" in any totalizing sense. Irigaray's critiques of Lacan all focus on highly problematical aspects of his thought, and have been and continue to be extremely useful and important for feminists. If Irigaray doesn't "get Lacan right," she certainly comes close to the mark on many points. I wonder if "getting Lacan right" does not really mean "making Lacan right," or at least "all right" for feminists.

ily the child's father, or even a man. "He" is rather a composite of both
parents or a

> coagulation of the mother and her desire. The imaginary father would
> thus be the indication that the mother is not complete but that she
> wants . . . Who? What? The question has no answer other than the one
> that uncovers a narcissistic emptiness; "At any rate, not I." Freud's
> famous "What does a woman want" is perhaps only the echo of the more
> fundamental "What does a mother want?" It runs up against the same
> impossibility, bordered on one side by the imaginary father, on the other
> by a "not I". And it is out of this "not I" . . . that an Ego painfully
> attempts to come into being . . . [12]

The imaginary father is then some object of desire for the mother,
apart from the child, signifying already prior to the mirror stage a limit
to union with the mother—in effect the incest taboo—and an "imaginary castration." That this preoedipal ternary structure is indeed constitutive of subjectivity can be shown by the pathology of its failure.

> If the mother clings to her offspring, laying on it the request that origi-
> nates in her own request as confused neotenic and hysteric in want of
> love, the chances are that neither love nor psychic life will ever hatch
> from such an egg. . . . Without the maternal "diversion" towards a Third
> Party, the bodily exchange is abjection or devouring; the eventual schiz-
> ophrene, whether phobic or borderline, will keep its hot-iron brand
> against which his only recourse will be hatred.[c]

While the borderline patient, the victim of such abjection, does not
suffer the psychotic foreclosure on the symbolic,[d] his or her relationship
to the symbolic will be painful and symptomatic. Abjection induces a
consistent detachment from and alienation in language, often used flu-
ently for all that, but functioning as a screen over nothingness, where
no subjectivity has come into being. The borderline patient's language

> is often abstract, made up of stereotypes that are bound to seem cul-
> tured; he aims at precision, indulges in self-examination, in meticulous
> comprehension, which easily brings to mind obsessional discourse. But

---

[c] Kristeva, "Freud and Love," p. 251. J. Laplanche and J.-B. Pontalis do not define
neotenic in *The Language of Psychoanalysis* (trans. Donald Nicholson-Smith [New
York: Norton, 1973]), so it is probably safe to assume that the term is something
of a "Kristevism." A "neotenic" exhibits the property of "neoteny," which Random
House defines as a "slowing of the rate of development with the consequent retention in adulthood of a feature or features that appeared in an earlier phase in the
life cycle," and Webster as "the retention of some larval or immature characteristics in adulthood." The "confused neotenic in want of love" would be the mother
who demands that her child fulfill her narcissistic need for love.

•
•
•

there is more to it than that. That shell of ultra-protected signifier keeps breaking up to the point of desemantization, to the point of reverberating only as notes, music, "pure signifier" to be reparcelled out and resemanticized anew. . . . With the borderline patient, sense does not emerge out of non-sense, metaphorical or witty though it may be. On the contrary non-sense runs through signs and sense, and the resulting manipulation of words is not an intellectual play but, without any laughter, a desperate attempt to hold on to the ultimate obstacles of a pure signifier. . . . It is a frantic attempt made by a subject threatened with sinking into the Void.[13]

Keeping Hold of the Phallus

Kristeva effectively moved the basis of the symbolic order back into the prephallic disposition, thereby inaugurating a liberation from absolute phallic domination. It would be a mistake, however, or at least overly simplistic to view this liberating enterprise as part of a feminist project. Kristeva's theorization of women, female sexuality, and motherhood are highly complex, and ambivalent. In Kristeva's thought, even though the preoedipal relation to the mother is more thoroughly explored and theorized than it had been by either Freud or Lacan, and even though the complex relationships of primary narcissism emerge from this explo-

---

[d] Laplanche and Pontalis define "foreclosure" as a "defense mechanism specific to psychosis" (Language of Psychoanalysis, p. 167), explaining that "foreclosure consists in not symbolizing what ought to be symbolized (castration): it is a symbolic abolition' " (p. 168).

For further clarification: Ragland-Sullivan writes that "the unconscious mechanism behind psychosis points to difficulties in learning to count to two. A foreclosure (*Verwerfung*), as distinct from a denial (*Verneinung*), of castration has occurred. . . . By rejecting the psychic split from the (m)other, the psychotic personality retains a sense of self-identity: a lack of lack (Desire). But the price paid is an incapacity to function in the Symbolic realm of displacement and substitutions" (*Jacques Lacan*, pp. 156–157).

For a complete work-up on foreclosure, which has the advantage of being very clear, see Michael Walsh, "Reading the Real in the Seminar on the Psychoses," in Patrick Hogan and Lalita Pandit, eds., *Criticism and Lacan: Essays and Dialogue on Language, Structure, and the Unconscious* (Athens: University of Georgia Press, 1990), pp. 64–83. Walsh writes of "foreclosure," or "*Verwerfung*": "[It] is a term deployed by Freud in his discussion of the Wolf Man's rejection of castration, and Lacan makes much of the point that this rejection passes beyond mere repression, treating castration as if it did not exist. . . . Lacan uses *Verwerfung* principally to denote the exclusion of fundamental signifiers from the Symbolic ordering of the Subject, and ultimately develops the term into the essential mechanism in the functioning of psychosis and the key to its understanding" (p. 73).

ration as essential to the development of subjectivity, the female body in its specificity is, one might say, repressed out of this articulation. So that finally, despite the newly established importance of the preoedipal *relation* to the mother, Mother's Body remains alienated from/in Father's Tongue. The Kristevan mother is the "phallic" mother. Elizabeth Grosz writes that " 'she' is thus the consequence of a *masculine* fantasy of maternity, rather than women's lived experience of maternity."[14] I would nuance this statement by noting, as Kristeva does, that the fantasy is not strictly a masculine one, but is cherished more generally by both men and women.[15] However, I agree with Grosz to the very large extent that the phallic mother is not a woman, or a body at all, but the image of an all-powerful completeness, the phantasmal recreation of the memory of the relationship of primary narcissism.

In the hauntingly beautiful "Stabat Mater" Kristeva tries to come to terms with this problem, which she herself acknowledges, even if only as a symptom of a regressive culture. She attempts to theorize the ideal of virginal maternity, as it exists in Western civilization, in "Stabat Mater" 's "phenotextual" development, while allowing some of the repressed lived experience of actual motherhood, her own and her memories of her mother's, to resurface through the semiotic rhythms of the deliberately offset "genotext."[e] While Kristeva has always predicated the difficulty for a woman, indeed the inevitable suffering and/or danger of psychosis, of trying to access the semiotic[16] through textual means, or artistic practice, rather than through motherhood alone, she would seem to be attempting precisely that in "Stabat Mater." So that, at least theoretically, what we read in the poetic part of the text is the recuperation, through semiotic representations, of an actual woman's experience of maternity. Ironically however, and I do not doubt that Kristeva herself was well aware of this irony, the semiotic subtext has a troubling way of confirming or even of illustrating the symbolic analysis of the image of the Virgin Mary. Thus, despite poetic representations of the mother's own sexuality,[17] of her suffering in labor and childbirth,[18] of her ambivalent feelings and the conflicts dividing her soul in child rearing,[19] the "repressed semiotic" of "Stabat Mater" resembles nothing so much as the "Madonna-ism," and the "*Mater Dolorosa*-hood" discussed in the phenotext. It would be difficult to find a more telling illustration of Judith Butler's claim that the semiotic is ultimately determined by the law of the symbolic.[f]

---

[e] The Kristevan terms phenotext/genotext are well known, and can be said to correspond roughly to "symbolic/semiotic." For a detailed explanation see "Revolution in Poetic Language" in Moi, *The Kristeva Reader*, in particular, pp. 20–123.

[f] See note e above.

Kristeva's poetically figured relationship to her baby son could even exemplify the Western tendency to overidealize the mother-son relation. Writes Kristeva:

> The lowered head of the mother before her son [Kristeva refers here to the iconography of the Virgin Mother who kneels down before the Christ child] is accompanied by the immeasurable pride of the one who knows she is also his wife and daughter. . . . Contrasted with the love that binds a mother to her son, all other "human relationships" burst like blatant shams.[20]

As daughters, and as mothers of daughters we may well wonder about that . . .

In fact, all relations between women, among women, are highly problematic in Kristevan theory. Daughters and mothers can "re-establish the contact," lost when the daughter entered the symbolic order, only through the daughter's own subsequent experience of motherhood.[21] In between is a "no woman's land" of hostility and conflict. The ambivalent complexities of this mother-daughter relation are played out and replayed in all women's relationships to each other. Although women among themselves, a "community of dolphins," experience a certain ease in nonverbal communication, about which Kristeva waxes rather lyrical,[g] their contacts with each other are in no way facilitated by this "semiotic style" of relating. Their relationships, according to Kristeva, harden into, at best, a contemptuous indifference, or, at worst, a deadly rivalry.

> Women doubtless reproduce among themselves the strange gamut of body relationships with their own mothers. Complicity in the unspoken, connivance of the inexpressible, of a wink, a tone of voice, a gesture, a tinge, a scent. . . . The community of women is a community of dolphins. Conversely, when the other woman posits herself as such, that is, as singular and inevitably in opposition . . . either, not wanting to experience her, I ignore her and, "alone of my sex," I turn my back on her in friendly fashion. It is a hatred that, lacking a recipient worthy enough of its power, changes to unconcerned complacency. Or else, outraged by her own stubbornness, by that other's belief that she is singular, I unrelentingly let go at her claim to address me and find respite only in the eternal return of power strokes, bursts of hatred.[22]

Kristeva's description of intrasexual female relations resembles Luce Irigaray's analysis of female relations under patriarchy in "Women on the

---

[g] Dolphins indeed! The image is seductive, but underlines a childish playfulness all too often considered to be "typical" of women.

Market" and "Commodities Among Themselves."[23] Nevertheless, ironically once again, this long quotation from the semiotic subtext of "Stabat Mater" functions as an illustration very nearly validating patriarchal images of maternity. Kristeva comes very close, dangerously close it seems to me, to concluding that Christianity, with its maternal virginity, represents a legitimate attempt to control, to sublimate, those impossible relations among women, so colored by violence and paranoia.[24] What is lacking in Kristeva's analysis is that which becomes clear in Irigaray's—these vitiated female relationships have as much, if not more, to do with the social and economic conditions of patriarchy as with any particular daughter's problems with her own mother—her "oedipus complex."

Kristeva staunchly maintains traditional psychoanalytic readings and interpretations of female sexuality as the "mirror image" of male sexuality, whose founding concepts are, precisely, "castration" and the oedipus complex.[25] While it is true that she "nuances" Freud with Ernest Jones,[h] and with Lacan,[i] there is no effort on her part to get beyond the mirror image, or to elaborate a sexual identity based on female parameters.[26] Kristeva has in fact characterized the search for feminine sexual identity as metaphysical and essentialistic. "The very dichotomy man/woman as an opposition between two rival entities may be understood as belonging to *metaphysics*. What can 'identity,' even 'sexual identity,' mean in a new theoretical and scientific space where the very notion of identity is challenged?"[27] Without trying to understand fully what feminists like Irigaray are doing, she simply dismisses them, in an anonymous mass, as regressive, not recognizing that getting beyond the "looking glass" does not mean searching for a biologically based predetermined female essence but rather the opening-up of a discursive space

---

[h] Kristeva uses Jones's concept of "aphanisis," rather than Freudian castration. She defines aphanisis as "the fear of losing the possibility of *jouissance*" ("About Chinese Women," in Moi, *The Kristeva Reader*, p. 150). Laplanche and Pontalis define it as "the disappearance of sexual desire," and write,

> Jones evokes the notion of aphanisis in the context of his enquiries into feminine sexuality. Whereas Freud had centered the development of the little girl—just like the little boy—on the castration complex and the predominance of the phallus, Jones attempts to describe the girl's development in more specific terms, laying the stress on a sexuality that has its own aims and activity from the outset. For Jones, therefore, the common denominator in the sexuality of the boy and the girl has to be sought at a more fundamental level than the castration complex, that level being the fear of aphanisis. . . . According to Jones aphanisis is the object, in both sexes, of a fear more profound than the fear of castration. (*Language of Psychoanalysis*, p. 40)

that would allow for the creation of a subjectivity (or for subjectivities) capable of expressing a sexuality or sexualities on its/their own terms. I would once again attribute Kristeva's lack of understanding of this project to her investment (overinvestment?) in psychoanalysis. Kristeva has up to now been unable or perhaps more precisely unwilling to radically refound her thought, and so it has remained quite orthodoxically psychoanalytic. It is as if the discovery of psychoanalysis, which came to replace her earlier Althusserian Marxist political position, satisfied a particular personal need; indeed certain of her writings of the eighties, "Psychoanalysis and the Polis" or *Psychoanalysis and Faith*, for example, are passionate apologies, sometimes quite aggressive in tone,[28] for this entrenched position of hers, of which feminists, particularly Anglo-American feminists, have generally been critical.

It is safe to say that, on the whole, Kristeva's relationship to feminism is a difficult one.[j] For Kristeva feminism is negative, a protest or a struggle, and unproductive, holding no promise of a new social order. It is, at best, "but a *moment* in the thought of that anthropomorphic identity which currently blocks the horizon of the discursive and scientific adventure of our species."[29] While playing down the subversive potential of feminism, Kristeva has consistently extolled and overidealized the revolutionary charge of avant-garde artistic and signifying practice. For Kristeva the promise of a new social order is to be found in the art of the avant-garde, where *all* identities are destroyed.[30] The "revolution" for Kristeva is truly in poetic language.[k] Ultimately, however, how much promise of a new social order does one find in Mallarmé, or in Céline—however great the appeal of their literary power might be?

---

[i] Faithful to a certain biblical tradition, Freud saw the fear of castration as the essential moment in the formation of any psyche, male or female. Closer to Christianity, but also to the post-Romantic psychology which defines all characters according to the amorous relations, Jones proposed to find the determining element in aphanisis (the fear of losing the possibility of *jouissance*), rather than in castration. Perhaps it would not merely be a resurgence of Greek or logico-phenomenological thought to suggest locating this fundamental event neither in castration nor in aphanisis (both of which would be only its fantasmic derivatives), but rather in *the process of learning the symbolic function* to which the human animal is subjected from the pre-Oedipal phase onward. . . . The symbolic order functions in our monotheistic West by means of a *system of kinship* that involves transmission of the name of the father and a rigorous prohibition of incest, and a *system of speech* that involves an increasingly logical, simple, positive and "scientific" form of communication, that is stripped of all stylistic, rhythmic and "poetic" ambiguities. (Kristeva, "Chinese Women," pp. 150–151)

Despite the refusal of the term *castration*, it is difficult to see how this differs in any significant way from the standard traditional Lacanian psychoanalytic position.

Kristeva herself recognizes the potentially "double-edged" threat of
avant-garde artistic activity, which, as Grosz writes, "risks co-option or
recuperation in functioning as a 'safety valve' or outlet for what may
otherwise have become a more disruptive political practice."[31]

A Kristevan advocate like John Lechte follows Kristeva in what I call
the overidealization of the avant-garde.[32] Lechte writes that Kristeva

> would advocate "aesthetic practices" which explore, and also construct,
> the singularity of every speaking being: that is, a being who is the out-
> come of a multiplicity of "possible identifications." Aesthetic practices
> here are equivalent to transcending difference as a battle between rival
> groups of all kinds (including that of the sexes), in order to turn it into
> the basis of new possibilities for subjectivity.[33]

---

[j] Elizabeth Grosz has called her "ungenerous" (*Subversions*, p. 94) to feminists and
feminisms, and it does seem an applicable epithet when we read in Kristeva's work
that, for example, "women are particularly susceptible to the seductions of terrorism" ("Women's Time," p. 204). The definition of what a *terrorist* is has become
increasingly muddled, as all political groups have come to apply it to their enemies
and rivals, even as they commit the exact same criminal acts of violence as those
enemies and rivals. Despite the muddle, it still seems safe to affirm however that
the vast majority of those prone to making themselves heard through violence are
male.

Kristeva has also written that "since the dawn of feminism, and certainly before,
the activity of exceptional women, and thus in a certain sense of liberated women,
has taken the form of murder, conspiracy and crime" (ibid). It might be useful to
point out that history has recorded the actions of the Charlotte Cordays of the
world—and passed less spectacular and grisly "exceptions" over in silence.

Perhaps we should not take too seriously Kristeva's references to suffragists as
"more threatening than the father of the primitive horde" or to active women in
general as "supermen" or as "homosexual women (whether they know it or not)"
("Chinese Women," p. 155). These possibly tongue-in-cheek labels do bear an
uncanny resemblance however to traditional scoffing male dismissals of feminists.
It seems clear in any case that Kristeva has made a deliberate effort to distance herself from feminism.

[k] Obviously here I echo the title of what is in many ways Kristeva's masterwork—
Revolution in Poetic Language, trans. Margaret Waller (New York: Columbia University Press, 1984)/ *La Révolution du langage poétique* (Paris: Seuil, 1974). I would
point out however that radical feminism has as much to do with artistic and signifying practice as any avant-garde movement. Kristeva does seem to recognize this
(see the conclusion of "Women's Time," pp. 209–211) when she is not blaming
bad feminist artistic practice on feminism. "Thanks to the feminist label, does one
not sell numerous works whose naïve whining or market-place romanticism would
otherwise have been rejected as anachronistic?" (ibid., p. 207). True enough. But
I fear the avant-garde label often produces the same effect.

.
.
.

The danger of "aesthetic practices" that seek new "possibilities for subjectivity" is underlined by Margaret Whitford in her article, "Irigaray's Body Symbolic." How are texts, works of art, etc., to be produced in which women's subjectivity and identity "are not immediately recaptured, or recapturable, by the dominant imaginary and symbolic economy, in which woman figures for-man"?[34] Kristeva has always posited the dependence of all aesthetic practice, even that of the avant-garde, on the symbolic order. Logically then, until the imaginary and symbolic economy can be changed, all aesthetic practices, and hence any new subjectivities developing therefrom, must necessarily remain at least theoretically problematical from a feminist standpoint.[35]

I would add as a final criticism of Kristeva's relationship to feminism the fact that a large body of Kristeva's work in psychoanalysis has been done since 1974, that is, since the publication of Irigaray's *Speculum*— to which I have found no reference *anywhere* in Kristeva's oeuvre.[36] This omission is particularly striking in the case of a woman in France working in postmodern theory and psychoanalysis who supposedly remains neutral and "eclectic,"[37] and aligns herself with no polemical position within the splintered, highly partisan French psychoanalytic scene. Talk about blind spots . . .

Luce Irigaray: Spaces, Intervals, and Mediations

The Placenta as Mediator

It is to Irigarayan theory we must turn for a radical rethinking in nonoedipal, nonphallic terms of the body's relation to subjectivity. In a special issue of *Langages* entitled *Le Sexe linguistique*, edited by Irigaray in 1987, there is an interesting article that has not attracted much attention among American feminists, "Le Placenta comme tiers" ("The placenta as third term") by Hélène Rouch. Rouch, a biologist, summarizes the current (for 1987) state of obstetrical research about the placenta and its role in pregnancy. She shows how the widespread conception of the placenta as the organ that nourishes the fetus is overly simplistic. Rouch demonstrates how much more complex the placenta's work is, and how its benefits accrue to both mother and offspring. The placenta regulates the immune system of the mother so that the newly implanted embryo is not rejected in the way that an organ transplant would be; at the same time it maintains a sufficient level of immunity in the mother's body to protect her from disease. In addition, during the hiatus in ovulation that is pregnancy, the placenta takes over the

production of the progesterone needed for the mucous lining of the
uterus, essential for both mother and child.

> The placenta is not only the essential organ that permits the embryo-
> fetus to develop. It is not only a strainer or a sucker, a selective filter or
> a perfected pump, as it is depicted by mechanistic medical language as
> well as by currently popular language which is less charged with deter-
> minist fantasies. The placenta establishes a *relationship*, a unique rela-
> tionship between mother and fetus, because it realizes neither separation
> nor fusion between them.[38]

Rouch further points out that the placenta is formed exclusively
from the genetic and cellular material of the embryo itself, and is never
part of the mother's body. So that when

> the umbilical cord is cut, the baby is not cut from the mother's body,
> but from the placenta, from something then that was part of itself. . . .
> Lacan insists on this point: "Here it is from its own partition that the
> subject proceeds to its parturition. Therefore, with the cutting of the
> cord, what the newborn loses is not, as analysts think, its mother, but its
> anatomical complement." That which made it a sphere, the image of
> completeness. In a certain way the anatomical dice is thrown: the lost
> placenta is possibly the primordial object *a* for whose loss the drive—
> which will always be partial—will seek, through other part objects, to
> compensate.[39]

The One was never a One, not even before parturition; nor was it a
Two, the infamous dyad; nor was it really a Three, despite Rouch's title,
since the placenta, although separate, is genetically part of the fetus.[1] The
One and the Two are imaginary numbers, covering over the only physical organ loss, that of the "anatomical complement," the placenta. The
Three, the sacred number of the oedipus complex, is also an imaginary
configuration, highly elaborated symbolically (and how!) in a multiplicity of contexts (in how many!), but an insufficient representation of the
type of mediation taking place between the mother's body, the fetus, and
the placenta. It is important to begin to make here an essential distinction between Kristeva, who never lets go of the strictly ternary oedipal
model, and Irigaray who strives to get beyond the number Three and
find new representations for mediation and entry into the symbolic.

---

[1] I am indebted to Elizabeth Grosz for her insight in helping me think through this
problem. Irigaray has always challenged the number One, and consequently any
logical system based off One + One + One . . . —so the numbers Two and Three
are immediately suspect. What really interests Irigaray is that which is "left over,"
that which lies between the integers, like a remainder in division perhaps—or like
the placenta.

- • Rouch goes on to discuss the breast and weaning as "postfigurations"
- • of the cutting of the umbilical cord, and "prefigurations" of "castration."
- •

> At the time of weaning, what constitutes the breast as lost object for the
> child is, as much as the separation between himself and the breast, the
> one that is effected in his fantasy between the breast and his mother. In
> this sense Lacan adds, "the function of weaning. . . prefigures castration."
> . . . Birth and weaning are the first points of entry into the symbolic.[40]

Weaning, the "postfiguration" of the cutting of the cord, is experienced
psychically as the separation of the body from that which was part of
itself—the mother from her breast—a structure identical to the original separation from the placenta. Irigaray makes use of Rouch's study as
empirical evidence in dealing with problems she had already begun to
theorize herself, several years prior to the publication of the special issue
of *Langages,* in the published series of lectures dating from 1982 that is
Ethique de la différence sexuelle (*An Ethics of Sexual Difference*) and in
one of her most abstruse and difficult texts, "La Croyance même"
("Belief Itself"), which was delivered as a conference paper in 1980, and
published in a collection of lectures appearing in 1987, *Sexes et parentés*
(*Sexes and Genealogies*).

In "Belief Itself" Irigaray proffers her own reading of Freud's grandson little Ernst's *fort-da* game,[41] a profoundly dialogic reading of a
whole series of intertexts dealing with little Ernst: Freud's, Derrida's,
Lacan's . . . Irigaray begins by repositioning our point of view on the
child's game, so that the spool comes to represent not the child's mother who is symbolically made to come and go at the child's whim, which
is the traditional interpretation of the bobbin, but rather the child himself endeavoring not only to recover his mother's presence but even to
regain access to his mother's body.[42]

> But is this spool really about her? or about him? He, the fetus, playing
> at going in and out of her with a cord, a veil-placenta, a womb-bed, for
> example.[43]

Irigaray further shifts the emphasis away from the bobbin or spool and
redirects our attention to the veil—to the bed curtains, across which
Ernst throws his toy/himself and out through which he pulls it/himself
back. Irigaray remarks that this veil, which has been "neglected, disregarded, censored, repressed, forgotten by Freud,"[44] is

> necessary as the milieu, the mediation for the staging of presence within
> absence, for the process of re-presentation. . . . The child sends it [the bob-
> bin] and sends himself away, beyond, but not behind a wall or a curtain,
> which hides, hides her or hides him definitively. He plays, does not risk

the definitive step. . . . What Ernst wants is to master presence-absence with the help of a more or less white veil, more or less transparent.[45]

For Irigaray the veil makes the game as much as the bobbin does. Without the veil the whole staging (mise en scène) would not work—or would be part of that other, first version of the game where Ernst simply tossed his toys away, and left to his parents and grandparents the trouble of bothering to find them. It is the veil along with the string (Irigaray calls it a cord [*cordon*]) that permits the spool to be lost or "gone," and then found or "here," alternatively, thus symbolically controlling presence and absence.

Irigaray reads Ernst's efforts to throw himself back across the veil as a symbolic return to the womb.[m] Like Rouch, Irigaray refuses to posit

---

[m] Irigaray calls the womb a first paradise, and relates it directly to the heavenly one.

> Le plus formidable *fort-da* s'envoie . . . de la présence de la mère, dans la mère, outre-voile, à celle de Dieu, outre-ciel, outre-horizon visible. . . . Tous les fils et les fils vont et viennent entre ces deux lieux de l'invisible, ces deux présences cachées, entre lesquelles tout se joue, en lesquelles tout se rassemble. . . . Cette vie-ci ne signifiant qu'une sorte d'exode entre deux paradis: l'un scindé entre la biologie et la mythologie ou laissé en silence, et l'autre dont un certain savoir prétend pouvoir rendre compte en totalité. Pour ces deux lieux, deux mesures et transcriptions différentes donc, du moins apparemment. Reste à savoir comment l'un se plie dans l'autre, est ployé dans l'autre, réserve immémoriale de fiction, de croyance, qui sous-tend secrètement sa vérité. ("La Croyance même," *Sexes et parentés*, pp. 44–45)
>
> The most important *fort-da* . . . refers, past the mother's presence, in the mother, beyond-veil, to the presence of God, beyond the sky, beyond the visual horizon. . . . All the threads and all the sons (*tous les fils et les fils*) come and go between these two places of the invisible, these two hidden presences, between which everything is played out, in which everything meets. . . . This life in turn becomes merely a kind of exodus between two paradises: the one split between biology and mythology or left in silence, and the other for which a certain knowledge claims to account. For these two places, there are therefore two different measures and transcriptions, or so it seems at least. It remains to be seen how the one is folded and bent into the other, as an immemorial store of fiction, of belief, that secretly underpins its truth.
> ("Belief Itself," trans. Gillian C. Gill, *Sexes and Genealogies*, pp. 32–33)

The divine aspirations of human beings are a sophisticated manifestation of the *fort-da* game. "Belief Itself" is also an account of the origin of religious belief—hence the title. Furthermore, in this extremely rich and complex text, Irigaray relates the mother's body, that which is most corporeal and material in traditional metaphysics, to God, that which is most spiritual and transcendental. Margaret Whitford writes that in order to create an ethics of sexual difference the construction of a "sensible transcendental" is necessary (Whitford, *Luce Irigaray*, p. 150). This too is part of the project of "Belief Itself." However, this aspect of the text cannot concern us here at length.

•
•
•
any direct access to the mother's body. The mother/child relationship is always already mediated by the veil, by the placenta, which originated as we have seen in the genetic and cellular material of the embryo.

> The placenta is without doubt the first veil belonging to the child. Doesn't he forget that it belongs to him, even if it is produced for him in her, even if she, through it, unceasingly gives herself to him without return, and even if this first home does adhere to her? . . . The string of the bobbin does *not* bring her into him like the first cord . . . and further the first abode was *not* simply commensurate with her.[46]

The Angel, the Mucous, and Love

In "Belief Itself" the reading of the *fort-da* game becomes the jumping-off point for a development on one of the most puzzling and profoundly original aspects of Irigarayan thought—her work on the angel. Elizabeth Grosz reads this rather unexpected theorizing of the angelic as a fascination

> with exploring the possibility of an intermediate . . . a middle ground between the bird and the fish, God and human, man and woman. . . . The angel traverses distinct identities and categories. . . . Although angels signify the possibility of a bridge between the mortal and immortal, the terrestrial and the divine, male and female, they are usually disembodied, sexually neuter, intangible, incorporeal.[47]

Grosz's reading underlines many of the traditional characteristics associated with angels in Western religious and artistic tradition, and indeed Irigaray exploits these traditional characteristics in her thought. But in so doing she also goes far beyond them. She makes her move in "Belief Itself," after having established the veil/placenta as mediating element.

> Before the son has perfected his staging we can try to sneak off with his veil, the curtain of his theater, the milieu or mediator of his *fort-da* and lend it or give it to the angels. The veil that playfully separates him from her, from him, from him in her, from her in him, this veil that will divide and surround his theater, calls up or recalls perhaps something of the angel, of angels, just as disregarded, forgotten as the nature of this first veil.[48]

This hint at an identification between the veil/placenta and the angel is made explicit a page or two later as Irigaray discusses the angel as messenger, particularly the Angel of the Annunciation who really

> always goes in the same direction, even in its comings and goings: from heaven, where God the Father is supposed to be, to her . . . in order to

give or entrust to her his descendants. Don't we have some sort of reversal here? When it goes toward her isn't it possible that it is coming back from her? Wasn't it from her that the angel was lifted? from her that it flew/was stolen away? Nearly imperceptible skin or membrane, nearly transparent whiteness, quasi-indecipherable mediation.[49]

The source of the angel is the mother's body, where mediation always already took place between the fetus, the mother, and the placenta. The angelic is then an imaginary and symbolically elaborated representation of this mediated communication and exchange.

The skin or membrane is "always at work in any process of language, of representation, assuring the link between the most terrestrial and the most celestial, the first abode in her, out of which he makes and remakes his bed, and the elaboration of the transcendence of the Lord."[50] Mediation, a certain type of nonoedipal, nontriangular mediation, becomes the possibility of the entire symbolic order. If we have not yet gotten beyond the phallus, its uniqueness and privilege have certainly been severely undermined. Margaret Whitford states explicitly: "One way of seeing the angel is to see it as an alternative to the phallus. In psychoanalytic terms, the phallus has sometimes been thought of as that which 'goes between,' creates a bridge."[51]

In *Ethique de la différence sexuelle* Irigaray once again takes up the angelic, this time in relation to the mucous rather than to the placenta. She writes, "The mucous should no doubt be pictured as related to the angel."[52] We are back in the slightly more familiar territory of the mechanics of fluids[53] in dealing with the mucous. It also functions like the placenta as a mediating membrane through which substances pass freely from any direction. It is a medium of exchange through which messages, communications may flow.[54] Irigaray writes of its effervescence during the sexual act: "The interval approaches zero when skins come into contact. It goes beyond zero when a passage occurs to the mucous."[55] She seems to envisage a new world, or, she says, a "new morning for the world," perceived across the "threshold"—another image of mediation[56]—of the female sex, which is after all, the "threshold that gives us access to the mucous. Beyond classical oppositions of love and hate, liquid and ice—a threshold that is always half-open. . . Both the threshold and reception of exchange."[57]

In the second essay of *Ethique de la différence sexuelle*, "L'Amour sorcier" ("Sorcerer love"), Irigaray writes of love itself as the "intermediary between couples of opposites."[58] She does not use the metaphor of the angel in this context, but there is enough basis in Western tradition for the association of the angel with love to justify such an extrapolation. Love itself, like the placenta, like the mucous, is a mediating element: "If

• the couple of lovers cannot establish the link of love as a third term
• between them, they can neither remain lovers nor give birth to lovers."[59]
• In Irigaray's 1990 article, "Questions à Emmanuel Levinas," love as
"third term" is even incarnated, so to speak, as a

> child prior to any child. In this relation we are at least three, each of
> which is irreducible to any of the others: you, me, and our work, that
> ecstasy of ourself in us. . . . Pleasure neither mine nor thine, pleasure
> transcendant and immanent to one and the other, and which gives birth
> to a third, mediator between us thanks to which we return to ourselves,
> other than we were.[60]

Margaret Whitford develops fully the Irigarayan theme of love as
mediator, using terms identical to those we have already associated with
the angel, the mucous, and the placenta:

> Love is the vehicle which permits a passage between, the passage to and
> fro between sensible and intelligible, mortal and immortal, above and
> below, immanent and transcendent. Instead of an abyss, or an enclosure
> which defines an inside and an outside, there should be a threshold, and
> the possibility of permanent passage in and out, to and fro.[61]

At the most basic level the body, its skin and orifices, function as
mediators between the self-conscious subject and the world. Further, it
is the positioning of the body that determines the organizing structures
most necessary to cognition and to existence itself—inside and outside,
above and below, open and closed. . . . This mediation by, of, and in the
body begins already in the womb of the mother through the operations
of the placenta, and the structures put in place there create the very possibility of human love, which Kristeva, Irigaray, and others can be said
to regard as necessary for the integration of the psyche and, perhaps, as
the pinnacle of human achievement.

Conclusion

I would like to place the angel, the placenta, the mucous, and love within a perspective created by Margaret Whitford in her article "Speaking
as a Woman: Luce Irigaray and the Female Imaginary." Whitford
works up a telling scenario wherein Irigaray acts the psychoanalyst to
a troubled and ailing Western culture, trying to liberate the repressed
from an overburdened unconscious in order to relieve certain painful
symptoms. Whitford argues that "only certain Imaginary objects are
taken up and symbolized; other objects, presently neglected *could be*
symbolized."[62] What Irigaray is interested in, then, is the neglected
imaginary, what our culture has chosen not to take up and symbolize;

this is one of the things she means by the "female" or "feminine" imaginary.[63] Just as she had done with the lips in "Quand nos lèvres se parlent" ("When Our Lips Speak Together"),[64] Irigaray continues to take previously unsymbolized aspects of feminine existence, female corporeality, and sexuality, aspects that had been lost in the silence of patriarchal taboo,[n] and bring them to the cultural order through the creation of images and symbols present to consciousness. Her theorizing of the angelic is somewhat more complex, and perhaps even more interesting. Irigaray has appropriated an image that had already been highly elaborated philosophically, theoretically, and artistically in the Western cultural order, and she anchors it in the female body, from which it had been carefully cordoned off before, since angels are supposed to have no sex. She relates it to maternity through the placenta and to feminine desire and sexuality through the mucous. Whether we think we can begin to take the problem of angels seriously or not, it seems clear that the concept of these entities, nearly forgotten since the death of God,[65] has been revived, rejuvenated through Irigaray's revolutionary meditations. She forces us to come to terms with that which we have repressed, or consciously ignored—for decades at least. We are forced to visualize and verbalize angels the way we were forced to visualize and verbalize the heretofore unmentionable lips.[66]

It might be useful to go back once again to Kristeva's concept of the semiotic in order to clarify what is meant by the new "female imaginary." Both the Irigarayan imaginary and the Kristevan semiotic are grounded in the female body, both bring to the light of the symbolic the inexpressible, giving form to the previously unformed or chaotic, and both constitute a link or a bridge of sorts between nature and culture. The semiotic and the imaginary[o] are both liberating, releasing energy bottled up in keeping the "repressed from returning," in maintaining certain silences and darknesses to keep order—in discourse and in society. It is significant however that the semiotic is a strictly individual phenomenon. It is recuperable *in* the works of the avantgarde artist, or in the language of the analysand in the transference, or possibly in the language (as, for example, in love letters) of the lover in the throes of that madness which is love,[67] and recuperable *by* the reader (who would really have to be more of a sophisticated literary

---

[n] Lacan discusses this lack of symbolization of female sexuality. In the vicious circle of the patriarchal symbolic order, it is one of the reasons for the privilege of the phallus. See Ragland-Sullivan, *Jacques Lacan*, p. 286.

[o] For the purposes of the ensuing discussion I will be referring to the Irigarayan imaginary, without necessarily specifying so each time.

critic and theoretician) skilled at "semanalysis,"[68] or by the analyst
attentive to the materiality of her or his patient's language. The new
imaginary on the other hand is a cultural, a political phenomenon,
independent of any particular individual's preoedipal (pre)history,
and recuperable immediately, by any and all, in images created and
recreated from a revolutionary perspective—that of a "philosopher in
the feminine," to paraphrase Margaret Whitford. The semiotic,
although anchored in the body of the mother, is neither specifically
male nor female, and is, in fact, as we have seen, more susceptible to
expression by males than females. Irigaray's imaginary is openly and
intentionally female, implying within itself a challenge to all philosophers and to all thinking subjects to carry on with the elaboration of
images and symbols appropriate for human, both female *and* male,
development into the future.

Irigaray's project is eminently ethical in the sense that what she seeks
through this imaginary is the founding of a feminine subjectivity capable of establishing new ways of relating to/being with the other. Her
work on love is an obvious extension of this same ethical project. Once
again here, on the subject of love, the contrast with Kristeva is illuminating, and relates directly to the distinction we have been articulating
between the Kristevan semiotic and the Irigarayan imaginary. Kristeva
finds in love an ideal or "model of optimum psychic functioning. . . .
The psyche is one open system connected to another, and only under
those conditions is it renewable. If it lives, your psyche is in love. If it is
not in love it is dead. 'Death lives a human life,' Hegel said. That is true
whenever we are not in love or not in analysis. . . . The effect of love is
one of renewal, our rebirth."[69] Irigaray also writes, using the religious
metaphor of transubstantiation, of love as a rebirth, a triumph over
death, through union—which is *not* necessarily procreative union—
with the other. "The act of love becomes the transubstantiation . . . of
oneself and one's lover (male or female) into spiritual body. It is festival,
celebration, rebirth. . . . Love is the redemption of the flesh by the transfiguration of the desire *of* the other (as object?) into desire *with* the
other."[70]

It is significant that for Kristeva love and psychoanalysis are more
or less interchangeable. The psychoanalytic relation is a closed-off
"openness," and love an integrating model for the "cure" of one individual, or, one supposes, perhaps, two. But for Irigaray love becomes
not only the source of our individual health/salvation, but of our collective health/salvation as well (*salut individuel et collectif*).[71] Love is
a community project. Love is advancement toward a goal for the
species.

[The] couple forms the elementary social community. It is here that the
desire of the senses must become potentially universal culture. It is here
that the gender of a man and a woman can become the model for the
human masculine or feminine gender, all the while remaining tied to the
singular task of being this particular man or that particular woman. Real-
izing this passage from nature to culture, from the singular to the universal, from sexual attraction to the effectivity of the gender, the couple
formed by a man and a woman assures the health/salvation of the community and of nature, the two together. It is not only their pleasure that
is at stake but the order of becoming-spirit of the entire community.[72]

It is important for us to tie together the elements of this new female
imaginary that is in the process of being forged. Irigaray has consistently foregrounded structures and images of mediation, from the placenta, to love, to the angel. She consistently discovers mediatory structures in relationships previously conceived as strictly binary: the angels
are messengers between god and man, the placenta regulates the flow
between mother and baby in the womb, love itself exists as a space or
even as an entity between lovers, the mucous establishes a less than zero-
degree interval between two different bodies in the sexual act. Kristeva's
work on the preoedipal disposition and particularly on the imaginary
father showed a similar preoccupation with founding mediation prior
to castration and the phallic metaphor. Kristeva however, still very
much within the institution of psychoanalysis, maintains the priority of
difference and loss, the ultimate difference and loss resulting from the
disruption operated by the phallic signifier. The phallus as third term
spells "prohibition, difference, and individuation by Castration."[73]

It is Irigaray who truly takes on the project of getting "beyond the
phallus." She consistently seeks the mediating term, but in so doing,
puts forth not the violent disruptive separation of the phallus but rather
an intermediary space through which passes a flow. Few would argue
against the femininity of such a metaphor. Could/Should an imaginary
of flow and exchange replace an imaginary of separation and loss? Or
might that not be the reversal of values that only maintains the status
quo? I propose we begin to think in terms of an imaginary of exchange
simultaneously with a phallic imaginary, but not as a binary pair
engaged in a philosophical battle of the sexes. Elizabeth Grosz has written that "to speak as a woman . . . means to evoke rather than to designate, to overflow and exceed all boundaries and oppositions. It involves
speaking from a position in the middle of the binaries (the so-called
position of the 'excluded middle'), affirming both poles while undoing
their polarisation."[74]

Is such a project utopian? There are undoubtedly many utopian fea-

•
• tures in Irigaray's thought,[75] but she never loses sight of the negative
• potential of the human psyche and of human development. There are
in her work no promises for a warm and glowing future of exchange and
communication. Margaret Whitford writes:

> Although some of Irigaray's formulations seem to imply a kind of belief
> in a utopian future of peace and harmony, she is too aware of the death
> drives (women's as well as men's) not to underestimate the need for their
> symbolic organization, and its sometimes inevitable failure. So I think
> we cannot take her visions as literal accounts of an imagined ideal future.
> But on the other hand, psychoanalysis also recognizes moments of inte-
> gration between different parts of the psyche; the unconscious may be a
> resource, and crossing boundaries in phantasy may have real and tangi-
> ble results in the world.[76]

We are split subjects, and despite her "utopianism" there is no doubt
that Irigaray recognizes the cleft in being on which human subjectivity
is constructed. Separation, loss, and emptiness are instrumental in
forming our identity, and our language can only demand that which
can never satisfy our desire, since what we desire is everything.[P] But
"everything" is a binary concept, making sense only when paired with
its other, "nothing." Somewhere between nothing and everything lies
language, flowing through the space of separation, making contact, ini-
tiating exchanges, articulating, if not what we "desire," at least certain
of our wants for ourselves and for others, and those of others for ourselves. In the inevitable absence of ultimate satisfaction we can still
exchange words. An imaginary of flowing mediation shifts the emphasis away from the tragedy of desire and its impossible satisfaction onto
the gratification of the exchange itself.

NOTES •

1. Jane Gallop, "Phallus/Penis: Same Difference," in *Men by Women:
   Women and Literature* (New York: Holmes and Meier, 1981); reprinted
   in Jane Gallop, *Thinking Through the Body* (New York: Columbia University Press, 1988).
2. That Kristeva has elaborated upon Lacan's work cannot be denied. Her

---

[P] "Desire is in principle insatiable. It is always an effect of the Other, an 'other' with
whom it cannot engage, in so far as the Other is not a person but a place, the locus
of the law, language, and the symbolic" (Grosz, *Jacques Lacan*, p. 67.) "Desire is a
fundamental lack, a hole in being that can be satisfied only by one 'thing'—anoth-
er('s) desire. Each self-conscious subject desires the desire of the other as its object"
(ibid., p. 64). See also Ragland-Sullivan, *Jacques Lacan*, pp. 69–89.

debt to him is immense. Nor can it be denied however that she has brought an articulation that was previously lacking to the preoedipal disposition.

3. For an introduction see Toril Moi, *Sexual/Textual Politics* (New York: Methuen, 1985), pp. 161–167. For a thorough presentation see John Lechte, *Julia Kristeva* (New York: Routledge, 1990), pp. 123–198. For more critical readings see Elizabeth Grosz, *Sexual Subversions: Three French Feminists* (Sydney, 1989), pp. 39–55; and Elizabeth Grosz, *Jacques Lacan*, pp. 147–167.

4. Grosz, *Sexual Subversions*, pp. 63–68. Grosz writes that in Kristevan theory "woman remains unable to speak her femininity or her maternity. She remains locked within a mute, rhythmic, spasmic, potentially hysterical—and thus speechless—body, unable to accede to the symbolic because 'she' is too closely identified with/as the semiotic" (Grosz, *Jacques Lacan*, p. 163).

5. Judith Butler, *Gender Trouble: Feminism and the Subversion of Identity* (New York: Routledge, 1990), p. 93, and in general pp. 79–93.

6. "Lacan upholds Freud's statement that repression (*Verdrängung*) requires the possibility of some prior repression as a foundation. Lacan makes *Urverdrängung* the equivalent of the fixing of a primary, signifying chain in the prespecular and mirror-stage periods, a phenomenon he renders into French as *refoulement*, or that which makes secondary repression or suppression (*Unterdrückung*) possible" (Ragland-Sullivan, *Jacques Lacan*, p. 113). I am drawing a parallel here between the concept of primal repression and that of Kristevan prephallic difference because, in both cases, phenomena that have been conceived as oedipal or postoedipal, are clearly anchored in the preoedipal disposition.

7. Julia Kristeva, "Freud and Love: Treatment and Its Discontents," trans. Leon S. Roudiez, in Toril Moi, ed., *The Kristeva Reader* (New York: Columbia University Press, 1986), p. 244.

8. Kristeva writes, "The whole symbolic matrix sheltering emptiness is thus set in place in an elaboration that precedes the oedipus complex" (ibid., p. 245).

9. In short, primary identification appears to be a transference to (from) the imaginary father, correlative to the establishment of the mother as "ab-jected." Narcissism would be that correlation (with the imaginary father and the "ab-jected" mother) enacted around the central emptiness of that transference. This emptiness, which is apparently the primer of the symbolic function, is precisely encompassed in linguistics by the bar separating signifier from signified and by the "arbitrariness" in psychoanalysis by the "gaping" of the mirror. (ibid., p. 257)

Primary identification creates the possibility of initiation into the symbolic, as well as the possibility of mirror-stage identifications.

10. Ibid.

11. Ibid.

- 12. Ibid.
- 13. Kristeva, *Powers of Horror*, trans. Leon S. Roudiez (New York: Columbia University Press, 1982), pp. 49–51.

14. Grosz, *Jacques Lacan*, p. 151.

15. "If it is not possible to say of a *woman* what she *is* (without running the risk of abolishing her difference), would it perhaps be different concerning the *mother*, since that is the only function of the "other sex" to which we can definitely attribute existence? And yet, there too, we are caught in a paradox. First, we live in a civilization where the *consecrated* (religious or secular) representation of femininity is absorbed by motherhood. If, however, one looks at it more closely, this motherhood is the *fantasy* that is nurtured by the adult, man or woman, of a lost territory; what is more, it involves less an idealized archaic mother than the idealization of the *relationship* that binds us to her, one that cannot be localized—an idealization of primary narcissism." (Julia Kristeva, "Stabat Mater," in Moi, *The Kristeva Reader*, p. 161)

16. See in Moi, *The Kristeva Reader*: "Women's Time," pp. 199–213; and "A New Type of Intellectual: The Dissident," pp. 297–298.

17. Kristeva, "Stabat Mater," p. 174.

18. Ibid., p. 168.

19. Ibid., pp. 174–175.

20. Ibid., p. 172.

21. See Kristeva, "Women's Time," p. 204. See also "Recovered childhood, dreamed peace restored, in sparks, flash of cells, instants of laughter, smiles in the blackness of dreams, at night, opaque joy that roots me in her bed, my mother's, and projects him, a son, a butterfly soaking up dew from her hand, there, nearby, in the night. Alone: she, I and he" (Kristeva, "Stabat Mater," p. 172).

22. Kristeva, "Stabat Mater," pp. 180–182.

23. Irigaray, "Women on the Market," and "Commodities Among Themselves," in *This Sex*, pp. 165–185, 187–193/*Ce Sexe*, pp. 170–191, 192–197.

24. Kristeva, "Stabat Mater," p. 182.

25. For the famous analysis of the mirror image see Irigaray, *Speculum*. Grosz claims that Kristeva is a "dutiful daughter" (Jane Gallop's term applied by Grosz to Kristeva—see Gallop, *The Daughter's Seduction* [Ithaca: Cornell University Press, 1982]), clinging to Lacan as "Law-Giver." The dutiful daughter

> claims that the Father's Law or the oedipal interdict is one of the necessary conditions for the existence of the social, in whatever form it may take. Each [dutiful daughter] affirms that the child must be definitively separated from its immediate, maternal dependencies, which threaten it with suffocation or annihilation and the loss of an independent position or place in the social. And

each affirms that, because of his purely cultural or significatory role in paternity, the father (or the Father's Name) is ideally placed to perform this operation. The institution of the Father's Law, while objectionable in some of its forms, is nevertheless regarded as the necessary condition of stable discursive and social relations. In short, their [the dutiful daughters'] adherences to psychoanalysis are framed (in various ways) in terms of the universality or cultural necessity of some oedipal-like structure. (Grosz, *Jacques Lacan*, pp. 184–185)

26. Her theorization of lesbianism in particular is very troubling. (See Kristeva, "Chinese Women," in Moi, *The Kristeva Reader*, p. 149.) See also Judith Butler's entire criticism of Kristevan theory (Butler, *Gender Trouble*, pp. 79–93).

27. Kristeva, "Women's Time," p. 209.

28. Julia Kristeva, "Psychoanalysis and the Polis," in Moi, *The Kristeva Reader*, pp. 301–320. Kristeva presented this paper at the University of Chicago in 1981 at a colloquium entitled "The Politics of Interpretation." The paper starts out by sharply criticizing American academic discourse in general (certainly *il y a de quoi* but that is not the point here) and American Marxist criticism in particular. Her aggressive stance would appear to be a defensive strategy. See also Kristeva, *Au Commencement était l'amour: Psychanalyse et foi* (Paris: Hachette, 1985)/*In the Beginning Was Love: Psychoanalysis and Faith*, trans. Arthur Goldhammer (New York: Columbia University Press, 1987), which is lyrically quite moving as well as being a lucid and well-argued defense of psychoanalysis.

29. Kristeva, "Women's Time," p. 211.

30. See Grosz, *Sexual Subversions*, pp. 91–99.

31. Grosz, *Jacques Lacan*, p. 165. See Kristeva, *Powers of Horror*, particularly the second half of the book.

32. Lechte tries to refute the arguments of feminism, largely through criticism of the work of Elizabeth Grosz. However, he uses only her older work, which is much less highly elaborated than either her *Sexual Subversions* or her *Jacques Lacan*. (See Lechte, *Julia Kristeva*, pp. 202–204.)

33. Ibid., p. 207. See also pp. 201–208.

34. Margaret Whitford, "Irigaray's Body Symbolic," *Hypatia* (Fall 1991), 6(3):97–110. I thank Margaret Whitford for letting me read this work before its publication.

35. The first to recognize and to try to come to terms with this dilemma was Irigaray, who has launched what I have called elsewhere a "three-pronged attack" on the main supporting pillars of the symbolic order—language, law, and religion.

36. Such a reference may exist. I have not found one. Of course in all fairness I should mention that Irigaray never refers to Kristeva's work either.

37. Edith Kurzweil, "An Interview with Julia Kristeva," *Partisan Review*

- (1986), 53(2):216–229. "My generation is more eclectic. For theoretical
  reasons, we feel we have to know what all the others have done, even the
  Kleinians, the Freudians . . . and the followers of Winnicott. So we have
  a sort of psychoanalytic Babylon, but it's useful: you no longer want to
  be pure, to belong to one and only one group. You want to know what
  all psychoanalysts have done, in the hope of someday hitting upon *the*
  pertinent synthesis" (p. 221). Claims of eclecticism are no guarantee of
  nonpartisan views however.

38. Hélène Rouch, "Le Placenta comme tiers," *Langages* (1987), 85:75. All
    translations from the Rouch article are my own.

39. Ibid., pp. 75–76. Rouch cites Jacques Lacan, *Ecrits* (Paris: Seuil, 1966),
    pp. 843, 845.

40. Ibid., p. 76. See also Lacan, *Ecrits*, p. 848.

41. In *Culture and Domination* John Brenkman points out the contingent
    nature of Freud's interpretation of his grandson's game, its dependence
    on historical and sociological conditions. Brenkman's deconstruction
    thus underlines the contingency of all subsequent interpretations of this
    interpretation. Irigaray's reading radically deconstructs all previous read-
    ings. John Brenkman, *Culture and Domination* (Ithaca: Cornell Universi-
    ty Press, 1987). Ernst's game is discussed by Freud in *Beyond the Pleasure
    Principle* (in James Strachey, trans. and ed., the *Standard Edition of the
    Complete Psychological Works of Sigmund Freud* [London: Hogarth,
    1955], 18:14–17).

42. "Belief Itself"/"La Croyance même" is not the only text where Irigaray
    takes up the problem of the *fort-da* game. It is a recurring theme of *Sexes
    and Genealogies/Sexes et parentés*, along with "Gesture in Psychoanaly-
    sis"/"Le Geste en psychanalyse" and "A Chance for Life"/"Une Chance
    de vivre."

    Margaret Whitford reads the two latter texts, where the *fort-da* game
    is analyzed by Irigaray as a paradigm for the male's relation to the moth-
    er. "Men's relationship to the phantasied mother is exemplified by the
    fort-da, the manipulable object which can be thrown away and then
    retrieved. They can relate to the phantasied mother as to an object, with-
    out their own subject-position being put into question. If women learn
    their identity in the same way, the results are disastrous for that identity"
    (Margaret Whitford, *Luce Irigaray: Philosophy in the Feminine* [New York
    and London: Routledge, 1991], p. 44.)

    This aspect of the question is obviously very important to Irigaray's
    thought, but is not directly related to the thematics and point of view
    developed in "Belief Itself." An integrated study of Irigaray's readings of
    the *fort-da* might be interesting—if perhaps anti-Irigarayan? . . . I have
    dealt with the problem of systematizing Irigaray's work in a previous arti-
    cle (Gail Schwab, "Irigarayan Dialogism: Play and Powerplay," in Dale
    M. Bauer and S. Jaret McKinstry, eds., *Feminism, Bakhtin, and the Dia-
    logic* [Albany: SUNY Press, 1991]), pp. 57–72.

43. Luce Irigaray, "Belief Itself," *Sexes and Genealogies*, p. 31/"La Croyance même," *Sexes et parentés*, p. 43. All translations from "La Croyance même" are my own, except where noted.

44. Ibid.

45. Ibid., p. 42/30.

46. Ibid., p. 46/33–34.

47. Grosz, *Sexual Subversions*, p. 161.

48. Irigaray, *Sexes and Genealogies*, p. 35/*Sexes et parentés*, p. 47.

49. Ibid., pp. 38–39/50.

50. Ibid., p. 39/50–51.

51. Whitford, *Luce Irigaray*, p. 163.

52. Irigaray, *Ethics*. p.17/*Ethique*, p. 23.

53. Irigaray, "The 'Mechanics' of Fluids," in *This Sex*, pp. 103–116/*Ce Sexe*, pp. 106–118.

54. Margaret Whitford has dealt extensively with Irigaray's interest in the mucus. In "Irigaray's Body Symbolic" she compares what Irigaray does for the mucus to her (in)famous treatment of the lips. In *Luce Irigaray* she sums up the properties of the mucous that make it appropriate to the "representation of the unthought" (p. 163). Those properties of the mucous particularly appropriate to the representation of the angelic would seem to be the following: "it is essential to the act of love, i.e., to exchange between the sexes. . . . It is neither simply solid nor fluid. . . . It is not stable, it expands, it has no fixed form; it expands, but not in a shape" (p. 163).

55. Irigaray, *Ethics*, p. 48/*Ethique*, p. 53.

56. See Whitford, *Luce Irigaray*, p. 162.

57. Irigaray, *Ethics*, p. 18/*Ethique*, p. 24.

58. Ibid., p. 24/p. 30.

59. Ibid., p. 27/p. 33.

60. Irigaray, "Questions to Emmanuel Levinas," pp. 180–181/"Questions à Emmanuel Levinas," pp. 912–913.

61. Whitford, *Luce Irigaray*, p. 164.

62. Margaret Whitford, "Speaking as a Woman: Luce Irigaray and the Female Imaginary," *Radical Philosophy* (Summer 1986), 43:4.

63. Ibid., p. 8.

64. See "When Our Lips Speak Together," in *This Sex*, pp. 205–218/*Ce Sexe*, pp. 203–217.

65. The angel, like the veil that represents it, has been "neglected, disregarded, censored, repressed, forgotten" (Irigaray, *Sexes and Genealogies*, p. 31/*Sexes et parentés*, p. 43).

66. The type of strategy put into operation by Irigaray corresponds to the reconceptualization of the body called for by Elizabeth Grosz in her "Notes Towards a Corporeal Feminism," *Australian Feminist Studies* (1987), 5:1–16. Grosz writes that "alternative models of corporeal or carnal existence . . . should place special emphasis on women's particular corporeal experiences. Specifically female processes like ovulation, men

•   struation, childbirth, lactation . . . have always been inscribed in patriar-
•   chal terms" (p. 14).
•
67. See the opening essay of *Histoires d'amour*, called "Eloge d'amour," trans-
    lated as "In Praise of Love" in Kristeva, *Tales of Love*, trans. Leon S.
    Roudiez (New York: Columbia University Press, 1987).

68. See Kristeva, "The System and the Speaking Subject," in Moi, *The Kris-
    teva Reader*, pp. 24–33.

69. Kristeva, *Tales of Love*, pp. 14–15.

70. Irigaray, *J'aime à toi*, p. 219. Translations from *J'aime à toi* are my own.

71. Ibid., p. 57

72. Ibid., p. 55.

73. Ragland-Sullivan, *Jacques Lacan*, p. 279.

74. Grosz, *Sexual Subversions*, p. 132.

75. It should be noted here, in all fairness, that Irigaray's thought comprises
    a highly practical political agenda. Her work on language (see in particu-
    lar *Sexes et genres à travers les langues*), law (see *Sexes et parentés*, *Le Temps
    de la différence*, and *Je, tu, nous*), and religion (see in particular "Body
    Against Body: In Relation to the Mother/"Le Corps-à-corps avec la
    mère," "Divine Women/"Femmes divines," and "Women, the Sacred,
    Money" "Les Femmes, le sacré, l'argent," in *Sexes and Genealogies/Sexes
    et parentés*, and *Le Temps de la différence* as well as *Je, tu, nous*) is only
    utopian in that it has so far been implemented "no-place." Over the next
    twenty years however it will certainly filter into mainstream feminist
    political thought and action.

76. Whitford, *Luce Irigaray*, p. 166.

IRIGARAY, UTOPIA,

AND THE

DEATH DRIVE

Tout change, tout passe, il n'y a que
le tout qui reste.
Everything changes, everything
passes, only the whole remains.
—Diderot, *Le Rêve de d'Alembert*

Made anxious by . . . inscrutable dis-
junctions, we invariably attempt to
mend them . . . with *love*, forced or
fantasized into the state.
—Gillian Rose, *The Broken Middle*

Je suis donc une militante politique
de l'impossible.
So I am militating politically for the
impossible.
—Luce Irigaray, *J'aime à toi*

The debates around the two poles of equality and difference have characterized women's politics for quite a long time. Biddy Martin, in her book on Lou Andreas-Salomé,[1] describes the arguments in nineteenth-century Germany as follows:

> Claims for political rights based on arguments of women's equal ration-
> ality with men were rejected by political conservatives within the
> women's movement and by those who believed that the suppression of
> difference amounted to a repression of woman and the body. Feminists
> who struggled for concrete social, legal and economic changes on the
> rationalist grounds of equal rights attacked proponents of what they
> considered to be romantic conceptions of difference for their complici-
> ty with reigning misogynist discourses.[2]

This is Martin's summary, and perhaps she is writing it with the benefit of hindsight, but it does sound just like the arguments between, say,
Irigaray and the *Questions féministes* collective, a hundred or so years
later. The persistence of this tension leads me to think that we should
try to hold on to both strands, and maintain the tension between them,
in the hope that the conflict will test the strengths and weaknesses of
each strand.[3]

.
. Irigaray is a thinker who has come to reject explicitly equality as an
. intelligible goal for women, on the grounds that the conditions for its
intelligibility have not yet been met. While she was willing in the seventies to accept the struggles for equal rights as a tactical necessity, in
her most recent book, *J'aime à toi* (published 1992), she writes that "to
want to be equal to men is a grave ethical fault";[4] in seeking equality
"woman contributes to the erasure [*effacement*] of natural and spiritual
reality in an abstract universal which is in the service of a single master:
death."[5]

I would nonetheless want to argue that, in the broadest sense, Irigaray is a political thinker who wants to transform the order of the polis
so that women can take their place in it. But she doesn't approach politics in a familiar manner; her terrain is the terrain of the symbolic. For
her symbolic change is the *precondition* of women's entry into the polis.

The kind of politics that Irigaray has been associated with is sometimes referred to as a "politics of the imaginary" or a "politics of the
unconscious." Without endorsing all the ramifications of these phrases, I will just adopt here a minimal definition:

1. On the one hand "the politics of the imaginary" contains the idea
   that imagination—the possibility of imagining that things might be
   different—could have a critical function in political thought.[6]
2. The flip side of the critical function is summed up nicely by Slavoj
   Žižek in the title of his book, *For They Know Not What They Do*,[7]
   which makes explicit the unpredictability of action. The phrase
   "politics of the unconscious" foregrounds the idea that there is a
   sense in which you cannot know exactly what you are doing. In vio-
   lating the symbolic limits of the community, for example,[8] an act
   can seem violent or criminal, but it may redefine the symbolic community: it will then retrospectively come to be seen as a founding
   act. Interpretation of such violence is always "after the event";
   whether it is destruction pure and simple or whether it is creative
   destruction, whether it is eros as thanatos or thanatos as eros—this
   often cannot be known except retrospectively.[9]

The issue is put in another way by Kristeva's remarks on feminism in
her remarkable essay "Women's Time":

> [Women] are attempting a revolt which they see as a resurrection, but
> which society as a whole sees as murder. This attempt can lead us to a
> not less and sometimes more deadly violence. Or to a cultural innova-
> tion. Probably to both at once. But that is precisely where the stakes are,
> and they are of epochal significance.[10]

Kristeva suggests that feminism can be seen as *either* or *both* resurrec-

tion and murder, innovation and violence, depending on where you
stand. The undecidability of interpretation leads to her second opposition, between women and society as a whole: "[Women] are attempting a revolt which they see as a resurrection, but which society as a
whole sees as murder." The question of women's position in relation to
society as a whole, at what points they are "inside" and at what points
they are "outside," seems to be a crucial question for thinking about
equality and difference. In Irigaray's account women are positioned *outside* the social contract, as its basis and foundation, and therefore it is
inevitable that women contesting their position will come to be seen as
violent and threatening, while, from women's point of view, it is *patriarchy* that is deadly. In the terms that I am going to be using in this
essay, it is a question of locating the source of destruction or death
drive. However, it may be that the radical uncertainty of interpreting
the death drive is paralleled by a radical uncertainty about the interpretation of feminist politics.

One of the things I want to suggest here is that Irigaray has dealt with
the problem of symbolic (and sometimes real) violence by moving from
a politics of desire to a politics of love; her most recent book, *J'aime à
toi*, exemplifies this move. By this I mean that she has moved from the
stress on *un*binding, or *un*doing (e.g., undoing patriarchal structures)
to a stress on binding (e.g., constructing new forms of sociality). What
has been described as the "philosophical terrorism" of *Speculum* has
given way to an apparently more law-abiding concern with citizenship
and rights, in which the central political concept is love between the
sexes. This essay is an attempt to offer a possible rationale for the transition. I want to approach it via the tension between Irigaray's psychoanalytic premises, in particular the notion of the death drive, which is
one of the more controversial aspects of Freud's theories,[11] and on the
other hand her appeal to utopian topoi; for among the critiques of
utopia psychoanalytic critiques have been the most prominent.

For example, Krishan Kumar, in his recent book *Utopia and Anti-
utopia*, writes that *Civilization and Its Discontents* (1930) is the key anti-
utopian text of the twentieth century:

> No one more than Freud has so powerfully and persuasively under-
> mined the intellectual and emotional foundations of utopian hopes. . . .
> In *Civilization and Its Discontents* . . . Freud portrayed a world in which
> pain and unhappiness are the norm and conflict and disintegration an
> ever-present tendency. All culture is reared on repression and instinctu-
> al renunciation. All civilized morality, all laws and institutions, are the
> necessary but precarious bulwarks against elemental biological drives
> towards aggression, destruction and domination. . . . The whole of

-
-
-

> mankind's development, as of life itself, was seen as a ceaseless war
> between Eros, the constructive "life instincts" and Thanatos, the
> destructive "death instinct."[12]

Slavoj Žižek puts forward one of the most explicitly psychoanalytically based arguments against the idea of utopia in his book, *The Sublime Object of Ideology* (1989): utopia is the idea that there can be universality without negation, a subject without a lack or a symptom, a society without contradiction; it is the idea that the death drive can be finally overcome.

There are two problems that concern me here. First, it must be noted that Irigaray draws heavily on a theory—psychoanalysis—that has mounted one of the most definitive critiques of utopianism, while at the same time she deploys a whole range of utopian references (whose interpretation is not at all obvious, despite their apparent limpidity, sometimes bordering on the simplistic). This ambiguity is nicely reflected in the following remark in which Irigaray both affirms and denies the utopian impulse:

> I am militating politically for the impossible, which doesn't mean I am
> a utopian. Rather what I want is what does not yet exist, as the only possibility of a future.[13]

Second, she both does and does not recognize the death drive. In explicit terms she tends to reject Freud's dualism of eros and thanatos, as in the following remark, for example:

> We cannot allow the vibrations of death to continue to drown out the
> vibrations of life, if I may use terms which are rather too dichotomized
> for my taste.[14]

And yet, despite her disclaimer, this particular dichotomy appears to be one of the structuring dualisms of her work. The duality that everyone refers to—including Irigaray herself—is that of sexual difference, man and woman, male and female. But her work is also informed by quite a number of paired terms, or concepts, of which it is arguable that the underlying pair is life and death, or eros and thanatos—for example, mobility/immobility, creation/destruction, movement/rigidity, (flowing) blood/sclerosis, and so on. These pairs are articulated to the sexual pair, male and female, but not in a simple one-to-one correlation, and "death" as the underside of love is a persistently sounded note.

I shall be taking as many of my examples as possible from work recently translated into English, that is, *Marine Lover*, which is virtually unexplored in English,[15] and the essays translated in *The Irigaray*

Reader. The essay is in two parts. In the first part I shall be looking at
utopias; in the second part, at the death drive.

I

Given the stress on the death drive in Irigaray's thought one might
expect Irigaray to be an anti-utopian too, whereas in fact there is an
almost profligate recourse to utopian topoi in her work. Let us look first
at some of these multifarious utopian elements; they can range from as
little as a phrase, mentioned almost in passing, to the evocation of a
whole social organization. This review will not by any means be exhaustive, but will show, I think, that Irigaray's use of utopian topoi is a quite
central characteristic of her work.

Perhaps the most well-known is the economy of abundance, mentioned for example in *This Sex Which Is Not One* and *L'Oubli de l'air*. It
is possible to interpret this as an echo and reworking of the ancient
theme of the Land of Cockaigne, a popular or folk utopia describing a
totally hedonistic or sybaritic existence.[16] It is a folk utopia that has
often found its way into literature; in the French tradition the most
well-known example is probably Rabelais's reworking of the cornu-
copian theme. From *L'Oubli de l'air* it becomes clear that for Irigaray
the fantasy underlying abundance is that of the maternal uterus,[17] a
kind of irrecoverable plenitude when want was unknown and there was
no question of debt. This is also referred to as the "gift." It is a theme
that can be seen as part of Irigaray's project to put the mother into symbolic circulation, by explicating the fantasies of Western civilization.

A second type of utopian topos is the evocation of religious, often
Christian images, and I want to spend a little time on this type for what
it reveals about Irigaray's purposes. These images range from "the dawn
of a new age" to the Parousia, or Second Coming. The "dawn of a new
age" appears notably in *An Ethics of Sexual Difference* and in *Marine
Lover*. In the third part of *Marine Lover*, in the section entitled "When
the Gods Are Born," Irigaray gives an account, from the perspective of
the forgotten woman, of the gods who figure so prominently in Nietzsche's work: Dionysus, Apollo, and Christ. Irigaray sees the Greek
myths as a record of the time when an earlier matriarchy was giving way
to patriarchy, and her interpretation indicates first the marks of the
struggle and then the more tranquil period of "oblivion" that has oblit-
erated and continues to obliterate the traces of a maternal genealogy. In
the myth of Dionysus, she suggests, we can still see the signs of the
deadly struggle between two conceptions of the world: "He participates
in both, and clearly shows he is torn apart by that double allegiance."[18]

Dionysus's mother was reduced to ashes by Zeus's thunderbolt before the birth of her son, who is implanted in Zeus's thigh, from which he is later born. In the case of Apollo the maternal genealogy will be supplanted by the patriarchal order. Apollo signifies the moment at which allegiance to both parents, so painfully experienced as conflict by Dionysus, is resolved by the installation of a single genealogy: "One kinship line submits to the other."[19] The split between men and gods, the material-sensible body and the immaterial disembodied spirit, is consolidated, and has marked Western civilization ever since. Just as Zeus had swallowed Metis in order to give birth to Athena (his thought or intelligence), so Apollo incorporates, as it were, his twin sister Artemis: "He takes from his sister what he needs to establish sovereignly his identity."[20] The face of Apollo, the beautiful and calm Olympian, hides the murderer. Finally Christ. The life of Jesus of Nazareth could be read as the last great founding tragedy of the West, Irigaray argues. In her interpretation the crucifixion, the culmination of Jesus's life and mission, is in fact a non-Christian accident that patriarchy has made central as a symbol because of the sacrifice upon which patriarchy founds itself. The patriarchal reading eliminates from the story first the significance of Mary and second Christ's sexuate embodiment—his possible carnal union with the other sex. In so doing it eliminates women yet again. In the Christian tradition of the West Mary is the receptacle for the divine child; her function is purely maternal. Nothing is ever said of Mary's sacrifice: the sacrifice of "her generation, her flowering,"[21] in short, of her own life, her own embodiment as a woman-lover, or the "movement of her becoming" (to quote a phrase that is a kind of leitmotif for Irigaray). "Physical embrace will be banned from this religion of love."[22] In Greek mythology, then, according to Irigaray what we see is the first indication of the split or *schize* that she diagnoses as the pathology of our civilization: the split between mind and body, ideal and material, On High and here below, Heaven and earth, Truth and error, good and evil, God and idols, Divine and human, eternal and transient/mortal, and, of course, male and female.

Now Irigaray writes that the moment of Apollo was a "new dawn, the flowering of an unexpected spring"[23] before it solidified into an order that we now describe as patriarchy but that could not have been foreseen. Irigaray sees us once more on the brink of a "new era"[24]—a phrase she uses frequently—whose advent will depend on restoring the maternal genealogy, recognizing once more the mother and daughter line, and giving it a symbolic existence. Interestingly, she draws here on the vocabulary of Christianity, for the reason that Christianity is the mythology of the West, the era in which we still live. "When are we to

have an 'Annunciation,' an 'Advent,' a 'Christmas' in which 'Mary' is
conceived and anticipated as a divine manifestation?"[25] This would be
not the matriarchy again but, for the first time, the divine couple, the
marriage of two genealogies, the retrieval of the woman from the darkness in which she has been buried so that a "new birth" can come about.

Irigaray returns to the image of the "new era" in *An Ethics of Sexual
Difference*, where it is a central theme. Again, the vocabulary that evokes
it is often Christian: the Parousia, or Second Coming,[26] the New Pen-
tecost,[27] "resurrection" and "transfiguration,"[28] the messianic "Coming" [*avènement*].[29] In one place the reference is explicitly millennial:
the suggestion that we are on the threshold of the "third era" of the
West, the era of the Spirit and the Bride[30] that follows the era of the
Father (the Old Testament) and the era of the Son (the New Testament). In another context Gillian Rose explains that "the idea of a
'third' testament is taken from Joachim of Fiore, c. 1132–1202, who
divided history into three periods: the Age of the Father (Old Testament), the Age of the Son (New Testament and 42 subsequent generations) and the Age of the Spirit, in which all humanity would be con-
verted."[31] Joachim, though not formally a millenarian, was interpreted
as such by a long succession of followers.[32] Irigaray's adaptation
includes the woman too, as the Bride.

The millenarian topos is connected by Irigaray to the vocabulary of
mystical eroticism. As I noted, Irigaray adds to the millenarian formula the figure of the Bride, specifically making a place for the woman. In
her erotico-mystical accounts this is imaged in terms of the nuptial or
ecstatic embrace. The best example of this is not yet well-known, so I
will give quite a long quotation, which comes from an essay entitled
"Questions à Emmanuel Levinas." In it Irigaray discusses the need for
women to have a divine ideal, in order to reclaim their body and their
sexuality from the degradation to which it is reduced by the dualism of
Western theology and philosophy. The following remarks, then, appear
in the context of a discussion subtitled "On the Divinity of Love." It is
part of a process of rethinking the divine, so that women's bodies are
not fantasized as "chaos, abyss or dregs":[33]

> He knows nothing of communion in pleasure [*volupté*]. Levinas does not
> ever seem to have experienced the transcendence of the other which
> becomes an immanent ecstasy [*extase instante*] in me and with him—or
> her. For Levinas, the distance is always maintained with the other in the
> experience of love. The other is "close" to him in "duality." This autistic,
> egological, solitary love does not correspond to the shared outpouring, to
> the loss of boundaries which takes place for both lovers when they cross
> the boundary of the skin into the mucous membranes of the body, leav-

•
•
•

ing the circle which encloses my solitude to meet in a shared space, a
shared breath, abandoning the relatively dry and precise outlines of each
body's solid exterior to enter a fluid universe where the perception of
being two persons [*de la dualité*] becomes indistinct, and above all, acceding to another energy, neither that of the one nor that of the other, but an
energy produced together and as a result of the irreducible difference of
sex. Pleasure between the same sex does not result in that immanent ecstasy between the other and myself. It may be more or less intense, quantita-
tively or qualitatively different, it does not produce in us that ecstasy
which is our child, prior to any child. In this relation we are at least three,
each of which is irreducible to any of the others: you, me and our creation
[*oeuvre*], that ecstasy of ourself in us [*de nous en nous*], that transcendence
of the flesh of one to that of the other become ourself in us [*devenue nous
en nous*], at any rate "in me" as a woman, prior to any child.[34]

I think we are no more intended to take this as a purely literal description than the account of women's sexuality in *This Sex Which Is Not
One.* Irigaray writes in *An Ethics of Sexual Difference* that the "copula of
the sex act" is the world's "essential symbol";[35] it is an imaginary and
symbolic union that she evokes here.

Yet another type of utopian topos is based upon the classical Arca-
dia, or the golden age, which may have been Christianized in the Garden of Eden. The most influential modern version is probably
Rousseau's evocation of the golden age when man was still close to
nature and had not developed all the vices and evils that civilization
brings. Modern ecotopias[36] probably draw on Rousseau and post-
Rousseauistic accounts for inspiration. The myth of the earthly paradise is one that Irigaray alludes to quite explicitly, as in this example
from a 1986 lecture written shortly after Chernobyl:

There was once a time when mother and daughter formed a paradigm
for nature and for society. This couple was the guardian of nature's fruitfulness in general and of the relation to the divine. During that era food
consisted of the fruits of the earth. Thus the mother-daughter couple
guaranteed human food supplies and was also the place where oracles
were spoken. This couple watched over the memory of the past: then the
daughter respected her mother, her genealogy. The couple also cared for
the present: food was brought forth by the earth in serenity and peace.
Foreseeing the future occurred thanks to women's relation to the divine,
to the word of the oracle.

Were men harmed by this organization? No. When life, love, and
nature are respected neither sex is destroyed by the other. The two sexes
loved each other without need of the institution of matrimony, without
obligation to bear children—though this never meant that no children
were born—without censorship of sex and body.

> This is probably what monotheistic religions tell as the myth of the earthly paradise. This myth corresponds to the many centuries of history that we now label prehistory, primitive times, etc. Those people who lived in those so-called archaic times were perhaps more cultivated than we are.[37]

The context of this mini-utopia is particularly relevant, since it comes in an essay that opens with the reference to Chernobyl, and the pessimistic statement that "nature" no longer represents a limit to human destructiveness. Since Chernobyl, and the contamination of rain, grass, and the food chain over thousands of miles, it is difficult to see nature as a refuge any more. So, like Rousseau, while evoking a past "golden age," Irigaray is not suggesting that we can in any sense "return" to it. The restored maternal genealogy, the symbolic mother-daughter relationship, have to be created in the present to bring about change in the future.

These utopian topoi, then, are so insistent that one is forced to ask what their function is in Irigaray's work. Perhaps there is no single, coherent, unifying explanation. I will hazard a few remarks, but only to open a debate.

The first thing that one notices above all is that these images are all mobilized, without exception, around fantasies of the maternal body, or the maternal genealogy, or the figure of the desiring woman. (I think we have to keep in mind here the two modalities of desire that Irigaray foregrounds. In the first place there is the desire of women for each other, which is explicitly linked to the divine: "What we lack as a goal . . . is that of loving and wanting ourselves and one another [*de nous aimer et de nous vouloir*]. That project can only be divine."[38] In the second place there is love between the sexes, which for Irigaray cannot really exist in a monosexual economy. For the sexual relation to take place, socially and symbolically, the woman must first exist.) I wonder therefore whether one function of Irigaray's utopias is to evoke desire— for example, women's previously unnamed desires—so that they may try to satisfy them. But then, in order to satisfy them they would need to change the social order.[39] One example of such a possible link between women's desire and social change can be found in the theory of the Milan Women's Bookstore Collective. They refer to the "immensity" of women's desire, and to "the real difficulty that a woman encounters in acknowledging the immensity of a desire she has no way of putting forward, openly, in full sight of society, without the disguise of some female virtue."[40] The "irruption of excessive claims in the given reality"[41] can lead to the experience of defeat, depression, and retreat into fantasy, or it can lead to a realistic confrontation and assessment of

•
•
•   what the possibilities are and what needs to be done. For women to take
the second path they need some kind of symbolic support: the images
of mothers and daughters that Irigaray suggests, in the Chernobyl article, we should put in public places may seem somewhat inadequate, but
the point is the need to construct the necessary symbolic systems that
would offer women the support that traditional systems of legitimation—principally religion and mythology—have offered certain men.
The Milan Women's Bookstore Collective suggests that when women
fight for emancipation they are almost always legitimated by "virtue";
they fight for a woman who is less fortunate, less liberated than themselves. They would need another woman—a mother or a symbolic
mother—to legitimate their own desires, which otherwise they can put
forward only "under the disguise of some female virtue"—which
means, I think, legitimated by the social order currently existing.
Whereas what has been excluded by the social order—the desires of
women, for example—appears as a threat. I will come back to this point
in the second part of the essay.

A second possibility is raised by what Irigaray says about mythology
in her recent work, particularly in *Le Temps de la différence* and *Je, tu,
nous*. Myths, including religious narratives, she says, are "one of the principal expressions of what orders society at any given time."[42] "Myths are
neither univocal nor transhistorical [*intemporels*], despite what is
claimed."[43] "Mythical stories are not independent of History, but
express it in narratives which illustrate the major lines of development of
a given period."[44] Myths, therefore, should be analyzed "with a mind to
change the social order."[45] As I mentioned earlier, Irigaray sees the Greek
myths as figurations of a struggle between matriarchy and patriarchy in
which patriarchy finally won. There is some suggestion that she sees the
struggle as being in some sense still with us: "All this is extremely topi-
cal. The mythology that underlies patriarchy has not changed."[46] Only
now instead of a struggle for dominance, she sees it more as a struggle
for the maternal principle to return to the light of day: "The relation to
the mother . . . remains in the shadow of our culture, it is night and
hell."[47] Thus one could see her as trying to rewrite the founding
mythologies of Western culture, in her reinterpretation of myth.

One of the purposes of this rewriting might be, as the Lacanian formula puts it, "something which will be realized in the Symbolic, or,
more precisely, something which, thanks to the symbolic progress
which takes place in the analysis, *will have been*."[48] Or, in other words,
rewriting history, determining what it *will have been*. This process is a
familiar one in psychoanalysis, in which the analysand's past is reconstructed so that unincorporated trauma from the past acquires, retro-

spectively, a meaning that brings to the analysand healing in the present.[49] It is partly this rewriting process that gives challenges to the symbolic order some of their undecidability. For whereas an analyst might
provide an interpretation the analysand might accept and use, society
has no analyst in any comparable sense. Interpretations compete with
each other, and it is not clear at what point they become temporarily
definitive. This lends to Irigaray's voice an increasing sense of urgency.
For without a receptive audience the (pre)history she is evoking *will*
precisely *not have been*, and, instead of a prophet heralding the new era,
she could become an emblem of women's madness.

This reconstruction can be described in a slightly different way, as
follows. Irigaray argues that the death drives are bound by a particular
symbolic economy, in which the woman's "castration" functions to
mask men's fear of death. This argument is made in both *Speculum* and
Marine Lover; here is an example from *Marine Lover*:

> Predicable *qua* object "in general," the/a woman remains exterior to the
> objective. From this exterior, she supports its economy—castrated
> [*châtrée*], she threatens with castration [*castration*]. To glimpse that she
> might subtend the logic of predication without that logic's functioning
> being in any way her own [*lui soit propre*] is to fear that her intervention
> will disturb its order; the death of the subject would not be anything
> other than this. A ground rises, a heap [*montage*] of forms collapses. The
> horror of the abyss, attributed to woman. The loss of identity—death.[50]

The emergence of the woman appears to threaten the male subject with
"loss of identity—death." My argument would be that Irigaray is
attempting to formulate the conditions of a different economy that
would bind the death drives in a different way and, in particular, symbolize women's death drives by providing women with a symbolic identity.[51] Thus one reason for the mobilization of the myths is to explore
the fantasies of male culture, specifically the fears that consign the maternal to "night" and "hell." Again, this is spelled out in *Marine Lover*:

> I want to interpret your midnight dreams and unmask that phenome-
> non: your night. And make you admit that I dwell in it as your most
> fearsome adversity. So that you can finally realize what your greatest
> ressentiment is. And so that with you I can fight to make the earth my
> own and stop allowing myself to be a slave to your nature. And so that
> you can finally stop wanting to be the only god.[52]

> You rub your eyes, anxious to know if I am a ghost or a living woman.
> If I have ever existed. . . . Have I ever been anything but your dream of
> midday or midnight?[53]

> For this flesh that is never spoken—either by you or by her—remains a
> ready source of credulity for your fantasies . . . your dream life.[54]

Irigaray is trying, then, to speak "this flesh that is never spoken," and,
through this "transfiguration" and "resurrection" of woman's flesh and
blood in language, to inaugurate a new era. The condition of this seems
to necessitate a twofold movement: on the one hand the interpretation
of the male fantasy of woman, on the other the attempt to construct
alternative fantasies, an alternative imaginary scenario—and perhaps
this too is one of the functions of the mini-utopias.

II

I turn now to the question of the death drive. The concept of the death
drive often seems to result in a contradiction as soon as one tries to pin
it down in a definition. The death drive is *both* what disintegrates and
also what immobilizes; it is what breaks things into fragments and what
prevents fragmentation. On the one hand the death drive can be interpreted as the drive toward an imaginary and lost wholeness, toward the
return to the bliss of the complete symbiosis of the womb. In this sense,
although it is often opposed to the pleasure principle, it can also be seen
as the drive toward the ultimate pleasure, so that the drives toward pleasure and death, which from one point of view would seem to be radically opposed, are from another point of view indistinguishable. On the
other hand death is that which fragments, castrates, and separates—it
is the fear of fragmentation or annihilation against which the ego
defends itself. But here, again, there is a problem, for although death
appears to be the opposite of life, it can also be seen as its condition, i.e.,
if the self achieved the pleasure of stasis, it would be equivalent to
achieving the death of nirvana or immobility. So death in its other
meaning, as castrating, separating, and fragmenting force, prevents this
immobility and allows life to continue, although too much fragmentation also immobilizes and destroys. The sexual drives, then, which are
often set in opposition to death, preserve life, but in the form of
destruction and division, by breaking up stasis and sclerosis. Insofar as
the sexual drives *unbind*, they can be seen as death drive; and insofar as
death drive allows for new creation to arise out of destruction, it can be
seen as eros.[55]

Richard Boothby's recent Lacanian interpretation of the death drive
shows some of the ambiguities at work.[56] Boothby argues that each of
Lacan's three registers—Symbolic, Imaginary, and Real—seems to
claim the death drive for its own.[57] Death, in the imaginary register,
can be, for example, the fixity or encrustedness of the imago, *or the*

aggressivity involved in images of the fragmented body.[58] But Booth-by also suggests that the imago or imaginary gestalt is subject to pressure from two sides. On the one side is the threat from what the image excludes in its primitive formation. What is excluded is named differently—it may be called unbound energy (Freud), it may be called the Real (Lacan), or it may be the abject (Kristeva), prediscursive experience (phenomenology),[59] excess, jouissance, or the immensity of women's desires and their excessive claims. It may be a *resource* as well as a danger; Irigaray, in more positive terms, sometimes sees it as a "reserve of power."[60] The point is that there is always an excess, a reservoir of energies or forces animating the body that are left outside of representation, not channeled by the image. "The human being is always something more than the sum of its representations," Boothby writes.[61] Imaginary identity involves exclusion and also violence. Its integrity and form are threatened by pressure from the unrepresented, to which it reacts with anxiety and aggression. On the other side the symbolic functions as a disruptive and disintegrative factor. Boothby calls this a sublimation of the death drive. The symbolic can negate or transform the imaginary, break up imaginary formations. The stability of the imaginary allows life to continue, but it impedes creation or transformation. Insofar as it breaks up fixed forms, the death drive as symbolic may be creative. However, this may also be experienced by the imaginary as symbolic violence. The death drive may be purely destructive, but it may also be creative.[62]

Now Irigaray reinterprets the Lacanian formulation in turn. Her account of the male imaginary sets out to show first the immobilizing character of cultural formations, particularly the way in which they hold women back from "the movement of their becoming." Their effects on women are described in the most negative terms: dereliction, exile, slavery, submission, degradation or fall [*déchéance*], self-obliteration [*oubli d'elle-même*].[63] The fantasy of the maternal-feminine, the woman as container, described in *Speculum, Marine Lover*, and *L'Oubli de l'air*, immobilizes the woman, who is not allowed to come alive or be sexual in other than male terms. The first part of *Marine Lover*, for example, is the lament of the woman who is held in a kind of living death, "dwelling in death without ever dying."[64] The figure of Antigone, evoked in many places in Irigaray's work, is an image of this entombed woman, buried alive, not put to death by violence, but deprived of air and sustenance. In this scenario the man's identity seems to depend on attaching death to femininity; he preserves himself against fragmentation by locating death in woman. It is always the woman who is fragmented; in the male imaginary woman is in bits and

•
• pieces: she is debris, shards, scraps (*This Sex Which Is Not One*) or the
• 1+1+1+ of the male fantasy described by Lacan.

Irigaray also draws on the idea of the death drive as symbolic, that is
to say, as the possibility of breaking up or disrupting imaginary formations in a creative way, and on the idea of the real, that is to say, on the
possibility of pressure from the "unsymbolized" from the "mute,"
"silent substratum of the social order"[65] outside the male imaginary.
But, reinterpreting these registers in terms of sexual difference, she diagnoses a failure to sublimate at a crucial point, owing to the nonrecog-
nition of woman as other.[66] For women the sexual drives in a monosexual economy are destructive:

> Destruction [is] at work in the life drives themselves, insofar as they fail
> to respect the other, and in particular the other of sexual difference.[67]
>
> Instead of being in the service of creation or recreation of human
> forms, [eroticism] serves destruction or the loss of identity in fusion.[68]

Love, she argues, is still "uncivilized" so long as it does not include
woman in her specific symbolic or civil identity.[69] Psychoanalytic theories—whether Freudian or Lacanian—"describe and perpetuate an
uncivilized state";[70] we are living in "a primitive chaos."[71]

To overcome the negative effects on women she mobilizes the image
of love, arguing that love is a philosophical issue: "we do not yet know
the salvation, both individual and collective, that love can provide."[72]
The emergence of the figure of Aphrodite, goddess of love,[73] in Irigaray's recent work picks up the image of the ecstatic union that I discussed in the first part of this essay. The point of civilization is in part
to tame the destructive energies of eros;[74] Aphrodite is love sublimated,
the union of spiritual and carnal, the death drive mediated by the symbolic. If the universal is not sexuate then women are effaced. While the
male universal is governed by death, Irigaray wishes to replace this with
eros—life or love.

At a certain point in her work, then, which is concerned from the
outset with the problem of the death drive and the sacrificial basis of
patriarchal culture, the image of nuptials or amorous exchange begins
to emerge more strongly. It corresponds to the idea that "*each* sex
should have access to life and to death."[75] "Our tradition has not taught
[women] to take responsibility for and watch over their own death."[76]
The image of the nuptials or wedding responds to several problems. In
the first place Irigaray needs an image that allows women to be subjects
in love—desiring women—but is not reducible to the degraded eroticism from which women suffer in patriarchy. Second, she needs an
image that binds the death drives of both sexes, in a way appropriate to

both of them. Third, she needs an image that represents two genealogies and two sexes. Fourth, she needs an image that represents incarnation, which overcomes the deadly split between body and spirit, an incarnation "without murderous or suicidal passion."[77] She considers the incarnation of Christ, as we saw, to leave out the physical embrace and embodiment of the woman lover and to lead to the patriarchal sacrifice of crucifixion. She requires an image without sacrifice, an image of fertility:

> A sexual or carnal ethics would demand that both angel and body be found together. This is a world that must be constructed or reconstructed. A genesis of love between the sexes has yet to come about in all dimensions, from the smallest to the greatest, from the most intimate to the most political.[78]

It is an image, then, standing both for relations between men and women at the level of sexuality ("the most intimate guise") or at the level of the polis ("the most political guise"): "It is up to us to make of this name [love] the designation of an amorous relationship which passes from the most intimate part of our life to a political ethics which refuses to sacrifice desire to death, power or money."[79] I'm not sure when the image of the nuptials appears for the first time; it can certainly be found in *This Sex Which Is Not One* and *Marine Lover* (parts 2 and 3); its fullest elaboration is in the essay on Levinas from which I quoted earlier. It is clearly and explicitly linked to the problematic of life and death: "To make the difference between the sexes the motor of the becoming of the dialectic, is also to be able to renounce death as sovereign master in order finally to concern oneself with the growth of life, natural and spiritual, individual and collective."[80]

In her recent work, what emerges, I think, is the idea that the transitional epoch in which we live is a dangerous one for women. It has involved bringing to the surface, in a sometimes cathartic way,[81] the previously hidden suffering and dereliction of women. But this also releases the hidden violence—primarily directed toward the mother, it can be deflected on to men and on to other women. There is some evidence to suggest that Irigaray considered the triumphal moment of feminism and its celebration of relations between women as too dangerous; relations between women became too readily fusional and evoked the murderousness of the primitive and unsymbolized feelings for the mother.[82] Not to mention men's counterviolence in response. This violence needs to be bound in a symbolic way. The dangers in feminism, as Irigaray sees them, lie in a politics that is heedless of the functioning of the patriarchal death drive. Such a politics risks an escalation and counterescalation of violence that leaves the sacrificial foundation untouched. I would suggest that Irigaray sees it as one of her tasks to work toward a new symbolization. In her attempt to rewrite a founding myth for the new era, she wants to bind the death drive with eros. Eros is also an *unbinding* force; there might seem to be a paradox here. But I think Irigaray would argue that this is because it remains primitive, "uncivilized," unsublimated, a purely private affair, when it should be a civil and social recognition of two generic identities.[83]

The question Irigaray negotiates is the tension between death drive as destructive and death drive as creative, or between eros as thanatos and thanatos as eros. On the one hand the imaginary formations of patriarchy need to be broken up, for something new—some new formation—to emerge. Yet there are problems with this. One is the aggression likely to be released by this pressure, and the need to bind aggression. The second is that one cannot remain indefinitely in the moment of negativity. A new formation must be a *formation*, it needs to stay constant long enough to have some effect. Hence the desire to give women a civil identity. Whereas Irigaray's early work—*Speculum*, "The Bodily Encounter with the Mother"[84]—belongs to a more disruptive moment, I see her images of utopias, the evocations of harmonious relations between mothers and daughters, the symbolization of the maternal body and the nuptial images as attempts to bind the death drive in a stable imaginary formation.

On the other hand any stable imaginary formation is itself implicated in the death drive in its other sense as stasis; this makes *any* image problematic. This problematic seems to be inherent in the economy of eros and thanatos. Their instability means that each can turn into its opposite; they can change places. The harmonious sexual relationship could equally well become the image of satisfaction, and absence of contradiction, and then one would expect the conflict that is expelled from the imaginary to return elsewhere.

For this reason it is problematic to read Irigaray's work as a source of images and symbols that we can simply take over.[85] It is equally problematic, however, to reject images altogether, since this merely leaves the terrain open for invasion by patriarchal images and symbols. The problem is how to keep the space open, how to hold the tension, without succumbing either to fixation or to uncontrolled and endless disruption. Different feminists have come up with different solutions to this problem, and Irigaray's solution is the necessity for sexuate rights and a sexuate civil code, giving women a distinct civil and generic identity. Some people may feel that in so doing she has lost the tension, and lost sight of eros as excess, disruption, and negativity. But death is on *each* side of the question, since, while stability immobilizes, perpetual disruption is immobilizing and also destructive.

In its feminist form the problem can be put like this: is feminism destined to remain contestatory—feminism as critique—or can it legitimately move to a more constructive moment? Can it settle into an order, or would that be to lose sight of its disruptive potential? From the angle I've been describing there is no definitive answer to this question. The mistake would be to identify feminism with either one side or the other, or with any one of the three Lacanian registers. The imaginary is both the condition of growth and what impedes growth. The symbolic is what disrupts stasis and what consolidates stasis. The real offers potential for new growth, but its irruption can also be shattering. Thus identity is both necessary and violent.

Strategically, in her most recent work, Irigaray has chosen to locate the violence in the system we know as patriarchy. But she is aware, as we know from her earlier work, that violence also comes from the real—from the excess, the silent substratum, women. And she is afraid, I think, that the irruption of the real can be dangerous to women too, because it is unsymbolized and unsublimated.[86] For those attracted to her earlier work, with its focus on the woman as "other" to the social order, and her potential for disruption, Irigaray's later work—with its stress on citizenship and rights—may come as something of a letdown. What has happened to the iconoclastic vigor of *Speculum*? I think there *is* a continuity, and it is provided at least in part by the need to address the death drive in its destructive as well as creative potential.

NOTES •

1. Biddy Martin, *Woman and Modernity: The (Life)Styles of Lou Andreas-Salomé* (Ithaca and London: Cornell University Press, 1991).
2. Ibid., pp. 142–143.
3. In this respect I am attracted by the epistemological and methodological model offered by Jennifer Ring in *Modern Political Theory and Contemporary Feminism: A Dialectical Analysis* (Albany: SUNY Press, 1991), which foregrounds conflict over harmony, and dialectic over unity, in an explicit critique of feminist epistemologies developed by Sandra Harding, Alison Jaggar, and Evelyn Fox Keller. (It is not a reinstatement of an adversarial model but rather the recognition of the *difficulty* of unity.)
4. Irigaray, *J'aime à toi*, p. 53.
5. Ibid., pp. 53–54.
6. This critical function is nicely summarized by Iris Marion Young in *Justice*

- *and the Politics of Difference* (Princeton: Princeton University Press,
- 1990), when she writes:

> With an emancipatory interest, the philosopher apprehends
> given social circumstances not merely in contemplation but with
> passion: the given is experienced in relation to desire. Desire, the
> desire to be happy, creates the distance, the negation, that opens
> the space for criticism of what is. This critical distance does not
> occur on the basis of some previously discovered rational ideas of
> the good and the just. On the contrary, the ideas of the good and
> the just arise from the desiring negation that action brings to
> what is given. Critical theory is a mode of discourse which pro-
> jects normative possibilities unrealized but felt in a particular
> given social reality. Each social reality presents its own unrealized
> possibilities, experienced as lacks and desires. Norms and ideals
> arise from the yearning that is an expression of freedom: it does
> not have to be this way, it could be otherwise. Imagination is the
> faculty of transforming the experience of what is into a projection
> of what could be, the faculty that frees thought to form ideals and
> norms. (pp. 5–6)

In contrast, see also Biddy Martin, who interprets Salomé's work as a
warning against the dangers of imagination. There is a danger that
women's socially imposed lack of access to purposeful activity will lead to
their containment and confinement in daydreams and fantasy. Desires
must have some purchase in reality. This point is taken up also by the
Milan Women's Bookstore Collective—see below, and note 40.

7. Slavoj Žižek, *For They Know Not What They Do: Enjoyment as a Political Factor* (London: Verso, 1991).

8. Ibid., p. 192.

9. "There is a difference between 'politics' as a separate social complex, a positively determined sub-system of social relations in interaction with other sub-systems (economy, forms of culture . . .) and the 'Political' [*le Politique*] as the moment of openness, of undecidability, when the very structuring principle of society, the fundamental form of the social pact, is called into question. . . . The 'political' dimension is thus doubly inscribed: it is a moment of the social Whole, one among its sub-systems, *and* the very terrain in which the fate of the Whole is decided—in which the new Pact is designed and concluded" (ibid., p. 193).

10. *The Kristeva Reader*, ed. Toril Moi (New York: Columbia University Press and Oxford: Blackwell, 1986), p. 200.

11. For discussion of the fate of Freud's theory of the death drive in psycho-analytic theory, see Richard Boothby, *Death and Desire: Psychoanalytic Theory in Lacan's Return to Freud* (London and New York: Routledge, 1991); and Marion Michel Oliner, *Cultivating Freud's Garden in France* (Northvale, N.J.: Jason Aronson, 1988).

12. Krishan Kumar, *Utopia and Anti-utopia in Modern Times* (Oxford: Basil Blackwell, 1987), p. 384.

13. Irigaray, *J'aime à toi*, p. 26.

14. In Raoul Mortley, ed., *French Philosophers in Conversation: Derrida, Irigaray, Levinas, Le Doeuff, Schneider, Serres* (London: Routledge, 1991), p. 78.

15. It is discussed in Ellen Mortensen's unpublished Ph.D. thesis, "Le 'féminin' and Nihilism: Reading Irigaray with Nietzsche and Heidegger," University of Wisconsin, Madison, 1989. See also her essay, this volume. See also brief discussions in Elizabeth Berg's review of *Amante marine* in "The Third Woman," *Diacritics* (1982), 12(2):11–20, and Sara Speidel's notes on her translation of extracts from "Lèvres voilées" in "Veiled Lips."

16. In which the inhabitants of Cockaigne lie around idly all day, while birds already roasted fly into their mouths (or variations on this theme). See Kumar, *Utopia and Anti-utopia*, p. 7. Irigaray does not seem to fit in well with the *masculine* utopian traditions as described by Kumar.

17. For this insight I am indebted to Agnès Vincenot, "Genèse," in Agnès Vincenot, Marion de Zanger, Heide Hinterthür and Anne-Claire Mulder, eds., *Renaissance: Drie teksten van Luce Irigaray vertaald en becommentarieerd* (The Hague: Uitgeverij Perdu, 1990), pp. 46–88. Anne-Claire Mulder of the University of Amsterdam kindly provided me with an English translation.

18. Irigaray, *Marine Lover*, p. 129/*Amante marine*, p. 137. All translations from *Marine Lover* are my own.

19. Ibid., p. 144/154.

20. Ibid., p. 151/162.

21. Ibid., p. 167/179. This notion of sacrifice is expanded in "Le Mystère oublié des généalogies féminines" in *Le Temps de la différence*, pp. 101–123.

22. Irigaray, *Marine Lover*, p. 168/*Amante marine*, p. 179.

23. Ibid., p. 154/165.

24. Ibid, p. 170/182.

25. Ibid., p. 171/183.

26. Irigaray, *Ethics*, p. 147/*Ethique*, p. 139.

27. Ibid.

28. Ibid., p. 129/p.124.

29. Ibid., p. 6/p. 13.

30. Ibid., p. 148/p. 140.

31. Gillian Rose, *Dialectic of Nihilism: Post-Structuralism and Law* (Oxford: Basil Blackwell, 1984), p. 91, note 26.

32. According to Kumar, *Utopia and Anti-utopia*, p. 16.

33. Irigaray, *Sexes and Genealogies*, p. 180/*Sexes et parentés*, p. 194; and Whitford, *The Irigaray Reader*, p. 151. The French word I am translating by "dregs" appears in *Sexes et parentés* as *rebus*, which is a misprint. It is not clear if this should be *rébus* (puzzle) or *rebut* (dregs, cast-off).

34. Irigaray, "Questions à Emmanuel Levinas," p. 913; Bernasconi and Critchley, *Re-reading Levinas*, pp. 110–111; Whitford, *Irigaray Reader*, p. 180. My reading here is confirmed by *J'aime à toi*, p. 163–164, where the same terms (*extase, enstase*) are taken up in a reading that is quite clearly concerned with the social and cultural sublimation and symbolization of love in sexual difference.

35. Irigaray, *Ethics*, p. 54/*Ethique*, p. 58; cf. *J'aime à toi*, p. 192.

36. I borrow this term from Ernest Callenbach's novel *Ecotopia: A Novel About Ecology, People, and Politics in 1999* (Berkeley: Banyan Tree, 1975; London: Pluto, 1978).

37. Irigaray, *Sexes and Genealogies*, pp. 191–192/*Sexes et parentés*, p. 206.

38. Ibid., p. 68/80; my translation.

39. My formulation of this point was assisted by Linda Williams, *Hard Core: Power, Pleasure, and the "Frenzy of the Visible"* (Berkeley: University of California Press, 1989), especially p. 155, and the Milan Women's Bookstore Collective, *Sexual Difference: A Theory of Social-Symbolic Practice* (Bloomington: Indiana University Press, 1990), especially chapter 4.

40. Milan Collective, *Sexual Difference*, p. 115.

41. Ibid., p. 118.

42. Irigaray, *Je, tu, nous*, p. 24/28.

43. Irigaray, *Le Temps de la différence*, p. 106.

44. Ibid., p. 112. With thanks to Luisa Muraro (this volume) whose essay drew my attention to these remarks on mythology in *Le Temps de la différence*.

45. *Sexes and Genealogies*, p. 73/*Sexes et parentés*, p. 86.

46. Ibid., p. 12/24.

47. Ibid., p. 10/22.

48. Jacques Lacan, *The Seminar of Jacques Lacan, Book I: Freud's Papers on Technique* (Cambridge: Cambridge University Press, 1988), p. 159, quoted in Slavoj Žižek, *The Sublime Object of Ideology* (London: Verso, 1989), p. 55.

49. See Dianne Chisholm (this volume) for a similar but alternative psychoanalytic reading. Žižek's account of the rewriting of history seems to me to apply quite well to Irigaray's project.

50. Irigaray, *Marine Lover*, p. 91/*Amante marine*, p. 97.

51. A longer version of this argument can be found in Margaret Whitford, *Luce Irigaray: Philosophy in the Feminine* (London and New York: Routledge, 1991); see especially chapter 6.

52. Irigaray, *Marine Lover*, p. 25/*Amante marine*, p. 31.

53. Ibid., p. 31/37.

54. Ibid., p. 33/39.

55. I am indebted here to Elisabeth Bronfen's entry "Death Drive (Freud)," in Elizabeth Wright, ed., *Feminism and Psychoanalysis: A Critical Dictionary* (Oxford: Blackwell, 1992), pp. 52–57. See also Elisabeth Bronfen,

Over Her Dead Body: Death, Femininity and the Aesthetic (Manchester: Manchester University Press, 1992).

56. I suspect that Boothby makes the mistake of trying to make Freud's theory coherent at the price of simply removing or cutting the bits that don't fit.

57. Boothby, *Death and Desire*, p. 19.

58. Ibid., chapter 2.

59. Cf. Irigaray, *Ethics*: "Up to this point, my reading and my interpretation of the history of philosophy agree with Merleau-Ponty: we must go back to a moment of prediscursive experience . . . and pause at the 'mystery, as familiar as it is unexplained, of a light that, illuminating the rest, remains at its source in obscurity' " (p. 151/143)

60. See Dianne Chisholm, this volume.

61. Boothby, *Death and Desire*, p. 64.

62. I set aside here the question of real as opposed to symbolic violence, although Boothby (p. 176ff.) gives a particularly grisly example of what happens when the symbolic framework is impaired or inadequate. His example is taken from a moment in recent Colombian history; I would have thought one could find examples closer to home.

63. See Irigaray, *Le Temps de la différence*, pp. 110–111.

64. Irigaray, *Marine Lover*, p. 28/*Amante marine*, p. 35. The woman as "container" is discussed in *An Ethics of Sexual Difference*.

65. See Irigaray, "Women-Mothers, the Silent Sub-Stratum of the Social Order" in *The Irigaray Reader*, pp. 47–52.

66. Irigaray, *Le Temps de la différence*, pp. 108–109. One might interpret in these terms the various manifestations of violence against women.

67. Ibid., p. 109.

68. Ibid., p. 110–111.

69. Irigaray, *J'aime à toi*, p. 201ff.

70. Ibid., p. 209.

71. Irigaray, *Le Temps de la différence*, p. 104.

72. Irigaray, *J'aime à toi*, pp. 56–57.

73. Ibid., p. 211ff.

74. Ibid., p. 212.

75. Irigaray, "The Limits of the Transference," in Whitford, *The Irigaray Reader*, p. 106; "La Limite du transfert," *Parler n'est jamais neutre*, p. 294. The original date of this remark is 1982.

76. Irigaray, in Whitford, *The Irigaray Reader*, p. 114; *Parler n'est jamais neutre*, p. 302.

77. Irigaray, *Marine Lover*, p. 201/*Amante marine*, p. 188.

78. Irigaray, "Sexual Difference," Whitford, *The Irigaray Reader*, p. 174; *Ethics*, p. 17/"La Différence sexuelle," *Ethique*, p. 23. On the angel see Gail M. Schwab, this volume.

79. Irigaray, *J'aime à toi*, p. 63.

80. Ibid., p. 107.

81. See Irigaray, *Je, tu, nous*, p. 131/107ff.

82. See Luisa Muraro, this volume.

83. This is the argument of Irigaray, *J'aime à toi*, passim.

84. Irigaray, "The Bodily Encounter with the Mother," in Whitford, *The Irigaray Reader*, pp. 34–46.

85. In particular there seem to be a number of problems with the image of the harmonious sexual relationship, for example: it gives offense to homosexuals, it appears to reintroduce romantic and traditional versions of patriarchal motherhood by the back door, fertility seems an eminently recuperable ideal, whose patriarchal reading may drown out its more spiritual or symbolic aspects.

86. Cf. Irigaray's warning to avoid "spontaneism" in "Creating a Woman-to-Woman Sociality," Whitford, *The Irigaray Reader*, p. 196.

BIBLIOGRAPHY:

LUCE IRIGARAY

This bibliography contains only the works of Luce Irigaray that are cited in this book. A longer bibliography of Irigaray's writing in French, including uncollected articles not translated into English, can be found in Margaret Whitford, *Luce Irigaray: Philosophy in the Feminine*, London: Routledge, 1991.

Entries in this bibliography are arranged in alphabetical order under French titles (except in the case of articles that have appeared only in English). Extracts are listed under the French collection from which they were taken. In the articles of this volume page references are to the English translations (where available), followed by the French reference.

Amante marine. De Friedrich Nietzsche. Paris: Minuit, 1980.
Marine Lover of Friedrich Nietzsche. Trans. Gillian Gill. New York: Columbia University Press, 1991.
Extract:
"Veiled Lips." Trans. Sara Speidel. *Mississippi Review* (1983), 11(3):98–119.

∘ *Le Corps-à-corps avec la mère.* Montreal: Editions de la Pleine Lune, 1981.
   Extracts:
   "The Bodily Encounter with the Mother." Trans. David Macey. In Margaret
      Whitford, ed., *The Irigaray Reader*, pp. 34–46. Oxford: Basil Blackwell,
      1991.
   "Body Against Body: In Relation to the Mother." Trans. Gillian C. Gill. In
      Sexes and Genealogies, pp. 7–21. New York: Columbia University Press,
      1993.
   "Women-Mothers, the Silent Substratum of the Social Order." Trans. David
      Macey. In Margaret Whitford, ed., *The Irigaray Reader*, pp. 47–52.
      Oxford: Basil Blackwell, 1991.

   "Créer un Entre-Femmes." *Paris-féministe* (September 1986),
      31(2):37–41.
   "Women-amongst-themselves: Creating a woman-to-woman sociality."
      Trans. David Macey. In Margaret Whitford, ed., *The Irigaray Reader*, pp.
      190–197. Oxford: Basil Blackwell, 1991.

   La Croyance même. Paris: Minuit, 1983. Reprinted with slight alterations in
      Sexes et parentés, pp. 35–65. Paris: Minuit, 1987.
   Extract:
   "Belief Itself." Trans. Gillian C. Gill. In *Sexes and Genealogies*, pp. 23–53.
      New York: Columbia University Press, 1993.

   "Egales à qui?" *Critique* (May 1987), 43(480):420–437.
   "Equal to Whom?" Trans. Robert L. Mazzola. *differences* (1989), 1(2):
      59–76.

   Ethique de la différence sexuelle. Paris: Minuit, 1984.
   An Ethics of Sexual Difference. Trans. Carolyn Burke and Gillian Gill. Ithaca:
      Cornell University Press and London: Athlone Press, 1993.
   Extracts:
   "Sexual Difference." Trans. Seán Hand. In Toril Moi, ed., *French Feminist
      Thought*, pp. 118–130. Oxford: Basil Blackwell, 1987. Reprinted in
      Margaret Whitford, *The Irigaray Reader*, pp. 165–177. Oxford: Basil
      Blackwell, 1991.
   "Sorcerer Love: A Reading of Plato's *Symposium*, Diotima's Speech." Trans.
      Eléanor Kuykendall. *Hypatia* (1989), 3(3):32–44.
   "The Fecundity of the Caress." Trans. Carolyn Burke. In Richard A.
      Cohen, ed., *Face to Face with Levinas*, pp. 231–256. Albany: SUNY
      Press, 1985.

Et l'une ne bouge pas sans l'autre. Paris: Minuit, 1979.
Extracts:
"And the One Doesn't Stir Without the Other." Trans. Hélène Vivienne
Wenzel. *Signs* (1981), 7(1):60–67.
"One Does Not Move Without the Other." Trans. Rosi Braidotti and Mia
Campioni. *Refractory Girl* (1982), 23:12–14.

"Interview." Interview with Raoul Mortley. In *French Philosophers in Conversation: Derrida, Irigaray, Levinas, Le Doeuff, Schneider, Serres,* pp. 62–78.
London: Routledge, 1991.

"An Interview with Luce Irigaray." Interview with Kiki Amsberg and Aafke
Steenhuis. Trans. Robert van Krieken. *Hecate* (1983), 9(1–2):192–202.

The Irigaray Reader. Ed. Margaret Whitford. Oxford: Basil Blackwell, 1991.

J'aime à toi: Esquisse d'une félicité dans l'histoire. Paris: Grasset, 1992.
Translation forthcoming, Routledge.
Extract:
"Love Between Us." Trans. Jeffrey Lomonaco. In Eduardo Cadava, Peter
Connor, and Jean-Luc Nancy, eds., *Who Comes After the Subject,* pp.
167–177. London: Routledge, 1991.

Je, tu, nous: pour une culture de la différence. Paris: Grasset, 1990.
Je, Tu, Nous: Toward a Culture of Difference. Trans. Alison Martin. New
York: Routledge, 1993.
Extracts:
"The Culture of Difference." Trans. Alison Martin. *Pli* (formerly *The War-
wick Journal of Philosophy,* special issue on feminist philosophy) (1990),
3(1):44–52.
Interview. Trans. Margaret Whitford. In Alice Jardine and Anne Menke,
eds., *Shifting Scenes: Interviews on Women, Writing, and Politics in Post 68
France,* pp. 97–103. New York: Columbia University Press, 1991.
"How to Define Sexuate Rights." Trans. David Macey. In Margaret Whitford,
ed., *The Irigaray Reader,* pp. 204–212. Oxford: Basil Blackwell, 1991.

Le Langage des déments. Collection "Approaches to Semiotics." The Hague:
Mouton, 1973.

"Language, Persephone, and Sacrifice." Interview with Heather Jon Maroney.
Trans. Heather Jon Maroney. *Borderlines* (Winter 1985–86), 4:30–32.

° "Luce Irigaray." Interview with Lucienne Serrano and Elaine Hoffman Baruch. In Janet Todd, ed., *Women Writers Talking*, pp. 230–245. New York and London: Holmes and Meier, 1983. Reprinted in Elaine Hoffman Baruch and Lucienne Serrano, eds., *Women Analyze Women*, pp. 147–164. London: Harvester Wheatsheaf, 1988.

L'Oubli de l'air chez Martin Heidegger. Paris: Minuit, 1983.
Extract:
"He Risks Who Risks Life Itself." Trans. David Macey. In Margaret Whitford, ed., *The Irigaray Reader*, pp. 213–218. Oxford: Basil Blackwell, 1991.

"Où et comment habiter?" *Cahiers du Grif* (March 1983), 26:139–143.

Parler n'est jamais neutre. Paris: Minuit, 1985.
Translation forthcoming, Athlone.
Extracts:
"Is the Subject of Science Sexed?" Trans. Edith Oberle. *Cultural Critique* (Fall 1985), 1:73–88.
"Is the Subject of Science Sexed?" Trans. Carol Mastrangelo Bové. *Hypatia* (Fall 1987), 2:65–87. Reprinted in Nancy Tuana, ed., *Feminism and Science*, pp. 56–68. Bloomington: Indiana University Press, 1989.
"The Poverty of Psychoanalysis." Trans. David Macey and Margaret Whitford. In Margaret Whitford, ed., *The Irigaray Reader*, pp. 79–104. Oxford: Basil Blackwell, 1991.
"The Limits of the Transference." Trans. David Macey and Margaret Whitford. In Margaret Whitford, ed., *The Irigaray Reader*, pp. 105–117. Oxford: Basil Blackwell, 1991.
"The Language of Man (The Sexuation of Discourse)." Trans. Erin G. Carlston. *Cultural Critique* (Fall 1989), 13:191–202.

Passions élémentaires. Paris: Minuit, 1982.
Elemental Passions. Trans. Judith Still and Joanne Collie. London: Athlone Press, 1992.

"Questions à Emmanuel Levinas." *Critique* (November 1990), 522:911–920.
"Questions to Emmanuel Levinas." Trans. Margaret Whitford. In Robert Bernasconi and Simon Critchley, eds., *Rereading Levinas*, pp. 109–118. Bloomington: Indiana University Press 1991. Reprinted in Margaret Whitford, ed., *The Irigaray Reader*, pp. 178–189. Oxford: Basil Blackwell, 1991.

Le Sexe linguistique. Ed. Luce Irigaray. Special issue of *Langages* (March 1987), vol. 85.

Ce Sexe qui n'en est pas un. Paris: Minuit, 1977.
This Sex Which Is Not One. Trans. Catherine Porter and Carolyn Burke. Ithaca: Cornell University Press, 1985.
Extracts:
"That Sex Which Is Not One." Trans. Randall Albury and Paul Foss. In P. Foss and M. Morris, eds., *Language, Sexuality, and Subversion*, pp. 161–171. Sydney: Feral Publications, 1978.
"This Sex Which is Not One." Trans. Claudia Reeder. In Elaine Marks and Isabelle de Courtivron, eds., *New French Feminisms*, pp. 96–106. Brighton: Harvester, 1981.
"When the Goods Get Together." Trans. Claudia Reeder. In Elaine Marks and Isabelle de Courtivron, eds., *New French Feminisms*, pp. 107–110.
"When Our Lips Speak Together." Trans. Carolyn Burke. *Signs* (1980), 6(1):69–79.

Sexes et genres à travers les langues: éléments de communication sexuée. Ed. Luce Irigaray. Paris: Grasset, 1990.
Translation forthcoming, Routledge.

Sexes et parentés. Paris: Minuit, 1987.
Sexes and Genealogies. Trans. Gillian C. Gill. New York: Columbia University Press, 1993.
Extracts:
Divine Women. Trans. Stephen Muecke. Sydney: Local Consumption Occasional papers no. 8, 1986.
"Women, the Sacred, and Money." Trans. Diana Knight and Margaret Whitford. *Paragraph* (October 1986), 8:6–18.
"The Gesture in Psychoanalysis." Trans. Elizabeth Guild. In Teresa Brennan, ed., *Between Feminism and Psychoanalysis*, pp. 127–138. London: Routledge, 1989.
"The Bodily Encounter with the Mother." Trans. David Macey. In Margaret Whitford, ed., *The Irigaray Reader*, pp. 34–46. Oxford: Basil Blackwell, 1991.
"The Necessity for Sexuate Rights." Trans. David Macey. In Margaret Whitford, ed., *The Irigaray Reader*, pp. 198–203. Oxford: Basil Blackwell, 1991.
"The Three Genres." Trans. David Macey. In Margaret Whitford, ed., *The Irigaray Reader*, pp. 140.

○

Speculum. De l'autre femme. Paris: Minuit, 1974.
Speculum of the Other Woman. Trans. Gillian C. Gill. Ithaca: Cornell University Press, 1985.
Extract:
"Any Theory of the 'Subject' Has Always Been Appropriated by the 'Masculine.' " Trans. Gillian C. Gill. *Trivia* (Winter 1985), 6:38–51.

Le Temps de la différence: pour une révolution pacifique. Paris: Librairie Générale Française, 1989.
Translation forthcoming, 1994. *Time for Change: For a Peaceful Revolution.* London: Athlone.

"Women's Exile." Interview. Trans. Couze Venn. *Ideology and Consciousness* (1977), 1:62–76. Reprinted in Deborah Cameron, ed., *The Feminist Critique of Language: A Reader*, pp. 80–96. London: Routledge, 1990.

CONTRIBUTOR'S

NOTES

Philippa Berry

is a Fellow and Lecturer in English Literature at King's College, Cambridge. She is the author of *Of Chastity and Power: Elizabethan Literature and the Unmarried Queen* (New York and London: Routledge, 1989) and the editor, with Andrew Wernick, of *Shadow of Spirit: Postmodernism and Religion* (New York and London: Routledge, 1992). She is currently working on two projects: a feminist reading of Shakespearean tragedy (forthcoming from Routledge, 1995) and a book on French feminism entitled "Dancing in Space: The Turns of Feminist Philosophy."

Rosi Braidotti

has been Full Professor and Chair of Women's Studies in the Humanities at the University of Utrecht since 1988. She received her Ph.D. in Philosophy from the Sorbonne in 1981, with a dissertation on Foucault and feminism, and taught for several years in the Columbia Programs in Paris (Reid Hall). She is the author of *Patterns of Dissonance/Beelden van Leegte*, a study of women in contemporary philosophy, and *Nomadic Subjects* (New York: Columbia University Press, 1994), a volume of collected essays. She has also published extensively on feminist theory in collections such as *Between Feminism and Psychoanalysis, Men in Feminism, Critical Dictionary of Feminism and Psychoanalysis*, and journals such as *differences, Gender Studies, Hypatia, Women's Studies International Forum, DWF, Les Cahiers du Grif*, and others. She coordinates an Erasmus exchange network for Women's Studies with European partners.

Carolyn Burke

has translated several texts by Irigaray, most recently *An Ethics of Sexual Difference* (with Gillian Gill), and has written extensively on French feminisms and modernist art and writing by women. Her biography of the modernist painter and poet, Mina Loy, is forthcoming from Farrar, Straus and Giroux.

Judith Butler

is Professor of Rhetoric and Comparative Literature at the University of California, Berkeley, and the author of *Gender Trouble: Feminism and the Subversion of Identity* (New York: Routledge, 1990) and *Bodies That Matter: On the Discursive Limits of "Sex"* (New York: Routledge, 1993).

Dianne Chisholm

is Assistant Professor of English at the University of Alberta. She is author of *H.D.'s Freudian Poetics: Psychoanalysis in Translation* (Ithaca: Cornell University Press, 1992) and advisory editor, with Juliet Flower MacCannell and Margaret Whitford, of *Feminism and Psychoanalysis: A Critical Dictionary* (Oxford: Blackwell, 1992). She is currently working on a new book, "Avant-Garde Sexualities: Eroticism in an Age of Barbarism."

Jean-Joseph Goux

is Lawrence Favrot Professor of Romance Studies at Rice University and Directeur de Programme at the College International de Philosophie in Paris. His most recent books include *Symbolic Economies: After Marx and Freud* (trans. Jennifer Gage; Ithaca: Cornell University Press, 1990) and *Oedipe philosophe* (Paris: Aubier, 1990; forthcoming in translation from Stanford University Press).

Elizabeth Grosz

teaches Critical Theory, Philosophy, and Women's Studies, and is the Director of the Center for Critical Theory and Cultural Studies at Monash University in Victoria, Australia. She is the author of *Sexual Subversions: Three French Feminists* (Sydney: Allen and Unwin, 1989) and *Jacques Lacan: A Feminist Introduction* (London and New York: Routledge, 1990) and has edited a number of anthologies on feminist theory.

Elizabeth Hirsh

is presently Assistant Professor at the University of South Florida, having taught previously at Swarthmore College and the University of Wisconsin. She is the author of the forthcoming "Re-Producing Modernism: Irigaray, Formalism, and the Place of the Woman Writer" and of articles on feminist theory and women writers such as H.D., Virginia Woolf, and Radclyffe Hall.

Joanna Hodge

wrote her doctoral thesis on Martin Heidegger's account of truth in *Being in Time.* She has rewritten her thesis for publication as a book under the title *Heidegger and Ethics* (forthcoming, Routledge, 1994). She is currently Senior Lecturer in Philosophy at Manchester Metropolitan University. She is currently working on a study of time and destiny in the writings of Nietzsche, Benjamin, and Heidegger.

Ellen Mortensen

is Associate Professor in Comparative Literature at the University of Tromso, Norway. She received her Ph.D. in Comparative Literature from the University of Wisconsin-Madison (1989). Her forthcoming book on Luce Irigaray, *Femininity and Nihilism: Reading Irigaray with Nietzche and Heidegger* (Scandinavian University Press), will be published in 1994.

Luisa Muraro

has been teaching Philosophy at the University of Verona since 1975. She is the author of *L'Ordine simbolico della madre* [The symbolic order of the mother] (Rome: La Tartaruga, 1987), and also contributed to *Il pensiero della differenza sessuale* [The thought of sexual difference] (Milan: La Tartaruga, 1987). She was one of the founders of the Milan Women's Bookstore Collective (whose book, *Sexual Difference: A Theory of Social-Symbolic Practice,* was published in 1991 by Indiana University Press), and has translated Luce Irigaray's major works into Italian. She is actively involved in the women's political movement.

Naomi Schor

is William Hanes Wannamaker Professor of Romance Studies and Professor of Comparative Literature at Duke University. Her most recent

° books include *Reading in Detail: Aesthetics and the Feminine* (New York: Routledge, 1987) and *George Sand and Idealism* (New York: Columbia, 1993). Along with Elizabeth Weed she coedits *differences: A Journal of Feminist Cultural Studies.*

Gail Schwab

is Associate Professor of French at Hofstra University. She has published on nineteenth-century French literature as well as on Luce Irigaray, and is currently doing research, under the direction of Irigaray, on gender difference in language use, for the Centre National de Recherches Scientifiques in Paris. She is also cotranslator of Luce Irigaray's *Sexes et genres à travers les langues* (forthcoming from Routledge).

Elizabeth Weed

is the Assistant Director of the Pembroke Institute at Brown University. She is the editor of *Coming to Terms: Feminism, Theory, Politics,* and is also the coeditor of *differences: A Journal of Feminist Cultural Studies.*

Margaret Whitford

teaches in the French Department at Queen Mary and Westfield College, University of London. Her recent publications include *Luce Irigaray: Philosophy in the Feminine* (London: Routledge, 1991) and *The Irigaray Reader* (Oxford: Basil Blackwell, 1991). She also coedited *Feminist Perspectives in Philosophy* (Indiana University Press) with Morwenna Griffiths. She is currently coediting a collection with Kathleen Lennon on feminism and epistemology.

INDEX

Page references enclosed in square brackets indicate textual references to end-notes. Luce Irigaray is abbreviated LI.

GENDER AND CULTURE •

A Series of Columbia University Press
Edited by Carolyn G. Heilbrun and Nancy K. Miller

Shifting Scenes: Interviews on Women, Writing, and Politics in Post-68 France
Edited by Alice A. Jardine and Anne M. Menke

Tender Geographies: Women and the Origins of the Novel in France
Joan DeJean

Modern Feminisms: Political, Literary, Cultural
Maggie Humm

Unbecoming Women: British Women Writers and the Novel of Development
Susan Fraiman

The Apparitional Lesbian: Female Homosexuality and Modern Culture
Terry Castle

Nomadic Subjects: Embodiment and Sexual Difference in Contemporary Feminist Theory
Rosi Braidotti

Designer: Linda Secondari
Text: 11/13 Adobe Garamond
Compositor: Columbia University Press
Printer: Edwards Brothers
Binder: Edwards Brothers